Political Accountability in Europe: Which Way Forward?

Europa Law Publishing, Groningen 2008

Political Accountability in Europe: Which Way Forward?

A Traditional Concept of Parliamentary Democracy in an EU Context

Luc Verhey, Hansko Broeksteeg and Ilse Van den Driessche

Europa Law Publishing is a publishing company specializing in European Union law, international trade law, public international law, environmental law and comparative national law.
For further information please contact Europa Law Publishing via email: info@europalawpublishing.com or visit our website at: www.europalawpublishing.com.

Typeset in Scala and Scala Sans, Graphic design by G2K Designers, Groningen/Amsterdam

NUR 828; ISBN 978-90-76871-82-0

British Library Cataloguing-in-Publication Data
A catalogue record for this book is available from the British Library

Acknowledgements

This book is the first publication under the responsibility of the Maastricht branch of the Montesquieu Institute, the Centre of Parliamentary History and Constitutional Development. This institute in which four Dutch universities (University of Leiden, Radboud University Nijmegen, University of Groningen and the University of Maastricht) are engaged and which intends to grow into a European network of scientific experts, is aimed, amongst other things, at stimulating comparative research into the different parliamentary systems in Europe. The institute was officially opened in spring 2007.

The research in this book forms part of the research program 'Political Control in a European and Constitutional Perspective'. This program was started in 2004 by the universities of Maastricht, Utrecht and Amsterdam. It tries to assess how political control can be organised in the (future) European Union. The program is financed by the Netherlands Organisation for Scientific Research (NWO). It is embedded in the Ius Commune research school, a cooperation of the mentioned universities, and is led by Luc Verhey (Professor of Constitutional and Administrative Law, University of Maastricht), Deirdre Curtin (Professor of International and European Governance, University of Utrecht) and Jit Peters (Professor of Constitutional Law, University of Amsterdam).

This research is one of the sub-projects of the research program. In this book we try to answer the question of how political accountability can be further developed in the future European Union. This answer is based on an 'ius commune' approach: we seek common constitutional principles and practices in the national political systems in the EU Member States and we try to assess to what extent these common principles and practices can be applied in the European Union. For that reason, we invited distinguished lawyers and political scientists to explore political accountability in their country. We like to thank the authors for their contributions to this book.

Furthermore, we needed the help and support of others to realise this project. First, we would like to thank the other members of the research group: Monica Claes, Deirdre Curtin, Jit Peters, Olaf Tans, Anchrit Wille and Carla Zoethout. Subsequently, we also want to mention Joop van den Berg, Philipp Kiiver, Sofie Polleunis, Naima Qoubbane, Walter van Gerven and Carol Harlow. Finally, we want to thank Marina Jodogne and Marjo Mullers of the METRO Institute of the University of Maastricht for their professional administrative and editorial support.

Luc Verhey, Hansko Broeksteeg, Ilse Van den Driessche
December 2007

Contributors

The editors

Luc Verhey is Professor of Constitutional and Administrative law at the University of Maastricht since 2000. He is the director of the Maastricht branch of the Montesquieu Institute and coordinator of the research program 'Ius commune and public law' of the Research School Ius Commune. In 1992, he defended his PhD-thesis on the Drittwirkung of fundamental rights, particularly the right of privacy. Between 1993 and 2000 and since 2007, he has worked as a senior legal adviser at the Dutch Ministry of Justice. He mainly publishes on issues of public accountability, democracy, legislation and human rights.

Hansko Broeksteeg is a Senior Lecturer of Constitutional Law at the Radboud University in Nijmegen since 2007. Between 2001 and 2007, he was lecturer at the University of Maastricht. In 2004, he defended his PhD-thesis on political and legal accountability of ministers and members of the local government. He mainly publishes on issues of parliamentary law and local government law.

Ilse Van den Driessche is a Lecturer of Constitutional Law at the University of Maastricht since 2002. In 2005, she defended her PhD-thesis on political accountability, a comparative research on the concepts of political accountability in the Netherlands, Belgium, Germany and France. She mainly publishes on issues of public accountability, comparative constitutional law and governance.

The authors

Enoch Alberti: Professor of Constitutional Law at the University of Barcelona.

Hansko Broeksteeg: Senior Lecturer of Constitutional Law at the Radboud University Nijmegen.

Monica Claes: Professor of Constitutional and Administrative Law at the University of Tilburg.

Mahulena Hofmann: Professor of European Law at the University of Giessen

Jørgen Albæk Jensen: Lecturer of Constitutional Law at the University of Aarhus.

Jiři Kopal: PhD candidate of International Public Law at the Masaryk University of Brno.

Veith Mehde: Professor of Public Law, especially Administrative Law at the Leibniz University of Hannover.

Joakim Nergelius: Professor of Law at the University of Örebro.

Stefania Ninatti: Associate Professor of Public Law at the University of Turin.

Ryszard Piotrowksi: Lecturer of Constitutional Law at the University of Warsaw.

Giulia Tiberi: Lecturer of Constitutional Law at the University of Como.

Adam Tomkins: Professor of Public Law at the University of Glasgow.

Ilse Van den Driessche: Lecturer of Constitutional Law at the University of Maastricht.

Luc Verhey: Professor of Constitutional and Administrative Law at the University of Maastricht.

Lorenza Violini: Professor of Constitutional Law at the University of Milan.

Jacques Ziller: Professor of Comparative Public Law at the European University Institute, Florence.

CHAPTER I

Introduction: Political Accountability in a European Perspective

Luc Verhey and Monica Claes

1 Introduction

1.1 The Question of Political Accountability

This book attempts to ascertain whether and how political accountability in the European Union can be further developed. As part of a wider project[1] it looks at political accountability from a particular perspective: it attempts to answer the question of whether and how political accountability in the European Union can be further developed by building on constitutional concepts, principles and practices relating to political accountability as understood within national legal systems. The concept of political accountability has a longstanding tradition in the Member States of the European Union. It is an essential element of democratic government in European democracies.

The research starts from the presumption, which will be explained further below, that the EU is challenged in terms of accountability, and that the concept of political accountability as it operates in national systems may contribute to address these challenges at the EU level. Some preliminary questions accordingly need to be addressed: Why should the concept of political accountability be further developed in the future European Union? In addition, why exactly could national experiences be relevant if we assume that the European Union is something else than a nation state?

1.2 Democratic Deficit of the EU

The question of the 'democratic deficit' of the European Union (EU) has been a major subject of public debate for many years now.[2] The European polity is, in the eyes of many, undemocratic and dominated by unelected officials in the European Commission and by the Member States acting together in the Council. In practical effect, the latter escape accountability both to the national parliaments and to the European Parliament. Many national parliaments appear unable or unwilling to influence the behaviour of their government in the Council. The European Parliament cannot hold the Council to account and is considered too weak to effectively monitor the accountability of the Commission. The result is non-accountable governance in the European context, with the machinery failing at all levels, both European and national.

---

1 This book is part of a wider project on political control and accountability in the European Union. Political control in the EU through the national parliaments is the central theme of the sub-project co-ordinated by the University of Amsterdam, while accountability issues in political administrative relations in the EU context will be looked into in the sub-project based at the Utrecht School of Governance. See for the outcome of the first project Tans, Zoethout, Peters (2007).

2 There is an abundant amount of literature on this issue. A summary can be found in Craig and de Búrca (2007) 133 ff (with many references) and Chalmers, Hadjiemmanuil, Monti, Tomkins (2006) 63 ff and 167 ff. For the theoretical background of the discussion on the democratic deficit Craig (1999) Ch. 1. See further Weiler (1999) 77 ff and 264 ff.

This perceived democratic deficit, in terms of accountability and responsibility of government to parliament becomes even greater when the national models of democracy are chosen as a yardstick for analysis. In the parliamentary systems in the Member States, government is accountable to a directly elected parliament, government can be censured by it, individual ministers can often be removed and the direction of government policy can directly be influenced by the people's representatives in parliament. Compared with such systems Eurodemocracy comes out relatively feeble.[3] Of course, the European Parliament's powers have been steadily increased and it can now effectively block legislation in some circumstances. In terms of political control, it has contributed to the resignation of the Santer Commission, and influenced the composition of the Barroso Commission. Yet, in terms of legitimacy and accountability Europe continues to struggle. The prevailing perception remains that allegations of democratic deficit and lack of accountability are general speaking more problematic at the European than at the national level.

1.3 The EU is not a Nation State

At first sight, therefore it may be assumed that lessons could be learned from democratic and accountable government in the national parliamentary systems. Nevertheless, it could be objected, Europe *is* not a State,[4] and national democratic and accountable government simply cannot be transposed to the European level.[5] When the European Communities were first established, they were not modeled after the example of the Nation States. Typical for the EU-framework as it still exists today is a mixture of intergovernmental and supranational elements. Especially because of the essential role of the Council, consisting of national governments, the EU differs considerably from traditional Nation States in the process of EU-policymaking.

The atypical character of the EU can also be illustrated by its supranational institutions. The Commission was set up to overcome the evils of traditional diplomacy. The members of the Commission would, accordingly, not be accountable to the Member States, either the national governments appointing them or to the national parliaments. This has been clearly expressed in the EC Treaty:

> 'The Members of the Commission shall, in the general interest of the Community, be completely independent in the performance of their duties. In the performance of these duties, they shall neither seek nor take instructions from any government or from any other body. Each Member State undertakes to respect this principle

[3] Although some authors argue that the problems with democracy in the Member States are no less than in the European Union. See for example Weiler (1998) 54-55.

[4] There is a difference of opinion on whether the European Union *should* be a state. See Mancini (1998) 29 ff and Weiler (1998) 43 ff.

[5] On the problem of translation, see for instance Walker (2003) 27 and other contributions in the same volume.

> and not to seek to influence the Members of the Commission in the performance of their tasks (..)'.[6]

Although the independence of the Commission has increasingly become a subject of debate, it would be too simple to equate the Commission with a regular national government.

The specificity of the European Communities and now Union in general and of the institutions specifically, does make it a dangerous venture to compare the European system with the national parliamentary model. However, the specific nature of the Commission as independent from the Member States should not mean that it should not be accountable at all. In a democracy, government must be *accountable:* government which is held to give account or explanations of actions and which can be forced to resign if it should appear that mistakes have been made. In addition, in parliamentary democracies as they exist in Europe, account is given to the directly elected representatives of the people, to parliament. Transposed to the European level, and given that the national parliaments cannot fulfill that role, it would appear self-evident that account should be given to the European Parliament.

1.4 European Parliamentary Democracy

In the aftermath of the difficult ratification of the Treaty of Maastricht the debate on the democratic deficit and the viability of real European democracy was re-launched. As the *Bundesverfassungsgericht* indicated in its *Maastricht Urteil,*

> 'It is first and foremost for the peoples of the Member States to provide democratic control via the national parliaments. Nevertheless, as the Community's tasks and powers are expanded, so the need grows to add to the democratic legitimacy and influence imparted through the national parliaments by securing the representation of the national populations of the Member States in a European Parliament, as a source of *additional* democratic underpinning for the policies of the European Union'.[7]

According to some, Europe simply lacks the *demos* and *ethos* that is indispensable for the functioning of any democratic system. There is still no real political debate in Europe, if only because of the lack of a common language and of pan-European media.[8] There is still no European functioning political system with European political parties and shifting majorities and minorities presenting

6 Article 213 EC Treaty.

7 BverfG, NJW 1993, 3047. For an English translation of importance of the judgment, CMLRev. 1994, 251 ff. Emphasis added.

8 So for instance Grimm (1995) 282. See also Habermas (1995) 303 ff and Van Gerven (2005) 41 ff.

themselves as such in the European Parliament. One could say that there is no Majesty's Government and Opposition in the European Parliament, and no real Parliament to which to give account.[9]

However in the last decade the power of the European Parliament has increased considerably. In particular the fall of the Santer Commission in 1999 can be seen as a turning point.[10] Its resignation 'was undoubtedly brought about by the activities of the European Parliament in seeking to reinforce real executive accountability'.[11] To what extent this will lead to a parliamentary system in a more traditional sense cannot be foreseen. However as the appointment of the Barroso Commission in 2004 shows the struggle for power has not yet come to an end.

1.5 Could the EU Learn From National Parliamentary Systems?

In trying to reduce the democratic deficit it may be useful to return to classic notions of constitutionalism like political accountability and parliamentary control. While recognizing that the EU will never become a traditional state or something similar one can reasonably assume that longstanding national traditions of parliamentary democracy are relevant with respect to finding a European model of democracy and accountability. The paradigm of the parliamentary system as it operates at the national level creates the expectation in the minds of many that when real power is executed at the European level and decisions are taken that influence their lives directly, this can only be done by accountable government, by institutions which must give account of their actions to the people's representatives in parliament, and which may ultimately have to step down when mistakes have been made. Although national systems in this respect do not operate perfectly, national experiences may offer inspiration to find solutions.

This suggestion can be further sustained by constitutional arguments. All Member States of the European Union have in common certain constitutional principles such as respect for the rule of law, separation of powers, democracy and accountable government.[12] These principles cannot be ignored in the debate on democracy in the European Union. On the contrary, the basic assumption of this book is that the democratic deficit in the European Union cannot be solved if European rules and mechanisms are not firmly rooted in the longstanding constitutional traditions of the Member States. That is also laid down in Article

9 However one could argue that the relation between political groups has gradually changed. A polarisation between the largest groups in Parliament has now emerged. See Harlow (2002) 101.

10 See for a detailed study: Craig (2000) 98-116 as well as Tomkins (1999) 744 ff.

11 Shaw (2000) 141. See also Weatherill, Beaumont (1999) 1064; Harlow (2002) 95.

12 Although the way in which these concepts are shaped in a particular political context and legal constitutional framework is not necessarily the same.

6 EU: the European Union is founded on the principles of freedom, democracy, human rights and the rule of law principles which 'the Member States have in common.' It may be assumed that this also applies to the issue of political accountability.

That is why in this research we want to have a closer look to national experiences with regard to the issue of political accountability. This type of research has never really been conducted in a comprehensive manner.[13] Arguments have often been used on whether national experiences are useful or not.[14] However, they are based on assumptions: they have never really and systematically been checked. Therefore in this research we want to focus in a more systematic way on the lessons Europe could learn from the Member States. Could their experiences with parliamentary democracy contribute to developing a European concept of accountability?

In this respect, there can be an important role for comparative constitutional research. What we are trying to achieve in this book is by comparative research trying to identify common principles ('*ius commune*') and practices which have been developed in different national systems with regard to political accountability and to see to what extent these principles and practices are relevant for the further development of the European constitutional system.

1.6 Scope of the Research

Given the multi-levels of the European Union the institutional structure is very complex and also quite different from the classical Montesquieuvian trias politica.[15] It involves institutions at various levels staffed by members who may execute mandates across these levels. Therefore the issue of political control and accountability is multi-faceted, raising questions as to who is accountable to whom, for what and under which mechanism. Should the

---

13 See Craig, Tomkins (2006). We can agree with their statement that 'public law research into the nature of executive power is only just beginning' (p. 15).

14 In discussing solutions the EU's 'democratic deficit' authors, while recognizing that the EU is not a traditional state, often explicitly or implicitly seem to fall back on or let themselves inspire by national models of representative democracy. Perhaps the clearest example is Van Gerven (2005). See further Dann (2003) 549 ff, Crum (2005) 452 ff and Follesdal, Hix (2005). Why There is a Democratic Deficit in the EU: A Response to Majone, Moravcsik (2002). Other authors however criticize traditional nation-state oriented ways of constitutional thinking and argue for new forms of constitutionalism. See for instance Maduro (2003) 73 ff. and other contributions in the same volume.

15 This is not to say the national systems still do conform in all respects to the classical Trias as originally presented. In reality, there is in most States much more fusion than the traditional representation of the system or the constitutional texts would make us believe. Political parties, administrations and civil servants, interest groups and civil society, committees and agencies all interfere with the original blueprint and confuse the original separation of powers, if any. In this respect, the focus should be on the checks and balances in any system, rather than in the theoretical separation of powers.

Council and/or the European Council, in addition to the accountability of its members to their respective parliaments, be accountable to the European Parliament, and how? Are there alternative mechanisms for accountability?[16] Should the Commission be accountable to the European Parliament (as representatives of the peoples of Europe to whom they are accountable through direct election) and/or to the Council (as representing the Member States acting in common, expressing the double legitimacy of the European Union, and whose members are in turn accountable to the respective national parliaments)? Should national parliaments play any role in holding the Commission to account? Which accountability mechanisms should apply to agencies and committees?

This book does not pretend to answer all these questions.[17] Its scope is limited; it concerns first and foremost the relationship between the Commission and the European Parliament. Its perspective is closely related to the tendency, expressed most prominently in the Reform Treaty,[18] to construe the Commission-European Parliament relationship more and more towards what is known as a parliamentary system in the relationship between governments and parliaments in national systems. This means a system where the composition of the government reflects the majority in Parliament, where the government is politically accountable to the Parliament and remains in office as long as it has the confidence of the majority in Parliament and until Parliament votes a motion of censure – or the government resigns.[19]

Given the peculiarities of the EU and especially the fact that the executive power within the EU is at the EU level divided between the Commission and the Council, its seems likely that the EU will not in the near future develop into a full-fledged parliamentary system. However, even if this is true, this does not make national experiences inadequate. Over the past decades the Commission-European Parliament relationship has developed more and more towards what is known at the national level as a parliamentary system. Given this fact national experiences could be relevant to draw lessons at a more operational level. National experiences with political accountability could for example be relevant to clarify specific constitutional concepts or to improve the quality of the account. In the last part of this book,[20] we will deal more comprehensively with this type of issues.

---

[16] On accountability of the Council see for instance Curtin (2004); Van Gerven (2005).

[17] As said before this book is part of a wider project on political control and accountability in the European Union. See note 1.

[18] See especially art. 9D Reform Treaty. Note however, that there is no explicit mention of Commission accountability to the European Parliament in the Title on the Provisions on Democratic Principles, in parallel to the democratic accountability of the heads of states and governments, represented in the European Council and the Council, either to their national Parliaments or to their citizens (see art. 8A Reform Treaty).

[19] These statements may seem overly simplistic and vague. The specification of the terminology and of the mechanisms involved are precisely the subject of this research project.

[20] See part III.

This introductory chapter will seek to define the general concept of political accountability (par. 2). Subsequently the chapter will describe the research method as well as a set of research questions. The latter has served as a guideline for the comparative research (par. 3).

2 What is Political Accountability?

2.1 Different Concepts

In the preceding pages, the notions of 'accountability', 'political accountability' and 'responsibility' have been used without further explanation and definition, and sometimes interchangeably. The haphazard way, in which these notions are often used in the debate on democracy at the European and the national level, is confusing. In these sections an attempt will be made to bring some clarity, and a working definition of 'political accountability' will be proposed.

The concept of 'accountability' is these days very much *en vogue* among constitutional lawyers, political scientists, managers in the public sector and politicians, often accompanied by that other notion of 'governance'. According to Richard Mulgan, it now crops up everywhere performing all manner of analytical and rhetorical tasks and carrying most of the burdens of democratic 'governance'.[21] However what is exactly meant by 'accountability' remains often unclear. Bovens claimed that the notion of 'accountability' turned out to be 'a garbage can filled with good intentions, loosely defined concepts, and vague images of good governance'.[22] This makes the concept less useful for analytical purposes.

However, the disadvantages of a blurred concept are not limited to a diminished capacity to make sound scientific analyses. The lack of clarity also has negative effects on the effectiveness of accountability mechanisms in practice. It can be used as an instrument to evade accountability. The Commission, for example, has mentioned in its White Paper on European Governance accountability as one of the principles that underpin 'good governance', but it does not explain what it means. It does not go further than to stipulate that 'each of the EU Institutions must explain and take responsibility for what it does in Europe'.[23]

The Report of the Committee of Experts took recourse to the notions of accountability and political responsibility in the relationship between parliaments and the executive branch, in addition to other types of responsibility,

21 Mulgan (2000) 479.

22 Bovens (2006) 7.

23 European Governance, A White Paper, COM (2001), 428 final, 10. In another document the Commission defines accountability as 'the obligation to answer for a responsibility that has been conferred'. See the Commission's White Paper, 'Reforming the Commission', Part I, 43. What the difference is between 'accountability' and 'responsibility' is not explained.

mainly ethical and legal. *'Accountability'*, then, was defined as the right to be informed by the Executive, which gives account of its action, while *'political responsibility'* related to the Parliament judging the ultimate political responsibility of the Executive and drawing the political consequences.[24]

Commenting on the Report of the Committee of Experts, Van Gerven has further defined the notions of responsibility and accountability.[25] He distinguished between *ethical, political* and *legal* responsibility, while the latter (defined as responsibility determined by a court of law on the basis of binding legal rules) could further be broken up into disciplinary, criminal and civil responsibility (or 'liability'). *Ethical* responsibility was concerned with the – non-legally binding – rules of good behaviour in public life. *Political* responsibility was about responsibility to be determined by political organs on the basis of rules of conduct on proper behaviour in public life. These rules are not necessarily legally binding, but are regarded by the organ determining political responsibility as deserving the imposition of a political sanction. One set of such rules related to the duty of accountability towards Parliament. He thus seemed to distinguish the types of rules on the basis of which responsibility is measured and depending on the perspective of the body or organ judging the relevant behaviour.

In her leading book on accountability in the European Union, Harlow has pointed out that the terminology of *'accountability'* is not in use everywhere, but in all systems its content is considered to be 'an essential element of the relationship between governors and governed'. Parliaments play some part in that relationship, normally through a process in which an explanation is offered by the government to a representative assembly. However Harlow stresses that the way in which that explanation is enacted and the terms on which it is offered, may vary from one system to another.[26]

2.2 Definition

It thus appears that the concepts of 'responsibility' and 'accountability' are used in various meanings, across but even within different legal systems, both as political and legal concepts. Generally speaking, this may not a major problem. However, in the framework of a comparative research project it is important to agree on a working definition of the type of relationship and the kind of rights and obligations coming with it.

The work of Richard Mulgan can be instructive in this respect.[27] Mulgan has analysed the concept of accountability both in the public sector (public sector or government accountability) and accountability in the private commercial sector and the private non-profit sector. The concept of 'accountability', he argues, has

---

24 Second report, at marginal number 7.14.2.

25 Van Gerven (2000a) 1-15.

26 Harlow (2002) 15.

27 See for example Mulgan (2003).

been expanded to perform all manner of analytical and rhetorical tasks, but it has along the way lost some of its former straightforwardness. To Mulgan,[28] 'accountability', in its core sense, is associated with the process of being called to account to some authority for one's actions. It is *external*, it involves *social interaction and exchange*, and it *implies rights of authority*.

In the context of a democratic state, the key accountability relationships are between the citizens and the holders of public office and within the ranks of office holders, between elected politicians and bureaucrats. Mulgan contrasts 'accountability' with 'responsibility' (which is internal), 'control' (a feature of checks and balances where there is no interaction or exchange), responsiveness, and dialogue (where there is no suggestion of authority or subordination). Accountability in its core sense is defined, then, as:

> 'the obligation to be called 'to account', as a method of keeping the public informed and the powerful in check'.[29]

The starting point for the debate on issues of 'accountability' in parliamentary democracies, in particular in Westminster jurisdictions, he says, has been the role of ministers in answering to Parliament for the actions of their departments, classically termed 'ministerial responsibility'.[30] Both notions have been developed from their core sense, to often overlap, and they are often used interchangeably.

Other definitions of 'accountability' are much in line with that of Mulgan, but more elaborate. For example, the British constitutional lawyer Oliver defines 'accountability' as:

> 'being liable to be required to give an account or explanation of actions and, where appropriate, to suffer the consequences, take the blame or undertake to put matters right if it should appear that errors have been made. In other words, it is explanatory and amendatory.'[31]

More recently Bovens launched a very similar definition. According to Bovens 'accountability' is:

> 'a relationship between an actor and a forum, in which the actor has an obligation to explain and to justify his or her conduct, the forum can pose questions and pass judgment, and the actor may face consequences'.[32]

---

[28] Mulgan (2000) and (2003).

[29] Mulgan (2003) 1.

[30] Mulgan (2003) 48-52.

[31] Oliver (2003) 48.

[32] Bovens (2006) 9.

Both Oliver and Bovens recognize different elements of accountability. On the basis of their definitions one could distinguish the following stages within the process of giving an account:

- the accountor fulfilling his obligation to inform the forum and to explain and justify his conduct;
- the forum interrogating the accountor and debating the adequacy of the explaining of its conduct;
- the forum passing judgment and the accountor facing the consequences.

Our hypothesis is that the process of political accountability in the Member States of the European Union to a large extent consists of the same stages. 'Political accountability' could then be defined in the same way as Bovens to be applied in the relationship between the executive[33] (the government) and the representative body (the parliament). This is however only a hypothesis. Accordingly, the national experts involved in the project (see hereafter par. 4), what the concept of political accountability in their system exactly means. As will become clear from the country reports there are major differences between the national systems; some systems strongly stress on the consequences the government could face due to political accountability, other systems pay more attention to the quality of the preceding process of giving an account by individual ministers.

The notions of 'political accountability' and 'political responsibility' are often used interchangeably. Some authors state however, that there is a distinction between accountability and responsibility. In this point of view, the latter term can be used, when a minister cannot be held to be responsible for the actions of every civil servant or, for example, agencies.[34] At the same time, the distinction has been criticised, because of its confusing and ambiguous character.[35] We will therefore not use this distinction, unless the context makes this necessary. We therefore will in principle use only the term 'political accountability'.

In the context of this project, the concept of 'accountability' will be used to denote *political* accountability, at the exclusion of legal and ethical accountability or responsibility. Other types of accountability such as organisational, administrative and professional accountability are not taken into account either. However, for a proper understanding of rules and practices on political accountability and of the debate on the strength and the weaknesses of the concept, it will sometimes be necessary to put the issue of accountability in a broader perspective.

33 We have to keep in mind that 'the executive' can be difficult to define. See Craig, Tomkins (2006) 4-6.

34 See for example: Gay, Powell (2004) 11-12.

35 Flinders (2001) 48.

3 Research Framework

3.1 General Approach

This book is aimed at identifying common principles and practices in the Member States on political accountability. In order to deal with the complexity of this concept of 'accountability' and to get a better view/understanding of the accountability mechanisms, the institutions and the actors involved, the functions political accountability fulfils and the means by which the executive is called to account, an elaborate research framework was provided. This framework had to be elaborated to minimize the chance that the descriptions and analyses of the national systems would be incomparable.

With a view to the comparative research, a position paper was drafted, setting out the research questions and putting them in a broader context. The paper went into the details of the project: it explained the immediate cause of the research, it analysed the concept of political accountability and other relevant notions and described the state of the art on political accountability within the European Union. Finally, a set of detailed research questions was formulated to be answered for every parliamentary system involved in the comparative part of the research (see the appendix).

In advance the assumption was that if we would look at the parliamentary systems on the national level, the differences would be substantial. One could not only expect differences between the parliamentary systems of the 'older' Member States, but also between these systems and the new Member States in Eastern Europe. Our assumption is that these differences are due to the fact that the concept of political accountability is closely interwoven with the political system and the parliamentary tradition of the particular Member State. As a result the concept of political accountability will presumably be strongly influenced by national circumstances.

Not all the Member States are involved in this book.[36] We have selected Member States with longstanding parliamentary traditions in which the concept of political accountability plays a key role.[37] Apart from five out of six of the first Member States (France, Germany, Italy, Belgium and the Netherlands) we chose one Member State from Southern Europe (Spain), one Anglo-Saxon Member State (the United Kingdom), two Scandinavian Member States (Denmark and Sweden) and two Member States from Eastern Europe (Poland and the Czech Republic). We realize that this selection sets limits on the representativeness of the research. We are however convinced that this research offers at least a clear indication of the most relevant parliamentary models.

The Maastricht research group worked closely together with national experts from the selected systems, who are constitutional lawyers and/or politi-

---

[36] For practical reasons, in order to keep the project manageable, and due to financial restrictions.

[37] Although one can assume that political accountability is important even in systems that are not parliamentary. See Craig, Tomkins (2006) 11.

cal scientists. Each of the experts drafted a national report on the basis of the questionnaire annexed to the position paper mentioned above. A conference was convened in Maastricht in 2005, bringing together the Maastricht group and the national experts in order to discuss the national reports and to address some of the key issues.[38] The reports, which can be found in part II of this book, were finalised after the conference.

3.2 Research Questions

As mentioned above there was a need for a research framework to get a clear picture of the accountability mechanisms, the institutions and the actors involved, the functions political accountability fulfils and the means by which the executive is called to account, in every parliamentary system involved in the research. A preliminary question that had to be answered for every individual system was whether a constitutional concept of political accountability could be identified and if yes, what it exactly means. Accordingly, the research framework began with the overall question on the constitutional status and content of the concept as such.

When it came to the details, the research framework consisted of five basic elements which were presumably relevant in the accountability mechanisms of each of the parliamentary systems. They were shaped in five key questions:

1) Who is accountable?
2) To whom one is accountable?[39]
3) For what one is accountable?
4) How one is made accountable?
5) What are the possible consequences of being accountable?

These five key issues were elaborated in a more detailed questionnaire,[40] which has served as a guideline for the research of the national systems. Some questions were formulated in general terms to leave room to particular developments on alternative types or mechanisms of accountability that possibly have occurred in a particular Member State.

The national experts were asked not only to give answers to the questions as mentioned above but also to involve the general context of the constitutional system in question where relevant. Moreover, it was indicated that it was important not only to give straight answers but also to provide an insight in prevailing problems and dilemmas, as well as debates among politicians and academics on issues relating to political accountability. Experts were invited to make reference to historical events or to recent political cases if useful.

---

38 The conference took place at the University of Maastricht during 8-10 February 2005.

39 The questions as to who is accountable to whom are often addressed jointly, as they also will be in the research questions in the appendix.

40 See the appendix of this chapter.

3.3 Structure

This book consists of three parts. Apart from the introductory chapter (part I), the contributions of the national experts can be found in part II, while the book finishes with two concluding chapters in part III.

Part III has two main objectives. In the first place the main issues on political accountability at the national level are analysed as they appear from the national reports and, where possible, formulate common principles and practices. Based on earlier research[41] we assumed that it would at least be possible to identify some basic models of political accountability in the Member States. We do not pretend to give an exhaustive picture of all the systems involved. It is our intention to search for the headlines: the general principles on which the systems are based. Further research will be required for a more detailed comparative analysis.

The second aim of part III is to ascertain what the results of the comparative research could mean for the further development of the concept of political accountability within the European Union. Despite the peculiarities of the European Union, lessons may be learned from national experiences; at the very least, these national experiences may offer a source of inspiration for future research on accountability in the EU, and indeed, for the development of accountability mechanisms at the EU level. Needless to say, this is a very complicated task, because, as already mentioned above, the European Union is not a nation state with a full-fledged parliamentary system and because the results of the comparative research are not entirely clear and unambiguous. Nevertheless, we think it is worthwhile to search for common principles and practices on the highly important issue of accountability in order to further develop the constitutional system of the European Union.

---

[41] Ziller (2001), Van den Driessche (2005).

Appendix

Research questions

1. Accountability: general aspects

a. How is the procedure of appointment of ministers? Does this procedure influence the concept and practice of political accountability?

b. Does the concept of political accountability exist as a legal constitutional concept and if it does, what does it mean exactly?

c. Do other relevant types of accountability exist and if so, which types? To what extent is there political or legal academic debate about these issues?

2. Accountability: the actors

a. Who within the government (the government as a whole, the prime minister, individual ministers, civil servants, agencies) is politically accountable to national parliament?

b. To whom the government or actors within the government (the prime minister, individual ministers, civil servants, agencies) are accountable: national parliament or otherwise?

d. Is political accountability collective of individual? What does collective accountability, if applicable, exactly mean?

3. The scope of accountability

a. Are ministers and/or the government only accountable for policy-making or for the execution of policy as well?

b. Is there a relation between the scope of political accountability of ministers and the scope of his legal powers?

c. Does the government make use of new policy instruments that are more or less comparable to European 'co-regulation' or the 'open method of coordination'? If yes, how is accountability achieved?

d. Do ministers have political advisers? To what are extent ministers accountable for their actions?

e. To what extent ministers are accountable for actions of governments departments? Do ministers have powers to give instructions to civil servants?

f. To what extent ministers are accountable for the actions of independent agencies? Which control powers do ministers or the government have with regard to agencies?

4. Activating accountability: parliamentary control and transparency

a. What means of political and/or budgetary control are at the disposal of Parliament?

b. What obligations result from rendering political account? Does it imply, for example, giving answer to Parliament or to give information? Does a minister have to appear in Parliament when rendering account?

c. Can the government refuse to give answer or to render political account?

If yes, what are the legal grounds to refuse to answer?

d. Does Parliament have the right to question or scrutinise civil servants or independent agencies? Is there a political or scientific debate about these issues?

e. Are there any other legal or other means to activate accountability of the executive?

5. *Consequences*

a. How can the prime minister and other ministers be dismissed?

b. What is the role of Parliament with regard to the dismissal of ministers? If Parliament has the power to dismiss, can the dismissal then be collective and/or individual?

c. Are there any parliamentary procedures in place with regard to the dismissal of ministers? Can Parliament pass a motion of no-confidence or censure and if yes, does a procedure for passing such a motion exist?

d. What is the role of the prime minister with regard to the dismissal of ministers?

Bibliography

ARNULL (2000)

A.M. Arnull (eds.), *Wyatt & Dashwood's European Union Law* (London 2000).

BOVENS (2006)

M. Bovens, 'Analysing and Assessing Public Accountability: A Conceptual Framework', (2006) *European Governance Papers* (EUROGOV), no. C-06-01, <www.connex-network.org/eurogov>.

DE BÚRCA (2003)

G. de Búrca, 'The constitutional challenge of new governance in the European Union', (2003) *ELR* 28 814-839.

CHALMERS (2006)

D. Chalmers, C. Hadjiemmanuil, G. Monti, A. Tomkins, *'EU-Law'. Text and Materials* (Cambridge 2006).

CHRISTIANSEN (2004)

Th. Christiansen, 'The European Commission: Administration in turbulent times', in J. Richardson (ed.), *European Union, Power and policy-making* (London 2004) 95-114.

CLEGG, VAN HULTEN (2007)

N. Clegg, M. van Hulten, 'Reforming the European Parliament', <fpc.org.uk/fsblob/130.pdf> (viewed December 2007).

CODE OF CONDUCT FOR COMMISSIONERS (2004) 1487/2.

Available on <http://ec.europa.eu/commission_barroso/code_of_conduct/code_conduct_en.pdf>.

COMMITTEE OF INDEPENDENT EXPERTS (1999)

Committee of Independent Experts, *Second Report on the reform of the Commission. Analysis of current practices and proposals for tackling mismanagement, irregularities and fraud*, Volume II (Brussels 1999). (Available on >http://www.europarl.europa.eu/experts/default_en.htm>).

CONSTANTINESCO (2000)

V. Constantinesco, 'La responsabilité de la Commission Européenne: la crise de 1999', in P. Albertini et. al., *Pouvoirs, La responsabilité des gouvernants*, n°92, (Paris 2000) 117-131.

CORBETT, JACOBS, SHACKLETON (2005)

R. Corbett, F. Jacobs, M. Shackleton, *The European Parliament*, Sixth Edition (London 2005).

CRAIG 1999

P. Craig, 'The Nature of the Community: Integration, Democracy and Legitimacy', in: P. Craig, G. de Búrca (eds.), *The Evolution of EU Law* (Oxford 1999) 16-54.

CRAIG (2000)

P. Craig, 'The Fall and Renewal of the Commission: Accountability, Contract and Administrative Organisation' (2000) *ELJ* 98-116.

CRAIG, DE BURCA (2007)
P. Craig, G. de Búrca, *EU Law. Text, Cases and Materials*, Fourth Edition (Oxford 2007).
CRAIG, TOMKINS (2006)
P. Craig, A. Tomkins (eds.), *The Executive and Public Law. Power and Accountability in Comparative Perspective* (Oxford 2006).
CRUM (2005)
B. Crum, ,Tailoring Representative Democracy to the European Union: Does the European Constitution Reduce the Democratic Deficit?' (2005) *ELJ* 452-467.
CURTIN (2004)
D. Curtin, *Mind the Gap: the Evolving EU Executive and the Constitution*, Third Walter Van Gerven Lecture (Groningen 2004).
CURTIN (2005)
D. Curtin, 'Delegation to EU Non-Majoritarian Agencies and Emerging Practices of Public Accountability', in D. Geradin, R. Muñoz, *Regulation through agencies in the EU. A new paradigm of European governance* (Cheltenham 2005) 88-119.
CURTIN, WESSEL (2005)
D. Curtin, R. Wessel (eds.), *Good Governance in the European Union. Reflections on concepts, institutions and substance* (Antwerp/Oxford/New York 2005).
DANN (2003)
P. Dann, 'European Parliament and Executive Federalism: Approaching a Parliament in a Semi-Parliamentary Democracy' (2003) *ELJ* 549-574.
VAN DEN DRIESSCHE (2005)
I.A. Van den Driessche, *Politieke ministeriele verantwoordelijkheid: Het Nederlandse begrip in rechtsvergelijkend perspectief* (Deventer 2005).
EDITORIAL COMMENTS (1999)
Editorial Comments, (1999) *Common Market Law Review* 39 269-272.
EDITORIAL COMMENTS (2004)
Editorial Comments, 'Power to the people of the European Union – Right on?' (2004) *Common Market Law Review* 41 1475-1479.
EUROPEAN COMMISSION (2001)
European Commission, European Governance, A White Paper COM (2001) 428 final, Brussels. (Available on <http://eur-lex.europa.eu/LexUriServ/site/en/com/2001/com2001_0428en01.pdf>).
EUROPEAN COMMISSION (2002A)
European Commission, *Code of Conduct for Commissioners* (Brussels 2002).
EUROPEAN COMMISSION (2002B)
Note European Commission, *Framework for European regulatory agencies*, Brussels, COM (2002) final.

EUROPEAN COMMISSION (2005)
European Commission, *Draft Interinstitutional Agreement on the operating framework for the European regulatory agencies*, Brussels, COM 59 final 2005.

EXTERNE COMMISSIE MINISTERIËLE VERANTWOORDELIJKHEID (1992-1993)
Externe Commissie Ministeriële Verantwoordelijkheid (commissie-Scheltema), *Steekhoudend ministerschap. Betekenis en toepassing van de ministeriele verantwoordelijkheid*, Tweede Kamer, vergaderjaar 1992-1993, 21427, nrs. 40-41.

FLINDERS (2001)
M. Flinders, *The Politics of Accountability in the Modern State* (London 2001).

FOLLESDAL, HIX (2005)
A. Follesdal, S. Hix, 'Why There is a Democratic Deficit in the EU': A Response to Majone and Moravcsik, European Governance Papers (EUROGOV) No. C-05-02, (Available on http:/www.connex-network.org/eurogov/pdf/egp-connex-C-05-02.pdf).

GAY, POWELL (2004)
O. Gay, Th. Powell, 'Individual ministerial responsibility – issues and examples', Research paper House of Commons Library 2004.

GERADIN, MUÑOZ, PETIT (2005)
D. Geradin, R. Muñoz, N. Petit (eds.), *Regulation through agencies in the EU: A new paradigm of European governance* (Cheltenham UK/ Northampton MA USA 2005).

VAN GERVEN (2000A)
W. van Gerven, Guest Editorial, 'Ethical and political responsibility of EU Commissioners' (2000) *Common Market Law Review* 1-15.

VAN GERVEN (2000B)
W. van Gerven, 'Managing the European Union: For Better or for Worse?', in B.S. Markesinis (eds.), *The Clifford Chance Millennium Lectures* (Oxford/Portland/Oregon 2000).

VAN GERVEN (2005)
W. van Gerven, *The European Union: A polity of states and people* (Oxford 2005).

GRIMM (1995)
D. Grimm, 'Does Europe need a Constitution' (1995) *European Law Journal* 1 282-302.

HABERMAS (1995)
J. Habermas, 'Remarks on Dieter Grimm's 'Does Europe Need a Constitution?' (1995) *ELJ* 303-307.

HARLOW (2002)
C. Harlow, *Accountability in the European Union* (Oxford 2002).

HARTLEY (2003)
T. Hartley, *The Foundations of European Community Law* (Oxford 2003).

HIX (2005)
S. Hix, *The political system of the European Union* (Hampshire/New York 2005).

KIIVER (2006)
Ph. Kiiver, *The National Parliaments in the European Union: A Critical View on EU Constitution-Building* (The Hague 2006).

LEQUESNE (2000)
Ch. Lequesne, 'The European Commission: A Balancing Act between Autonomy and Dependence', in K. Neunreither, A. Wiener (eds.), *European Integration After Amsterdam* (Oxford 2000).

MADURO (2003)
M.P. Maduro, 'Europe and the constitution: what if this is as good as it gets', in J.H.H. Weiler and M. Wind (eds.), *European Constitutionalism Beyond the State* (Cambridge 2003) 74-102.

MAGNETTE (2001)
P. Magnette, 'Appointing and Censuring the European Commission: The Adaptation of Parliamentary Institutions to the Community Context' (2001) *European Law Journal* 292-310.

MAJONE, EVERSON (2001)
G. Majone, M. Everson, 'Institutional reform: independent agencies, oversight coordination and procedural control', in O. De Schutter, N. Lebessis and J. Paterson (eds.), *Governance in the European Union*, Luxembourg 2001.

MANCINI (1998)
G.F. Mancini, 'Europe: The Case for Statehood' (1998) *European Law Journal* 4 29-42.

MEHDE (2003)
V. Mehde, 'Responsibility and Accountability in the European Commission' (2003) *Common Market Law Review* 40 423-442.

MÖLLERS (2006)
C. Möllers, 'European Governance: Meaning and Value of a Concept' (2006) *Common Market Law Review* 43 314-336.

MULGAN (2000)
R. Mulgan, 'Accountability: An ever expanding concept?' (2000) *Public Administration* 78 555-573.

MULGAN (2003)
R. Mulgan, *'Holding Power to Account': Accountability in Modern Democracies* (Basingstoke 2003).

NUGENT (2001)
N. Nugent, *The European Commission* (New York 2001).

NUGENT (2003)

N. Nugent, *The Government and Politics of the European Union* (New York 2003).

OLIVER (2003)

D. Oliver, *Constitutional Reform in the UK* (Oxford 2003).

RAPPORT-DEHAENE (1999)

Rapport-Dehaene, *Rapport à la Commission Européenne, Implications institutionnelles de l'élargissement* (Bruxelles, 18 octobre 1999).

DE SCHUTTER, LEBESSIS, PATERSON (2001)

O. de Schutter, N. Lebessis, J. Paterson (eds.), *Governance in the European Union* (Luxembourg 2001).

SHACKLETON (1998)

M. Shackleton, 'The European Parliament's New Committees of Inquiry: Tiger or Paper Tiger?' (1998) *JCMS* 115-130.

SHAW (2000)

J. Shaw, *Law of the European Union* (New York 2000).

TANS, ZOETHOUT, PETERS (2007)

O. Tans, C. Zoethout, J. Peters, *National Parliaments and European Democracy. A Bottom-up Approach to European Constitutionalism* (Groningen 2007).

TOMKINS (1999)

A. Tomkins, 'Responsibility and resignation in the European Commission' (1999) *Modern Law Review* 62 744-765.

TURPIN, TOMKINS (2007)

C. Turpin, A. Tomkins, *Political accountability and British government: Text and Materials (Law in Context)* (Cambridge 2007).

VOS (2003)

E. Vos, 'Agencies and the European Union', in L. Verhey, T. Zwart (eds.), *Agencies in a comparative and European Perspective* (Antwerp 2003) 113-147.

WALKER (2001)

N. Walker, 'The White Paper in Constitutional Context', in Symposium: Mountain or Molehill? A Critical Appraisal of the Commission White paper on Governance, Jean Monnet Working Paper No. 6/01.

WALKER (2003)

N. Walker, 'Postnational constitutionalism and the problem of translation', in J.H.H. Weiler and M. Wind (eds), *European Constitutionalism Beyond the State* (Cambridge 2003) 27-54.

WEATHERILL, BEAUMONT (1999)

S. Weatherill, P. Beaumont, *EU Law* (London 1999).

WEILER (1998)

J.H.H. Weiler, 'Europe: The Case against the Case of Statehood' (1998) *European Law Journal* 4 43-62.

WEILER (1999)
J.H.H. Weiler, *The Constitution of Europe. 'Do the new clothes have an emperor?' and other essays on European Integration* (Cambridge 1999).
WEILER (2001)
J.H.H. Weiler, 'The Commission as Euro-Skeptic: A Task Oriented Commission for a Project-Based Union. A Comment on the First Version of the White Paper', in Symposium: Mountain or Molehill? A Critical Appraisal of the Commission White Paper on Governance, Jean Monnet Working Paper No. 6/01, 2001 (available on <http://www.jeanmonnetprogram.org/papers/01/013401.html>).
WEILER, WIND (2003)
J.H.H. Weiler, M. Wind (eds.), *European Constitutionalism beyond the State* (Cambridge 2003).
WESTLAKE (1994)
M. Westlake, *The Commission and the Parliament* (London/Dublin/Edinburgh 1994).
WESTLAKE (1997)
M. Westlake, 'The Commission and the Parliament', in G. Edwards, D. Spence (eds.), *The European Commission* (London 1997).
ZILLER (2001)
J. Ziller, ''European Models of Government': Towards a Patchwork with Missing Pieces' (2001) *Parliamentary Affairs* 54 102-119.

CHAPTER 2

Political Accountability in Belgium

Ilse Van den Driessche

1 Origin and Embedment of Political Accountability in the Belgian Parliamentary System

Throughout history, the territory of Belgium has always been under the reign of foreign sovereigns. By the end of the 18th century, the territory was annexed by France and became part of the French Empire under the reign of Napoleon. The defeat of Napoleon however resulted in the unification of the Southern Netherlands with the Northern Netherlands. In 1830, after merely 15 years of unity under the reign of the Dutch King William I, the southern provinces of the Netherlands called for independence, renamed themselves Belgium and drafted a – for that time very – liberal Constitution. Although many aspects of French and Dutch law inspired the new country, the new Constitution made it possible to renounce the Dutch constitutional system and to draw up a new institutional structure based upon democratic principles. To restrain the power of the King, as head of state in a parliamentary system, and to introduce a form of political accountability were some of the main objectives of the drafters of the Constitution. Their motives were based on their experience with the overall repressive power of the Dutch King and the lack of accountability for the King's policy. Etienne de Gerlache, president of the National Congres and later first Prime Minister of Belgium, described the Constitution as following: '*Notre constitution respire partout la haine du roi passé, et la peur du roi future*'.[1] The primary principle for the power of the King from then on was: '*pas de pouvoir sans responsabilité*'. However, since it was generally accepted that, because of his immunity, parliament could not criticise a king directly for his policy and the execution thereof, accountability for the king's actions was to be redirected to his ministers.[2] In addition, to avoid that a king or any group of people would be able to claim the sovereign power in the state, the Constitution explicitly states that sovereign power is in the hands of the Nation.[3] The parliament, as representative of the Nation,[4] is thereby bestowed with a central role in the parliamentary structure. The cabinet in its turn, receiving its legitimacy from the Nation through the parliament, has to retain that confidence to remain in office and

---

1 'The hatred for the previous king and the fear for the future king is shown throughout the Constitution', De Gerlache, as quoted in Alen (1984) 56. The hatred for the King's policy was mainly based on the introduction of the freedom of religion, which was not to the liking of the catholic elite, and the King's economic and linguistic policy in the southern provinces, which resulted in strong resistance from the French-speaking liberal elite, and eventually leaded to the secession of the southern provinces.

2 Moreover judicial review of governmental acts, the so-called '*exceptie van onwettigheid*', was established to make sure that the judiciary could check the legitimacy of governmental acts.

3 Art. 33 Constitution: 'All power emanates from the Nation. This power is exerted in the manner established by the Constitution'. The Nation is a contrived concept that contains all generations of the present, the future and the past. The relevant provisions in the constitution have not been altered since 1831. I use the current numbering of articles in the Constitution, unless otherwise specified.

4 Art. 42 Constitution: The members of both the House and the Senate represent the Nation, and not only those who elected them.

therefore accounts to the parliament. The introduction of ministerial accountability is a consequence of both the limitation of the King's competences and the sovereign power of the Nation.[5]

The concept of accountability has evolved in the last 175 years, but the historical context and the key constitutional articles still provide for its basic principles. When reading the Belgian Constitution, one cannot help but notice that the King to this day still seems to have a lot of formal power bestowed on him: 'The federal executive power, as stipulated by the Constitution, belongs to the King' (art. 37 Constitution); The federal legislative power is exerted collectively by the King, the House of Representatives and the Senate (art. 36 Constitution); Judiciary power is exerted by the courts and tribunals. Rulings and court decisions are carried out in the name of the King (art. 40 Constitution). However, the King's competences are strictly demarcated in the Constitution.[6] Moreover, ministerial accountability for the King's actions is introduced in the general clause of art. 88 Constitution in a single phrase: 'The King can do no wrong; his ministers are accountable'.[7] This provision is completed with art. 106 Constitution: No actions of the King may take effect without the countersignature of a minister, who, in doing so, takes responsibility upon himself.[8] These articles remain the key provisions that establish political accountability. They mean that, although the powers of the executive – and some other powers – are all formally concentrated in the King, these are not personal powers and under no condition can the King act alone. By countersigning the King's decisions and supporting his actions, his ministers become accountable to parliament. Political accountability is up to this day still organised with this theoretical framework in mind, although the focus has shifted from accountability for the acts of the King to accountability for the acts of the ministers and their departments, now called services. Indeed, in practice, the functioning of the executive is in the hands of the ministers and the King's role herein is reduced to a minimum.[9]

2 Terminology and Definition

Nowadays, defining the term 'political accountability' in legal terminology is difficult and there is no such thing as a common definition. In colloquial language, '*politieke verantwoordelijkheid*' or '*responsabilité politique*' is

5 Van den Driessche (2005) 71.

6 Art. 105 Constitution: The King has no powers other than those formally attributed to him by the Constitution and by specific laws established by virtue of the Constitution itself.

7 Art. 88 Constitution: '*De persoon des konings is onschendbaar; zijn ministers zijn verantwoordelijk*'.

8 Art. 106 Constitution: '*Geen akte van de Koning kan gevolg hebben, wanneer zij niet medeondertekend is door een minister, die daardoor alleen reeds, ervoor verantwoordelijk wordt.*'

9 His role is reduced to the formal forming of the cabinet, signing of governmental acts and giving royal assent to legislation; his overall role has in fact reduced to 'the right to be consulted, the right to encourage, the right to warn' (Bagehot).

often equated with 'having to take the blame' and, consequently, 'being forced to step down'. Within the Belgian discourse, the Flemish-Belgian term '*verantwoordelijkheid*' is equated with the French-Belgian term '*responsabilité*', but – as in France – no differentiation is made between accountability and responsibility[10] and the term itself seems to refer to both. In fact, attempts at defining the term in legal literature are usually not more than a description of the means that parliament has to oust the cabinet, rather then defining the term itself. Van Impe describes the term as following: '*La responsabilité politique consiste dans l'obligation qu'ont les ministres de démissionner lorsque la Chambre des représentants ou le Sénat manifeste de façon non équivoque sa désapprobation* .[11] Political accountability then solely means that ministers are required to step down, when dismissed by parliament. However, in order to retain the parliament's confidence, the ministers have to account to parliament.[12] Usually, when political accountability is described in the context of the Belgian parliamentary system, one will not only find references to the motions of (no) confidence and their consequences, but also to the rendering of account by ministers.

One can conclude that the focus in Belgian legal literature when describing political accountability is mainly on the parliament as the forum and on the means parliament has to make ministers accountable and to dismiss them.

3 The Forum

3.1 *Kamer van Volksvertegenwoordigers* as the Political Chamber

Up until 1993, ministers were accountable to the 'parliament'. The Belgian parliament is composed of two assemblies, and the ministers were accountable to both assemblies. On the one hand, there is the *Kamer van volksvertegenwoordigers* (House of representatives), the directly elected assembly, on the other the *Senaat* (Senate), comprised of senators who are indirectly chosen in a number of ways. In 1993, the Constitution was amended to enforce stability of the government: the parliamentary system is now *rationalised*, after the example of the French and German parliamentary systems. This means that parliament is restricted in its possibilities to control, or more specifically, to oust the government. The focus is now on the House of representatives, which is – as directly elected assembly – the so-called 'political chamber', reducing the Senate to a so-called 'chamber of reflection'. The Constitution was amended to this end and article 101.1 now states that Ministers are accountable before the House of representatives. Only the House therefore has to its disposal the means to ask

10 See for a discussion on the terms accountability and responsibility: Allen, Thompson (2005) 250-287. For the discussion in the UK, Harlow (2002) 6-24, for a comparative discussion.

11 Van Impe (1968) 126: Political accountability consists of the obligation of ministers to resign when the House of representatives or the Senate unambiguously expresses disapproval.

12 Van den Driessche (2005) 66-69.

for information and to require of ministers that they account for their actions and policy. Also the (constructive) motion of confidence and of no-confidence can only be introduced in the House. The Senate retained its right to ask questions, but since it no longer constitutes a political chamber, senators can merely ask, but cannot require of ministers that they account for certain policies, nor can they oblige the cabinet or individual ministers to step down. The focus hereafter will therefore, within the context of accountability, mainly be on the position of the House.

3.2 Questions and Interpellations

With the constitutional amendment of 1993, the incompatibility of the mandate of a representative in the parliament and the office of minister was also introduced. Ministers therefore have to give up their seat in the parliament when they come into office. A member of the government can however be present in the plenary assembly and a specialised committee, and usually is when the topic of the day regards a matter attributed to the minister. The House can request the presence of the members of government when it sees fit to do so (art. 100.1 Constitution). The Senate can only request the presence of a minister in certain procedures (art. 100.2 Constitution); in all other cases the Senate can *ask* for the presence of the minister. In the latter case, the minister is not required to attend the meeting. There is however no (legal) sanction whether the presence of the minister was asked for or was requested. The right of the House of representatives to request the presence of ministers is by some scholars considered the basis for the right to submit interpellations and the right to submit questions to the government.[13] The right to submit questions and interpellations are not expressly provided for in the Constitution, but are mentioned in the standing orders of the houses of parliament. Others consider these rights to be a direct consequence of the principle of political accountability.[14]

3.2.1 Questions

Both Houses have the right to submit questions to receive information. Questions are addressed at a minister, usually not at the government as a whole, and are answered orally during a weekly question hour. The more technical answers are usually provided for in written form and published. Questions do not generate the possibility to oust the government or one of its members: they are not followed by a debate, or by the possibility to invoke a vote on a motion. There are also no legal rules for the refusal of answers. This implies that questions are meant to ask for information and not to demand explanation on the policy choices. This is also the reason why the *Senaat* still retains the right to ask questions, while it is no longer a political chamber. How-

[13] Van Impe (1972) 2.

[14] Van der Hulst (1996) 16.

ever, in practice it is difficult to differentiate between giving information and giving an explanation.

Aside from the weekly question hour, there is also the possibility of a debate on a pressing topic. As is the case for questions, this type of debate cannot be concluded by a vote.

3.2.2 Interpellations

The right of submitting interpellations is a means of calling the government to account for its policy. Because the House of representatives is the political chamber, only this assembly has the right to submit interpellations. Interpellations are followed by a debate and the possibility to conclude the debate with an evaluation of the given explanation. These votes can vary from a vote on a *simple motion*, in which parliament acknowledges the answer of the government and proceeds to the next item on the agenda, to a vote on a *reasoned motion*, being either a (constructive) motion of censure – emanating from the members of the House – or a (constructive) motion of confidence – emanating from the government. Simple motions prevail over reasoned motions, when several motions are handed in. This consequently means that reasoned motions are rarely voted on. The parliamentary majority would most likely want to dismiss a reasoned motion when the reasoned motion was handed in by the opposition, and try to move on to the next item on the agenda without destabilising the position of the government. Interpellations are directed at the government, and addressed to the Prime minister, although he can decide which minister will account for the subject matter at hand. Since the government can only be ousted collectively according to the Constitution, an interpellation should legally only be directed at the government as a whole. The House however wanted to be able to express the loss of confidence in single minister, which is why a motion following an interpellation can be addressed at a single minister according to the standing orders of the House of representatives (see under Consequences). Expressing the loss of confidence can however not formally prompt the dismissal of a minister, since that would be unconstitutional. An adopted motion will however be a powerful signal to the government and the public from the House and will in practice result in the resignation of the minister in question. The House has never adopted a motion in this sense; usually the minister will resign in advance.[15]

[15] Some examples of ministers resigning in the last decade are: Stefaan De Clerck and Johan Vande Lanotte (1998), Louis Tobback (1998), Marcel Colla and Karel Pinxten (1999), Magda Aelvoet (2002), Isabelle Durant and Olivier Deleuze (2003).

4 The Actors and the Scope of Political Accountability

4.1 Accountability for Governmental Acts

Political accountability covers both accountability for policy-making and the execution of policy. Theoretically and in origin, it applies to all decisions and acts of the King that might have any political impact. In practice, the state is governed by the ministers,[16] but this is formally done in the name of the King. The King is head of the executive[17] and all executive powers are constitutionally attributed to the King.[18] This includes the power to make *Koninklijke Besluiten* (governmental acts) and this also includes that he organises the executive: the King formally appoints and dismisses his ministers, and has the power to organise the ministerial departments. This is however theory. It is the parliamentary majority that provides the government and it is the ministers who are head of the ministerial departments.

Ministers are still explicitly mentioned in the Constitution as ministers *of the King*. They are however no longer *his* ministers, but are in fact ministers of the parliamentary majority. The ministers are formally appointed and dismissed by the King (art. 46 Constitution), but ministers no longer formally rely on the confidence of the King, but on the confidence of the majority in parliament (in fact of the House of representatives). The House of representatives has the so-called *government making power* and it is towards the House of representatives that ministers are politically accountable. The King still has the formal power to appoint the members of the government, and upon their appointment, the government can act. However, the government refrains from acting as long as it lacks democratic legitimacy, i.e. as long as there is no explicit vote of confidence by the House of representatives.

The governmental acts are signed by the King and countersigned by the ministers and/or secretaries of state. Not only does this countersignature constitute political accountability for the act, it is also a condition for the legality of the act. No act of the King can have any effect if it is not countersigned by a minister (art. 106 Constitution). The King does not have any political influence,[19] therefore he cannot sign any act without his ministers, who take on the accountability for these acts. This also means that there is a unity between the King and his ministers, and that all powers attributed in the Constitution to the King, are in fact attributed to the King and his accountable ministers. Therefore a countersignature is interpreted widely, meaning that not only written acts by the King have to be countersigned to have any effect; also all other actions by

---

16 Unless mentioned otherwise, secretaries of state are considered to be ministers and the rules relating to ministers also apply to them.

17 Article 37 Constitution.

18 Article 105 Constitution.

19 The King has to remain neutral and should stand above politics, therefore the rather active role of the King during the difficult formation of the 2007 cabinet has been criticised.

the King that can have a political effect have to be (pre-) approved by a minister. This means in theory that ministers are accountable for all acts of the King, be they written or not.

The Prime Minister is considered to be *primus inter pares*.[20] He has no more powers than other members of the government. He heads the government and presides over the council of ministers, although this latter presidency is formally a task of the King. The King has not taken up this task for decades. One of his primal tasks is to coordinate the government. This is not an easy task when one considers that the government always consists of several political parties that form a coalition. The Prime Minister is also the main link of the government to the King and to the parliament.

4.2 Reform of the Departmental Structure

The Belgian departmental structure was long in need of a restructuring, a change of management culture and an overall modernisation. In 2000 a major reform, strongly influenced by the New Public Management discourse, called '*het Copernicusplan*' changed the departmental structure of the so-called '*Ministeries*' into '*Federale Overheidsdiensten*' (FGS; i.e. Federal Government Services) and '*Programmatorische Overheidsdiensten*' (PGS; i.e. Program Oriented Government Services). The new structure intends to solve the problem of the departmental structure before the reform: policy matters were sometimes scattered over several departments, making civil servants report to several ministers at the same time. The basic principle of the Copernicus reform was that only one minister would be accountable for an entire service.

The FGSs are now services that specialize in a specific policy area, e.g. finance, internal affairs, foreign affairs, justice, defence, social security, economy, etc.[21] These are the vertical FGSs. The horizontal FGSs coordinate matters common to the other FGSs.[22] The Prime minister has a Chancellery, which is a 'horizontal FGS, at his disposal.

The PGSs are more diverse and cover larger policy areas, mainly a crossovers of several or all policy areas, e.g. telecommunication, integration, poverty and social economy, ICT, ... etc. PGSs can be erected according to the policy of each new cabinet in office.[23] Ministers are politically accountable for the FGS and PGS assigned to them. Each service consists of a *Beleidsraad* (Policy Board), a *Directiecomité* (Management Committee) and a *Beleidscel* (Policy Unit). The *Beleidsraad* is presided by the minister and is considered to be the link between the government and the civil service. Its main function is to prepare policy.

20 He is in fact '*primus inter primi*', when one considers that there are also vice-prime ministers from every coalition party.

21 There are 10 vertical FGSs.

22 There are 4 horizontal FGSs: personnel and organization, budget, information and communication, and the Chancellery of the Prime minister.

23 There are at the moment 4 PGSs.

The *Directiecomité* covers the management of civil service and is presided by a manager with a temporal contract of 6 years.[24] The *Beleidscel* assists the minister in preparing and evaluating the policy and coordinating that policy within the FGS/PGS. The *Beleidscel* was introduced to take over the function of the ministerial cabinets. These are personal advisers of the minister, which prepare policy outside of the civil service. The advisers are contracted on a personal and temporal basis. One of the focuses of the Copernicus reform was the diminishment of these personal cabinets, which consist of sometimes hundreds of personnel members per minister. The problem was, and to this day still is, that these highly politicised cabinets took over most of the policy and coordinating functions of the civil service, and even mingled in the policy executing function of the civil servants. By abolishing the ministerial cabinets and introducing the *Beleidscel* within the administration, the policy role of the administration would be strengthened. However, the ministerial cabinets were in the end not abolished and attaining the goal of a diminished ministerial cabinet has now been omitted from revision. The Copernicus reform was halted in 2004. How all of this now reflects onto the accountability of the ministers is not clear. In fact, although at the beginning of the Verhofstad, II cabinet (2004) ministers were heading their respective service, some policy areas were later on again scattered over several ministers, which devalued the overall effect of the reform.

4.3 The Scope of the Accountability for Civil Servants

Neither civil servants, nor members of a ministerial cabinet are accountable towards parliament; it is the minister – as head of the FGS/PGS and his personal cabinet – who is accountable. Secretaries of state are considered to be a sort of under-ministers. They are allocated to a certain minister and FGS/PGS, but have a specific policy area attributed to them. They are accountable for this area towards the parliament, not withstanding the accountability of the minister responsible for the entire FGS. Wigny (1952) stated that the parliament could only control the general policy of the government; therefore (minor) incidents in the ministerial departments were under the control of the government and not so much within the scope of parliamentary control. Nowadays there is hardly a legal debate on whether a minister is accountable to parliament for the actions of his civil servants or the members of his political cabinet; the minister is at the top of the hierarchy and is therefore accountable. The debate rather concerns the question when it is politically appropriate that a minister resigns. Prime minister Dehaene considered it appropriate for ministers to resign when: 'a minister has made a personal mistake, when a minister can no longer fulfill his function and when it is necessary for the continuation of the government's general policy that a minister resigns'.[25] Delpérée has rephrased this in light of recent resignations implying that ministers lately resign, not so much because

[24] Not all PGSs have a *Directiecomité*.

[25] Jean-Luc Dehaene during a debate in the Senate in 2002, 28 February 2002, no. 2-184/704.

they were personally responsible, but mainly because they became 'vulnerable' in the eyes of the media and the general public.[26] Especially cases with a high symbolic value seem to result in resignations.[27]

4.4 Independent Agencies

Independent agencies[28] exist in many forms within the federal executive and it is hardly possible to classify these forms.[29] The general idea is that the minister to which the agency is attributed remains fully accountable for the agency, even if he does not have any competences to regulate the decision making by that agency.[30] The reasoning behind this is that of democratic legitimacy and parliamentary control: ministers have to account to parliament for everything within the executive. Ministers have in the past tried to avoid parliamentary questions about the independent agencies, by refusing to answer[31] or reading out loud the answer given by the agency itself.[32] The debate on independent agencies is a hot topic on the Flemish level of government. In 2000, the Flemish government started a major reform of the Flemish administration structures, called *Beter Bestuurlijk Beleid* (better administrative policy).[33] The debate also includes the possibility of shifting several policy-executing matters to independent agencies as a means to create more transparency in the administration. The idea is to leave the full accountability with the minister for the department and the independent agencies, regardless of the internal relation of the minister with the manager of the department.[34] The reform is approved and partly in effect as of 1 January 2006.[35]

5 The Consequences

Since the rationalisation of parliament in 1993, the House only has a constructive vote of censure to its disposal. This means that only in

---

26 Delpérée (2000) 900.

27 The ministers Vande Lanotte and De Clerck resigned after the escape of Belgium's main criminal Marc Dutroux in 1998.

28 See extensive on this topic: Alen, Devroe (1997).

29 There are *'openbare instellingen'*, *'parastatalen'*, *'intercommunales'*, *'gepersonaliseerde overheidsdiensten'*, *'publiekrechtelijke of gemengde verenigingen'*, *'autonome overheidsbedrijven'*, etc.

30 Alen, Devroe (1997) 124.

31 The information was either too sensitive, it was within the commercial strategy, it would take too long to gather the information, etc.

32 Alen, Devroe (1997) 123.

33 See for an extensive report: <http://www2.vlaanderen.be/ned/sites/bbb/krachtlijnen/index.htm>.

34 See for the background of this reform: <http://www2.vlaanderen.be/ned/sites/bbb/documenten/organisatie/decreten/kaderdecreetbb_memorie_bespreking_dispositief_211103.pdf>.

35 <http://www2.vlaanderen.be/ned/sites/snelinfo/snelinfo2005/0523.htm>.

certain, well-defined cases is the government as a whole obliged to hand over its resignation to the King. Therefore, the government is only collectively accountable towards parliament. This means that ministers give account in name of the government and that the government can only as a whole be ousted by the House of representatives.

The constructive vote of censure works as following (art. 96 Constitution):

1) the House of representatives, when casting a vote of censure towards the government, has to nominate a new Prime Minister;
2) the House of representatives, when rejecting a motion of confidence, has three days to nominate a new Prime Minister.

In both cases, the King can decide to dissolve the House of representatives when no new Prime Minister is nominated. The Senate is dissolved together with the House of representatives. A government can of course decide to resign itself, but this does not automatically provide for new elections. The House of representatives has to approve its dissolvement in such a case.

Although the Constitution does not mention the consequences for the loss of confidence in an individual minister, the standing orders do mention a vote of confidence and a vote of censure directed at individual ministers (art. 135.1 and 138.1 Standing Orders of the House of representatives). However, these individual votes of censure, since they are not mentioned by the Constitution, cannot compel a minister to resign. It is however in practice very difficult to continue in office when confidence is lost by the parliament.

The constructive vote of censure was introduced after a period of instability of the government (mainly in the 1970s and '80s). The idea was to strengthen the government and to clearly define the powers of the parliament. It is not clear how a constructive vote could better the stability of the government since governmental crises were – and still are – almost always due to internal rivalry within the government and political bickering, rather than a conflict with the parliament. Since 1993, no government was ousted by the parliament, nor did an individual minister explicitly lose the confidence of the parliament. Ministers do resign on an individual basis, usually because of pressure, either from the media, from within their political party or from the Prime Minister. Although the Prime Minister is head of the government, he does not legally have the power to compel one of the ministers to hand in their resignation to the King. It is however politically accepted that the Prime Minister can pressure a minister to resign. This was the case after the escape of Belgium's number one criminal Marc Dutroux from prison. It was expected that this would eventually bring the government to resign, be it initiated by the parliament or not. To save the government, and more importantly to safeguard the major reform of the police and justice departments that was about to start, in 1998, Prime Minister Jean-Luc Dehaene pressured the ministers of interior affairs and justice to resign.[36]

[36] Johan Vande Lanotte, minister of interior affairs and Stefaan De Clerck, minister of justice, resigned in 1998. Especially Vande Lanotte saw it as his duty as head of the department of interior affairs to

Another form of parliamentary control that can eventually lead to a motion of censure can be found in the establishment of parliamentary committees of inquiry.[37] Especially in recent years, many inquiries were held on topical matters.[38] Both members of the House and of the Senate are entitled to request that an inquiry be held. A member can introduce the topic of an inquiry in a commission, which will be discussed and then sent to the plenary meeting for further discussion. The introduction of the inquiry will be voted upon by majority. An inquiry may be held by the House or the Senate in their entirety or a special committee, but it is in practice always conducted by a special committee.[39] An inquiry may take anywhere from 1 month up to 2 years. A *rapporteur*, designated by the committee, gives an account of the inquiry to the plenary session upon conclusion of the investigation. The plenary then makes a statement about the possible conclusions, recommendations or resolutions of the committee of inquiry. This may lead to a legislative initiative or even the indication of political accountability of ministers. If the latter is the case, only the House – as political chamber – can sanction the minister by approving a motion of censure.[40] This however has never happened.

6 Other Forms of Accountability

Ever since the birth of the Belgian parliamentary system, political accountability has been the main form of accountability for actions by the executive. For over a century, neither criminal nor civil ministerial liability was of any practical importance. However, criminal ministerial accountability has known a revival at the end of the twentieth century due to some corruption scandals and the consequent amendment of the Constitution.

---

step down, when the police failed to prevent the escape of Dutroux. However, both resignations where considered to be the solution to prevent a (forced) resignation of the entire cabinet.

37 Article 56 Constitution and Law of 3 May 1880 on parliamentary inquiries, amended in 1996.

38 List of inquiries established by the House since 1880 include in recent years: 1988: Committee of inquiry in charge of banditism and terrorism (Bende van Nijvel I); 1992: human trafficking; 1993: weapons trade; 1996: investigation in sects; 1996: investigation in the disappearance of children; 1996: Bendecommissie II; 1999: dioxine; 1999: Lumumba; 2002: SABENA; List of inquiries established by the *Senaat* since 1880 include in recent years: 1990: Committee of inquiry in charge of the investigation of the recent unveiling of the existence of a clandestine international intelligence network, known as 'Gladio'; 1996: Committee of inquiry in charge of the investigation of the organized crime in Belgium; 1997: Committee of inquiry in charge of the investigation of the events in Rwanda; 2001: Parliamentary committee investigating the legal and illegal exploitation and trade of natural resources in the Great Lakes region in view of the current conflict situation and Belgium's involvement.

39 See for procedure Law of 3 May 1880, amended by Law of 30 June 1996, and Standing Orders of the House of representatives (23 October 1997).

40 Vos (1999) 101.

Criminal and civil liability of ministers was introduced in the 1831 Constitution in the same single phrase as political accountability. A separate article in the Constitution mentioned the basic rules of the procedure for criminal liability of ministers, which deviated from the civil procedure. The House of representatives had to indict; the trial was to be held by the *Hof van Cassatie* (Supreme court). Especially criminal liability was, in theory, considered of great importance, since there was little experience with political accountability at that time. Comments were made in the constituting assemblies that additional rules on criminal liability, i.e. the definition of criminal acts done by a minister; the proceedings in detail and the conviction were to be elaborated on in a parliamentary act set up '*in the near future*'. Meanwhile a transition procedure was proposed in the Constitution. Several proposals were introduced, but a parliamentary act never came into force. This however did not seem problematic until the end of the twentieth century.[41] The transition procedure was amended in 1993 to comply with the principle that there cannot be a punishment without a stipulation by law.[42] This however was not enough. In 1996, minister Coëme, was indicted and tried for corruption. The case was appealed at the European Court for Human Rights and the Court condemned Belgium in 2000 for not having a legal basis for the specific procedure for ministers. Consequently, the Constitution was again amended and a new parliamentary act on criminal liability for ministers was approved to comply with this decision.[43] The last case of criminal liability was that of the Ministers Claes and Coëme in yet another corruption case, the so-called 'Agusta-Dassault case'. Both ministers were convicted by the *Hof van Cassatie* and appealed the decision at the ECrtHR. This time the Court did not decide in their favour. Although the said Belgian legislation on the criminal procedure was at the time of the facts (at the end of the 1980s) and at the start of the proceedings not yet amended, the Court decided in 2005 that the previous decision by the *Hof van Cassatie* in the first Coëme case of 1996 constituted enough facts for the parties to be acquainted with the specific procedure for ministers in a criminal liability case.[44]

Civil liability of ministers is still a vague concept. As was the case with criminal liability, civil liability was mentioned in the 1831 Constitution. There was however never a parliamentary act that elaborated on the procedure and other rules.[45] The parliamentary act of 1998 regulating the criminal liability of ministers does not mention any form of civil liability. There is also no clear doctrinal understanding of the proceedings: some scholars conclude that this

---

41 Until 1996, a minister was only once indicted and tried, namely in 1865, for engaging in a pistol fight with a representative of the House.

42 See Article 15 of the International Covenant on Civil and Political rights and article 7 European Convention on Human Rights.

43 Parliamentary Act of 25 June 1998.

44 Van den Driessche, Broeksteeg (2005) 713.

45 Vande Lanotte, Goedertier (2003) 775-776.

means that ministers can be held liable under the common civil rules;[46] others conclude that in fact ministers cannot be held liable and enjoy civil immunity,[47] yet others conclude that the minister cannot be held liable on a personal basis, but only as an organ of the state (state liability).[48]

7 Conclusion

To conclude one would have to point out that to this day political ministerial accountability is the form of accountability that is pivotal to the Belgian constitutional system. A clear definition of political accountability is lacking in Belgian legal literature, although one could say that political accountability refers to the obligation of ministers to step down, after having lost confidence of the House. However, formally losing confidence by the House after losing a vote of censure has not occurred in the last decades. Indeed, ministers and cabinets step down before a debate even occurs in the House. One could therefore conclude that political accountability is weak. However, political accountability underpins the constitutional system in Belgium, and it is not so much the ousting of the government that is central to the principle, but the retaining of the confidence by the House. Therefore, the government-making power of the House, and the means the House has, not only to ask for information in the form of questions, but also the right to interpellate the government and the possibility to vote on a motion, are of more importance to the principle of accountability.

46 Popelier (1999) 5-12.

47 *Parl. St. Kamer* 1997-98, nr. 1258/5, p. 17; 1997-98, nr. 258/8, p. 2; Advies Raad van State 1 December 1997, *Parl. St. Kamer* 1997-98, nr. 1274/6, p. 4.

48 Hugo Vandenberghe, Hand. Senaat, 11 June 1998.

Bibliography

ALEN (1984)

A. Alen, *Rechter en Bestuur in het Belgische Publiekrecht. De grondslagen van de rechterlijke wettigheidskontrole* (Antwerpen 1984).

ALEN, DEVROE (1997)

A. Alen, S. Devroe, *Verzelfstandiging van bestuurstaken* (Zwolle 1997).

ALLEN, THOMPSOM (2005)

M. Allen, B. Thompson, *Parliamentary Government at Work, in Cases & Materials on Constitutional and Administrative Law* (London 2005).

DELPÉRÉE (2000)

F. Delpérée, *Le droit constitutionnel de la Belgique* (Brussels 2000).

VAN DEN DRIESSCHE (2005)

I. Van den Driessche, *Politieke ministeriële verantwoordelijkheid. Het Nederlandse begrip in rechtsvergelijkend perspectief* (Deventer 2005).

VAN DEN DRIESSCHE, BROEKSTEEG (2005)

I.A. Van den Driessche, J.L.W. Broeksteeg, 'Annotation of the Case Claes e.a. 2 juli 2005' (2005) *EHRC* 713-716.

HARLOW (2002)

C. Harlow, *Accountability in the European Union* (Oxford 2002).

VAN DER HULST (1996)

M. Van der Hulst, 'Vragen, interpellaties en moties na regeringsverklaringen in het federale parlement: naar een politieke controle 'nieuwe stijl?' in K. Leus, L. Veny (red.), *Het federale België in de praktijk, de werking van wetgevende vergaderingen na de verkiezingen van 21 mei 1995* (Bruges 1996) 11-60.

VAN IMPE (1968)

H. Van Impe, *Le régime parlementaire en Belgique* (Brussels 1968).

VAN IMPE (1972)

H. Van Impe, *Het interpellatierecht in het Belgisch parlement* (Bruges 1972).

LANOTTE VANDE, GOEDERTIER (2003)

J. Vande Lanotte, G. Goedertier, *Overzicht Publiekrecht* (Bruges 2003).

POPELIER (1999)

P. Popelier, 'De burgerlijke aansprakelijkheid van ministers voor onrechtmatige daden begaan in de uitoefening van de ministeriële functie' (1999) *TBP* 5-12.

VOS (1999)

I. Vos, 'Kan een parlementaire onderzoekscommissie individuele verantwoordelijkheden vaststellen?' (1999) *TBP* 95-114.

CHAPTER 3

Political Accountability in the Czech Republic

Mahulena Hofmann and Jiří Kopal

1 Introduction

The constitutional and legal system of the Czech Republic has a long tradition and democratic roots. One should keep in mind, however, that its development was interrupted for more than fifty years and that after Word War II, the first democratic Constitution based on the system of the separation of powers was adopted in 1993. Nevertheless, and perhaps because of this fact, the question of accountability of the executive power to the legislature was one of the most significant issues in the process of drafting the constitutional design of the then new state mechanism. Today, the Czech legal system provides for all current attributes of the Government's accountability to the Parliament which, if necessary, is still open to further developments.

A surprising contrast to this rather positive situation is a relative lack of academic interest in this constitutional issue: With two exceptions[1] known to the authors, the information is scattered in numerous commentaries on the Constitution, and the scholarly literature offers hardly any substantive critical discussion on this subject.

2 Accountability: General Aspects

The main features of the legal and political accountability of the Government to the Parliament are stipulated in the 1993 Constitution of the Czech Republic.[2] Its basis is the principle of the separation of powers (Art. 2 para. 1 Const.) and the accountability of the executive power to the legislative power. The relation of the executive to the legislature is constructed so as to achieve two main aims – the continuity of performance of state power and the balance between the organs of the executive and legislature. The term 'organs of executive power' is usually defined by a negation: They are considered to be all state organs which do not belong to the legislative or judicative powers.[3]

2.1 The Procedure of Appointment of Ministers

The Prime Minister and the ministers are to be appointed by the President of the Republic (Art. 68 Const.). Regarding the appointment of the Prime Minister, the President is free in his decision; only from a political point of view does he have to choose a person able to form a Government with the confidence of the Chamber of Deputies.

Other members of the Government will be appointed by the President of the Republic on the Prime Minister's proposal. In this case, the President is obliged

---

1 Filip (1997) 46; Pavlíček et al. (2003) 342.

2 Constitutional Act No. 1/1993 Coll. of the Czech National Council of 16th December 1992, as amended by Acts Nos. 347/1997 Coll., 300/2000 Coll., 448/2001 Coll., 395/2001 Coll., and 515/2002 Coll.

3 Pavlíček et al. (2003) 390.

to respect the proposal of the Prime Minister.[4] The same principle applies to the act of entrusting the members of the Government with leadership of individual ministries or other agencies; also here, the President has no discretion and has to follow the proposal of the Prime Minister.

2.2 The Concept of Political Accountability as a Constitutional Aspect

The Constitution is based on the parliamentary system combined with – in the view of some scholars[5] – a strong position of the President of the Republic. The Head of State is formally part of the executive power, together with the Government.[6] Optically, it is stressed by including the provisions on the powers of both these state organs in Chapter 3 of the Constitution, 'Executive Power'. The legal position of the President is defined as 'Head of State', and as such he is not legally accountable for the performance of his own office to any State bodies (Art. 54 para. 3 Const.). Instead, his constitutional accountability is transferred to the Government through the countersignature of the Prime Minister or other members of the Government.

The Government is vested with concrete executive powers defined in the Constitution; for their implementation it is accountable to the 'lower' chamber of the Parliament of the Czech Republic, the Chamber of Deputies (Art. 68 para. 1 Const.).

2.3 The Political and Legal Academic Debate and Other Relevant Types of Accountability

There is no unity and clarity in the Czech legal terminology regarding the accountability of the executive to other state powers. The literature refers to political, ministerial, governmental or constitutional accountability, indicating the relation in which a term has been used.[7] Moreover, there is usually no strict borderline between accountability and responsibility (both '*odpovědnost*').

Currently, there still has been only little academic debate on this issue. In his book *Ústavní právo* of 1997, the Czech author J. Filip writes on the 'as yet hardly analyzed problematic....'[8] In his pioneer work on this subject, he considers it, however, important to draw a distinct line between the legal and other than legal forms of responsibility, the first one being connected with the existence of legal relations, the second one occurring on the basis of other form of relations – political, ethical or moral. As a consequence, he differentiates between

---

4 *Ibid.* 345.

5 See Zoubek (1994) 99.

6 Kolář, Pecháček & Syllová (2002) 179.

7 Filip (1997) 46.

8 *Ibid.* 48.

a 'narrow' constitutional – legal responsibility which arises as a consequence of violation of specific constitutional provisions, and a 'wider' constitutional – political responsibility based on relations not necessarily following a breach of legal norms, e.g. on the relation of a parliamentary confidence to the Government.

From the viewpoint of the time factor, he identifies two forms of responsibility in constitutional law. The first one is a 'positive' responsibility which is directed into the future and is connected with a fulfillment of a particular aim (e.g. the appointment of the Government). The second one is called a 'retrospective' or 'penal' responsibility and is connected with a negative evaluation of a certain behavior in the past (e.g. the expression of a non-confidence to the Government).

Generally, he treats the responsibility in constitutional law as a special form of legal responsibility in the legal order: From the responsibility in other legal branches (such as criminal, proprietary, administrative or disciplinary responsibility), the constitutional accountability or responsibility differs primarily in its aim, which is the protection of the whole state and legal system. Its preconditions and attributes are generally identical with those of other forms of legal responsibility: It arises as a consequence of a wrongful behavior (delict) which infringes certain values protected by law; its consequence is a sanction imposed by a competent organ. It can occur in the form of a subjective responsibility based on the existence of guilt, and an objective responsibility which can be exculpated through a proof of spending all effort for avoiding its negative consequences. This second form of responsibility can occur also in the form of an absolute responsibility for which solely the result plays a decisive role and which cannot be exonerated by any means.

According to Filip, in contrast thereto, other forms of accountability, such as a political or moral accountability, do not necessarily have to be (but can be) the consequence of a violation of legal norms and, thus, do not necessarily have legal consequences. For example, the political accountability of the members of the Government can result from a violation of the rule that the members of the Government may not be engaged in activities which contradict the performance of their office (Art. 70 Const.), as well as a from a violation of the principle that they may not misuse their position (Art. 69 para. 2 Const.). The violation of these rules does not imply the loss of their position as members of the Government; it has consequences 'only' in the political sphere: The members of the Government are obliged to cease these activities 'as early as possible'. [9]

Additionally, the oath taken by the ministers on entering their offices stresses their 'civic accountability' or responsibility to act in accord with legal acts. In the oath, they swear, *inter alia*, to uphold the Constitution and laws and implement them (Art. 69 para. 2 Const.).

---

9 See the Act on the Conflict of Interests No. 238/1992 Coll.

3 Accountability: The Actors

3.1 Who Within the Government is Politically Accountable to the National Parliament?

The Prime Minister of the Czech Republic has a role of *primus inter pares* in the Government. He has neither a legal nor a practical capacity to intervene in the activities of the ministries. Therefore, the Government as a body is accountable to the national parliament (Art. 76 para. 1 Const.).

3.2 To Whom is the Government or Actors Within the Government Accountable?

Article 68 para. 1 Const. reads: 'The Government is accountable to the Chamber of Deputies'. The Chamber is entitled to exercise a political control of the Government. The Government is dependant on its confidence.

This relation is drafted as an 'exclusive' accountability; the Government is accountable 'only' to this chamber of the Parliament. This Chamber is entitled and obliged to control the activities of the Government and to express its confidence or lack of confidence in it. The Government is accountable neither to the Parliament as a whole, nor to the Senate (second Chamber), even in case of dissolution of the Chamber of Deputies,[10] nor to the President of the Republic. The Senate has no direct constitutional relation to the Government.

There are basic and complementary instruments for the accountability of the Government to the Chamber of Deputies. The basic tools are the votes of confidence or no confidence, which are supplemented by the right of Deputies to interpellations, information and explanations.[11] Concerning the vote of confidence, a new Government is obliged to ask the Chamber of Deputies for a vote of confidence within thirty days after its appointment (Art. 68 para. 3 Const.). Because the Constitution does not prescribe any qualified majorities necessary for the expression of confidence, the Chamber is able to vote if at least a third of the Deputies (of 200) is present; the vote of confidence is expressed if approved by the majority of the present Deputies (Art. 39 Const.). If the Government fails to win the confidence of the Chamber, the same procedure is repeated. If a thus appointed Government again fails to win the confidence, the President of the Republic must appoint a Prime Minister on the proposal of the Chairman of the Chamber of Deputies (Art. 68 para. 4 Const.). Also, this Government has to win the confidence of the Chamber. If it fails, the President of the Republic may (but does not have to) dissolve the Chamber of Deputies according to Article 35 para. 1 lit. a Const.

In other cases, the Chamber of Deputies may express a vote of no confidence in the Government on the motion of no less than fifty Deputies. Further, the

---

10 Kolář, Pecháček & Syllová (2002) 172.

11 Zoubek (1994) 90.

Government may ask the Chamber to complete its consideration of a Government bill within three months of its introduction, provided that the Government attaches its request for a vote of confidence (Art. 44 para. 3 Const.). The motion is admitted when approved by the majority of all Deputies.

All cases of lacking confidence of the Chamber of Deputies lead to the resignation of the Government through the Prime Minister (Art. 73 Const.). The President of the Republic has no discretion to reject such a resignation.

One of the forms, by which the Chamber of Deputies monitors the Government, is its oral or written interpellation of the members of the Government (Art. 53 Const.). As a complement to interpellations, the Chamber of the Deputies can ask the members of the Government for information and explanations. Both procedures are regulated in the Rules of Procedure of the Chamber of Deputies.[12]

The accountability of the Government to the Chamber of Deputies reflects also in the constitutional duty of the members of the Government to appear personally at its meetings if it so decides (Art. 38 para. 2 Const.). The fact that this duty does not extend to the meetings of the Senate is connected with the concept of the legislative process in the Czech Republic: A member of the Government – a potential author of a draft of a legal act – would be obliged to explain and defend the draft in the session of the Chamber of Deputies. However, the draft could subsequently be modified in the Chamber during the legislative process; also, the Senate could deviate from the original governmental text substantially. If this member of the Government were obliged to defend this final, modified text in the Parliament, he could become disloyal to the original governmental draft.[13]

According to Article 42 Const., the Government submits the Draft Act on the State Budget, as well as the Draft Final State Budgetary Account to the Chamber of Deputies for its approval. The Chamber considers and decides upon them at a public meeting. Moreover, the Chamber may request further governmental reports, such as annual reports on migration, drugs, law and order, extremism and others.

The next aspect of the governmental accountability to the Chamber of Deputies includes the responsibility for the appointment of the judges of the general courts. The right to appoint them is, indeed, vested in the President of the Republic (Art. 63 para. 1 Const.), but this act requires the countersignature of the Prime Minister and, as such, implies the Government's accountability of to the Parliament for this act.

The Chamber of Deputies has no executive power, and as such it is not entitled to charge the Government with any duties. However, in its resolutions, it can call on the Government to carry out particular activities, such as to initiate the legislative process on a concrete issue or to report on particular problems. Only rarely does the Chamber of Deputies openly recommend any particular

[12] Act No. 90/1995 Coll., as amended.

[13] Pavlíček et al. (2003) 367.

activities to the Government. Despite the fact that the second Chamber of the Parliament, the Senate, does not have any direct constitutional relation to the Government, in practice it adopts recommendations to the Government relating to the legislative process, too.

3.3 The Collective or Individual Form of the Accountability

The Government is a collective organ; it makes its decisions as a body (Art. 76 para. 1 Const.). In order to be adopted, a decision of the Government has to be approved by the majority of all its members (Art. 76 para. 2 Const.); in the course of the voting procedure, no substitution of ministers by other persons is allowed. Therefore, the accountability of the Government is constructed as a collective accountability; any individual accountability of the ministers is excluded.[14] The Government bears the responsibility for the execution of powers of each of its members.

This collectivity applies also to the responsibility for decisions made by the President of the Republic which have to be countersigned by the Prime Minister or a member of the Government authorized by the Prime Minister: In this case as well, the Government as a whole is responsible for the decision of the President (Art. 63 para. 4 Const.). The same rule applies to the performance of presidential duties by the Prime Minister in case of the vacancy of the office of the President of the Republic (Art. 66 Const.). In such situations, the decisions of the Prime Minister are not countersigned. The Government is also collectively accountable for the implementation of governmental decrees.

4 The Scope of Accountability

4.1 The Accountability of the Government and/or Ministers for Policy-making and for the Execution of Policy

Neither the Constitution nor any statute defines exhaustively a scope of the relation of the accountability of the Government to the Chamber of Deputies. The competencies of the Czech Government are based on the principle that the Government's competence comprises everything in the executive branch that the Constitution or a statute does *not* vest in the President of the Republic or in ministries or other administrative subjects.[15] Thus, the Government's setting the aims of state policy is hardly dividable from its execution through sub-statutory acts and the coordination of the activities of state administration. All these activities can be reviewed by the Chamber of Deputies.

---

[14] *Ibid.* 346.

[15] Filip (1994) 168.

According to § 28 para 1 of the 1969 Act on the Ministries and Other Central Organs of the State Administration[16], the activities of the ministries are 'directed, controlled and unified by Government'. The ministries are subordinated to the Government and can be managed not only by generally binding legal acts but also by internal normative instructions and individual acts. The Government as the supreme body of executive power (Art. 67 para. 1 Const.) represents the ministries in relation to other state organs, especially to the Chamber of Deputies.

According to Article 79 para 1 Const., the scope of competence of ministries may be established only by law. The general descriptions of their competencies are laid down by the 1969 Act on the Ministries and Other Central Organs of the State Administration, their detailed description can be found in special statutes which regulate the execution of their powers in various branches of State administration. In principle, the scope of their activity encompasses both policy-making and the execution of the State policy in their particular area (§ 22 – 25 of the 1969 Act on the Ministries and Other Central Organs of the State Administration).

The ministers are heads of the ministries; they can act as representatives of the ministries, as well as in other roles such as vice-prime-ministers, if appropriate. They are bearers of the constitutional – political responsibility for the activity of the ministry as a whole to the Prime Minister; this follows from the fact that the Prime Minister can propose to recall the minister from his/ her position to the President of the Republic (Art. 74 para 1 Const.).

Concerning their legal responsibility, in contrast to the President of the Republic and the members of the Parliament, the ministers do not differ substantially on account of their office from other citizens of the Czech Republic.[17] In contrary to the situation between the years 1920 – 1960, the 1993 Constitution does not provide for any special criminal responsibility of the Ministers.

The only differences concern their status as 'public actors' according to the Czech penal law and their position stipulated by the 1994 Act on the Conflict of Interests. However, the infringement of this second statute does not lead to any constitutional responsibility of the ministers; this breach has consequences only in the area of their political accountability.

4.2 Political Advisers of the Ministers

The term 'political adviser of a minister' is not common in the Czech political and legal language. The Act on State Service[18] mentions 'the advisors of the members of the Government' (§ 2 (3) b) only in order to exempt them from the scope of this Act.

---

16 Act No. 2/1969 Coll., as amended.

17 Filip (1994) 171.

18 Act No. 218/2002 Coll., as amended.

4.3 The Extent of the Accountability of Ministers for Functions of Governmental Departments: The Powers to Give Instructions to Civil Servants

The ministries of the Czech Republic are built as monocratic organs. They constitute central organs of the state executive headed by ministers who act on their behalf. The ministers bear political accountability for the activity of the ministry as a whole to the Prime Minister. An activity of the minister can be reviewed by the usual means of parliamentary democracy, such as interpellations or the duty to attend the session of the Chamber of Deputies or its organs. However, the Chamber of Deputies has no power to express a vote of no confidence in individual ministers; this can be proposed only by the Prime Minister (the President must follow the Prime Minister's proposal) (Art. 74 Const.).

The legal status of governmental employees in the ministries is defined by law (Art. 79 para. 2 Const.): The Act on State Service[19] stipulates that the instructions to civil servants can be given by the members of the government (usually ministers) as well as by other persons enumerated in § 68 of the Act.

4.4 'Other Administrative Agencies'

'Other administrative agencies' have their legal basis in Article 79 Const. The scope of their competence is usually narrower than the areas of activities of the ministries. The 1969 Act on the Ministries and Other Central Organs of the State Administration[20] introduced a differentiation among these institutions: Only the twelve agencies enumerated in the Act are classified as 'central' administrative agencies[21] which belong into the structure of the 'central administration of the State'. These central administrative agencies are governed by the Government as the supreme body of executive power, in the framework stipulated by special legal acts. The decrees of the Government are generally binding on the activities of these agencies.[22] They are not headed by ministers or other members of the Government; instead, their presidents are appointed by the Government or, in case of the Czech Statistical Authority, by the President of the Chamber of Deputies. The ministers influence the activities of these agencies only indirectly, by means of their membership in the Government and its collective form of activity.

In contrast thereto, several central administrative bodies have been established such as the Council for Radio and TV Broadcasting, the Office for Personal Data Protection, the Council for Czech TV and others. Their heads and members are usually elected as well as dismissed by the Chamber of Deputies

19 *Ibid.*

20 See Fn. 16.

21 E.g. the Czech Statistical Authority, Czech Mining Authority, Industrial Property Authority, National Security Authority, and Czech Telecommunications Authority.

22 Pavlíček et al. (2003) 360.

or appointed (and dismissed) by the President of the Republic on the proposal of the Senate. Their relative legal independence from the Government derives for the most part from the special acts that set down their competencies, special constitutive procedure and the fact that governmental decrees can be binding on their activities only if stipulated by law. They are usually accountable either to the Chamber of Deputies or both to the Chamber of Deputies and the Senate and are obliged to submit annual reports to one or both of the legislative bodies, or only in exceptional cases to the executive.

5 Activating Accountability: Parliamentary Control and Transparency

5.1 Means of Political and Budgetary Control at the Disposal of Parliament

The basic means of political and budgetary control have already been briefly outlined above in Part 2. The details of this procedure are stipulated in the Rules of Procedure of the Chambers of Deputies.[23]

5.1.1 The Right to Interpellate the Government

According to § 110 para. 1 of the Rules of Procedure of the Chamber of Deputies, any Deputy has the right to interpellate the Government or its members regarding issues over which they have authority. The Deputies interpellate through the Chairperson of the Chamber of Deputies either orally or in writing.

The Rules of Procedure set down in detail the time and procedure for interpellations. For *oral* interpellations of the Prime Minister, a period from 14:30 to 15:15 o'clock is set aside on the stipulated meeting day which falls on Thursday. The time set aside for interpellations of other members of Government is from 15:15 to 16:15. In case the interpellations of the Prime Minister are finished earlier than 15:15, the interpellation of other members of Government may begin immediately afterwards. The last parliamentary question may be submitted by 16:10 at the latest. The Deputies must apply to the Chairperson of the Chamber of Deputies in writing, no later than 11:00 of the day on which they wish to interpellate. The presentation of an oral interpellation may not exceed two minutes and that of a supplementary question one minute. After the expiry of these time limits, additional interpellations may not be posed; however, after the response to the last interpellation has been delivered, a supplementary question may be submitted, even after the expiry of the time limit.

The Chairperson of the Chamber of Deputies is to send *written* interpellations to the Prime Minister without delay and, if addressed to a member of the

[23] Act No. 90/1995 Coll., as amended.

Government, to this member as well. In case the Government or a member of Government fails to answer, the Deputy notifies the Chairperson of the Chamber of Deputies this fact; the Chairperson must inform the Chamber of Deputies about the failing answer in its next meeting. If the response to the interpellation is unsatisfactory, the Deputy may ask the Chairperson of the Chamber of Deputies to include it on the agenda of its next meeting. In this case, the interpellation and the response are printed out and sent to all Deputies.

In the respective parliamentary debate, a resolution may be adopted which expresses the satisfaction or non-satisfaction with the response to the interpellation. If the resolution expresses disagreement with the response, the member of Government to whom the written interpellation was submitted has to prepare a new response within thirty days from the date of the resolution.

5.1.2 The Approval of the State Budget

Article 42 Const. stipulates that the Government introduces the Draft Act on the State Budget as well as the Draft of the Final State Budgetary Account. These drafts are to be debated in a session open to the public, and only the Chamber of Deputies may adopt resolutions concerning them.

The legislative process connected with the approval of the state budget deviates from the ordinary legislative process and is described in Part Thirteen of the Rules of Procedure of the Chamber of Deputies. It is discussed separately from other drafts and may not contain any amendments relating to other acts.[24]

The Government is expected to submit the Draft Act on the State Budget to the Chairperson of the Chamber of Deputies no later than three months prior to the start of a governmental fiscal year. It may submit addenda to such a draft no later than fifteen days prior to the meeting of the Chamber of Deputies at which the first reading of the act is to take place. The Chamber of Deputies either approves the 'substantial information'[25] of the Draft Act on the State Budget or recommends to the Government changes thereto and sets a deadline for submitting a new draft. The given period cannot be shorter than twenty days and cannot exceed thirty days after the delivery of the resolution of the Chamber of Deputies to the Prime Minister. In case the Chamber of Deputies approves the substantial information in the Draft Act on the State Budget, it may not be changed during further discussion of the act.

After this step, the Chamber of Deputies assigns individual chapters of the Draft to committees, which may propose changes only to those chapters of the state budget assigned to them. If a committee wishes to change another chapter, it has to ask the committee to which the chapter has been assigned to discuss

[24] Kolář,Pecháček & Syllová (2002) 188.

[25] The 'substantial information' includes the amount of revenues and expenditures, the balance (surplus or deficit) and the manner of addressing the balance, the overall relationship to the budgets of higher territorial self-administered units and municipalities and the scope of the authority given to executive bodies (§ 102 para. 2 of the Rules of Procedure).

the changes. The minimum period for discussing a chapter of the Draft Act on the State Budget in a committee is thirty days.

In the second reading of the Draft Act on the State Budget, detailed parliamentary debate is to be held on the draft itself and on the corresponding resolution of a parliamentary Budget Committee. During the detailed debate, amendments and other proposals can be submitted. The third reading may be started no earlier than forty-eight hours after the second reading has been completed. At the conclusion of this reading, the voting on amending proposals and other proposals to the act takes place. In conclusion, the Chamber of Deputies decides whether it will express its agreement with the Draft. In case the Chamber of Deputies refuses the Draft Act on the State Budget and the amended version is not approved until the beginning of the Government's fiscal year, a provisional expenditure follows.[26]

5.1.3 The Right to Require Information for Carrying Out the Duties Associated with Parliamentary Membership

The Deputies (§ 11 Rules of Procedure of the Chamber of Deputies) and also the Senators (§ 12 para. 1 Rules of Procedure of the Senate[27]) have a right to require from the members of the Government and the heads of administrative agencies information and explanations which they (that is, the Deputies or Senators) 'require for carrying out the duties associated with their post'. Correspondingly, the members of the Government and the heads of administrative agencies have a duty to provide information and explanations to the Deputies within thirty days, unless they are prevented from doing so by law. Czech constitutional theory,[28] however, stresses that the Senate has no authority to monitor the Government. In practice, a Senator's request for information or explanation, as well as the fulfilment or refusal of the request, might lead to factual discoveries which in turn could trigger serious political accountability, as well. For not fulfilling the duty to inform and explain, no sanctions are envisaged by law. Therefore, the respective procedural provisions can both be considered *leges imperfectae*.[29]

5.2 Obligations Resulting from Political Accountability

The Constitution and the Rules of Procedure of the Chamber of Parliament stipulate the means by which the Government gives political account to the Parliament.

---

[26] The first experience with the provisional expenditure in the Czech Republic came during the first term of the minority Social Democrats' Government in the year 1999; the revised draft was not passed until January 15, 1999.

[27] Act No. 107/1999 Coll.

[28] Filip (1994) 162.

[29] Adamus (1995) 370.

5.2.1 The Duty to Attend Personally the Meeting of the Chamber of Deputies

The members of the Government are obliged to attend in person the meeting of the Chamber of Deputies, if it so resolves. For the adoption of a corresponding resolution, a simple majority of the Deputies is necessary (Art. 39 para. 2 Const.).

This duty, which is derived directly from the responsibility of the Government to the Chamber of Deputies (Art. 68 Const.),[30] is not limited to the sessions of the Chamber of Deputies: The Prime Minister and the ministers also may have to appear at the meetings of committees, commissions, or commissions of inquiry of the Chamber of Deputies. In such cases, however, a member of the Government may be represented by an associate or another member of the Government provided that personal participation has not been explicitly demanded. As a rule, no substitution by lower-ranking Government officials (e.g. a director of the section) is permitted, not even based on power of attorney.[31]

5.2.2 The Duty to Respond Interpellations

The Government's (and its members') duty to respond to interpellations corresponds to the right of the Deputies to submit interpellations. According to the Rules of Procedure of the Chamber of Parliament (§ 111 para. 5), the Prime Minister or other members of the Government have to respond to *oral* interpellations immediately after they have been posed. The time limit for the answer of the Government member is set at five minutes, or two minutes for a supplementary answer (§ 111 para. 6 of the Rules of Procedure). In case the interpellated person is not present or declares that it is not possible to respond immediately, he or she has to respond to the Deputy in writing within thirty days.

The procedure for answering the *written* interpellation is set down in § 112 of the Rules of Procedure of the Chamber of Deputies: The Government or the member of Government must respond to a written parliamentary question at a meeting of the Chamber in writing within thirty days of its submission. If a parliamentary resolution is adopted expressing dissatisfaction with the response, the member of Government has to prepare a new response within thirty days from the date of the resolution.

---

[30] Pavlíček & Hřebejk (1994) 112.

[31] Hendrych & Svoboda (1997) 60.

5.2.3 The Duty to Appear before the Committees and Commissions of the Chamber of Deputies

As a rule, the members of the Government and the heads of other central administrative agencies are obliged to attend in person a meeting of a committee if it so requests, and to provide information and explanations demanded by the committee. However, a member of Government may be represented by another member of Government or an associate, unless the committee insists on the member's personal attendance. Members of Government, their representatives and the heads of central administrative agencies may be accompanied by experts.

Besides establishing the committees, the Chamber of Deputies may also establish from its Deputies and others permanent or temporary commissions and vest them with certain powers within the scope of its own authority. Those Deputies who are also members of the Government may not then be members of a commission. The present permanent commissions include commissions on Banking, on the Oversight of Military Intelligence Activities, on the Oversight of Security Information Service Activities, on the Oversight of Employment of Operational Technique, on the Media, on Family and Equal Opportunities, as well as on the Monitoring of the Process of Accessibility of the Volumes Developed from the Activities of State Security (during the period of communism). Each of these commissions has certain means of governmental monitoring at its disposal, including requesting information and explanation from the representatives of state bodies and invited experts (cf. § 47 para. 2 Rules of Procedure of the Chambers of Deputies).

5.3 Legal Grounds for Refusing to Answer

Neither the Constitution nor the Rules of Procedure of the Chamber of Deputies contain any provision on the right of the members of Government to refuse to answer in the interpellation procedure in the Chamber of Deputies. However, during meetings of parliamentary committees, a member of Government or a head of a central administrative agency does have legal grounds to refuse, based in § 39 para. 2 of the Rules of Procedure of the Chamber of Deputies. According to this provision, the member of the Government has to avoid in particular any information specified in the legislation on state secrecy or in further legislation that prohibits disclosing information. The scope of this legislation is very wide: According to the Explanatory Opinion of the Supreme Prosecutor No. 30/2000 on the Authorisation of the Deputies, Senators and the Investigative Commission, in relation to institutions of criminal justice, there are around ninety acts and decrees that contain duties of secrecy published in the official Collection of Acts. For example, they regard information defined by the Act on the Protection of Classified Information[32] as any information that could either endanger the course of a criminal procedure that is still ongoing according to the Criminal Procedure Code[33] (§ 8) or endanger the protection of citizens' right to privacy according to the Act on the Protection of Personal Data.[34]

5.4 Right to Question Heads of Central Administrative Agencies and Civil Servants

The Rules of Procedure of the Chamber of Deputies assume that not only members of Government but also the heads of other central administrative agencies have a duty to attend in person a meeting of a committee if the committee so requests (§ 39 para. 2). According to § 41 para. 2, the committees must submit such resolutions to the appropriate member of Government or head of the central administrative agency. Unless the committee sets a longer period, the members of Government and heads of other central administrative agencies have a duty to deliver the requested information and explanations within thirty days, unless they are prevented from doing so by law. However, some constitutional scholars[35] suggest that the Chamber of Deputies or its committees may exceed their powers in requiring the attendance, information, or explanation of the heads of central administrative agencies. After all, they argue, this right is foreseen not in the Constitution but only in the Rules of Procedure of the Chamber.

Also the possibility to question lower-ranking civil servants can be only indirectly deduced from the § 39 para. 4 Rules of Procedure of the Chamber of Deputies. As already mentioned, the members of Government, persons representing them and the heads of central administrative agencies may be accompanied by experts to meetings of the Chamber of Deputies' committees or commissions. In practice, the experts can also be civil servants responsible for a particular sector of scrutinized activity. However, this construction cannot be interpreted the right of parliamentary committees to have the civil servant attend the particular session. It is rather the right of the minister, his or her

---

32 Act No. 148/1998 Coll. § 3 of this act reads as follows:

Classified Information

1. Classified information is information the unauthorised disclosure of which could cause detriment to the interests of the Czech Republic or to those interests which the Czech Republic has undertaken to protect, or which could be unfavourable to these interests, and which is included in the register of classified information. 2. Registers of classified information shall be processed by the Authority on the advice of central authorities. 3. Registers of classified information shall be issued by the Government in the form of a decree.

33 Act No. 141/1961 Coll.

34 Act No. 101/2000 Coll.

35 Hendrych & Svoboda (1997) 48.

associate or the head of a central administrative agency to be accompanied by these persons.

5.5 Commission of Inquiry – An Instrument for Activating Political Accountability?

One of the strongest means of activating political accountability seems to be the institution of Commission of Inquiry.

The Commission of Inquiry foreseen in Article 30 Const. can be established on the basis of a proposal by at least one-fifth of all Deputies (40 of 200). Its aim is to investigate matters in the public interest. The Chamber of Deputies determines what constitutes 'matters in the public interest'.[36] The chairperson and other members have to be Deputies elected by the Chamber of Deputies. No Deputies who are also members of Government may be members of this commission. For its purposes, the commission may obtain necessary information, demand explanations, examine witnesses and hear experts. The Commission of Inquiry's own rules of procedure are to regulate, *inter alia*, the duty to testify, summoning of witnesses, prohibiting examination, the right to withhold testimony, the entitlement to receive compensation for acting as a witness or the hearing experts.

According to § 48 para. 6 of the Rules of Procedure of the Chamber of Deputies, the meeting of an investigative commission is, as a rule, public. Its members and other persons in attendance are obliged to maintain in secrecy the facts which they discover during the meeting. If these facts indicate that a criminal act has been committed, the institutions responsible for carrying out criminal proceedings may be informed.

Furthermore, there have been more than ten *ad hoc* Commissions of Inquiry established since 1993 in the Czech Republic on the basis of § 47 of the Rules of Procedure of the Chamber of Deputies. This number includes in particular commissions for the investigation and clarification of unsuccessful cases of privatization, disadvantageous public contracts and the responsibility of Government members, bankruptcies of banking institutions and the relationship between organized crime and state administration. The experience of the past twelve years nevertheless shows – according to the many experts and journalists, including investigators – that these Commissions are hardly ever able to investigate anything essential.[37] Many politicians and state officials regularly argue that this institution is often abused by the parliamentary opposition for its political purposes.

---

36 Pavlíček & Hřebejk (1994) 102.

37 <Http://www.radio.cz/cz/zpravy/54687>.

5.6 Transparency in the Chamber of Deputies and its Openness to the Public

All plenary discussions in the Chamber of Deputies, as well as the meetings of committees, are generally accessible to the public, unless the Rules of Procedure of the Chamber of Deputies stipulate otherwise or unless the Chamber decides that a meeting or portion thereof shall be non-public, especially if the agenda includes secret issues connected with the protection or defense of the state or other serious or confidential matters. Discussions concerning the Draft Act on the State Budget, the Draft Final State Budgetary Account, drafts concerning tax policies or fees must always be public (§ 56 para. 1).

The interpellations of the members of Government are regularly broadcasted on Czech public TV at night. The provisions on interpellation contained in the Rules of Procedure of the Chamber of Deputies were amended 2004[38] with the aim of making the process of interpellations – after eight years of experience with longer interpellations without the time limit for the responses from the Prime Minister and ministers – more valuable, quicker and more engaging for TV broadcasting and the public.[39]

The meetings of the committees of the Chamber of Deputies are also usually public. This rule does not apply, however, to proceedings regarding disciplinary matters which are always non-public. The chairpersons of the committees may allow, with the agreement of the committee, other persons to speak at the meetings of the committee (§ 39 para. 5); under the term 'other persons', the general public including representatives of civil society can be heard.

The work of the Commission of Inquiry has been made more transparent in recent years, as well. The original rule of § 48 para. 6 of the Rules of Procedure of the Chamber of Deputies stipulating that the meetings of the Commission of Inquiry were generally non-public[40] was amended in 2005[41] on the basis of the draft of a group of Deputies. In the explanatory report to this amendment, they explained that their draft was submitted in order to achieve transparency in the proceedings of state institutions.[42] They considered the proceedings of the

---

38 Act No. 359/2004.

39 The Draft of the Deputies Lubomír Zaorálek, Václav Exner, Vojtěch Filip, Michal Hašek, Jan Kasal, Jitka Kupčová, Ivan Langer, Hana Marvanová, Miroslava Němcová and Jan Vidím on amendment of Act. No. 90/1995 Coll., Rules of Procedure of the Chamber of Deputies as amended, No. 418/0, Explanatory Report, 4. Electoral Term, 2003.

40 *'The meetings of an investigative commission shall be non-public and may be attended only by its members. Other persons may attend or participate at meetings of an investigative commission only with its agreement or if legislation so stipulates'.*

41 Act No. 167/2005 Coll.

42 The Draft of the Deputy Martin Říman and others on amendment of Act No. 90/1995 Coll., on the Rules of Procedure of the Chamber of Deputies as amended, No. 670/0, Explanatory Report, 4. Electoral Term, 2004.

Commissions of Inquiry too strictly concealed,[43] in contrast to the practice of the states such as the USA, Canada, the UK, France, Germany and Austria, where, as a rule, the meetings of Commissions of Inquiry are open to the public.

Article 6 of Appendix No. 1 to the Rules of Procedure of the Chamber of Deputies, the 'Rules of Procedure for the Commission of Inquiry', states that the Commission must inform the public about its activities, primarily through the media. The disclosure of this information should, however, neither endanger the clarification of facts important to the investigation nor make public information on persons participating in the investigation when such information is not directly connected with the investigated matter or when disclosure could cause them needless harm. Additionally, state, economic and corporate confidentiality and the prohibition of disclosure of sensitive information protected by law have to be respected.

6 Consequences

In the most serious cases, the interpellation of a member of the Government or his or her unsatisfactory explanation could lead to the establishment of a Commission of Inquiry which performs its investigation by the above-mentioned means. Its conclusion can lead to the adoption of a resolution demanding appropriate measures from the Government, the dismissal of the responsible civil servant, the recall of the Minister or even an expression of no confidence in the Government.[44]

According to Article 72 Const., the Chamber of Deputies may adopt a resolution of no confidence in the Government which may be debated only if submitted in writing by at least fifty of two hundreds Deputies. For adoption of the resolution, an absolute majority of all Deputies is necessary. A vote of no confidence in a particular member of Government including the Prime Minister is not possible; rather, such a vote may only be as to the entire Government. Corresponding to this rule, an individual minister may not ask the Chamber of Deputies for its vote of confidence.[45]

Article 73 para. 2 Const. stipulates that the Government must submit its resignation if the Chamber of Deputies rejects its request for a vote of confidence or if it adopts a resolution of no confidence. The Prime Minister submits his resignation to the President of the Republic, and other members of the Government through the Prime Minister. The President can accept the resignation of a member of Government, even despite the opposition of the Prime

[43] Authors of the publications Parlament České republiky 1993-2001 wrote as late as 2002 without further explanation that the 'meeting of the commission of inquiry is *naturally* non-public' (emphasis added), Kolář, Pecháček & Syllová (2002) 128.

[44] *Ibid.* 128.

[45] Filip (1994) 165.

Minister. It is only logical that, for this act, the President of the Republic does not require the countersignature of the Prime Minister.[46]

In all cases when the Government submits its resignation through the Prime Minister, the President is obliged to accept it. Otherwise, as J. Filip concludes, he or she could be accused of high treason.[47] The Head of State must also recall a Government that has not submitted its resignation, even though obliged to do so. This rule stems from the nature of the President's role as a 'guarantor' of the constitutional principle that a Government that does not enjoy the confidence of the Chamber of Deputies cannot stay in power.[48]

7 Conclusion

The Czech Republic has opened up both its constitutional system and the legal relationships between the legislative and executive powers to the prevalent elements of accountability that are common in Western democracies. The institutions of parliamentary interpellations, right to request personal attendance and obtain information and explanations from the members of Government, special procedure for the approval of the state budget and the authority of setting up the Commission of Inquiry should be seen as necessary powers of the parliamentary organ, the Chamber of Deputies, to whom the Government and other administrative agencies render political account.

As the Chamber of Deputies cannot execute effective sanctions, with the exception of a vote of no confidence in the Government, the accountability of the Government has to be assessed as predominantly political. It is constructed as a collective one, without individual responsibility of members of the Government. However, the Czech Republic is a young democracy, and the repeated, politically motivated motions of no confidence against particular members of Government can be seen as serving short-sighted political purposes, continually overloading the agenda of the Chamber of Deputies, destabilizing the Government as well as aggravating the parliamentary culture.

The increased need of different administrative agencies with broader independence, diverse competencies and special tasks, in addition to the 'more traditional executive bodies' enumerated in the 1969 Act on the Ministries and Other Central Organs of the State Administration, has led to the establishment of different regimes of accountability for these agencies. Of particular consequence, are not only the powers of the President or the Chamber of Deputies to dismiss the heads of such agencies, but also the duty to report regularly to legislative and sometimes even to executive bodies. The question of accountability of particular civil servants vis-à-vis the Chamber of Deputies and its organs

[46] *Ibid.* 179.

[47] *Ibid.* 165.

[48] *Ibid.* 180.

has not yet been tackled in the Czech Republic in any way that would lead to any new concepts or legal regulation.

The problem of the occasional refusal to provide information on the basis of various legal grounds seems to be rather uncontroversial. The legislation on the protection of information and personal data does not differ significantly from other democratic states. Only perhaps the limited amount of legislation on confidentiality reflects some relics from the Austro-Hungarian and communist eras. But it is, of course, difficult to assess the frequency with which members of Government abuse the legal bases for refusing to provide information or explanation.

In general, the model of accountability of the executive power to the legislature chosen by the authors of the 1993 Constitution has proved well-balanced and not so rigid as to prevent necessary modifications by simple laws. Many of its aspects, such as the publicity of the sessions of the Commission of Inquiry, started to play an important role in public life. It is not excluded, however, that the interest of the public in even more transparent information by the members of the Government or the strengthening of the position of independent administrative bodies might lead to further legislative steps.

Bibliography

ADAMUS (1995)

V. Adamus, Jednací řád Poslanecké sněmovny a právo poslanců na informace (jakož i kontrolovat vládu), (1995/6) *Správní právo* 370 ff.

FILIP (1994)

J. Filip, *Ústavní právo, II.* díl (Brno 1994).

FILIP (1997)

J. Filip, *Ústavní právo*, Bd. I (Brno 1997).

HENDRYCH & SVOBODA (1997)

D. Hendrych & C. Svoboda, *Ústava České republiky – komentář* (Praha 1997).

KOLÁŘ, PECHÁČEK & SYLLOVÁ (2002)

P. Kolář, Š. Pecháček, J. Syllová, *Parlament České republiky 1993-2001* (Praha 2002).

PAVLÍČEK ET AL. (2003)

V. Pavlíček et al., *Ústavní právo a státověda*, Bd. II, 2001 (Praha 2003).

PAVLÍČEK & HŘEBEJK (1994)

V. Pavlíček, J. Hřebejk, *Ústava a ústavní řád České republiky, Svazek I. Ústava České republiky* (Praha 1994).

ZOUBEK (1994)

V. Zoubek, 'Moc výkonná', in A. Gerloch, J. Hřebejk, V. Zoubek, *Ústavní systém České republiky* (Praha 1994), 99 ff.

CHAPTER 4

Political Accountability in Denmark

Jørgen Albæk Jensen

1 Introduction to the Danish Political System

The Danish democratic system goes back to 1849 when the first Constitution was enacted and gave Denmark one of the most liberal constitutions of that time. The Constitution has of course been amended several times since then, but many of the basic features of the Constitution can be traced back to 1849.

In the present Danish Constitution from 1953, Denmark is described as a constitutional monarchy. This implies that the head of state is still the monarch ('King'), but also that the powers of this head of state are limited by the Constitution. In fact, according to the Constitution (articles 12-14), the monarch has no political power at all, the consequence of this being that wherever the Constitution mentions the powers of the King, it should be interpreted as powers of the government. Looking at the Danish political system from a more realistic point of view, the system can thus be described as a uni-cameral,[1] parliamentary democracy where the monarch has now only ceremonial functions, but at the same time has an important role as a symbol of the unity of the Danish nation.

2 Political and Legal Accountability

A basic feature of a parliamentary political system is that the executive branch of government is dependent on the support of the publicly elected legislature – or in other words that the government is politically accountable to Parliament.

First of all, this is demonstrated by the rules governing the formation of government in Denmark. After a prolonged constitutional crisis in the last fourth of the 19th century, the King and the minority party in Parliament finally in 1901 accepted that a government must in some way enjoy the support of the publicly elected chamber of Parliament. The model that gradually evolved in the following years was one of 'negative' parliamentarism where the government could stay in office as long as it did not receive a vote of no-confidence from the lower chamber of Parliament. However, this principle of negative parliamentarism was also reflected in the formation of governments as no government could be formed which could envisage a vote of no-confidence when it presented itself to Parliament.[2]

---

1 Denmark had up until 1953 a two-chamber Parliament, but with the acceptance of parliamentarism in 1901, the influence of the upper chamber (with a limited electorate) gradually declined. With the passage of the Constitution of 1953, Parliament became a one-chamber assembly (the *Folketing*).

2 On the other hand, there was no 'positive' parliamentarism in the sense that a new government was required to pass a vote of confidence in Parliament before taking office. In most situations, the difference between a positive and negative parliamentarism is quite small, as most governments actually have some kind of majority behind them, but in marginal cases with very unclear parliamentary situations, it might be easier to form a government in a system that adheres to the negative parliamentary

Although the Constitution was changed in 1915 and again in 1920, the principle of parliamentarism was not laid down in the Constitution itself. However, most constitutional theory claims that the parliamentary principle had become customary law during the first half of the 20th century, and in fact, no government was formed in the period between 1901 and 1953 that was not in accordance with the parliamentary principle.[3]

With the latest constitutional change in 1953, the parliamentary principle was finally written into the constitutional text as article 15. This article reads as follows:

> '(1) A minister shall not remain in office after the Folketing has approved a vote of no-confidence in him.
> (2) When the Folketing passes a vote of no-confidence in the Prime Minister, he shall ask for the dismissal of the Ministry unless writs are to be issued for a general election. Where a vote of censure has been passed on a Ministry, or it has asked for its dismissal, it shall continue in office until a new Ministry has been appointed. Ministers who remain in office as aforesaid shall perform only what may be necessary to ensure the uninterrupted conduct of official business.'

As can be seen, nothing in this article explicitly concerns the appointment of ministers. However, there is general agreement that article 15 implies that the negative parliamentary principle must be followed also in the formation of a government. Thus, a Prime Minister to be must make sure that he does not have a parliamentary majority *against* him before asking the King (Queen) to appoint him as the new Prime Minister.

The only article of the Constitution that explicitly mentions the formation of government is article 14, para. 1 stating that 'The King shall appoint and dismiss the Prime Minister and the other Ministers.', but this article should be interpreted in the light of article 15 as mentioned above. However, article 14, para. 1, reflects the process of appointment of ministers in another way, as it indicates that the process of formation of government is a two step process.

The first step is to establish which political composition a new government should have, and thus to determine who the new Prime Minister should be. This step involves negotiations between the parties in Parliament, and the result of these negotiations is then presented to the Queen who formally appoints the

system. This was for instance the case after the general elections in 1973 and 1975 where no clear majority was visible in either case.

3 In 1920, the King tried to form a government that was opposed by the majority of (the lower house of) Parliament. However, after a short crisis the King had to give in and appoint a government that enjoyed the confidence of Parliament. The crisis of 1920 thus actually strengthened the principle of parliamentarism. In the beginning of the German occupation of Denmark from 1940 to 1945, certain national-conservative forces in Denmark put pressure on the King to appoint a government without any parliamentary backing. The King, however, in this case publicly declared his support of the parliamentary principle and refused to do so.

new Prime Minister.[4] When the Prime Minister has been appointed, he then chooses the other ministers. The only legal requirement he has to observe in his choice of ministers is the same as applies to the government as a whole: No minister can be appointed if he will be met by a vote of no-confidence when presenting himself to Parliament.

Article 15 of the Constitution and its implications for the formation of government thus clearly shows that the government is politically accountable to Parliament. The political accountability of the government in relation to Parliament is, however, not the only form of accountability that is included in the Danish Constitution. Article 16 of the Constitution reads as follows:

> 'Ministers may be impeached by the King or the Folketing for maladministration of office. The High Court of the Realm shall try cases of impeachment brought against Ministers for maladministration of office.'

The responsibility contained in article 16 is normally called the *legal responsibility* (accountability) in Danish legal theory (in contrast to the *political accountability* of article 15). Further provisions concerning the legal responsibility are contained in articles 59 and 60 of the Constitution and in the Act on Ministerial Responsibility.

In total there have only been 5 impeachment cases during the time of the Danish Constitution (since 1849) – the second latest in 1910. Many legal theorists actually had projected that in reality the institution of impeachment had disappeared from the Danish constitutional system for good (as being replaced by the possibility of a binding vote of no-confidence), but in the late 1980's a situation occurred where a majority of Parliament decided to instigate an impeachment procedure against a former minister, and this impeachment case led to the conviction of the minister and 4 months of imprisonment.[5] Even if such impeachment cases will certainly also in the future be rare, there is thus still reason to consider the rules and practices governing impeachment cases.

---

4 In theory, it might be possible to form more than one government that meets the negative parliamentary requirement (if one or more parties are indifferent to which government is formed, or at least will not vote for a motion of no-confidence). In such a case, some have suggested that it should be left to the Queen to choose between the two possibilities. However, in a democratic society this would be totally unacceptable according to Danish constitutional theory, as the Queen always acts on the responsibility of a minister. In the mentioned situation, it must therefore be the retiring Prime Minister who 'advises' the Queen on who to choose, and thus in reality decides the composition of the new government. Even if such advice is a highly political matter, there is general agreement that such advice is 'necessary to ensure the uninterrupted conduct of official business', cf. article 15 in fine.

5 According to the Danish legislation on foreign citizens at that time, a legal permanent resident had a right protected by the Foreigners Act to bring his family to Denmark. The Minister of Justice, however, had obstructed this right in order to diminish immigration to Denmark. This was clearly a breach of the provisions of the Foreigners Act, and the (then former) Minister of Justice was consequently convicted of violating the Act on Ministerial Responsibility,

As can be seen from the wording of article 16 of the Constitution, impeachment cases can be started by either the government ('King') or Parliament. All five impeachment cases that have actually occurred were started by Parliament.[6] Only a simple majority in Parliament is needed to impeach a minister.

According to article 5, para.1, of the Act on ministerial responsibility a minister can be punished for putting aside the duties laid on him by the Constitution, by ordinary acts, or by the 'nature of his position as a minister'.[7] The acts to be punished must have been committed intentionally or due to gross negligence. According to article 5, para. 2, a minister can also be punished for misinforming Parliament, or for withholding important information in connection with matters being debated in Parliament.

As stated in art. 16 of the Constitution, the court that decides in impeachment cases is the High Court of the Realm (not to be confused with the ordinary Supreme Court). The High Court of the Realm is only used for impeachment cases, and further provisions on this court are contained in articles 59 and 60 of the Constitution and in a special act on the High Court of the Realm.

The court is composed of up to 15 of the members of the Supreme Court and an equal number of lay judges. The lay judges are elected by Parliament (in proportion to the relative size of the parties in Parliament), but cannot be members of Parliament, and the lay judges are elected for a six year period, but can be re-elected. The reason for the inclusion of lay judges is that impeachment cases often were supposed to lie in the border area between law and politics, and that consequently a case should be decided by a group of judges who had knowledge of both. After the introduction of parliamentarism, however, impeachment cases have not been considered unless the case involved a more traditional legal problem, so today there is widespread consensus that the special composition of the court is outdated,[8] and that impeachment cases should probably be decided by the ordinary Supreme Court.

---

6 On the face of it, it might seem odd to give the government the possibility of impeaching ministers. However, it should be kept in mind that according to article 8 of the Act on Ministerial Responsibility the period of limitation can be no shorter than 5 years, meaning that there will always be at least one general election between a possible breach of the Act on Ministerial Responsibility and the end of the limitation period, and that a new government might therefore find it necessary to start an impeachment case against members of the former government.

7 What is actually contained in the last part of article 5 (the nature of his position as a minister) might seem a little unclear. An example that has been recognized in court practice is the duty of the Prime Minister to scrutinize the work of the other members of government, even if the Danish Constitution rests on a presumption that the individual ministers are equal and not subject to instructions from the Prime Minister in their daily work. However, the duty of the Prime Minister is based on his power to appoint and dismiss the other ministers, which is construed to include a duty to oversee the work of the government in general.

8 As the composition of the court is determined in the Constitution itself, it would, however, require a constitutional amendment to change it, and as the Danish Constitution is very difficult to amend, a

With the inclusion of up to 30 judges (and a number of high-ranking lawyers), it is quite obvious that an impeachment case is only started in the gravest cases. This could be another reason for simplifying the procedures concerning impeachment cases, as the practical problems involved in such cases might in themselves mean that such cases are not raised – even if there was ample legal reason to do so.

Questions have been raised as to whether the composition of the High Court of the Realm is in accordance with the demands of article 6 of the European Convention of Human Rights (ECHR) on fair trial. More specifically the problem discussed is whether the fact that the 'prosecutor' (Parliament) also elects half of the judges is in conflict with fair trial. The High Court of the Realm had to decide on this question in connection with the latest impeachment case in the beginning of the 1990's and concluded unanimously that the High Court of the realm lived up to the standards of impartiality and independence required by article 6 of the ECHR.[9] The reason for this was that the lay judges are elected at fixed intervals and independently of any possible impeachment cases, and that the choice of judges cannot consequently be influenced by the knowledge of the contents of pending impeachment cases. Had the lay judges been elected to participate in a concrete case, it would have been illegal according to the Danish Constitution article 61 which forbids 'extraordinary courts[10] with judicial authority' – and probably also according to article 6 of the ECHR.

In conclusion, the political accountability of the government towards Parliament is by far the most important kind of accountability in the Danish political system, but can in rare cases be supplemented by the legal accountability of the ministers according to the Constitution and the Act on Ministerial Responsibility.

---

change in the composition of the High Court of the Realm will have to await that a new Constitution is enacted for other reasons.

9 The decision of the High Court of the Realm was brought to the European Court of Human Rights which concluded in 1999 that article 6 had not been violated by the composition of the High Court of the realm.

10 'Extraordinary courts' in Danish constitutional language means a court established to adjudicate a specific case that has already occurred. As can be inferred from the wording of the article, extraordinary courts for investigative purposes may be established, and in fact also have been established, thus for instance giving witnesses a legal duty to give evidence. The reports of such investigative extraordinary courts have been used by the prosecutorial authorities to determine whether they wanted to raise an actual case at the ordinary courts.

3 Who is Accountable for What?

The Danish executive system is a so-called ministerial system where the basic principle is that all administrative activities[11] take place within ministries with a politically and legally responsible minister as the head of it. In principle, each minister is responsible for his own ministry and the activities that take place there. However, the picture of who is responsible for what is somewhat more complicated in practice.

As has already been mentioned, article 15 of the Constitution makes clear that both the individual minister and the government as a whole are politically accountable to Parliament as a vote of no-confidence can be directed to an individual minister (who must resign if the motion is passed) or to the Prime Minister (with the effect that the government as a whole must resign or writs of elections must be issued).

In principle, a minister is accountable for everything that goes on within the framework of his ministry, and according to article 15 there are no limitations as to what the minister can be held accountable for. However, in practice a minister will only be held accountable for actions that can reasonably be attributed to his own conduct (or lack of conduct). In article 3 of the Act on Ministerial Responsibility (which concerns the legal responsibility of ministers, cf. above) it is laid down that a minister is legally responsible for the acts of the employees of the ministry if a) he has been aware of the illegal act and has not taken action to prevent it, if b) the action of the employee is a necessary or natural means to carry through a decision of the minister, and if c) he has promoted the illegal action by lack of supervision and directions to his employees.

Even though these provisions are not directly applicable to the political responsibility of article 15, it is probably a fairly accurate description of the actual limits of the political responsibility. Thus, no vote of no-confidence would probably be passed because of actions of ministerial employees unless it fell within one of the three categories mentioned above.

On the other hand, the responsibility of the ministers is not limited to policy making, but also applies to day-to-day administration (provided that it falls within one of the three categories of article 3 of the Act of Ministerial responsibility).

A growing number of administrative actions have during the years been removed from the ordinary ministerial system and have been placed within independent administrative agencies, complaint boards and the like. A consequence of that has been that the minister – in accordance with the guidelines mentioned above – is no longer in practice held politically accountable for the actions that take place within such administrative bodies, as he has no influence

[11] What is said in the following concerns administrative activities within the *State*. However, an increasing part of the administrative activities take place within municipalities ('local government') (as foreseen in article 82 of the Constitution).

on what is going on within such bodies, and it would thus seem unfair to hold him accountable for their actions.

This development can be attributed to several reasons. One reason has been to keep the ministers (and the ordinary ministerial systems) free of dealing with individual cases in order to give more time to strategic (policy making) tasks. Another reason is the lack of administrative courts in the Danish system, which makes it natural to create last instance authorities that are not dependent on the minister – in order to secure the rights of the citizens in relation to the ordinary administrative authorities. Both these reasons are generally acknowledged as well-founded, and there is also general agreement that the goals pursued by the 'out-sourcing' of administrative tasks to independent boards and the like have been achieved to a great extent.

However, this development where more and more administrative tasks are placed outside the ordinary ministerial system, has also given rise to some worry in another respect – exactly because accountability in such a system seems hard to find. There is general agreement that the transfer of administrative power to independent agencies and the like is not unconstitutional (even though the Constitution rests on the principle of a ministerial system), as long as this transfer of power is authorized by parliamentary act. The provisions on ministerial responsibility have primarily been put into the Constitution to benefit Parliament, so if Parliament – after weighing the pros and cons of such transfer of administrative power – decides to deviate from the basic principle, that is the sovereign right of Parliament.

As the benefits of placing ultimate administrative responsibility in independent agencies are widely acknowledged, the problem of accountability must be solved in other ways. A very important role in this respect is played by the Parliamentary Ombudsman (see further below) who also supervises the independent agencies. The decisions of the administrative boards are also subject to ordinary judicial review in accordance with article 63 of the Constitution (also dealt with below)

The Danish Constitution only envisages political accountability to Parliament. The general political accountability of article 15 has already been dealt with. On financial matters the control powers of Parliament are exercised by a National Auditing Agency, which is, however, an organization subjected to Parliament, and by six 'State Auditors' elected by Parliament. However, the final approval of the accounts of State lies with Parliament, cf. article 47 of the Constitution.

Another control mechanism that plays an important role in practice in holding the administration in general accountable is the above mentioned Parliamentary Ombudsman who – on behalf of Parliament – considers complaints from citizens who think that theirs rights have been infringed by the administration.[12]

---

[12] The Parliamentary Ombudsman supervises all kinds of public administration. Although the Constitution (article 55) only mentions the supervision of state administration (which also includes independent

In many respects the Parliamentary Ombudsman (together with the independent administrative boards etc. mentioned above) has taken the place of administrative courts as Denmark is one of the few countries in Western Europe that do not have such courts.[13] Such courts are foreseen in article 63, para. 2, of the Constitution, but have never actually been established – one of the reasons for this exactly being that the Ombudsman institution is generally considered to function extremely well as a easily accessible mechanism to hold the administration accountable.

Finally, it should also be mentioned that even though there are no special administrative courts, all administrative decisions can be tried by the ordinary courts according to article 63 of the Constitution. Even though such cases of review of administrative decisions are rather rare, the possibility of having their decisions reviewed probably acts as an important preventive incentive to the administration, and also as an important corrective means in concrete cases.

Apart from the ministers themselves, all parts of the administration are employed civil servants.[14] Such civil servants are of course accountable according to the rules that are in force for all other employees and the special rules laid down in the Civil Servants Act. This means that if they do not fulfil their jobs, or if they abuse their powers or make mistakes, they can be sanctioned by their superiors – ranging from warnings through transfer to another job to removal from office. It should be stressed, however, that Parliament cannot hold civil servants accountable, as only the ministers are responsible to Parliament. Indirectly Parliament can of course interfere also with the work of the civil servants by threatening to censure the minister.

A special category of civil servants – political advisers – ought to be mentioned in this connection as in some respect they are quite different from traditional civil servants in the Danish administrative system. Political advisers were not introduced into Danish politics until the late 1990's where a few ministers began to employ such advisers. At that time it created a lot of discussion as the phenomenon of politically appointed civil servants was quite unfamiliar in Denmark (cf. note 14), and resulted in a committee report which recommended some basic rules to govern the subject of political advisers. Such advisers are still employed as civil servants and must be hired for their qualifications (and not *only* for their political points of view), but unlike other civil servants they are expected to – and allowed to – advise the minister on purely political premises. As a reflection of that, such political advisers do not take part in the ordinary daily life of a ministry (cannot decide administrative cases, have no instructional power in relation to any subordinates in the ministry), and they are dismissed

boards as mentioned above), the competence of the Ombudsman has been enlarged by parliamentary Act to cover also local government.

13 Norway is another example of a country that has no special administrative courts.

14 In Denmark there are no politically appointed 'state secretaries', 'under secretaries', 'junior ministers', or the like. This has the effect that all employees of a ministry – with few exceptions, cf. below on political advisers – continue in their jobs even if the political colour of the government is changed.

from their job together with the minister who employed them in the first place. Most ministers now employ one or (in a few cases) a few political advisers – mostly for communication purposes (press secretaries or 'spin doctors' as they are termed in the media). With the generally accepted rules on political advisers and the relatively small number of such advisers, the issue does not seem to be controversial any more.

4 Holding Formally Independent Authorities Accountable

The government of course has the final responsibility for the public financial situation, and can be held accountable for that. However, a substantial part of the public economy lies with the municipalities, so the financial decisions of local government play an important part in determining the overall financial situation of the country. Consequently, the government is very interested in keeping some kind of control over the economy of local government.

According to article 82 of the Constitution local government is subject to the provisions of parliamentary acts, so at the end of the day government (and the parliamentary majority behind the government) can always force local government to get into line with the general policies of the government. However, article 82 reflects a value of local self-determination, so in practice the government negotiates with the organizations representing local government in order to find an agreement that will make legislation unnecessary,[15] and such agreements are normally achieved.

Such agreements between the national government and the organizations of local government are not necessarily subject to the ordinary control mechanisms of Parliament. However, in practice, such agreements must be approved by the Finance Committee of Parliament to have effect, and also in this quite important respect the government is thus accountable to Parliament (as the Finance Committee reflects the political composition of Parliament as a whole cf. below).

As already mentioned a minister is responsible for the actions within the framework of the ministry to the extent that he can actually influence the actions in question. This means that he will be responsible for the actions of ordinary government departments as he has the power to give instructions to all civil servants within such departments. On the other hand it also means that he is not accountable for the actions of independent government agencies, as it is exactly the lack of instructional power on the part of the minister that make such agencies independent.

As a basic principle, independent agencies cannot be controlled by the government – at least not directly. However, the government has a number of 'tools' that can be used to control such agencies. First, government controls the

[15] If such negotiations fail, legislation can – and has been – used to make the municipalities act in accordance with the general economic policy of the government.

budgets of the independent agencies, as appropriations to the agencies are part of the yearly budget.[16] Secondly, normally the civil servants employed within the agencies are appointed by the government, so at least over time the government can influence the policies of the agencies by its appointments for such jobs. Finally, the government can threaten to change the status of the agencies if they deviate too far from government policies. Even though this would also require a parliamentary act, a government would normally be able to rely on the majority supporting it in Parliament if it wanted to change the status of an agency for political reasons.

All this does not mean that independent agencies are normally in reality directed by government, but only that both the agencies and the government know that if it should come to a stand off between the two, the government can in most instances carry through its policies. This is in my opinion quite reasonable as the role of the agencies is to *execute* policies – although independently, e.g. to protect the rights of the involved citizens – but not to *make* policy.

5 Day to Day Parliamentary Control and Transparency

Besides the ultimate means of control – a vote of no-confidence (which is rarely activated, but acts as a potential threat at any time) – Parliament in its daily cooperation with the government has at its disposal a number of other ways to control government. In a situation like the one that has existed since 2001 in the Danish Parliament where a minority government is backed by a firm majority of MPs, it is inconceivable that a vote of no-confidence should be passed, or that a majority should vote for starting an impeachment case, and consequently the only means of control left to the opposition are the ones mentioned below.

Article 53 states: '*With the consent of the Folketing, any member thereof may submit for discussion any matter of public interest and request a statement thereon from the Ministers.*' The consent required for raising a debate of a matter of public interest is traditionally always given if the request comes from one of the opposition parties.

As can be seen from the actual wording of the constitutional provision, the relevant minister in such debates is obliged to answer the questions raised. This is supplemented by the provision of article 5, para. 2, of the Act on Ministerial Responsibility, according to which legal responsibility can be incurred if a minister gives information to Parliament that is not correct or misleading or withholds relevant information.[17]

16 The budget is formally enacted by Parliament, but is always a result of negotiations between the government and its parliamentary majority, thus giving government a great say on the budget.

17 The provision of the Act on Ministerial Responsibility not only applies to debates according to article 53 of the Constitution, but to every part of a minister's relationship with Parliament, for instance when answering questions from Parliament in writing, and when appearing in committees.

Debates according to article 53 of the Constitution are normally reserved to more general and broad questions. However, more specific questions can be raised in the parliamentary question time which takes place every Wednesday.[18] The formals details on the parliamentary question time are regulated in the Order of Business of Parliament (article 20 of the Order of Business). It follows from the provisions of the mentioned article 20 that a minister can refuse to answer such questions, but it is quite obvious that in practice a minister who does that will have to justify his refusal in some way, and also that a minister who abuses his right to refuse to answer questions could easily face a vote of no-confidence. Thus, there is also a near-duty to answer questions in the parliamentary question time.

Another way of controlling the work of the government, which has become more prominent, is for the parliamentary committees to call the relevant minister to a consultation with the committee. The ministers have always been called to consultations with the committees in connection with the committees' discussions on government bills, but it has also become common to call the ministers to consultations on administrative matters, so that not only the policy-making functions of the ministers, but also the specifically executive functions are increasingly controlled by Parliament. Furthermore, such consultations often attract much public attention, and in this way also act as a form of control from the general public and the press vis á vis the government.

When it comes to control of the budget, the basic provisions are laid down in the Constitution itself According to article 45 the annual budget must be passed as a parliamentary act, thus in effect giving Parliament the full control of the incomes and expenditures of the government for the coming year. In practice, no government can stay in office, if it cannot get its budget through Parliament in some form.[19] Furthermore, no expenditures can be paid, and no income collected, unless it is part of the parliamentary enacted budget, according to article 46 of the Constitution.

This means that if it is necessary to deviate from the figures of the budget, this must be approved by Parliament – in principle by the enactment of a supplementary budget. In practice, this has proven to be too unrealistic, so it has become customary law that the Finance Committee of Parliament can – on behalf of Parliament – approve expenditures not listed in the budget during the

---

[18] Questions are always raised in writing, but initially most such questions were answered orally in Parliament itself. However, with the growing number of questions this has become practically impossible, so nowadays the overwhelming majority of questions are answered in writing, and only a few – normally those touching on more general aspects of government policy – are answered orally and subject to a subsequent debate in Parliament.

[19] Some constitutional theory has even suggested that a government whose budget proposal was defeated in Parliament, had a legal obligation to resign, cf. article 15 of the Constitution. However, most theorists do not adhere to such a point of view although there is general consensus that in practice the resignation of the government would always be the effect of such a defeat.

fiscal year. Parliament then – after the end of the year – formally approves such expenditures by passing a supplementary budget act.[20]

Parliament thus retains full control over the budget – both before and during the fiscal year. Finally, Parliament must also approve the State Accounts after the end of the fiscal year (cf. article 47 of the Constitution). In that connection Parliament can make use of the National Auditing Agency and the six parliamentary elected State Auditors mentioned earlier. The approval of the accounts and the work connected with this also give Parliament a powerful control tool.

Parliament does not have any direct control power in relation to civil servants, as the basic presumption of the ministerial system is that it is the minister who is responsible for what goes on in his ministry. Thus, all contact between Parliament and civil servants goes through the minister. If a civil servant must be held accountable for his actions, it is the minister who must do so, as he is the employer of the civil servant and has the ordinary powers in relation to an employee.

Indirectly, however, Parliament can – as mentioned – to a certain extent also control civil servants, as it may be the basis of some kind of responsibility for the minister if – to the opinion of Parliament – he does not live up to his obligations as head of the ministry and its civil servants.

Independent agencies can in principle be controlled by Parliament as they are part of the public administration and as such subject to parliamentary control. In relation to budgetary control, there is no great difference in practice between the ordinary government departments and the independent agencies. In relation to other forms of control, it naturally affects the possibility of Parliament to control that the relevant minister has no instructional power over these independent agencies. However, the minister can still obtain information on what goes on in the agencies and pass it on to Parliament, and even independent agencies are required to give relevant information to the minister, unless specifically protected by special provisions or the general rules on professional secrecy.

6 Consequences

As mentioned in the first section of this paper, Parliament has the power to dismiss both individual ministers and the government as a whole[21]

[20] There is general agreement that this procedure does not cause any democratic or constitutional reason for concern. With the firm party discipline that is common in Denmark, a majority in the Finance Committee will almost always reflect a majority in Parliament proper – and if in rare circumstances that should not be the case, Parliament can always take up the matter and reverse the decision of the Finance Committee.

[21] As mentioned the passage of a vote of no-confidence to the Prime Minister must result in the resignation of the whole government, unless the Prime Minister decides to call for general elections. If such elections show a majority against the government, the government is at that time undoubtedly legally obliged to resign.

by passing a vote of no-confidence. There are no actual examples of votes of no-confidence to an individual minister. In the cases where there seemed to be a majority for such a proposal, the minister has either resigned himself before the debate in Parliament or has been dismissed by the Prime Minister, cf. article 14 of the Constitution, in order to diminish the political embarrassment for the government.

Since the introduction of parliamentarism in 1901, there have only been 3 examples of regular votes of no-confidence being passed (1909, 1947, and 1975) – all three times directed against the Prime Minister or the government as a whole. However, in a number of other cases Parliament has voted against the government on important pieces of legislation, and in most of these cases the government has chosen to either resign or call for elections, thus in effect perceiving such votes as votes of no-confidence. In a few other instances where it was certain that a vote of no-confidence would be passed in Parliament, the government has chosen to resign in advance – again probably to diminish the political embarrassment of the situation. It should be stressed that in neither of the two situations mentioned in this paragraph is there any legal obligation for the government to draw any consequences of the situation.[22]

As indicated above the Prime Minister has the possibility to dismiss a minister at any time and for whatever reason, even if Parliament has not shown any kind of dissatisfaction with the minister in question. However, in practice dismissal of a minister is often the result of some kind of criticism from Parliament, as a minister – even though there is no risk of a vote of no-confidence – can be a political liability to a government.

According to the Order of Business of the Danish Parliament proposals for a vote of no-confidence can only be raised in connection with certain debates in Parliament, i.a. debates on the basis of article 53 of the Constitution, cf. above. In practice, this places no limitation on the possibility of a majority in Parliament to pass a motion of no-confidence, as such debates are rather frequent, and the majority of Parliament can at any time put such a debate on the agenda of Parliament.

7 Concluding Remarks

Looking at the rules governing the relationship between the government and Parliament, it seems as if Parliament prevails over the government. When it comes to the end of the day, there is no doubt that Parliament can always carry through its will if it is determined to do so.

22 Actually, in the period between 1982 and 1988 the government was defeated in Parliament on a number of occasions without drawing any consequences of its defeats. The reason for that was that the government had a firm majority behind its economic policy, which the government had declared to be its top priority, and it was therefore willing to tolerate being defeated in a number of other policy areas. Although this differed substantially from ordinary practice in Danish parliamentary life, the government undoubtedly acted constitutionally.

However, in practice the problem has often been that the government with all its administrative resources behind it has too much power compared to the publicly elected Parliament – especially if the government has a stable majority behind it in Parliament. In such situations the role of Parliament could be reduced to appointing a government and to 'rubber stamp' the initiatives of that government.

Parliament has always been aware of the dangers of such a role, and in recent years has increased its possibilities of control of the daily work of the government, for instance by hiring its own professional staff of lawyers, economists, etc., and by increasing the funds paid to the political parties to make it possible for them to match – at least to a certain degree – the administrative resources of the government.

In recent years, further proposals have been put forward to strengthen Parliament, or more correctly, the opposition in Parliament. As demonstrated above, many of the control mechanisms of the Danish system are dependent on a majority in Parliament to be activated, so if the government commands a firm majority in Parliament, the possibilities of opposition are clearly diminished.[23] This has led to reform proposals involving that a 'qualified minority' (for instance 40% f the MPs) could demand that certain control procedures were initiated (the creation of investigative committees of the like), but such proposals have not been carried through so far.

The relationship between Parliament and government in Denmark is thus not one in which one or the other party prevails, but rather a delicate system of checks and balances, which has probably struck a reasonable balance between effectiveness of government and democratic control.

[23] One recent example of this is the Danish involvement in Iraq that was opposed by the opposition in Parliament. Even though the background for the involvement seems to be dubious, the government has consistently opposed the creation of an investigation committee to scrutinize the events leading up to the Danish involvement in the war.

Bibliography

GERMER (2001)

P. Germer, *Statsforfatningsret* 3. udgave (2001).

JENSEN (1997)

J.A. Jensen, *Parlamentarismens statsretlige betydning* 2. udgave (1997).

ZAHLE (2003)

H. Zahle, *Dansk forfatningsret I – Institutioner og regulering* 3. udgave (2003).

ZAHLE (2006)

H. Zahle (ed.), *Grundloven – Danmarks Riges Grundlov med kommentarer* 2. udgave (2006).

CHAPTER 5

Political Accountability in France

Jacques Ziller

1 Introduction

In May 2006, Robert Badinter, Former President of the Constitutional Council (*Conseil constitutionnel*) and former Minister of Justice of François Mitterrand in the nineteen eighties, gave an interview to the newspaper 'Le Monde', which was published with the title 'Political accountability has vanished' (*La responsabilité politique a disparu*). He was referring to the 'Cleastream' case, where Prime Minister Dominique de Villepin was suspected to have been involved in a case of fake computer listings which could have damaged the career of his rival, the Minister of the Interior, Nicolas Sarkozy. Badinter's declarations about political accountability are worthwhile reproducing,[1] as they are extremely typical of the French debates about this topic, amongst politicians and amongst academics.

> "Political accountability has vanished in the Republic as it functions now. Outside of 'cohabitation' the President of the Republic has powers without any equivalent in any democracy, without accountability. The Prime minister and members of government are appointed by him and are in practice only accountable to him. Since 1962 no government has been forced to resign by the National Assembly. Parliament has abdicated its function of controlling and possibly recalling government. "
>
> "Deputies should not remain machines which record the will of the Elysée.[2] Enquiry committees should be multiplied. In a public opinion democracy, citizens have to be directly informed. Enquiry committees should organise public hearings similar to those which were organised in the Outreau case,3 and which have been followed with passion by the public. And we need a modest presidency instead of an imperial one. The President should play his eminent role on the international scene, especially in Europe. He should be the warrant of the few important options which led to his election. He should look after the respect of the institutions and fundamental freedoms. For the remaining, it should be up to government to act, under Parliamentary control."

Quite similar declarations had been made forty and thirty years earlier by the leader of the opposition François Mitterrand, criticising the functioning of government during the presidential terms of Charles de Gaulle (1959-1969), Georges Pompidou (1969-1974) and Valéry Giscard d'Estaing (1974-1981). And the leader of the opposition, Jacques Chirac, made the same solemn criticism during the presidential term of François Mitterrand (1981-1995) – outside of 'cohabitation' periods where government was led by Chirac himself (1986-1988) or his fellow party member Edouard Balladur (1993-1995). As a matter of fact, most constitutional lawyers would make the same kind of declaration.

---

1 Published in Le Monde, 19 May 2006, translation by the author of this chapter.

2 The '*Palais de l'Elysée*' is the residence of the President of the Republic.

3 A case of malfunctioning of criminal justice which was very much discussed in France in 2005-2006.

To the journalist who went on asking him whether the Clearstream Case could have occurred in the same way under any regime, Badinter answered:

> "In many governments, there are conflicts of powers and of persons, sometimes serious. There exists a pathology of governments, which is illustrated by the present affair. It seems to me exaggerated however to say that it is linked to our institutions and to the practice of the Fifth Republic. What is genuine to this regime is the absence of political solution outside of a sovereign decision of the President of the Republic. In a system where the accountability of government is never challenged by Parliament, the only thing which eventually matters to ministers is the confidence of the President."

In a nutshell these declarations touch upon most aspects of political accountability in France. The following will mainly serve to explain it in more detail.

2 The Notion of Political Accountability in French Law and Politics

Using the English language formulation of 'political accountability' generates conceptual problems which come to the forefront when using the French language, though these problems are certainly not specific to France: as explained by Carol Harlow, the concept of accountability is not especially clear in the English language either.[4] The common translation of political accountability into French would be *'responsabilité politique'*. But *'responsabilité'* (like the Dutch *'aansprakelijkheid'* or the Italian *'responsabilità'*) is often considered in a stricter sense than accountability, although the literal meaning is exactly the same. This is due to the fact that the legal notion of *'responsabilité'* is threefold, linking in a single word the concepts of political accountability (*responsabilité politique*), with criminal liability (*responsabilité pénale*) and civil liability (*responsabilité civile*).

This is not specific to France, as demonstrated by the origins of political accountability in the British system: impeachment, which was a means of ensuring criminal liability of ministers has evolved into Parliamentary responsibility. Accountability, not being a legal concept, encompasses other phenomena and thus may have a broader and more vague scope than *'responsabilité'*. In order to cover the same ground as the broad concept of accountability, French language usually uses the plural *'responsabilités'*, or other expressions like *'imputabilité'* (the French Canadian translation for accountability) or the somewhat longer *'reddition de comptes'*, which is deemed to become the official equivalent of 'accountability'.

---

4 As Carol Harlow explains it, the concept of accountability is not especially clear in the English language (Harlow (2002) 6-24).

The concept of political accountability (*responsabilité politique*) is the central legal constitutional concept of the Parliamentary system of the Vth Republic. It is decomposed into:

i) political accountability of the government which needs to be supported by the National Assembly on one side and accepted by the President on the other, and
ii) political accountability of the Nation's representatives (President and Parliament) on the other side.

In the strict sense, political accountability of the government means that members of government need the approval/acceptance of the President in order to be appointed, and the acceptance of the National Assembly to keep their function. The President may refuse to appoint somebody as minister or even as Prime minister, and the National Assembly may adopt a vote of diffidence which obliges the Government to withdraw.

In a broader sense, political accountability means that Government has to give account. In order to ensure this, Parliament has the power to question government and to get answers, and to enquire into the actions of the executive. The political accountability of the Parliament stems from direct election and that of the National Assembly is reinforced by the President's power to dissolve it. The President's accountability only stems ex-ante from his election.

As mentioned earlier, civil and criminal liability are two other classical types of accountability, which are discussed as well in literature as in the political debate, especially as far as criminal liability of elected officials is concerned. The reform of the criminal code in 1992 has led to numerous cases involving mainly locally elected officials. The scandals around AIDS and other contamination of blood donors in the early nineties has involved heavy discussions and has led to a constitutional reform with the creation of a specific court (*Cour de Justice de la République*) to deal with the criminal and civil liability of ministers for the decisions they have made in the exercise of their official duties. This Court is made of ordinary independent judges, but prosecution is opened by decisions of Parliament.

The recent development of a 'law of regulation' (*droit de la régulation*) linked to the establishment of independent regulatory authorities, especially as a result of privatisations and the reorganisation of network industries, has led academics and practitioners to debate the ways and means of insuring accountability of independent authorities.

3 Accountability in the French Parliamentary System

The French Parliamentary system differs from the standard Westminster model which is present in most European countries, because it is a form of dual Parliamentary system (*parlementarisme dualiste*). This type of system was common to most Parliamentary monarchies in Europe until the second half of the XIXth Century and later for some countries. It implies a dual accountability of government: towards Parliament on one side, and towards the Head of State on the other. This dual Parliamentary system had seemed abandoned in France after the crisis of 16 May 1877.[5] Dual parliamentarism came to a strong revival with the Constitution of the Fifth Republic of 4 October 1958, or to be more precise, with the practice of General de Gaulle as President of the Republic, and the direct election of the President which was established by constitutional amendment in 1962.

The qualification of the French political regime of today's as a dual Parliamentary system means that Government is accountable both to Parliament and to the Head of State, the two institutions which represent the people. In strict constitutional terms, accountability to Parliament has precedence over accountability to the President, as demonstrated by the so-called '*cohabitation*' periods of 1986-1988,[6] 1993-1995[7] and 1997-2002.[8] In political terms however there are two totally different situations. When the President stems from the coalition which has a majority in the National Assembly, accountability to the President clearly prevails, whereas accountability to Parliament prevails when the coalition which opposes the President has the majority in the National Assembly. The constitutional reform of 2 October 2000, by cutting the President's term from 7 to 5 years – i.e. the same length as the National Assembly's mandate – coupled with the change of calendar by a statute of 15 May 2001, which led to the Presidential election of 2002 being held before the election of the National Assembly, has been designed to ensure as far as possible coincidence between the President's electoral majority and the majority in the National Assembly. This is however by no means guaranteed by the Constitution, and a premature end of a President's mandate or the dissolution of the National Assembly could restore the political conditions which led to '*cohabitation*' in the past. This is why it is and remains inaccurate to qualify the French political system as a 'presidential' system – as opposed to a parliamentary system.

---

5 On 16 May 1877 the president of the French Republic, Marshall Mac Mahon, a monarchist, forced the republican Prime Minister Jules Simon, whose cabinet still enjoyed the confidence of parliament, to resign. According Mac Mahon, in the parliamentary system instituted by the constitutional laws of the Third Republic, the cabinet not only needed the (political) confidence of parliament, but also that of the head of state. However, he overplayed his cards and lost the ensuing battle with parliament. Two years later a republican majority in both houses of parliament forced him to resign. Since then, and until 1958, the French heads of state have only played a marginal and essentially ceremonial role in French politics.

6 With François Mitterrand (Socialist Party) as President and Jacques Chirac (RPR – neo-Gaullist party) as Prime Minister.

7 With François Mitterrand (Socialist Party) as President and Edouard Balladur (RPR – neo-Gaullist party) as Prime Minister.

8 With Jacques Chirac (RPR – neo-Gaullist party) as President and Lionel Jospin (Socialist Party) as Prime Minister.

The Constitution of the Fifth Republic has been drafted in a context of remembrances of the Parliamentary system of the IIIrd Republic (1875-1940) and of the IVth (1946-1958) Republic. During that period, the French political system was characterised by the domination of Parliament over the executive without party discipline, which led to a very high degree of instability of Cabinets (22 from 1946 to 1958, the shortest lasting 10 days, and the longest one year and four months). The procedures laid down in the Constitution of 4 October 1958 can only be understood in this context: whereas they had been designed in order to introduce checks and balance in a system of high fragmentation of political parties, the bipolar political scene which has been consolidated by the direct election of the President – a reform adopted in 1962 – has led to a strong imbalance in favour of the Executive, whenever the government of the day may count upon an absolute majority in Parliament.

The President of the Republic's solid political power is hardly due to the constitutional text: his competences in foreign policy are submitted to the countersign of the ministers as are almost all his formal powers in the framework of internal politics. Apart from the direct election of the President, the only constitutional mechanism which contributes to his power is the fact that he may dissolve Parliament without countersign. No President could exercise leadership in politics without the agreement of the Prime Minister he has appointed, and of the coalition which has the majority in the National Assembly.

At the end of the day, elections to the National Assembly have a more determining impact than the election of the President. This is perfectly demonstrated since 1995: the Governments serving President Chirac under his second term represent the majority at the National Assembly, not the voters who preferred Jacques Chirac to Jean Marie Le Pen (extreme right) in 2002, in the same way as the Governments of his first term represented the majority which was first that of his own political coalition from 1995 to 1997 and than that of the opposition, led by Lionel Jospin, from 1997 to 2002.

Major issues of political accountability in the French political and constitutional debate are related to the lack of accountability mechanisms for the President of the Republic, who is elected for 5 years (7 years until 2002), with a mandate that may be renewed without limitations, and cannot be dismissed for any other reason than for high treason.

The dominant thesis in both doctrine and political live is that the President's political accountability is only at stake if and when he runs for a new term. In recent debates, attention shifted to the problems due to the classical immunity of jurisdiction which the President enjoys during his term and which protects him from civil and criminal prosecution as well as from the duty to testify. The many cases involving the municipal administration of Paris at the times when Jacques Chirac was Mayor point to the problems which may result from his immunity. The President's immunity is still considered by a majority of both constitutional doctrine and the political class to be inherent to the function of Head of State – provided obviously that it ceases with the President's term.

The French Parliamentary system is asymmetric – like most European systems apart from the Italian system (and the Belgian until 1993). The Government is only accountable to the directly elected National Assembly – not to the Senate whose election is indirect, based upon representation of local and regional governments – and it has the means to give the last word to the National Assembly in legislation. The Senate's collaboration is however necessary to amend the Constitution and some 'organic laws' (*lois organiques*) implementing the Constitution: this means that left wing Presidents have had to overcome more important obstacles than right wing Presidents in implementing their political programme, because the electoral system of the Senate invariably leads to a conservative majority. This demonstrates the existence of specific mechanisms of accountability towards the Senate, which do not necessarily appear through reading the Constitution.

Ministers are appointed by the President of the Republic, upon proposal of the Prime Minister. The latter is appointed by the President himself, but may be forced to withdraw by a vote of the National Assembly, which may be initiated by the Prime Minister's request of a vote of confidence, or by one tenth of the members of the Assembly. There is no formal need of Parliamentary approval of the composition of government, but the political practice is for Prime ministers to ask for a vote of confidence in the weeks which follow their appointment by the President.

According to practice the composition of government takes only a few days and is determined by discussions between the Prime minister and the President, not by discussions between the parties of the coalition which supports government. This procedure influences both the concept of a dual Parliamentary system and the practice of dual political accountability which it embeds. A Prime Minister cannot appoint a minister which has not been agreed to by the President – there are numerous precedents of Presidents refusing the appointment of a Minister proposed to them by the Prime Minister, both in periods of coincidence of Presidential and Parliamentary majority and in periods of cohabitation.

In addition to the specific constitutional mechanisms designed to ensure accountability, it has to be borne in mind that French administrative law has since long (from 1872 onwards) developed a regime of 'administrative liability' (*responsabilité administrative*) for acts of the public administration – national, local and regional – as well as independent agencies, based on the distinction between 'personal negligence' (*faute personnelle*) which leads to civil liability of the relevant official – and possibly criminal liability – and 'service negligence' (*faute de service*) which leads to 'administrative liability' of the legal person (State, local authority, agency). For the purpose of this regime, Ministers and the President as well as elected officials of local and regional government are considered as officers of public administration. The French notion of administrative acts (*actes administratifs*), submitted to judicial review by administrative courts, is very broad and includes not only individual decisions but also all regulations adopted by executive organs as well as local and regional authorities and autonomous or independent agencies, and contracts. Hence judicial review by administrative courts extends to *'décrets'*, *'arrêtés ministériels'* and circulars, which are the expression of a considerable amount of governmental policy-making and implementation. The administrative courts and specially the *Conseil d'Etat* as a supreme administrative court therefore play a role which is not marginal in political accountability mechanisms, even though limited to legal matters.

It should however be noted that decisions relating to the relationship between Government, Parliament and the President (*'Organstreitigkeiten'* as they are called in German constitutional law) are not submitted to judicial review by administrative courts, due to the jurisprudential theory of *'actes de gouvernements'*. They may not either be submitted to the Constitutional council.

4 Accountability: The Actors

Political accountability of the government and Prime minister is collective. Only the Prime minister and the government as a whole are politically accountable to the National Assembly in the strict sense, i.e. may be forced to resign by the adoption of a vote of diffidence. They are also politically accountable to the President, who is in a position to force them to resign if he has the support of the majority in the National assembly. This means that the National Assembly can only adopt a vote of diffidence against the whole government, not against a single minister. This means also that the resignation of the Prime minister automatically leads to the termination of the office of other ministers. Since 1958 there are no cases of an indirect vote of diffidence against a single minister, as the Constitution has prohibited votes on 'resolutions' which were the means by which formerly Parliament forced ministers to resign.

There is however a form of individual accountability of ministers, who are individually accountable to the Prime minister and, indirectly to the President of the Republic: the Prime minister may revoke a minister and the resignation of a minister has no consequences on the rest of government members. In practice resignation of ministers has also been requested and obtained by the President.

The French administrative system is characterised by the importance of the *'cabinet ministériel'*. The *cabinet* is a group of political advisers who support the Minister and may get delegation to sign a number of decisions in the name of the Minister. The *'directeur de cabinet'* is particularly important as he very often gets a quite general delegation from the Minister. In theory a Minister may choose anybody to become part of his *cabinet*; in practice, the overwhelming majority of *cabinet* members are civil servants who get a leave of absence from their administration for the time they serve in the *cabinet*. *Directeurs de cabinet* are usually experienced but still rather young civil servants coming from the most prestigious *'corps'* (careers) of civil servants. It also happens that a minister involves non-civil servants as members of their *cabinet*, but this is only a very small minority.

Their fate as members of *cabinet* is directly linked to that of the minister: a minister's resignation or the end of office of a government automatically puts an end to the functions of the members of *cabinet* and to any delegation of signature they might have. The position of higher civil servant at the will of government is different: the resignation or end of office of the government has no legal influence on their position, although the government of the day is free to appoint them and dismiss them at will.

Ministers are thus in theory fully accountable for the actions of the members of their *cabinets*. In practice however, most politicians prefer dismissing a member of their cabinet or its director rather than offer their own resignation in case of failures of the administration they are leading.

The importance of *cabinets* in the French administrative system is very much criticised by doctrine and by practitioners. The two main lines of criticisms are:

- the presence of the *cabinet* as an interface between the Minister and line managers impedes direct contact between the politician and civil servants and thus does not allow for a clear system of accountability of ministers for their services;
- *cabinets* tend to give precedence to short term actions they deem rewarding from the point of view of political image, and impede the long-term actions of administration and policy making to develop well.

A big number of those who criticised the *cabinets* – be it academics or civil servants – have at one moment or another ended up taking part in a *cabinet*.

The phenomenon of the '*cabinet*' is diffused in France well beyond Ministries. Almost all executives of regional and local governments, of government agencies as well as those of medium sized and big private businesses have a *cabinet*. I think this is due to a preference for individual decision-making at the top – as opposed to collegial management – which has its roots in Napoleonic France and is being fostered by the French educational system which favours competition between individuals rather than cooperation amongst them.

High ranking civil servants are politically accountable to their Ministers and to the Prime minister (and indirectly to the President): the law establishes a strictly defined list of functions of civil servants dismissible at will (*fonctionnaires à la discrétion du gouvernement*) which includes ambassadors, prefects and the highest level of ministerial hierarchies. Civil servants are accountable to their minister or their head of agency. Agencies are either accountable to the ministry or local or regional authority which has established them, or independent.

In a broad sense, all the abovementioned actors are politically accountable, i.e. they have to give account to Parliament, who may enquire about their activities. If needed these enquiries may lead to criminal prosecution by justice.

5 The Scope of Accountability

According to legal theory ministers and government are accountable for policy making as well as for the execution of policy. In practice however, ministers rarely offer their resignations because of failures in execution, they rather tend to require the resignations of their political advisers or of higher officials in the administrative hierarchy.

The scope of political accountability of ministers and the scope of their legal powers coincide, as the decisions of state administrations are signed by, or upon delegation of, the minister. This does not however lead in practice to the resignation of ministers. On the contrary, openness of public administration leads to the possibility of identifying the real author of a decision and hence often encourages ministers not to back their subordinates' failures.

The classical French administrations are based upon hierarchy, which means that Ministers have powers to give instructions to civil servants, and have also the power to reform decisions made by civil servants – subject to remaining in a strict framework of legality as determined by acts of Parliament and government regulations. This is why in theory Ministers are fully accountable for all actions of the government department they are heading.

Two elements however have an attenuating effect :

i) it is a civil servant's duty to disobey if he gets an unlawful instruction from his superiors, including the Minister; criminal and disciplinary liabilities ensure enforcement of this principle;
ii) civil servants are liable for their own mistakes: even if the victims of these mistakes receive compensation on the basis of administrative liability due to the fact that there is a link between the mistake and the civil servant's official function, disciplinary sanctions may be adopted against the culprit, and part or the total of the damages paid to the victims by administration may be subtracted from the civil servant's salary.

There is hardly any discussion of the question of political accountability of civil servants in France: the main topic is for decades the question of the role of *cabinets ministériels* (see above paragraph 4), which is sometimes confused with the question of political accountability of civil servants by the press, but not by academic literature nor by politicians.

In order to understand to what extent ministers are accountable for the actions of independent agencies and which powers of control do ministers or the government have with regard to agencies, a clear distinction is to be made between independent authorities (*autorités administratives indépendantes*), most of which are regulatory authorities, and autonomous agencies (*établissements publics*), which are not integrated into the hierarchy or ministerial departments, but are not fully independent either.

Independent authorities (like the competition authority *Conseil de la Concurrence* or the data protection authority *Commission nationale de l'informatique et des libertés*, as well as more recent sectoral authorities like the telecommunication or energy authorities) are not submitted to control by ministers or the government. The only influence of government is in the choice and appointment of the regulators or of some members of the regulatory board. Accountability of these independent authorities is ensured mainly by two mechanisms: i.) their decisions and regulations are submitted to judicial review either by administrative courts or in some specific cases by the *Cour d'Appel de Paris*, and ii.) in last instance, Parliament might amend the legislative basis of the authorities' independence.

Autonomous agencies (*établissements publics*) are linked to government or to the local and regional authorities which have set them up. There are thousands of *établissements publics* at state level as well as regional or local level: secondary schools and universities, musea, hospitals, to name just the most numerous ones. Contrary to ministerial departments, autonomous agencies are not subordinated to the executive by way of hierarchy. Ministers and government (or regional and local executives) usually appoint the top executive of the *établissement* and may give him/her a 'lettre de mission' which states in general terms what his/her goals should be. But Ministers and government may not give instructions to officials of public establishments whose accountability is to the board of the authority. Membership of the boards varies and is established by statute or regulation. The most common pattern of membership is composed of four types of board members: i.) representatives of the executive, appointed by different ministries, ii.) staff representatives appointed upon the proposition of the trade unions, iii.) representatives of the relevant user categories, and iv.) individual experts appointed on the basis of their relevant merits. The decisions of agencies are sometimes subject to control by the Ministers or government upon appeal by the addressees, and always to judicial review by administrative courts.

Different from autonomous agencies (*établissements publics*) which have a legal personality separate from that of the state or the local or regional authorities which have established them, there are also executive agencies, very similar to British executive agencies, which are called '*centres de responsabilité*'. They are not separate legal entities, but parts of ministerial departments which receive a rather important degree of managerial financial autonomy. Accountability of their top officials is to the minister or to the top hierarchy of the ministry, based upon quantified objectives set-up in an agreement between the ministry and the agency, but political accountability as well as legal accountability through judicial review lies with the relevant ministry.

There is no discussion in literature and politics about the political accountability of *établissements publics* and *centres de responsabilités*, for which the issue is that of managerial accountability. As far as independent regulatory agencies are concerned, both legal literature and a number of politicians are voicing the question of the compatibility of their independence with the constitutional power of the Prime Minister as Head of the executive.[9] A very recent report of the Parliamentary Evaluation Office gives a thorough overview of the issues debated in France.[10] It underlines the fact that independent regulatory agencies being established by Parliament are ultimately accountable to Parliament – which might suppress them; it also stresses the fact that the independent regulatory agencies request being accountable to Parliament, and that a yearly accounting to Parliament would reinforce their legitimacy.[11]

6 Parliament's Means of Political and Budgetary Control

The National Assembly may force the government to resign by the adoption of a motion of censure – which needs the support of the absolute majority of its members in order to be considered as adopted. Only once such a motion has been adopted since the Constitution of 1958 came into force: against the government of Georges Pompidou in 1962, leading to the dissolution of the National Assembly by President de Gaulle.

Both houses of Parliament may control government through refusing to pass legislation proposed by the government, including the budget; this however plays only a marginal role in accountability, as governments usually have support of a coalition which benefits from absolute majority in the National Assembly. The latter may be given the last word in case the Senate does not accept a legislative proposal. Only the governments of Michel Rocard and his successors Edith Cresson and Pierre Bérégovoy from 1988 to 1993 did not rely upon an absolute majority in Parliament – only relative majority – and thus had to negotiate supplementary support in Parliament for each single proposal, because they did not want to abuse the means given by the Constitution to have bills passed by asking votes of confidence.

Members of both houses may ask oral or written questions on the action of government, ministers, their departmental services and agencies; responses are published in the official journal. Ministers have to answer questions of Parliament in writing or orally. There is a weekly session of oral questions in the presence of television, where the Prime minister decides which minister should answer questions. There is however no real practice of 'surprise questions'. There is no strict legal obligation for ministers to appear in Parliament when rendering account, but practice is now well established that they do. The

9 Article 20 of the Constitution states that *'Art. 20. –Le Gouvernement détermine et conduit la politique de la Nation. Il dispose de l'administration et de la force armée'*. This is seen by some authors as a principle that impedes the possibility of having administrative bodies which are not hierarchically subordinate to the Prime minister – with the exception of local and regional government, for which the Constitution states the principle of freedom of local administration.

10 See Office parlementaire d'évaluation de la législation , *Les autorités administratives indépendantes: évaluation d'un objet juridique non identifié, 2006* <http://www.senat.fr/rap/r05-404-1/r05-404-11.pdf>.

11 *Op. cit.* 118.

problem is more on the side of members of Parliament: while attendance to standing committee meetings is good, attendance to plenary sessions is always problematic apart from the weekly session of oral questions. Therefore the personal appearance of Ministers in Parliament has a minor function in their accountability.

Government may refuse to give answer on the basis of the protection of official secrets. Legal grounds are the protection of state security and foreign relations, protection of privacy and pending judicial proceedings. However if government refuses to answer without having grounds the only real sanction would be a motion of censure of the National Assembly, which has no chance to be adopted if government has a reliable majority, which is usually the case.

Both houses may set up committees in order to enquire upon specific government actions or in order to inspect government departments or agencies; there are limitations to the scope of their enquiries in case of pending judicial proceedings; the threshold for the establishment of these committees is however rather high and it is not easy for opposition to use this tool in order to control government. Parliament has the right to question or scrutinise civil servants of government departments as well as of autonomous and independent agencies. They in turn may refuse to reply on the basis of the protection of state security and foreign relations, protection of privacy and pending judicial proceedings, or professional secrecy. Furthermore a minister may forbid a civil servant to answer parliamentary questions or scrutiny – on the basis of the same grounds. The sanction is again only political: as long as government is supported by the majority of the National Assembly and as long as civil servants are supported by their ministers there is no means of enforcement to ensure that Parliament gets the answers it is entitled to.

The organic law which establishes the framework for the budget has very recently been fundamentally reformed, in order to replace the classical division of budgetary chapters and lines according to the organogram of expenses by a budgetary division based upon objective and actions. This reform has a double aim:

i) increasing accountability by enabling parliament to concentrate on the allocation of finances to actions based upon objectives instead of being lost in the details of budgetary lines;
ii) modernising financial management by changing from an input based financial system to an output and objectives based system.

While this reform says a lot about the lack of accountability and transparency of the previous system, it is too new to allow for any evaluation of its implementation.

7 Supplementary Means to Ensure Rendering Account

Three other series of means to activate accountability of the executive should be taken into account in order to understand fully the French system: judicial accountability, the *Médiateur de la République* and the press.

Judicial accountability is ensured by three ways:

i) judicial review of administrative action – which includes the possibility to annul acts of ministers, the government as well as government regulations; since 1995 the administrative courts have the powers to give injunctions to administration and to impose provisional or even definitive financial sanctions;
ii) criminal and civil liability of civil servants and members of the executive are often sought for, and tend to have more and more impact, with the reform of the criminal code in 1992, which has considerably developed liability of elected officials; furthermore, the judiciary tends to go far more deeply into the control over actions of politicians;
iii) the establishment of a specific court for the criminal and civil liability of Ministers in cases of actions accomplished in exercising their functions. The *Cour de Justice de la République* has already judged ministers in cases such as the contamination by AIDS of transferred blood. The case of the President of the Republic is however specific as he enjoys an immunity during his mandate which would only fall in the case of high treason, where a mechanism of impeachment might be activated by parliament: this has never happened.

Giving account is also facilitated by the institution of the *Médiateur de la République* (Ombudsman), which is an independent authority who may enquire in all cases of misadministration which are not of the competence of courts. This is a rather effective means of accountability for two types of failures in executive action:

i) bad will on the part of civil servants, be it genuine or based on the lack of clear ministerial instructions in how to handle cases; this includes thus indirectly the accountability of ministers in that the *Médiateur* may recommend not only a solution to a specific case but also the adoption of a general instruction by the relevant ministry;
ii) incoherence of regulations, policies or legislation, which may lead the *Médiateur* to recommend reform at the level of regulation or legislation.

Last but not least, the press is obviously one of the most powerful alternative means to activate accountability. While television and radio remain rather deferential towards ministers and the President of the Republic, written press has started to develop enquiries in the last decades, which have led to revealing a number of scandals or policy failures leading to some resignations of ministers. This is no longer the monopoly to the satirical weekly '*Le Canard Enchainé*', which has had this function since World War One, but prestigious independent newspapers like '*Le Monde*' have developed into powerful organs of investigation.

8 Discrepancies between Law and Practice of Accountability

The only legal way to dismiss the Prime minister is the adoption by the National Assembly of a motion of censure. The motion of censure is regulated in detail by the constitution. It needs one tenth of the members of the National Assembly to be debated. 48 hours have to elapse between the presentation of the motion and the vote. The vote is secret. Only votes against the government are counted: abstentions and votes in favour of government are counted together. In order to pass, the motion needs to be voted by the absolute majority of members of the National Assembly.

When the President of the Republic enjoys the support of the majority of the National Assembly, he has the de facto power to dismiss his prime minister, as has been done by all Presidents – with the exception of periods of 'cohabitation' where the opposition to the President had the majority in the National Assembly.

Ministers may be dismissed individually by the President of the Republic upon request of the Prime minister (and vice-versa when the President enjoys the support of the majority of the National Assembly). There is no possibility for Parliament to dismiss an individual minister; it might only use the menace of a motion of censure against the entire government in order to prompt the Prime minister and President to dismiss someone; this has never happened. The Prime minister is free to dismiss ministers whenever he wants, provided the President accepts to sign the decree. In practice the weight of a minister in the parties of the governmental coalition will have an important weight upon the choice of the Prime minister. Rather than dismissing a specific minister, Prime ministers and Presidents usually proceed to a government reshuffle, which may take the form of a resignation presented by the Prime minister, which automatically terminates all ministers' mandates, and the immediate nomination of a new government including those ministers which the re-appointed Prime minister wants to keep.

All this explains that *de facto* and out of the period of '*cohabitation*', accountability of governments is to the President, who is hardly accountable himself. The President of the Republic can only be forced to resign in case of high treason, by a mechanism of impeachment which is controlled by the majorities in both houses of Parliament (the *Haute Cour*), and which has never been activated. Charles de Gaulle felt bound to resign if a referendum that he would organise had a negative outcome. Indeed after a series of successful referendums, which he used in order to consolidate his power as against parliament in 1962, the referendum he organised in 1969 had a negative outcome. But as far as his successors are concerned, they always made it clear that a negative referendum would have no consequence on their position. Indeed President Chirac remained in office after the referendum of 29 May 2005 on the ratification of the Treaty establishing a Constitution for Europe, although he had campaigned in favour of ratification.

When it comes to rendering account, Parliament is one of the weakest players if the majority supports the President in both houses – as was the case from 1959 to 1981 and again since 2002.

Bibliography

AVRIL (1977)

P. Avril, 'Pouvoir et responsabilité', in *Mélanges Burdeau* (Paris 1977).

BIDÉGARAY & EMÉRI (1998)

Ch. Bidégaray & C. Eméri, *La responsabilité politique* (Paris 1998).

BEAUD (1997)

O. Beaud, 'Le traitement constitutionnel de l'affaire du sang contaminé'(1997) *Revue du Droit public* 995 ff.

BEAUD & BLANQUER (1999)

O. Beaud & J.-M. Blanquer (dir.), *La responsabilité des gouvernants* (Paris 1999).

EMÉRI (1987)

C. Eméri, 'De l'irresponsabilité présidentielle'(1987/47) *Pouvoirs* 133 ff.

HARLOW (2002)

C. Harlow, *Accountability in the European Union* (Oxford 2002).

MATHIEU (1990)

B. Mathieu, 'La haute cour de justice ou comment se servir d'un sabre de bois' (1990) *Revue française de Droit constitutionnel* 735 ff.

MATHIEU & MAUS (2000)

B. Mathieu & D. Maus (dir.), *La Cour de justice de la République, et après?* (Paris 2000).

SÉGUR (1998)

P. Ségur, *La responsabilité politique* (Paris 1998).

SÉGUR (2001)

P. Ségur, 'Faute et responsabilité politique – sur quelques distinctions élémentaires' in J.-J. Sueur (dir.), *Juger les politiques* (Paris 2001) 83-119.

CHAPTER 6

Political Accountability in Germany

Veith Mehde

1 Introduction: Specific Problems of Accountability in the German Constitutional Structure

The English words 'accountability' and 'responsibility' both translate into the German word '*Verantwortlichkeit*'. The word is frequently brought into play in political debates. First, it is used to blame the government and individual ministers for virtually all things that go wrong in the country – economically, socially, etc. In political clashes between government and opposition, it is used in order to define who has to take the blame for problems that are seen to have a political dimension. The home minister therefore will always be criticised for high crime rates although he or she is only one of many actors that take decisions with repercussions in the field of internal security. In the same way, the German federal Government is under pressure to justify why political aims have not been achieved although the complicated German constitutional system gives power to a large number of different levels and institutions. The opposition always blames the government as a whole for high unemployment, small growth, etc. The second dimension that has to be mentioned is the one regarding the role Ministers play in regard to his or her department. This is underlined by the fact that there have been cases in which ministers resigned not only because of personal wrong-doings but because of deficiencies in their departments.

Both dimensions of the concept are very difficult to specify in a coherent and, therefore, scientifically satisfactory manner. This is not only due to a lack of precise rules in relation to the concept as such. Additionally, the complex constitutional structure of multi-level governance in Germany has to be borne in mind. The above-mentioned mechanisms by which the government of the day is regarded as being responsible for all bad things must be understood to relate to governments at the local, state (i.e. *Länder*) or federal level. For the electorate, it is very difficult to get a realistic view of where responsibilities for policy failures as well as successes realistically lie. This leads to a constellation in which responsibility that is attributed to a certain level of governments often is not necessarily matched by the scope this government actually has for political decision-making. Parties normally become unpopular because of policies they pursue in the federal Government. This unpopularity might lead to them losing state or local elections. State governments might be voted out because of high unemployment and a bad economic situation; although, in fact, they have very little powers to legislate in matters relevant for growth and job creation. Even matters with immediate budgetary relevance cannot be decided by the respective level of government alone.

If, for example, the federal government wants to raise taxes, it generally needs the consent of the *Bundesrat* in which the *Länder* governments are represented. The position of the *Länder* is even worse. They have virtually no power at all regarding taxation and they must pay for costs that follow from federal legislation which they have to implement. The reason for the latter is that in Art.

104a GG, the obligation to bear the cost caused by legislation is assigned to the entity that has the power to implement the laws, which in most cases is not the same as the one that has also the power to pass them. Although legislation is dominantly federal, implementation generally falls into the responsibility of the *Länder*. Considering further that education and policing are tasks that must be fulfilled by the *Länder* and which therefore need to employ a large number of teachers, professors and policeman, the scope for budgetary decision-making is very restricted.

Despite the importance of the lower levels of government, the focus of public attention lies on the federal level. In recent years, state governments led by the Social Democrats (SPD) had little chance to be re-elected because of the unpopularity of the welfare state reforms initiated by the federal government which was also led by the SPD. It is a rule whose validity has often been proven in the German political system that new governments normally are not voted into office, but that the old ones are voted out. Opposition parties are very rarely voted in on the basis of their election manifestos. At least with regard to the *Länder* level one has to add that normally the success or failure of a government are not determined with regard to the scope for decision-making they actually had. Expectations tend to be very unrealistic taken the constitutional structure governments work within. Therefore, one has to say that, in the first dimension, political accountability is compromised by a number of effects that make it a quite imperfect and especially imprecise instrument. Its precision certainly does not equal the relevance it obtains in political debates.

The second dimension of the concept offers better prospects as far as the application of clear guidelines is concerned. Rules are easier to develop and they induce a greater hope for compliance when they are meant to be implemented by a professional group rather than by the general electorate that of course is free to decide on the basis of whatever reason it finds appropriate. While there are no provisions in the constitution with regard to the basis on which voting should take place, the relation between the executive and Parliament is regulated in a number of articles of the constitution. Also, the accountability ministers are obliged to accept for their departments is put into practice on a regular basis while elections are taking place far less regularly. Therefore, the following analysis will mainly focus on this mechanism that is meant to guarantee accountability permanently while general elections will normally not be a subject.

2 Accountability: General Aspects

Irrespective of the prominent role accountability plays as a political concept, the legal side of the topic is difficult to assess. With regard to the general public and to media debates, it is hard to imagine legal scholars being asked if a particular aspect of administrative malfunctioning provides a legal case for a minister resigning or taking the blame for things that went wrong in his or her department. It is no coincidence that, generally, political scientists are regarded as the experts for this kind of question. Taken the highly legalistic tradition and the importance of the German constitution, the *Grundgesetz* (in the following: GG), this appears to be a very unlikely constellation. This is due to the fact that there are not many rules that actually help to determine which consequences have to be drawn from a specific type of malfunctioning in a department.

The lack of precise rules concerns written ones as well as constitutional conventions. The latter, of course, exist but they are not regarded as a binding source of law. Conventions are almost exclusively evoked when they seem to support a certain political claim. After the 2005 election, the Christian Democrats asserted that there was a constitutional convention giving the bigger one of two coalition partners the right to name the person to be elected Chancellor. This was the main argument supporting their claim that their candidate, Angela Merkel, had to be accepted by the Social Democrats as the new leader of the government, despite the fact that the Social Democratic Chancellor, Gerhard Schröder, had ruled out any talks leading to his counterpart becoming the new head of government. Of course, Angela Merkel won this conflict, although this does not serve as evidence of a constitutional convention being regarded as binding by the political actors. First of all, the case for determining such a rule is very weak, since there is only one precedent for a 'grand' coalition between the two biggest parties which lasted for only three years. Second, even the people using the argument did not claim that it would be illegal to elect a member of the smaller parliamentary party. Altogether, this episode shows that the notion of a constitutional convention is not a legal but a political concept in the German system. Therefore, one has to be very clear whether or not a certain aspect of the concept of political accountability is a strictly legal one or rather a consequence of political traditions and political prudence.

Of course, in actual fact, choosing the ministers is an entirely political affair. As other coalitions before, the present grand coalition agreed that all three parties involved had the right to choose the people that were to become 'their' ministers. The other parties – and indeed the Chancellor-designate – seemed to have had no chance to interfere with the decision of the respective other side. Obviously, this is not what the constitution says about forming the government. Under the German constitution, only the Chancellor is elected by Parliament. The ministers are picked by the Chancellor and then – as the Chancellor him- or herself – are appointed by the President. Since the President plays no political role, the legal power regarding the members of his or her government rests entirely with the Chancellor.[1] The Chancellor has also the exclusive power to induce the President to dismiss ministers. Here again, the President has no discretionary power.[2] This constellation could well be understood to imply that

1 Zippelius & Würtenberger (2005) 369.

2 *Ibid.*

the ministers are not accountable to Parliament but to the Chancellor.[3] Nevertheless, this should not be seen as an argument against ministers being also accountable to Parliament.[4] To a certain degree though, it does influence its practical implications. Undoubtedly, the Chancellor plays a pivotal part in the German political system. It is 'his' or 'her' government that is blamed for whatever goes wrong in society. He or she is expected to act whenever the public sees a case for political action.

In addition to Art. 65 s. 1 and s. 2, the democratic principle (Art. 20 s. 2 ss. 1 GG) generates the third pillar of the constitutional concept of political accountability under the German constitution. According to this principle, all state power must emanate from the people. The Constitutional Court has developed certain modes of legitimacy that play together in guaranteeing a sufficient level of legitimacy in administrative decision-making.[5] One central element of this concept is the notion of 'chains of legitimacy'. The personal legitimacy of the acting officials is regarded as deriving from the fact, that they were appointed by a minister, who him- or herself was chosen by the Chancellor, who was elected by Parliament, which was elected by the people.[6] On the material side of decision-making – i.e. the question of what decision is being taken rather than of who takes it – a similar notion exists. Every official has to be part of a hierarchy on top of which a minister accountable to Parliament has every right to give orders even in individual cases. As a consequence of the cited rulings of the Constitutional Court, this power is at the heart of any notion of ministerial accountability. Since he or she has the power to influence all cases in the department, there is a justification for holding ministers accountable for everything concerning their portfolios. In the end, Parliament can be held accountable by the electorate. In this way, again a link between decisions taken by state institutions and the people can be established.[7] In that sense, accountability is at the very heart of the democratic principle in the German constitution.

As a general rule, the Constitutional Court is mainly concerned with excluding external elements from becoming part of the decision-making system. This concerns actors that are neither appointed by a minister accountable to Parliament nor elected by the people and that consequently would destroy the described chain of legitimacy. This legal argument might be the main reason why Germany has no tradition of transferring powers to independent agencies. In fact, giving powers to officials that are not integrated into the hierarchical structure would have to be regarded as a breach of the chain of legitimacy and would, therefore, need special justification which can only be accepted in very unusual cases. An example of this unlikely constellation is the data commissioner who is independent in a way to allow him to become an espe-

3 See Oldiges (1983) 448; Maunz & Dürig-Herzog (1984) Art. 65, n. 65.

4 Maunz & Dürig-Herzog (1984) Art. 65, n. 66.

5 BVerfGE 83, 60 (72 f.); 93, 37 (66 ff.); 107, 59 (87 f.).

6 See Wolff, Bachof & Stober-Kluth (2004) n. 148.

7 Mehde (2001) 15.

cially efficient tool for optimising data protection. Germany has also problems justifying the idea of an independent regulatory agency[8] which in Europe has become the standard organisational setting for dealing with markets dominated by former state-owned monopolies in areas as telecommunication, electricity, etc. Up to now the legislature has been very cautious to write into German law explicitly what is called for by EC legislation,[9] namely that there is a functional separation between the regulatory function on the one hand and representation of the owner on the other hand. One proof of the resulting lack of experience with independent agencies can be seen in the fact that the regulatory agency for telecommunication now has been given responsibility also for electricity, gas, and the railways.[10]

The academic debate about political accountability in Germany is very much focused on specific questions like the legal feasibility of independent agencies or other forms of non-ministerial administrations. It is generally not a debate about the actual duties and the position of the ministers. Political accountability of ministers in relation to the administrations they are in charge of is taken for granted. With regard to the actual meaning of the concepts, a more thorough discussion seems to be prevented by the fact that – for different reasons – neither political nor legal scientists regard it as the fundamental question. From a point of view of legal science, the subject seems odd because no matter what the rules are, there are hardly any constellations in which courts would have to apply them. Taken the lack of judgements by the courts and the absence of any noteworthy doctrine of constitutional conventions, legal science cannot build on much substance for such an academic debate. The only exception from this rule might be seen in the fact that, as will be shown, there are some procedural elements in the constitution that provide the Bundestag with the means of holding the government to account.

Nevertheless, the question, although apparently legal in character, is regarded as a dominantly political one. Of course, as will be shown there are certain legal requirements regarding whether and how the government has to answer questions that are brought forward by MPs. Nevertheless, it is very unlikely that German lawyers would ever regard legal norms as the main aspect leading to the resignation of an individual minister or even to a government loosing an election. Political scientists instead seem to be less interested in formulating abstract rules that might be applied in the process of determining responsibilities. Rather, from their point of view, questions of political power and of the backing a minister has from the Chancellor and his or her party are the dominating aspects in this process. In a sense, the rule-based approach to

8 See e.g. Schmidt (2005) 1029 f.; Pielow (2005) 1018 ff.

9 See e.g. Art. 3 s. 2 of the directive 2002/21/EC on a common regulatory framework for electronic communications networks and services (Framework Directive), *OJ L108, 24.4.2002, p. 33.*

10 Gesetz über die Bundesnetzagentur für Elektrizität, Gas, Telekommunikation, Post und Eisenbahnen vom 7.7.2005, BGBl. I S. 1970.

this subject obviously is too formalistic to be of interest for political scientists or, indeed, to guide the public debate.

3 Accountability: The Actors

As already mentioned in the introductory remarks, political accountability is mainly a matter concerning Parliament (the Bundestag) on the one hand and the government (the *Bundesregierung*) and its members (the *Bundesminister*) on the other hand. The German constitution creates the rules of a parliamentary system of government. In this system, both, the *Bundesregierung* and the *Bundestag*, are constitutional actors. No actor is per se superior to the respective other one; no hierarchy exists between the two.[11] Therefore, the following rules are rules governing the interaction of two actors that perform diverse functions while being essentially equal constitutional actors.

Both in legal and political terms, the strong position of the Chancellor is mediated by a very strong notion of ministerial accountability regarding the portfolio of the relevant minister. While the Chancellor has the legal power to choose any person that he or she wants to become minister, the constitution gives him a rather restricted role in determining the policies pursued by the respective departments. According to Art. 65 s. 1 GG, the Chancellor establishes the guidelines of politics. Obviously, he or she can be held accountable for them.[12] Within these guidelines, the ministers supervise their departments independently and in this capacity, they are exclusively accountable. Therefore, political accountability is divided. As far as the guidelines and the overall performance are concerned, the Chancellor is subject to the respective claims; while regarding the individual departments, ministers are solely accountable.

Collective accountability does not feature prominently in the German constitutional system.[13] As has been shown, the main focus lies with the accountability of individual ministers. In regard to the accountability effectuated in general elections, the attention is on the parties and their leaders. They are blamed for a lack of success or are subject to the hopes for better future developments respectively. In the constitution, the cabinet as a whole is mentioned in Art. 65 ss. 3 GG as the actor that has to take the decision whenever ministers disagree. Furthermore, some functions can only be fulfilled by the cabinet as a whole. For example, bills cannot be introduced by individual ministers but only by the upper house, by MPs or by the cabinet (Art. 76 s. 1 GG). If the government wants to have the constitutionality of a law examined by the constitutional court, this is subject to a prior decision by the cabinet. In these cases, of course, the government as a whole can be held accountable for these decisions. Apart from this, there are not many rules that can be regarded as being an expression of the

[11] Zippelius & Würtenberger (2005) 365.

[12] See Brauneck (1994) 104.

[13] See Oldiges (1983) 449 ff.

doctrine of collective ministerial accountability. S. 6 of the *Bundesministergesetz* (federal ministers law) states that the ministers – even after having left the cabinet – are obliged to keep secret all facts they obtained in their official capacity. Nevertheless, there is an exemption concerning facts that are of such nature that secrecy is not required. In addition to this strictly legal side, it is quite clear that politically all ministers are expected to support policies formulated by the college of ministers. Failure to fulfil this expectation must be regarded as a political problem, not as a legal one – as a lack of loyalty, not as a neglect of laws.

4 The Scope of Accountability

As far as the Chancellor is concerned, it is obvious that he or she is held accountable for all decisions he or she takes him or herself. The same holds true for the ministers in regard to all decisions taken in their departments. That is to say that ministers are answerable to Parliament and that this duty relates to the whole amount of tasks fulfilled or illegally not fulfilled in their departments.[14] They can be held accountable even if they never actually got involved in a particular case and even if it had been inappropriate to interfere in administrative decision-making in that particular instance. Therefore, ministerial accountability is the instrument enabling Parliament to control the executive as a whole. This includes both, the strictly political part and the area of administrative decision-making. The justification for accountability being so far-reaching is the power of ministers to instruct all civil servants that are working in their departments. This power is a direct consequence of the hierarchical structure of government departments.

Despite this principle, it is also true to say that accountability is restricted to matters the minister can influence.[15] However, this logical connection relates to the legal powers of ministers rather than to their factual capacity to influence administrative decisions. Taken the complexity of matters departments have to deal with and considering the sheer number of decisions taken, the amount of cases a minister can take notice of is of course marginal. Still, the above described model of democratic legitimacy of state actions demands a more or less uninterrupted connection between the administration and Parliament. Since the link between the two is established by the minister, accountability has to cover the whole range of legal powers the minister has.

Nevertheless, in the German system of executive federalism, this rule does not necessarily imply that the minister is also accountable for the execution of policies. This is due to the fact that the federal level acts mainly by passing legislation while implementation falls into the responsibility of the *Länder*.[16] The federal level has very little powers to guarantee that laws are complied with

[14] Mehde (2001) 17 f.

[15] Mehde (2003) 426 f.

[16] Maurer (2005) 312.

in accordance with the original policy decision. Therefore, it is a very unlikely thought and indeed a rather improbable political conduct to hold a federal minister accountable for the implementation of laws in the states. Yet, as far as the implementation of policies by the federal administration is concerned, ministers as the head of the departments are fully accountable for the actions taken.

Ministers receive advice in different organisational settings. In the traditional German system, advice was meant to be given exclusively by the civil servants working in the respective departments. In the 1960s, the need was felt to increase the capacity of politicians to work through a large amount of information and thereby to increase the steering capacity of democratically elected political actors as opposed to unelected civil servants.[17] It is now generally acknowledged that ministers need to rely on a small cabinet of personal advisers as – on a larger scale – known from the French system. It is also accepted that the minister should have the chance to employ political advisers that are recruited on the basis of political trust rather than of the qualifications normally required in the civil service. There is no doubt that the minister is fully accountable for their actions. On the federal level, there is also the *Parlamentarischer Staatssekretär* (parliamentary junior minister) – an MP who is appointed to serve in a ministry without becoming a part of the departmental hierarchy.[18] Normally, at least one *Parlamentarischer Staatssekretär* is appointed to each ministry where he or she is expected to support the minister, especially by strengthening relations to the public and to Parliament.[19] Since he or she has to be an MP, there is some likelihood that Parliament would hold him or her directly accountable. Nevertheless, there is no legal basis for stopping Parliament from blaming the minister for actions taken by the *Parlamentarischer Staatssekretär* if he or she has some direct involvement in any wrongdoings.

Forms of co-regulation and – rather not 'open' – co-operation are well known in the German system. This co-ordination mainly takes place between the federal level and the *Länder* governments as well as between the *Länder* governments without involvement of the federal level. While ministers of different *Länder* mainly co-operate in order to support mutual recognition of standards and to share experiences, the interaction between the two different levels is a political necessity based on the constitutional setting. Most federal laws have to be passed by both Houses of Parliament. In the upper house, the *Länder* governments are represented. Therefore, co-operation is essential in order to gain majorities for bills. There is no direct accountability of these bodies for the decisions taken in these settings. This is acceptable because the decisions have no direct effect and are not binding. Hence, the institutions that implement these agreements can be hold accountable. The same can be said concerning the agreements that have been drawn up in recent years between the government and certain groups. In these agreements, the groups affected by certain poli-

17 See Rudloff (2003).

18 Bogumil & Jann (2005) 130.

19 Maurer (2005) 12.

cies agreed to take actions promoting these policies.[20] Examples include the one resulting in the ultimate closure of atomic energy plants in Germany and the one promoting gender equality. When they lead to policy decision, the political actors are fully accountable irrespective of the co-operative procedure.

5 Activating Accountability: Parliamentary Control and Transparency

Parliamentary control takes various forms. The Basic Law states in Art. 43 s. 1 that the Bundestag and its committees can demand the presence of any member of the government. The provision is not very clear as far as the duties of the ministers are concerned. Nevertheless, it does seem obvious from the wording of the provision that the minister has no right to ask someone else to represent him if the Bundestag has not accepted this in advance. Therefore, he or she must appear in person and is then obliged to answer all questions that the MPs put to him in relation to the subject named as the reason for calling him. The minister must tell the truth, although a wrong statement as such will bear only political but not legal consequences.[21] It is debated if reasons are conceivable that give ministers the right to reject answering a certain question. While a need for protection of state secrets is regarded as such a reason by some authors,[22] others claim that secrecy rules cannot apply in relation to Parliament since there are options to guarantee that the wider public is excluded.[23] The practical relevance of this debate should not be overestimated. It is very difficult if not practically impossible to claim that a ministerial answer was illegal since politicians normally are experienced enough to depict facts in a way that is imprecise but not insufficient.[24]

In any case, the fact that the *Bundesregierung* is a constitutional actor in its own right gives its members the power not to answer questions relating to topics that are still under review so that no official policy has yet been adopted.[25] The reason for this is that the operational capacity of the government needs to be preserved.[26] Since the powers following from Art. 43 s. 1 can only be exercised by the majority of MPs in Parliament or in one of its committees – which by definition supports the government of the day – calling Ministers to attend meetings is not very relevant in real-life parliamentary proceedings.[27] Its use would come very close to an expression of lack of confidence. Art. 43 s. 2 GG guarantees the

---

20 See Mehde (2002) 655 ff.

21 Ipsen (2005) 201.

22 See e.g. Maunz & Dürig-Maunz (1960) Art. 43, n. 8.

23 Alternativkommentar GG – Schneider (2002) Art. 43, n. 8; see also Ipsen (2005) n. 201.

24 Ipsen (2005) n. 201.

25 See BVerfGE 67, 100 (139).

26 Alternativkommentar GG – Schneider (2002) Art. 43, n. 8.

27 Mehde (2001) 14.

power of all members of the government to take part in all meetings of Parliament and of its committees.

Personal appearance in the Bundestag is not the only and certainly not the most important element of the system of political accountability in Germany. Generally, control is exercised by asking written questions that have to be answered by the government either in writing or during question time in Parliament. In contrast to the procedures following from Art. 43 GG, the so called '*Interpellationsrecht*' is an individual right of MPs, so that no majority decision is required. The right is regarded as a consequence of the constitutional position of MPs (status right) and the importance of the relevant information for exercising control over the government.[28] The rules structuring the process can be found in the GO BT, the *Geschäftsordnung* des *Deutschen Bundestages* (rules of procedure of the German Parliament), that govern the internal working of Parliament and that is no law in the sense that it would be binding for any other group of people than members of the *Bundestag*.[29] The government has a constitutional duty to answer these questions, although the above-mentioned exemption regarding the internal functioning of the government applies here as well.

Three different forms of parliamentary questioning are described in s. 100 ff. GO BT.[30] The most elaborate one is the *Große Anfrage* (major question), which concerns major political issues. The answer to this question is debated in Parliament, although it needs five per cent of MPs to enforce this rule if its application meets resistance. The *Kleine Anfrage* (minor question) does not lead to a debate, although, of course, in political statements MPs can use the information gained. The third option is to put forward short oral question during question time. In contrast to the Westminster tradition,[31] question time does not feature very prominently in Germany. This might be due to the fact that it is general practice not to let ministers answer in person but rather the *Parlamentarischer Staatssekretär*. In fact, the whole process takes place literally unnoticed by the wider public and by the national media. Not surprisingly, the total number of questions asked in all these different forms is traditionally far lower than in the British Parliament.[32]

Two means of holding a government to account are feasible but play – for different reasons – no role in the German system. The first one is to make civil servants answerable to Parliament. This would be an infringement of the role ministers play in establishing a link between Parliament and the executive. Nevertheless, civil servants might be called to answer the questions of parliamentary inquires which will be dealt with below. Also, the top civil servants can answer questions in parliamentary committees on behalf of the minister. The second aspect is the relation between ministers and the *Bundesrat*. Art. 53 GG points out that the *Bundesrat* and its committees can call any member of

28 Zippelius & Würtenberger (2005) 330 f.; Raap (1997) 508.

29 See Badura (2003) n. E 43.

30 See Ipsen (2005) n. 203 ff.

31 For an analysis of the historical reasons for this difference see Oldiges (1983) 443 ff.

32 Krause (1999) 547.

the Government to take part in their meetings. In this respect, the *Bundesrat* is in a position similar to the one of the Bundestag, although it has already been mentioned that the powers of the Bundestag expressed in Art. 43 s. 1 GG are of little practical relevance. In actual fact, the *Bundestag* is the institution that holds the Government to account while the *Bundesrat* concentrates on its role in the legislative process. It also has to be taken into account that the *Bundesrat* is not involved in the process of forming a federal government.

A mechanism that has been used quite frequently is the investigation committee as provided for in Art. 44 GG. Conceptually, there is no doubt that this parliamentary committee bears all the elements needed for a very forceful and efficient investigation into political or administrative malfunctioning.[33] It has to be established by the Bundestag when so demanded by one quarter of its members. In other words, it is a minority right which neither the government nor the majority in Parliament can escape from. Moreover, the Basic Law grants quite remarkable powers to these committees. In the course of the investigation, the rules of the Criminal Proceedings Act are applied analogously. Since these provisions did not fit in all cases of parliamentary inquiries, this provision led to many difficult questions.[34] Therefore, a special law concerning the role of these committees was – unanimously[35] – passed in 2001[36] resolving many of the problems lawyers had to deal with as long as there were no precise rules for this not so frequent kind of investigation.[37]

Witnesses that are found lying when being interviewed can be punished, as would be the case in the proceedings before a court of law. Courts and administrative agencies have the duty to assist in the investigation. There is no possibility to challenge the findings of the committee as such before the courts (Art. 44 s. 4 GG). The proceedings take place in public although the committee may choose to proceed confidentially. The committee can ask for a court decision ordering the seizure of relevant evidence, the search of witnesses' homes, and even the imprisonment of people refusing to make a statement as a witness without having a right to do so. Since Art. 44 GG establishes a minority right, exercising these powers does not require the majority decision.[38] The government must hand over the relevant files. Reasons for rejecting disclosure have to be of constitutional relevance. There is, for example a core area of decision-making in the government that has to be free from external scrutiny.[39] There are further restrictions when disclosure would lead to a violation of basic rights of the people named in the files.[40]

---

33 See BVerfGE 49, 70 (85 ff.).

34 See e.g. Arloth (1987); Hilf (1987).

35 Schneider (2001) 2605; Wiefelspütz (2002) 10.

36 Gesetz zur Regelung des Rechts der Untersuchungsausschüsse vom 25.6.2001, BGBl. I S. 1142.

37 Maurer (2005) 464 f.

38 BVerfGE 105, 197 (222 ff.).

39 BVerfGE 67, 100 (139); 110, 199 (214 ff.).

40 BVerfGE 77, 1 (53 ff.), see also Arloth (1987) 812.

The year 2005 saw the first live showing of parts of proceedings on national television. It was agreed between the parties that only the hearings of ministers and of *Staatssekretäre* should be televised while the other witnesses were interviewed in public with the press, but no television cameras present. This occasion was a sort of ultimate evidence of the fact that these committees are heavily influenced by party politics and that they are far from being the neutral investigator one might expect them to be when reading the rules governing the process. The majority of the committee – which was nominated by the governing coalition – decided to stop the investigation shortly after the Chancellor had announced that he was seeking an early election.[41] The argument for this was that one needed time to write the final report. This attempt was stopped by the constitutional court. The court did not accept this argument and decided that the work had to be continued.[42] Ultimately, it ended with the report being presented. The one written by the majority was apologetic with regard to the alleged mistakes made by the political leadership. Not surprisingly, the minority report blamed the political leadership of the ministry. Both were published when the election campaign had already started and was absorbing all political interest. Moreover, the attention span of the wider public had already been exhausted. The televised hearings drew so much attention and they led to so many accusations and excuses that it was impossible to present the reports as a new development worth any attention at all.

Ultimately one might well conclude that the enormous interest that was a consequence of the television coverage backfired because there was no way to set a new 'highlight' after these events. Additionally, experience shows that the government and the parliamentary parties supporting them have a lot of strategies at hand to diminish the political consequences of the investigation. Therefore, the hopes and expectations connected with parliamentary inquiries seem at best moderate. They are, undoubtedly, an important instrument at the disposal of the opposition.[43] Not many months after the described end of the inquiry into the visa problems, the three small parties in opposition to the 'grand coalition' which was formed in late 2005 decided to launch a investigation committee with regard to the case of a possible co-operation of German intelligence services with the CIA in the context of the war in Iraq.[44] Nevertheless, in the academic debate, disappointment regarding the effectiveness of these inquiries has been expressed.[45] They are regarded as means of political confrontation – a function that must be seen in stark contrast to the prerequisites of an objective investigation.[46] The above-mentioned new law has not changed this situation as it was mainly concerned with solving legal problems rather than with increasing the

41 For a description of the events see Lenz (2005) 2495.

42 BVerfGE, Beschluss vom 15.6.2005, 2 BvQ 18/05, *Neue Juristische Wochenschrift* 2005, 2537.

43 Arloth (1987) 808.

44 Deutscher Bundestag, Drucksache 16/1179 vom 7.4.2006.

45 Wolf (2005) 876; see also Hilf (1987) 545.

46 Schneider (2001) 2605.

effectiveness of the procedure. In fact, it is more a written version of rules that had already been the basis of parliamentary proceedings but that up to then had not been summarised in one law.[47]

6 Consequences

While it is a well-founded principle in the constitutional system that ministers can be held accountable for mistakes made in their department, it is less clear which sanctions can or even have to be inflicted on the respective minister as a consequence of these mistakes. In the general public, political accountability is almost exclusively associated with ministers resigning or being dismissed at the request of the Chancellor. When, for example, in early 2005 the national media started to ask questions with regard to a mishandling of visa applications in one German embassy in Eastern Europe, the foreign minister at the time, Joschka Fischer, felt the need to express that he was accepting political responsibility for mistakes made by the civil servants in the foreign office. In public debates, this was not depicted as a noble position but rather as a cheap escape from the questions that really were to be answered. First of all, the phrase in fact put the blame on the administrative staff rather than accepting that political decisions had been wrong. Second, there was a general mood that the notion of accountability is useless unless it leads to the minister's resignation. This is an expression of the fact that the political or legal concept is often mistaken to be a question of penal responsibility.[48] Even the fact that for several hours the acting foreign minister was grilled by a parliamentary committee set up to investigate the case was not seen as a satisfactory manifestation of political accountability. This, of course, makes things much more difficult. In fact, there is no legal rule as to whether or not a minister has to resign. It is rather a question of the remaining trust in his capacities and of the political support the minister can gather in his or her party in order to remain in office.[49] While some ministers have not 'survived' the first scandal that has come up, others have stayed in office although they were faced with quite a few.

For the sake of political stability in government,[50] the German constitution provides for only one possibility to dismiss the Chancellor during the election period of Parliament. That is by electing a successor (Art. 67 GG). The president is obliged to appoint the newly elected Chancellor. This is called the constructive vote of no confidence. Apart from this, general elections are the only event that can endanger the position of the incumbent. If he or she asks for a vote of confidence, Parliament can, of course, refuse to express such confidence. In that

47 Wiefelspütz (2002) 10 f.

48 For an analysis of 'political' as opposed to the various aspects of 'legal' responsibility see Masing (2001); see also Brocker (1999) 743; Nicolaus (2000) 393.

49 See Masing (2001) 42.

50 See Maurer (2005) 489 f.

case, he or she has the power to ask the president to dissolve Parliament (Art. 68 ss.1 GG). In any case, the Chancellor stays in office with all powers until the new Parliament meets for the first time. At this moment, his or her time in office ends. The president will then ask him or her to hold on until a new Chancellor is elected. Therefore, no time without a government can occur.

The position of ministers is tied to the one of the Chancellor. Art. 69 s. 2 GG makes sure that the time in office for ministers does not go on for longer than the one of the Chancellor. The provision therefore states that the time in office for each minister ends when a new Parliament meets for the first time. Again as the Chancellor, at the request of the president, the ministers are obliged to stay in office until a successor is being appointed. As a rule, this is generally applied although exceptions are possible. Even when the time until the election of a new Cabinet – as after the 2005 election – is rather long, it is not unusual for ministers to leave their offices before their successor is appointed – for example to take up new ones. After the 2005 election, the minister for consumer protection and the environment, Renate Künast, was elected chairwoman of the Green parliamentary group. She therefore resigned from the office that she would otherwise have led until swearing-in of the new government. In this case, another minister was asked to administer her ministry. As a general rule, though, ministers agree to stay in office until they can hand it over to their successor.

Additionally, Art. 69 s. 2 GG states that the ministerial term also ends in any other case in which the Chancellor looses his or her office. As has been said above, the time in office ends for the Chancellor when a new Parliament meets for the first time or whenever a new Chancellor is elected. The other cases include resignation, death, and the extremely unlikely case of a ruling by the criminal court in which as a side effect of the punishment, the incumbent looses the capacity to serve in public offices.

Therefore, there is no constitutional provision that gives Parliament the power to dismiss an individual minister. Of course, nobody can prevent Parliament from passing a motion that disapproves of the minister's conduct or that calls on the Chancellor to ask for dismissal or for his or her resignation. There is no specific constitutional provision regarding motions of censure aiming at individual ministers.[51] Nevertheless, to put forward such a request is not unusual,[52] since it is a possibility for the opposition to increase the pressure on the government and to grasp additional public attention for their condemnation of the minister. In any event, such motions are not binding – neither for the Chancellor nor for the minister.[53] Moreover, it is quite clear that no government would let itself be embarrassed in such blatant way. As this motion can only be passed when the majority of the government is not firm, there will be massive efforts to solve the problem politically – as a last resort also by asking the minister to resign.

---

51 See Mehde (2001) 14.

52 Badura (2003) n. E 17.

53 Zippelius & Würtenberger (2005) 330.

Ministers can only be dismissed by the federal president at the request of the Chancellor. As the role of the president is a formal one and as he or she has to oblige when asked to do so,[54] it is obvious that the political decision must be taken by the Chancellor. Normally, of course, the Chancellor will ask the minister to resign, since resignation is regarded as more honourable than dismissal. Indeed, it would be extremely unusual for a minister not to resign despite being asked by the Chancellor to do so. In that case, the Chancellor could ask the president to dismiss the minister. In 2002, shortly before the general election, the minister of defence, Rudolf Scharping, was dismissed because his close relations to a commercial political consultancy firm were regarded as improper. In a press conference, Chancellor Schröder explicitly claimed that Scharping had not resigned, but had been dismissed. At that time, this was probably due to a political consideration and was meant to portray the Chancellor – who was hoping for a rather unlikely re-election – as a strong leader.

A new aspect was added to the debate by the decision of the constitutional court concerning the vote of no confidence. The question arouse because the Chancellor and the party chairman of the biggest party decided that after a historical defeat in the elections in the state of North Rhine Westphalia, the 'heartland' of social democrats and the most populous state in Germany, the government needed to renew its legitimacy. The Bundestag, though, has no right to dissolve itself and to call for new elections.[55] The only way the constitution enables a new election before the end of the electoral period and after a Chancellor has been elected, is by loosing a vote of confidence. Under these circumstances, Art. 68 GG gives the Chancellor the right to ask the president to call an election. Since the parties supporting the government still had a small but sufficient majority of seats, the only way was to ask coalition MPs to abstain irrespective of whether or not they were still supporting the government. Such 'unreal' vote of no confidence had been applied before in 1982 when one coalition partner had left the government in order to form a new one together with the opposition party. In that case, the constitutional court developed very strict principles which it then went on to apply in a very generous fashion[56] so that in the end dissolution was ruled to be legal.[57] This precedent made it difficult to assess the rules applying in a new case. Two MPs who expected to lose their seats applied for an order by the constitutional court quashing dissolution. The court decided that it had very little power to control the decisions taken by the political actors.[58] After this judgement it is very clear that it is above all for the Chancellor to decide whether or not he or she still has enough support in Parliament to pursue his or her political intentions. This again shows the strong

---

54 Maurer (2005) 492.

55 For a description of the events see Feldkamp (2006).

56 See e.g. Pestalozza (2005) 2819.

57 BVerfGE 62, 1.

58 BVerfG, Urteil vom 25.8.2005, 2 BvE 4/05; 2 BvE 7/05, printed in: *Neue Juristische Wochenschrift* 2005, 2669.

constitutional position of the Chancellor – a position that is at the very heart of the German system of political accountability.

Bibliography

ALTERNATIVKOMMENTAR (2002)

Kommentar zum Grundgesetz für die Bundesrepublik Deutschland, Art. 46, Neuwied und Kriftel, 2002.

ARLOTH (1987)

F. Arloth, 'Grundlagen und Grenzen des Untersuchungsrechts parlamentarischer Untersuchungsausschüsse' (1987) *Neue Juristische Wochenschrift* 808-812.

BADURA (2003)

P. Badura, *Staatsrecht – Systematische Erläuterung des Grundgesetzes für die Bundesrepublik Deutschland* 3rd ed. (München 2003).

BOGUMIL & JANN (2005)

J. Bogumil & W. Jann, *Verwaltung und Verwaltungswissenschaft in Deutschland – Einführung in die Verwaltungswissenschaft* (Wiesbaden 2005).

BRAUNECK (1994)

J. Brauneck, *Die rechtliche Stellung des Bundeskanzleramtes – Rechtliche Grenzen für Organisation, Handeln und Kontrollierbarkeit des Bundeskanzleramtes* (Baden-Baden 1994).

BROCKER (1999)

L. Brocker, 'Parlamentarisches Untersuchungsverfahren und Zurückhaltungsgebot', (1999/30) *Zeitschrift für Parlamentsfragen* 739-747.

FELDKAMP (2006)

M.F. Feldkamp, 'Chronik der Vertrauensfrage des Bundeskanzlers am 1.Juli 2005 und der Auflösung des Deutschen Bundestages am 21.Juli 2005' (2006/37) *Zeitschrift für Parlamentsfragen* 19-28.

HILF (1987)

M. Hilf, 'Untersuchungsausschüsse vor den Gerichten – Zur neueren Rechtsprechung zum Recht der Untersuchungsausschüsse' (1987) *Neue Zeitschrift für Verwaltungsrecht* 537-545.

IPSEN (2005)

J. Ipsen, *Staatsrecht I – Staatsorganisationsrecht* 17th ed. (München 2005).

KRAUSE (1999)

J. Krause, 'Der Bedeutungswandel parlamentarischer Kontrolle: Deutscher Bundestag und US-Kongreß im Vergleich', (1999/30) *Zeitschrift für Parlamentsfragen* 534-555.

LENZ (2005)

C. Lenz, 'Verpflichtung zur Fortsetzung der Beweisaufnahme im Visa-Untersuchungsausschuss', (2005) *Neue Juristische Wochenschrift* 2495-2497.

MASING (2001)

J. Masing, 'Politische Verantwortlichkeit und rechtliche Verantwortlichkeit', (2001) *Zeitschrift für Rechtspolitik* 36-42.

MAUNZ & DÜRIG-HERZOG (1984)
T. Maunz & G. Dürig-Herzog, *Grundgesetz Kommentar, Art. 65* (München 1984).

MAUNZ & DÜRIG-MAUNZ (1960)
T. Maunz & G. Dürig-Maunz, *Grundgesetz Kommentar, Art. 43* (München 1960).

MAURER (2005)
H. Maurer, *Staatsrecht I – Grundlagen, Verfassungsorgane, Staatsfunktionen* 4th ed. (München 2005).

MEHDE (2001)
V. Mehde, 'Die Ministerverantwortlichkeit nach dem Grundgesetz – Dogmatischer Kernbestand und aktuelle Herausforderungen', (2001) *Deutsches Verwaltungsblatt* 13-19.

MEHDE (2002)
V. Mehde, 'Kooperatives Regierungshandeln – Verfassungsrechtslehre vor der Herausforderung konsensorientierter Politikmodelle', (2002/127) *Archiv des öffentlichen Rechts* 655-683.

MEHDE (2003)
V. Mehde, 'Responsibility and Accountability in the European Commission', (2003/40) *Common Market Law Review* 423-442.

NICOLAUS (2000)
H. Nicolaus, 'Politische Verantwortung im demokratischen Verfassungsstaat. Kritik des aktuellen "Staatstheaters" aus dem Geist des Grundgesetzes', (2000/31) *Zeitschrift für Parlamentsfragen* 391-400.

OLDIGES (1983)
M. Oldiges, *Die Bundesregierung als Kollegium – Eine Studie zur Regierungsorganisation nach dem Grundgesetz* (Hamburg 1983).

PESTALOZZA (2005)
C. Pestalozza, 'Art. 68 GG light oder Die Wildhüter der Verfassung', (2005) *Neue Juristische Wochenschrift* 2817-2820.

PIELOW (2005)
J.-C. Pielow, 'Wie "unabhängig" ist die Netzregulierung im Strom- und Gassektor? – Anmerkungen zum neuen Energiewirtschaftsgesetz', (2005) *Die Öffentliche Verwaltung* 1017-1025.

RAAP (1997)
C. Raap, 'Grundrechtsschutz bei der Information des Parlaments durch die Bundesregierung', (1997) *Neue Juristische Wochenschrift* 508-509.

RUDLOFF (2003)
W. Rudloff, '*Verwissenschaftlichung der Politik? – Wissenschaftliche Politikberatung in den sechziger Jahren' in P. Collin & T. Horstmann (Hrsg.), Das Wissen des Staates – Geschichte, Theorie und Praxis* (Baden-Baden 2003) 216-257.

SCHMIDT (2005)
C. Schmidt, 'Von der RegTP zur Bundesnetzagentur: Der organisationsrechtliche Rahmen der neuen Regulierungsbehörde', (2005) *Die Öffentliche Verwaltung* 1025-1032.

SCHNEIDER (2001)
H.-P. Schneider, 'Spielregeln für den investigativen Parlamentarismus – Das neue Untersuchungsausschuss-Gesetz des Bundestages', (2001) *Neue Juristische Wochenschrift* 2604-2608.

WIEFELSPÜTZ (2002)
D. Wiefelspütz, 'Untersuchungsausschuss und öffentliches Interesse', (2002) *Neue Zeitschrift für Verwaltungsrecht* 10-15.

WOLF (2005)
G.A. Wolf, 'Die Optimierung von Auskunftspflichten im parlamentarischen Untersuchungsverfahren', (2005/36) *Zeitschrift für Parlamentsfragen* 876-887.

WOLFF, BACHOF & STOBER-KLUTH (2004)
H.J. Wolff, O. Bachof & R. Stober-Kluth, *Verwaltungsrecht Band 3* 5th ed. (München 2004).

ZIPPELIUS & WÜRTENBERGER (2005)
R. Zippelius & T. Würtenberger, *Deutsches Staatsrecht – Ein Studienbuch* 31rst ed. (München 2005).

Table of Cases

BVerfGE 49, 70 – Untersuchungsausschuss Schleswig-Holstein
BVerfGE 67, 100 –'Flick' Untersuchungsausschuss
BVerfGE 69, 1 – Vertrauensfrage 1
BVerfGE 77, 1 – Untersuchungsausschuss 'Neue Heimat'
BVerfGE 83, 60 – Ausländerwahlrecht für Bezirksversammlungen in Hamburg
BVerfGE 93, 37 – Schleswig-Holsteinisches Personalvertretungsgesetz
BVerfGE 105, 197 – Rechte der Minderheit in Untersuchungsausschüssen
BVerfGE 107, 59 – Wasserverbände in Nordrhein-Westfalen
BVerfGE 110, 199 – Aktenvorlage Schleswig-Hostein
BVerfG, Beschluss v. 15.6.2005, 2 BvQ 18/05, printed in: *Neue Juristische Wochenschrift* 2005, 2537 – Visa-Untersuchungsausschuss
BVerfG, Urteil v. 25.8.2005, 2 BvE 4/05, 2 BvE 7/05, printed in: *Neue Juristische Wochenschrift* 2005, 2669 – Vertrauensfrage 2

CHAPTER 7

Political Accountability in Italy

Lorenza Violini, Stefania Ninatti and Giulia Tiberi*

1 The Complex Configuration of Political Accountability: The Italian Legal Perspective

1.1 Preliminary Remarks: The Role of the Political Configuration and Dynamics in the Italian System of Government

The defining traits of the Italian legal system belong to the classical principle of parliamentary government. In fact, we have a parliament composed of two elective chambers exercising legislative power and political control over the executive, a collective government appointed by the Head of State and accountable (through the mechanism of the vote of confidence) only to the Parliament and a President of the Republic elected by Parliament and not politically accountable.

As will be detailed below, these are the general features of our system of government. In practice, however, the system is strongly dependent on the configuration and dynamics of the political system (i.e., general outlines and stability of parliamentary forces). It is well known that the fragmentation of our political system is due to the longstanding tradition of the proportional voting system that made it impossible for one party to gain the absolute majority in Parliament. However, the profound changes in the political landscape through the adoption of a system that essentially ensured a majority during the early 1990s provoked a shift in the political order towards a two opposing coalition system, composed basically of centre-left and centre-right parties. Just a few very small groups could manage to survive outside of these two coalitions.[1]

While one might expect that the longstanding fragmentation of the Italian system would decrease with the new electoral system, instead, it became even worse. In fact, we can easily observe the presence of many different parties inside both coalitions. What is really different from the previous era is the stronger polarization of the system: there is no valid alternative between the centre-left and centre-right coalition and this fact splits out the voters in a striking way, as we witnessed in the recent national election (9 April 2006).[2]

---

[*] This article although the fruit of a combined and coordinated effort was written separately. Section 1 was written by Stefania Ninatti, section 2 by Lorenza Violini and section 3 by Giulia Tiberi.

[1] It is possible to understand, in this way, why the Italian Parliament is generally seen as the one major exception to the thesis of the decline of Parliaments during the XX century: 'if not unequivocally 'powerful', it is at least argued to be central to the political process' and it appears to be 'a far more formidable obstacle to the concerned will of the political executive than in any other West European democracy' (Hine (1993) 166).

[2] As a matter of fact the recent electoral result showed a highly divided political situation. The general election for the renewal of the two Chambers of the Parliament held on April 9 and 10, 2006 showed incumbent prime minister Silvio Berlusconi, leader of the centre-right party, facing Romano Prodi leader of the centre-left party. In the Chamber of Deputies the votes were distributed 49.81% for the coalition lead by Prodi to 49,74% (without considering the majority bonus): at the opposite, in the Senate

It is therefore important to underline that the functioning of the Italian system is affected by political factors much more than by legal rules.[3] For example, the well-known instability of our governments has led to countless governmental crises. These crises most often resulted in the spontaneous resignation of the government due to political conflicts rather than an invocation of the procedures provided by the Constitution.

Returning to political accountability in general, this is a contentious issue that we will examine in the next section regarding the resignation of individual ministers (both at national and regional levels). Furthermore, in contrast with other legal systems, in Italy some relevant cases have been decided by our Constitutional Court that settles litigation between ministers and the head of the government.[4]

Before dealing with the specific issues regarding political accountability in the Italian system, it is necessary to recall that our system is a multilevel one. Even if we will approach this topic only at the national level, nevertheless it is very important to briefly recall the experience of the regional government. Italian regions, in fact, are endowed with political autonomy and they have represented in recent years ideal laboratories in which new mechanisms of political accountability, aimed at satisfying the growing need for good governance, were tested.

---

the 'House of Freedoms' had secured a slight majority of seats elected within Italy (155 seats to 154), but 'The Union' won 4 of the 6 seats allocated to voters outside Italy, giving them control of both chambers.

3 From another point of view, a good example of the predominance of political life over the institutional one is the frequent case of members of Parliament shifting, during their parliamentary mandate, from the political group in which they were elected towards other political groups. This trend reached an alarming extent in the last legislature, affecting more than the 20% of the parliamentary members. It's important to stress that, despite the fact that they clearly disobey the voter's will there is no sanction for this irregular event. More precisely, see Curreri (2001) 189.

4 Even if we are not going to deal with the regional level, it is important to recall an important decision of the Constitutional Court on this matter. In fact, the new regional constitutions introduced many variants of the rule of confidence, resignation etc.: for this reason the Constitutional judge was forced to settle litigation dealing with these issues. Recently we had a relevant decision (Constitutional Court, 20 January 2006, case nr. 12/2006), in which Regione Abruzzi tried to establish a new rule of resignation of an individual member of the executive and a new hypothesis of removal of the entire executive. On one hand, one regional minister could have been dismissed by the Council, on the other the non-approval of the political program of the President at the beginning of the mandate was equivalent to a vote of no-confidence. Both rules were struck down. The constitutional judge remarked, very clearly, that the structure of political accountability derives directly from the form of government. When both the president of the region and the legislative Council are elected by the people there is a contextual confidence deriving directly from the election. According to the Constitutional Court, the election establishes a 'political consonance' between the two bodies, thus preventing one of them to prevail over the other as it would have been the case if the legislative Council could oblige regional member of the executive (nominated by the President) to resign.

As to the regional governments, the Constitution expresses a series of principles defining, in broad terms, their form of government. The Regional Council is the legislative assembly within which are represented the different political components of the regional community. The Regional Government, representing the political majority, is the executive branch, atop of which sits the President of the Region. Unless the regional constitution provides differently,[5] the President is elected by a popular and direct vote, and nominates or recalls the members of the Regional Government. In addition, the President is endowed with the general power of representing the Region, which makes him very similar to the Head of State. While we may be tempted to link these features to the presidential form of government, the Constitution establishes an institutional relation between the President and the legislative body, typical of the parliamentary systems. Indeed, thanks to art. 126, the Regional Council may express a vote of no-confidence to the President of the Region. The consequences of the no-confidence vote are the resignation of the government and the dissolution of the council. This rule was introduced in order to guarantee the stability of a directly elected government and to avoid circumventing the will of the electorate. This is the so-called *aut simul stabunt aut simul cadent* principle: where the council revokes its confidence in the executive (more specifically, its President), the council thereby must accept its own dissolution, so that the choice of the government may return to the electors. At the same time, the President may achieve the same result by resigning.

1.2 Setting the Scene: The Constitutional Framework

'A fundamental principal in constitutional states is that accountability follows power.'[6] In fact, the principle that there cannot be an exercise of power without corresponding mechanisms aimed at holding responsible those who exercise that power is widely accepted in today's democratic systems.

In the Italian legal order – as in almost all systems with written constitutions – this principle of accountability is expressly provided for in the Constitution (art. 95 It. Const.) and, where there are provisions that do not conform, they are conceived as exceptions to the general rule and deal only with processes of legal accountability (civil, criminal and administrative) without affecting those relating to political accountability. So it is, for example, the role of the President of the Republic or for the free parliamentary mandate, cases in which, due to the

[5] The regional form of government provided for in the Italian constitution could be changed in the regional constitutions (so called '*Statuti regionali*'). In other words, since the Regions have political autonomy they are not bound to the form of government 'suggested' by the Constitutions. Nonetheless, if they choose to accept the constitutional proposal, they are not entitled to introduce 'personal modifications' in the proposal itself. For an interesting overview of the Italian regional system see Grottanelli De Santi (2006) 3 ff.

[6] See Volpi (2003) 24 and also Azzariti (2004) 846.

special function performed by the Head of State and by the deputies, a certain lack of legal accountability is foreseen.

Article 90 – *Presidential Indemnity* – (1) The president may not be held responsible for exercising his duties, except for high treason and attempts to overthrow the constitution.[7]

Article 68 – *Indemnity, Immunity* – (1) Members of parliament may not be called to answer for opinions expressed or votes cast in the exercise of their office.

The general rule, therefore, is one of accountability for political power exercised, as evidenced by the formulation of article 95:

Article 95 – *Responsibilities* – (1) The prime minister conducts and is responsible for the general policy of the government. He ensures the unity of general political and administrative policies, promoting and coordinating the activities of the ministers. (2) The ministers are jointly responsible for decisions of the council of ministers and individually (responsible) for those of their ministries. (3) Rules concerning the role of the prime minister and the number, responsibilities and organization of the ministries are determined by law.

According to art. 94, the key moment of this responsibility is the vote of confidence of the Parliament, and more generally, art. 94 establishes this relationship between Parliament and Government.

From our constitutional map, though, we cannot infer a clear definition of political accountability.[8] In its classic meaning, political accountability is the relationship between the Parliament and the Government and it manifests itself in the ability of the former to condition the activities and indeed the very tenure

7 As it is well known, in the parliamentary system of government established by the Italian Constitution, the President of the Republic plays a central role. In the minds of the Framers, the President of the Republic was to play a 'rationalizing' role in the parliamentary system, acting as mediator between the Government and the Parliament and protecting the Government from the potentially destabilizing effects of an excess of parliamentarism. Even if it's not possible in this article to deal with the separate issue of the Head of State's accountability, it's important to stress that in the face of a series of significant powers provided by the Constitution, which make the President a difficult figure to place in the institutional framework – straddling two different functions, a more 'political' function and 'neutral' function of control, while at the same time apparently lacking in accountability – scholars have wondered what the President's real position is and about the meaning of his accountability/lack of accountability. More precisely on this matter, in the history of the Italian Republic one question remains to be resolved: if the Head of State intervenes illegitimately in the realm of the political direction, what legal instruments could the other constitutional bodies use (principally the Parliament, but also the Government) to sanction this 'political' interference? Given that art. 90 appears to be a tough road to pursue, the only alternative route seems to be that of inducing an appeal on grounds of conflict between the branches, leaving it for the Constitutional Court to declare its position on the alleged breach of constitutional competence.

8 See, foremost, art. 95, 94, 55 ff. on Parliament election and 83 on the Head of the State. See also art. 77 about law by decree.

in office of the latter based on institutions which depending on the historical period have assumed different formulations and varying degrees of intensity.[9] In order to clarify this statement we draw attention to the fact that the Government-Parliament circuit, and consequently the outline of the Government's political accountability in front of the Parliament, is strongly dependent on external factors such as the type of electoral law adopted.

From this point of view the change from a proportional electoral law to a majority system 'caused impressive effects on the political accountability issue, either on the institutional and diffuse side' in Italy.[10] Nowadays, the head of the government enjoys a higher degree of independence (since he is 'quasi-directly' elected) and this provokes also a different degree of political accountability. In a certain sense, the head of government is more directly accountable to the electors than the other political parties of the coalition.[11] A second effect that stems from this change is the increasing relevance of exit polls and, by and large, the media. Nevertheless, this is just one of the possible examples of the diverse formulation and varying of intensity of political accountability in different historical periods.

Returning to the central issue, the defining trait of political accountability in a democratic system is the active role accorded to the governed in controlling those who govern them and in utilizing the instruments of political accountability. If these are the principles in force within the Italian constitutional system on the subject of political accountability, we must now clarify what is meant in the constitutional realm by 'exercise of political power,' or, according to the wording of the Italian legal system, what is meant by responsibility for the '*indirizzo politico*' (general policy).

1.3 The Role of '*Indirizzo Politico*' as a Means for Identifying Individuals Subject to Political Accountability.

The function (and relative notion) of general policy arises in Italy with the establishment of a certain category of executive actions (either political or governmental) that are removed from the control of administrative judges. This was created during the preparatory work for the l. 31.3.1889, n. 5992, establishing the fourth section of the Council of State,[12] and explicitly

9 This is the definition commonly adopted: see Caretti: '*la mutevolezza delle forme e dei modi attraverso i quali può essere fatta valere la responsabilità politica di un soggetto, le une e gli altri legati non solo a regole costituzionalmente codificate, ma anche a quelle regole convenzionali dettate dalla prassi e diverse a seconda dei vari ordinamenti, dei vari assetti politici, delle varie epoche storiche*'.

10 Rescigno (2005) 13.

11 Prior to 1993, when the proportional regime was in effect, we would argue the Head of Government was more accountable to the political parties of the governing coalition.

12 In Italy, the Council of State is the court to which the citizen or the administrative authority – if they have lost the case in the first instance – can appeal. Its judgement cannot be object of further appeal, except for ground of jurisdiction.

excludes from judicial control those acts and measures promulgated by the Government in exercising its political power.

It immediately became apparent that such an assertion was not devoid of problems, *in primis* with regard to the difficulty of discerning a clear criterion for distinguishing political acts from administrative acts. Further, creating a category of actions that are beyond the reach of judiciary breaches the principle of separation of powers and takes a step towards forms of public activity typical of absolutism. Not by chance, in Italy, the theory of '*indirizzo politico*' (general policy) was fully realized during the Fascist period, when the head of the government possessed powers that were considerably greater than those held by prime ministers of democratic states. The theory of 'general policy' thereby took shape as the most immediate expression of a political regime characterized by an extremely high degree of political discretion, although its actions still had to fall within the limits of the material constitution.[13]

It's important to recall the origin of '*indirizzo politico*' because it marks the boundaries of the discussion of political accountability in Italy. In fact, in the Italian system there is a debate about the boundaries of accountability: on one hand, '*indirizzo politico*' is purely political; on the other, perhaps it closes off the mechanism of legal review. In other words, does it belong to the realm of political questions – and, for this reason, is not subject to judicial review – or is it also, in a certain limit, legal?[14]

Today, the constitutional meaning of '*indirizzo politico*' refers to government actions in a broad sense and is defined as that activity directed at defining the objectives that the government must pursue during its term in office. In identifying such objectives, the Government is limited to the fundamental norms of the Constitution: art. 1 on popular sovereignty, art. 49 on the multi-party system, art. 5 and Title V on decentralization, art. 13 et seq. on fundamental rights and the institutions of direct democracy (art. 71, 75, and 138). The Govern-

[13] More precisely, see Grottanelli De Santi (1990). When we use the expression 'material constitution', it is a reference to the noted theory of C. Mortati who distinguishes between a formal constitution and a material one, which coincides with the essential nucleus of tasks and powers that upholds a system of values advanced by a dominant political group (Mortati (1962)). It's clear, therefore, that in the concept of material constitution is implied in the idea of a predominant political group which manages to prevail on the others and to impose its Weltanschaung: at length see Catelani & Labriola (2001).

[14] Critics about the predominant thesis stressing the difficulty of a judicial review of political accountability (see for all Rescigno, later on), Angiolini (2001), *passim*, charges it to leave political accountability in the realm of politics and its virtue. But, suggests Angiolini, '*la politica anche quando è democratica e si esprime attraverso deliberazioni della maggioranza assunte in ottemperanza al principio del suffragio universale, è perfettibile ed esposta all errore. L appassimento del mito per cui nella politica si manifesterebbe una supposta sovranità dello Stato sembra doversi altresì accompagnare al definitivo tramonto del mito della volontà generale à la Rousseau, portandoci diritti alla riscoperta di posizioni individuali e collettive da garantire anche a fronte di deliberazioni a maggioranza ineccepibili dal punto di vista delle regole e dei principi sulla democrazia.*' (11-12). Also Ferrara (2005) 35, underlines in this issue '*La cattura della sovranità nel più stretto ambito giuridico*'.

ment, moreover, shares the power to exercise this function with other constitutional bodies, especially Parliament-- the primary representative of popular sovereignty.

In addition, one may ask whether other constitutional organs cooperate in the formulation of the 'general policy' (the Head of State, for example, or the Constitutional Court). In response to this question, doctrine replies that because the aforementioned organs serve a control function – which is not altogether devoid of characteristics that are *latu sensu* political – one can attribute to them a function of 'constitutional general policy' ('*indirizzo politico costituzionale*') still characterized by a power to identify the state's objectives, but less tied to political majorities in a strict sense.[15]

The clarification of which bodies participate in defining the 'general policy' is not merely of theoretical importance, but of practical significance even beyond this particular research paper. Indeed, identifying the bodies/individuals who hold this power is decisive in determining how the mechanisms of political accountability should be organized.

1.4 Main Features and Limits of Political Accountability

Difficulty arises when we try to define in the abstract what is meant by political accountability because of the multitude of forms that it takes in different systems and periods. Nevertheless, two aspects of political accountability are constant: its tight nexus with the principle of popular sovereignty and its connection with the organs entitled to exercise the general policy.

If an abstract explanation is not possible, the introduction of the principle of political accountability has nonetheless assumed a precise definition from a historical perspective. It marks the beginning of a movement to subject constitutional bodies that carry out political activities to established rules of a constitutional system. Therefore, with the multiplying of organs that cooperate to formulate the 'general policy', there is a corresponding multiplication of forms of political accountability.

According to the prevailing doctrine, two forms of political accountability may be distinguished: on the one hand, so-called *institutional political accountability*, fixed in conventional rules or codified; on the other, a sort of *diffuse political accountability*, inherent in the freedom of political criticism. In this day and age, this latter form of political accountability has developed the most. This is evident in the Italian republican experience, since, as will be discussed in subsequent sections, crises of parliamentary governments are very rare while extra- parliamentary crises are increasing.

---

[15] We are here referring to those majorities which may be ascribed to the current legislature which in Italy lasts 5 years (while the President serves a term of 7 years and judges on the Constitutional Court serve for 9 years). We will not elaborate here on the notion, initially explained by P. Barile, of a constitutional political agenda (that corresponds to objectives of constitutional implementation) and a contingent or majoritarian political agenda.

More simply, according to Rescigno's thesis, political accountability appears when one who exercises political power is exposed to criticism aimed at altering that person's conduct, removing that person from power, or reducing that person's power.

Institutional political accountability occurs when the active and passive entities in the relationship are identified, and in this a relationship, the former enjoys a qualified power to criticize and remove for political reasons the passive entity. To sum up, we could define this kind of accountability as a formalized one, in which there is a stable and definite relationship between the two subjects: the classic example is the Parliament-Government circuit. In fact, the Government is accountable to the Parliament and the Parliament is in charge of controlling the Government's actions (as we will see in the next part). This relationship is crowned in the sanctioning of removal of the Executive through a no-confidence vote.

Separate from this, diffuse political accountability is marked by a relation of the Executive with the polity. It occurs when a political individual is exposed to the common criticisms that anyone (the public or political parties, for example) could make without holding a power of removal.[16] The relevant trait of diffuse political accountability is its vagueness. In other words, the effects of this criticism are unpredictable. Possible outcomes range from the benign to the possibility that the Government will be forced to resign. A problem exists because there is no legal settlement for this kind of political accountability. What could derive from the above-mentioned criticism is, in a certain sense, spontaneous.[17] A classic example of this type of political accountability is the Government-public opinion circuit.

It is interesting to highlight that, even if we can legally distinguish the main features of political accountability, it is not equivalent to state that we also have the criterion for the legal review of political accountability. As a matter of fact, political accountability is often more about the person '*a tutto tondo*' who is in charge of certain activities than the activities themselves or specific acts. That means that we can review how the person acted in relation to the programs and aims he promised at the moment of the election or at the moment of the vote of no-confidence. It is, in a certain way, a judgement on the person overall.

Rescigno's thesis – that infers from the power to select a government an additional power to criticize, remove, or replace it – has been accused of partial-

[16] According to Rescigno, this form of accountability cannot be considered judicial since there is no visible, certain, predetermined link between the imputation and the sanction. This thesis, moreover, has been strongly opposed by doctrine.

[17] Prof. Angiolini underlines that the diffuse political accountability should not be considered at the same condition of the institutional one, since it is not a legal political accountability but just a *de facto* situation: according to him the principle of institutional balance could be really damaged if we consider in the same way both the type of political accountability (Angiolini (1998) 63). Similarly, Ferrara states that we can have political accountability only in the case that it is legally provided for that means that only the institutional political accountability is included in the public law discipline.

ity by some scholars since it is limited to the two types of political accountability mentioned above. However, political accountability is far more complex.[18] Referring to government as a whole, for example, Giovanni Sartori asserts that an 'accountable government' is one that attempts to meet two different requirements: first, to be sensitive and responsive to particular interests, and second, to behave responsibly, operating with efficiency and competence. Still this is not enough. In reality, we demand more from the government. Specifically, that it act efficiently and competently in pursuing the collective interest.[19]

A system of representative democracy has therefore to balance a variety of constitutional principles. It was thus correctly observed that in constructing the notion of political accountability, different impulses and needs come into play. The protection of political liberty excludes the irrevocability of those who govern while the need for democratic legitimization of the government postulates a certain degree of control by the governed over the government's actions.

All that being said, political accountability presupposes the existence of institutional mechanisms that put the government in a position to 'act responsibly' and permit the government to be called to account for its actions (a sort of explanatory accountability). Further, these mechanisms provide for the government's removal in the event it is unable to carry out the collective interest or guarantee the existence of a certain level of competition between political individuals so as to make substitutions possible.[20] We can, therefore, conclude that political accountability is a special type of legal accountability, and for this reason can be subject to juridical control.

The problem of political accountability is in large measure resolved by searching for institutional techniques through which to render it effective. There is a need to protect the collective interest and the conditions that permit the voters to evaluate the actions of the government and, where their judgment shall be negative, not affirm the government's mandate.

It cannot be denied, however, that in recent times the traditional models of political accountability (with the classic institutions of confidence) seem to be waning. In fact, cases of parliamentary crisis are very rare in western democracies (not just in Italy). If in the past, the game of political accountability was played primarily between the Parliament and the Government, today the game is played directly to the electorate. Therefore, we are facing a profound transformation in the methods for achieving political accountability. Ultimately, instead of a decline in the principle of political accountability, we are facing a profound transformation of it.[21]

---

18 See Pitruzzella (1998) 290 ff.

19 Sartori (1987) 282.

20 More fully, Pitruzzella (1998) 298.

21 Pitruzzella (1998) 294.

2 The Government-Parliament Circuit

2.1 Political Accountability in the Italian System: Rules *vs.* Practice

The following sections focus on the Government's and individual ministers' political accountability in the Italian system. Let us first operationalize this concept of accountability by specifying who is accountable to whom.

In Italy, the Government is accountable to the Parliament that has the task, among others, of controlling the conduct of the executive. Furthermore, it is important to point out that the Government is accountable to the people even though in the Italian system there is not any direct instrument, apart from the political election, that can immediately sanction a government that has failed to pursue its political program.

The Italian concept of Government's and ministers' accountability is based on the idea of sanctioning the Government or the individual ministers. Indeed, it can be argued that the question of confidence and the vote of no-confidence are the last steps of a process whereby the Government 'gives account' to the Parliament. However, these instruments, which represent the only possibility for the Government or an Italian Minister to be held accountable, are not widely used because in the Italian system many of the crises are so-called 'extra parliamentary,' born in the Government itself and not in the Parliament.

As stated earlier, the last step of the accountability process is the so-called question of confidence which can represent a pathological moment. Typically, by this time the Parliament has already used all the instruments it has in order to check and balance the actions of the Government. However, it is clear that these actions differ from the political program presented by the Government on which the basis of the fiduciary relationship between the executive and the legislative power has been established. Thus the vote of no-confidence can be seen as the ultimate sanction either to the Government or to an individual minister.

Yet, it must be noted that reality in the Italian system is often different from what we have just explained. Indeed, the question of confidence and the vote of no-confidence – that should represent sanction to the Government or to the individual Ministers – works just on paper. In practise, things work differently.

Actually the question of confidence is often used by the Government itself as a tool to strengthen its coalition and, in this way, obtain further consent on the political program which it pursues. Only once has the no-confidence procedure described in the Constitution been used (it happened in the 1998). Yet, this is not because Governments are so strong and fulfil their political programs presented but because many Italian Governments have resigned due to pressures or decisions of the political parties.

According to this perspective, it can be said that the political accountability of the Government and individual ministers is very much self-referential. The institutional political accountability of the Government before the Parliament has been replaced by a political accountability before the Italian political parties – a sort of diffuse political accountability.

Nevertheless, questions remain. How does the oversight of the Government's policy work? What can Parliament do in order to control the Government's actions? How do the instruments available to sanction either the Government or the individual Ministers function? Is there any evidence of a process of giving an account?

The following sections take up these issues more specifically. In particular, we examine the relationship between the Government and the Parliament stated in article 94 of the Constitution, point out in more detail the 'question of confidence' and the 'vote of no-confidence.' We look at the idea of a vote of no-confidence for individual ministers, and finally, detail one of the Parliament's instruments for exercising political control over the Government through emphasizing transparency and 'answerability' as part of accountability.

2.2 Political Accountability in Italy in the Constitutional Design: A Bi-Directional Relationship Between the Government and the Parliament

Moving now more specifically to the relationship between the Government and Parliament reveals the main task of the Italian Parliament in checking the existence of the fiduciary relationship between itself and the election of a new Government. It is as a result of that fiduciary relationship that the Parliament is able to check the Government's activity and, more specifically, hold the government accountable for fulfilling the political program which it presents within 10 days of its formation. This control should represent one of the best guarantees of democracy, at least on paper.

Because the Italian constitutional system is set within a parliamentary government, the fiduciary connection between the government and the parliament represents the primary circuit of political accountability. This fiduciary relationship is regulated at a constitutional level by art. 94, which provides:

1) the Government must have the confidence of both chambers;
2) each chamber accords or revokes confidence through a motion which is justified and voted upon;
3) within ten days of its formation the Government must go before both chambers to obtain a vote of confidence;
4) a contrary vote on a government proposal by one or both chambers does not require obligatory resignation;
5) the vote of no-confidence must be signed by at least one-tenth of the chamber's members and cannot be discussed until three days after its presentation;

The fiduciary relationship, and therefore the circuit of accountability, exists primarily between the Government and both chambers of Parliament, of which the Parliament can decide on the existence of fiduciary bond and reciprocal autonomy, each with binding results on the life of the Government. A decision by the majority of those present (simple majority) in one of the two chambers is sufficient to oblige the Government to resign. In particular, here is how the Constitution outlines the juridical regime of the Government's responsibility. In practice these rules have been changed and supplemented several times.

First of all, the Government, elected after consultations[22] between the President of the Republic and the various political parties, must – as provided in the Constitution – present itself to the chambers within 10 days of its formation to present its program and obtain the endorsement and formal seal of approval for its inauguration. This means, first of all, that a Government awaiting a vote of confidence cannot perform all of its functions, but is limited to those identified as 'of ordinary administration' which usually does not involve any assumption of political accountability.[23] In this way the Constitution seems to confirm the necessary connection explicated in art.94 between power and accountability. In other words, the moment confidence is granted is the moment that the Government assumes its full powers and corresponding accountability. It further implies that the Government should be held principally accountable for the program that it solemnly promised before the houses of Parliament to undertake.

It must be emphasized that the Constitution calls for a public vote of confidence so that the electorate may identify (and therefore eventually sanction) the political choice made by individual parliamentarians with respect to the Government. The Constitution also requires that the chambers' motion according or denying confidence be justified. In this way the relationship between the Government and the Parliament is characterized by a series of reciprocal rights and duties between these two political branches.

In reality, these two requirements have not always sufficed to achieve greater transparency and a clear assumption of responsibility. Particularly during the experience of national solidarity, (1976-1979) a very peculiar use of the abstention, during the vote of confidence in the House of Delegates and the exit of the Senators from the Senate chamber, led to the emergence of executives that weren't much more than a minority (so-called 'not-no-confidence') supported more by the mere non-opposition of the majority in the houses of Parliament

[22] In the early 1990s, one observed extreme extensions of Presidential consultations during which the proportional electoral system coupled with the peculiarity of our political system combined to prevent a clear configuration of the future government from emerging from the elections. Starting in 1996, we observed a sort of contraction. Rather than individual parties facing off in elections, entire coalitions squared off. The President reduced the number of individuals he consulted with, meeting with, for example, only 'the delegations of the two freely formed coalitions and not individuals groups in Parliament which comprised the coalitions'. De Caro Bonella (1996) 384.

[23] With the exception of some interventions dictated by extreme necessity and urgency.

rather than the explicit support of political movements. Moreover, during those years, approval for the Government was separated from approval of the Government's program. In July 1977, for example, the political parties presented their program (binding for the Government) directly to the House of Delegates, without the Government's participation in either the drafting or subsequent debate of the program.[24]

Beyond these excesses, and the frequent occurrence of cases of motivations *ob relationem* for a vote of confidence, the constitutional doctrine of confidence allows us to postulate a sort of bidirectional relationship between these two branches and consequently the existence of reciprocal responsibilities. In fact, one can say that not only 'must the government have the vote of confidence *of* the two chambers. The government must have confidence in the two chambers.'[25] This means that on the one hand, the Parliament must have faith in the Government's ability to achieve its declared political aims – the specific realization of which the Government assumes. On the other hand, the Government must have faith in the Parliament's (or perhaps more specifically, the majority in Parliament's) support and collaboration for the program. It is not by chance that Article 94, c.4 excludes the mandatory resignation of the Government in the case of a contrary vote by one or both chambers on a single Governmental initiative. In other words, a rejection of a single government act does not jeopardize the Government's overall agenda and therefore does not trigger mechanisms for imposing liability.

2.3 The Question of Confidence and a Vote of No-Confidence: Between Normative Elements and Constitutional Practice

From the co-dependence of the fiduciary relationship between Government and Parliament stems an equally bidirectional possibility of activating the mechanisms of responsibility. A verification of the existence of confidence can be put in motion either by parliamentary initiative (by 1/10 of the members of one chamber signing a vote of no-confidence, followed by a vote not less than three days later) or by the Government's own initiative (by posing a question of confidence on a matter that the Government believes is essential for achieving its political agenda). It is true that this latter mechanism is not recognized in the Constitution, having been formalized only in parliamentary rules (art. 116 reg. cam. and art. 161 reg. sen.). Nonetheless, it has been universally recognized as being in consonance with the overall constitutional framework. Through the vote of confidence, the Government commits itself – on its own initiative – to political accountability. The Parliament's rejection of the Government's proposal, like a vote of no-confidence, mandates the resignation

---

[24] Rescigno (1977) 9 observes that this split between program and government (by which one can approve the former without approving the latter and vice versa) produces 'a complete overturning of the political accountability of the government'.

[25] Manzella (1969) n. 5-6, 43.

of the Government. In the extreme case, when it is impossible to form a new Government supported by a parliamentary majority, both chambers could be dissolved.[26] As stated by Rescigno, when the Government poses the question of confidence:

> the political responsibility [becomes] a claim of responsibility' by the [Government] and in so doing reaffirms its political leadership. Such a claim is typically made when the executive threatens to resign and in so doing rallies support of his followers and obligates all to openly declare their support, in the name of accountability. Thus, if a majority is verified it reconfirms the Government's power and associated responsibility. If instead, a loss of a majority is apparent, responsibility causes the executive to resign and delivers to the Government's successor an unprejudiced situation.[27]

Realization of a political responsibility for non-fulfilment due to a rupture in the fiduciary tie comports the resignation of the Government and possibly even the dissolution of both chambers of Parliament.

Although we can observe that this mechanism has functioned very little in our system in such a linear manner there have been results more or less predicated upon it. On the one hand, the Government has increasingly utilized votes of confidence more as an anti-obstructionist instrument of blackmail vis-à-vis the parliamentary assembly than as a way of imposing its own responsibility in cases of particular importance. The discipline of this institution contained in the parliamentary rules provides – with some important differences between the two chambers – that when the Government poses a vote of confidence on a proposal subject to a vote in one of the chambers, a voice vote must be held on this proposal, with a resulting obvious and pronounced acceleration of the procedure.[28]

---

[26] This majority – at least from a normative perspective and excluding the judgment from considerations of opportunity and political legitimization could even be different from the majority which supported the previous Government.

[27] Rescigno (1988) 1351.

[28] It must be noted that a broad derogation from this rule is still contained in art. 116, c. 2, reg. cam., regarding a vote of confidence posed on a legal framework composed of only one article, in which case the a final vote is nonetheless saved. In this case, there ends up being two votes on the same object, with important repercussions on fiduciary constraints and on the eventual assurance of governmental responsibility (though this 'juridical monster' had greater practical relevance prior to the reform of parliamentary voting modalities, secret ballots were always prescribed for the final decision on a proposed law). If, in fact, the vote of confidence yielded a positive result for the Government, but then a subsequent vote on the same issue produced a negative result, what was the Government to infer about the existence or non-existence of confidence? As observed by Pezzini (1985) 181, 'either the Government remains in charge, implicitly contradicting the theory that led it to ask for a vote of confidence – thereby inevitably leading to a further loss of power and authority – or the Government resigns, in so doing contradicting the result of the vote of confidence that had officially confirmed it, and essentially

Moreover, in the course of our entire history as a republic, characterized by short-lived government bodies, in only one case did a Government's resignation result from a formal no-confidence vote by the Parliament, setting off a parliamentary crisis in the strictest sense of the term. The case involved the Prodi Government which, upon being defeated on its financial proposal by a single vote during the vote of confidence, was forced to resign in October 1998, opening the door for the formation of the D'Alema Government. This new government was supported by a somewhat different majority than the coalition that had originally won the election.[29] In all other cases, technically speaking, governmental crises could be defined as extra-parliamentary, since the voluntary resignations of the Government were not provoked by a formal vote of no-confidence, but rather by political problems within the majority coalition itself.

The latest example came very recently and regarded a crisis in the second Berlusconi Government, weakened by the unfavorable result of regional elections in April 2005. Following this crisis a new government was formed which, although led by the same President of the Cabinet and supported by the same majority, attested to a 'a 'discontinuity' with respect to the previous Government'.[30] It is true that in these cases, resignations by the Government can probably best be attributed to a sort of 'widespread' responsibility, characterized by the impossibility of effectively carrying out the government's functions, rather than to a true institutional political responsibility. It is also true that the frequent attempts effectuated by the President of the Republic, especially since the early 1980s, to parliamentarize governmental crises, encouraging the resigning executive to present himself to the chambers and opening debate on the reasons that induced the resignation constitutes a symptom, not so much of the will to end the crisis, but to bring it back within the normal mechanisms of political accountability.[31]

The powers of a resigning government are reduced correspondingly more than those of a government awaiting a vote of confidence. Most significantly, the resigning government is limited to the carrying out of daily affairs. Moreover, given the previously stated difficulty in identifying routine administrative actions which will not call into question political responsibility, the current practice (beginning with the resignation of the second Cossiga Government in 1980) is for resigning Governments to specify their 'auto-limits' set forth in Prime Minister's Directives at the time of the resignation. For example, Spadolini, in an effort to specify what was meant by routine administrative actions, excluded from this definition approval of new governmental bills, the presentation of

legitimizing a procedure which allows Government crises to be precipitated without explicit reasons or taking of sides (to the contrary, veiled in maximum ambiguity) in stark contrast to the constitutional discipline imposed by votes of confidence and no-confidence'.

29 With the exit of the Bertinotti's followers of Rifondazione came the entry of Cossiga's UdR.

30 R. Bin & G. Pitruzzella (2005) 128.

31 One can see this phenomenon in certain instances of parliamentarization in the crisis in Armaroli (1983) 400 ff, Calandra (1985) 551 ff, De Caro Bonella (1985) 551 ff, Traversa (1992) 335 ff.

new decrees to substitute decrees which did not become law, and the approval of new nominations with the exception of deadlines imposed by law. Furthermore, activities in foreign affairs were to be limited to non-deferrable acts, and, in Parliament, the Government could only work toward the approval of decrees-law, the budget, and fiscal law.

2.4 A Vote of No-Confidence for an Individual Minister

As previously asserted, political accountability involves, first of all, the Government as a whole. Nevertheless, it must also include political accountability for individual ministers. This interpretation is supported by art. 95, c. 2 Cost., which states 'ministers are accountable collectively for the acts of the Council of Ministers, and individually for the actions of their own ministry.'

More problematic, however, is identifying the consequences of such individual accountability as the Constitution does not include any suitable instrument for sanctioning a minister. In particular, without an express provision granting a power for the President of the Council of Ministers (or perhaps for the President of the Republic upon his request) to recall individual ministers, the prevailing school of thought is that such a use of power is not possible, even though this power might be considered inherent in the power to propose a list of ministers and more consistent with a majoritarian electoral system.[32] The only remedy for removal of an individual minister seems to be to induce his or her 'voluntary'[33] resignation or to adopt a 'motion of individual no-confidence,' not provided for in the Constitution, but recognized by parliamentary rules and confirmed as legitimate by the Constitutional Court in the only case that such a motion was effectively utilized (sent. n. 7/1996).[34] This ruling was established the noteworthy incident involving the Minister of Grace and Justice, Mancuso, who having received a vote of no-confidence in the Senate, created a conflict of power between the branches when he contested the legitimacy of the Senate's action before the Constitutional Court.

Such an event raises concerns of considerable interest regarding political accountability, both in constitutional and 'political' terms. From a constitutional perspective, the decision of the Court clarified that an individual motion of no-

[32] Carlassare (2001).

[33] An innovative solution to this problem was reached in the Amato government, when in order to overcome the obstacle of the Minister of Industry and State-Owned Enterprises, Guarino, who refused to resign, (who openly opposed the President of the Council and the Minister of the Treasury regarding a question of privatization of state-owned enterprises) and to prevent the crisis from affecting the entire Government a decree-law was approved separating the Ministry of Industry and State-Owned Enterprises and permitting the President of the Council to entrust the ministry's responsibilities to another minister.

[34] As a matter of practice in the Senate, and through a specific provision in the House of Delegates, that under art. 115, c. 3 extends to motions of no-confidence for individual ministers the rules generally envisioned for votes of no-confidence on the entire Government.

confidence is 'an institution which is innate in a parliamentary system ... and represents the instrument through which the fiduciary relationship between the Government and the Parliament is safeguarded, in the event that the Government is put in jeopardy by a single minister.'[35] The consequences of an individual vote of no-confidence can be nothing other than the mandatory resignation of the minister affected, except that the minister may raise a question of separation of powers, so long as it is aimed at the regularity of the procedure followed, and not at contesting the merits of the motion itself, which, as a *political act*, is beyond the competence of the Court. Yet, from the political perspective, we must emphasize the peculiarity of the particular case, which saw Minister Mancuso, a member of the 'technical' government (the Dini Government), in a position of absolute isolation with respect to the majority supporting the Government.

Apart from the importance that a *political* mechanism was utilized here for the first and only time with respect to a *technical* minister, the event under consideration suggests that only the absence of support from the majority allows this mechanism to function without triggering the otherwise typical intra-governmental solidarity that typically prevents the censure of a single minister.[36]

2.5 The Problem of Transparency in Parliament and the Influence of the Government in Parliament

We now consider whether there exist transparency mechanisms in the ordinary activities of Parliament that allow for greater transparency of the various political components and a more efficient operation of accountability mechanisms.

In this regard, it must be noted that, until the reform of parliamentary rules in the 1980s, the influence of the Government in Parliament was very limited and its visibility practically nil. This was a consequence of a rigorous application of the doctrine of the 'centrality of the Parliament;' a doctrine which postulated that only the legislative body had the capacity to represent social pluralism and achieve an effective compromise among various political views.

A particularly strong example of this philosophy was seen in the original method for planning the legislative program. In particular, the House of Delegates (art. 23 reg. cam.), where decisions on the proposed program were made during a meeting of the presidents of the various parties, decisions had to be made unanimously among groups with equal representation. Thus, beyond impeding the planning of the legislative program, due to the absolute veto power enjoyed by each parliamentary group, this method of decision-making barred any opportunity or initiative by the Government in selecting the issues to be

35 Caretti & De Siervo (2004) 226.

36 Confirmation of this observation can be seen in the fact that in all other cases of potential individual votes of no confidence, the motions were either repelled or withdrawn (for a recent example see the rejection of the motion against Scajola followed by the grave events at Genova during the G8 conference).

discussed. Compounding the difficulty of holding Parliament accountable for their actions was the secrecy under which these negotiations often took place.

Only in the 1980s did Italy begin to move past this vision of the role of the Parliament, gradually granting the Government specific powers that allowed it to impact the work of the Parliament and open the functioning of the Parliament to more scrutiny. In this way, through a series of progressive modifications,[37] there was introduced first, the necessity to 'take into account the recommendations of the Government,' and eventually, the formulation of the legislative program 'on the basis of the Government's recommendations *and* the proposals of the parliamentary groups.' These reforms assigned to the executive the additional responsibility of establishing the priorities in negotiating various issues with Parliament.

2.6 The Parliament's Instruments for Exercising Political Control over the Government

In addition to this enhanced transparency in establishing the legislative program, which, among other governmental priorities, today reserves time for opposition groups, one may also observe a more effective regulation of the Parliament's usual control instruments.

Apart from a full-fledged parliamentary inquiry,[38] (which does not accord minority groups in Parliament the independent power to launch an inquiry[39] and therefore seems to favour a view that investigations are political tools of the majority[40]) is the important '*interrogazioni a risposta immediata*' (so-called *Question Time* (art. 135-bis reg. cam.).[41] These interrogations, which usually occur weekly, have as their privileged addressee the President of the Council, (something similar to the *Prime Minister's Question Time* in the English tradition) and provide that in the course of each legislative calendar the President of the Council shall appear twice to answer questions within the President's area of competence as identified in art. 95 Cost. For their part, ministers whose responsibilities relate to subjects being discussed by the Parliament must appear once. Moreover, the pace of the debate (which is televised at the request of the President of the Chamber) is extremely fast and should make for a very high intensity engagement between the various political factions. Yet, in reality, the application of this institutional practice has not proved altogether satisfying principally due to the lack of a true obligation for the Government and its principal members to present itself to answer questions raised. Similar concerns arise in the context of the so-called 'urgent' or 'weighty' questions, provided for in art. 138-bis. reg.

37 Art. 23 reg. cam.

38 Governed in our system by art. 82 Cost.

39 Art. 82 provides in fact only that 'each chamber can order inquiries about public interest subjects'.

40 Pace (1979) 272.

41 The '*interrogazioni a risposta immediata*' which take place in the parliamentary committees are provided by the art. 135-*ter* reg. cam.

cam., following a model already in use by the Senate since 1988.[42] Instead, one may highlight the development of other institutions which, in the ordinary activities of the Parliament, can more appropriately be placed at the halfway point between the control function and the function of 'co-legislation'.[43]

Apart from the traditional co-legislative function effectuated in our system by the decree-law, which allows the Government to legislate by calling on its own majority and allows parliamentarians to use the decree as a vehicle for advancing additional amendments, of particular importance are parliamentary opinions on the drafts of normative acts. In this case, the Government is permitted to draft laws or administrative rules and regulations once the Parliament delegates him to enact them. In the Italian system, it is now common practice to call on the Government to submit drafts of legislation or new regulations to the competent parliamentary commissions. These commissions, in turn, may express an opinion that is obligatory but not binding.[44] Recurring examples of this are the programs that follow many legislative decrees implementing new community directives. In all of these cases, in fact, legislative delegation itself allows for more shared participation in normative activities between the Parliament and the Government. The subsequent 'return' to the chambers of the Government's drafts allows for further cooperation and ensures transparency – 'especially when the guiding principles and criteria of the act enabling delegated legislation are rather vague, the parliamentary commissions tend to collaborate in editing the draft of the legislative decree as if it were an ordinary bill.'[45]

Finally, of some interest, are the new rules and regulations for legislative investigation in the committees, (*'istruttoria legislativa in commissione'* art. 79 reg. cam.) that attributes to the Government the role of 'principal producer of information in the legislative process.'[46] 'Through the procedure of the legislative investigation, the Parliament recognizes that the Government does in fact have a right to play a decisive role in the legislative process ... but at the same time the procedure establishes that parliamentary minorities within the commissions have a right to know which factual elements form the basis for the normative texts and possession of which allows the Government to exercise its role in the legislative process. Parliament, in substance, forsakes part of its exclusive exercise of the legislative function in exchange for the ability to control those key factual elements upon which the exercise of the legislative function is based.'[47]

---

42 Sicardi (2004) 139 et seq.

43 Lupo (2004) 125 et seq.

44 Art. 96-*ter* reg. cam.

45 Lupo (2004) 128.

46 Lupo (2004) 130.

47 Lupo (2004) 131.

3 Beyond Political Accountability: The Separation Between General Policy *(indirizzo politico)* and Administrative Responsibilities (*responsabilità dirigenziale*) Within the Public Adminstration; the Italian Independent Regulatory Agencies

3.1 The Separation Between General Policy (*indirizzo politico*) and Administrative Responsibilities (*responsabilità dirigenziale*) in the Public Management Reform

Traditionally, Ministries and public administration in Italy were organised according to a hierarchical structure, reflecting the 19th century model of the Kingdom of Piedmont and Sardinia. This model was characterised by different Directorates General, both run and co-ordinated by one Secretary general for each Ministry. The Minister was thus responsible for the acts adopted by the public officials of his ministry.

In the late 1980s, as in several industrialised countries, Italy started a governmental reform. The reasons included the urgent need to cut the budget deficit by rationalising the expenditure on the public administration, and the need to restore citizens' trust in the institutions and in government. The struggle for meeting the Maastricht standards, in particular, widely invested the Public Administration both at the central and local level, imposing budget cuts and corrective measures to fight the state deficit throughout the decade.

In 1993 a Legislative Decree[48] grounded the status of civil servants by the concept of the separation between policymaking and administration, and ensured the basis for introducing private management approaches and techniques in the bureaucratic system, particularly at the level of human resource management.

The reform of 1993 sought to establish a clear separation of the functions of directing policy, which are entrusted to the organs of government, from those of its execution, for which managers are responsible. Managers are required to pursue the objectives and implement the programmes laid down by the policymaking bodies, but within these limits they act with discretionary powers. Thus the principle of distinction between the two spheres was emphasized: political organs identify aim s and priorities (and appoint top managers), public managers have responsibility in the management of resources, after they have been allocated.

Legislative Decree n. 29/1993 made a distinction between senior managers (*dirigenti generali*) and other managers, charging both with important personnel management functions. From the viewpoint of the legislators, all managers are required to act in the capacity of employer in regard to the employees of the public authorities. They are responsible for the results of the activity carried on by the departments they head and are subject to scrutiny by appropriate assess-

48 Legislative Decree n. 29 of 1993.

ment bodies which report to the policy-making bodies. Direction tasks, however, are only temporary, and the tenure is contractually defined. However, if their management leads to negative results, the sanctions applicable differ between the two categories and may extend to compulsory retirement for senior managers and dismissal for other managers.

Legislative Decree n. 29/1993 introduced also a new agency, ARAN, which represents the public employer in negotiations with unions and is responsible for drafting collective bargaining agreements. Moreover, it developed an interministerial pool of executives responsible 'for the results of the activity managed by their offices and the execution of programmes and projects entrusted to them in the light of productivity objectives and for financial, technical and administrative management results, including organisational and personnel management decisions.'

In 1997 the Public Administration's restructuring reached its acme with the Bassanini Reform,[49] a multifaceted normative corpus named after the Public Administration Minister who introduced it, that became a milestone in the modernization process of the Italian public administration.

With the Bassanini Reform, a new organisation of central Government and public administration was introduced.[50] The office of the Secretary general, as well the traditional subdivision into Directorates General has been suppressed and has been replaced by the Departments, whose role is to guarantee an integrated exercise of the respective governmental functions. Departments are charged with tasks concerning comprehensive groups of matters and relevant instrumental tasks including the orientation and coordination of the units of which Departments are composed, and with the organisation and management of instrumental, financial and human resources which are available to them. A Head of Department will replace the Secretary general for each Ministry, charged with co-ordination, direction and control functions. Whenever the Secretary General is eliminated, his functions are shared by the Heads of Departments. Only the Ministry of Foreign Affairs, the Ministry of Defence and the Ministry of Cultural Heritage and Activities have maintained their traditional internal organisation.

The reform of the Ministries has also introduced a new body in the organisation of the central government – the Agency – whose responsibility includes technical and operational tasks of national interest, which used to be carried out by the Ministries (among them, Agency for environmental protection and technical services, the Agency for Defence Industries, the Agency for civil defence). Agencies work for the benefit of public government institutions, also at a regional and local level. They enjoy full autonomy, within the limits set by law and they are placed under the supervision of the Corte dei Conti as well as of the Ministers concerned in accordance with their orientation and monitoring powers. Agencies must achieve the objectives set by the Ministers. They are also

49 See laws n. 59 and 127 of 1997.

50 Implemented by Legislative Decrees n. 300 and n. 303 of 1999.

subject to governmental inspections to verify that ministerial guidelines are duly implemented.

The goal of accountability of public administration was linked to previous efforts in reforming the personnel system, while trying to provide concrete managerial tools and contractual instruments for realizing the separation between policy-making and administration.[51] The competencies for political leaders, both at the national and at the local level, were preserved and included the definitions of goals and programs, the allocation of resources, the monitoring of performance and results and the appointment of managers (see Legislative Decree n. 165/2001, art. 4 and 14). The managers, on the other hand, were asked to run the agency or the city or the department, also adopting administrative measures not reserved for political bodies. Their appointment is not permanent, though they can be removed only if controlling and evaluating mechanisms assess their performance as ineffective or insufficient. The reform also called for a re-definition of the salary system, with the possibility of linking a share of the remuneration to performance measurement, as the incentive per results.

Following these reforms introducing a separation between general policy (*indirizzo politico*) and administrative responsibilities (*responsabilità dirigenziale*), a Minister can no longer annul an act adopted by officials and managers, or decide to take upon himself the right to adopt the act.

While the decree of 1993 remains the basis for every public management reform, three periods can be distinguished, each of which raised contractualisation to a new level:

a) 1993 to 1998: the 'privatisation' did not yet apply to senior executives. Their appointments and performance obligations remained the minister's responsibility. Their pay reflected standard scales. Other managers were governed by collective bargaining agreements;
b) 1998 to 2002: collective bargaining agreements became applicable to senior executives. They signed fixed-term contracts under private law specifying objectives and pay. The reform created an inter-ministerial management structure. In principle, all executives should have been lumped in this pool, which the ministries could have sourced for needed profiles. In fact, the ministries remained in control, trying to keep their best executives. Mobility was boosted by the development of an inter-ministerial database with the resumes of all senior executives and a list of available positions updated in real time. The years ahead can be expected to lead gradually to the creation of a genuine labour market;
c) since October 2002: the appointment and objectives of senior executives are fixed by decree (unilateral public act). Their pay is negotiated bilaterally and laid down in a private contract signed for the term of their appointment (3 years or less). The '*ruolo unico dei dirigenti*' has made way for ministerial pools but the inter-ministerial database continues to be used. The objective remains to promote mobility.

---

[51] Mussari (1997) and Bassanini (2000).

3.2 The Institution of Independent Authorities in the Italian Experience: A Brief Overview

While the preceding sections have dealt specifically with political accountability in the Italian system, Italy also features a number of independent authorities, many newly created, that challenge the notion of political accountability. These authorities allow us to draw some parallels between the Italian system and EU insofar as these commissions perform binding governmental and regulatory functions yet under most circumstances are not subject to any particular system of political accountability. However, a closer examination of these authorities and the rules that impact their operation may provide an entry point for further discussion on creating political accountability mechanisms that will be relevant in the EU. The following section is divided into three parts. The first outlines the establishment and competencies of independent authorities in the Italian system. The second part describes more specifically how the independent authorities function within the Italian system. Lastly, we examine some of the ways that Italy has tried to guarantee accountability and transparency within these bodies.

3.3 Independent Authorities in Italy: Their Establishment and Responsibilities

The Italian legal system enables non-governmental bodies to regulate certain specific fields such as competition, telecommunication, finance, and merchant banking, within rules coming from primary and secondary legislation. Delegation of such power is normally connected to a prevailing governmental regulation so that supervision and effective oversight of the regulatory policy created by these independent bodies is ensured. Those bodies are properly defined as 'Independent Authorities' ('*Autorità indipendenti*'), for which not only structural separation is provided by law, but also a certain degree of insulation from governmental control and policy. These authorities were set up during the last twenty five years, and following the Anglo-American model, share the following characteristics: They carry out, independently from the Government and ministers' daily activity, a surveillance function with regard to important economic sectors ensuring loyalty, fairness and honesty in order to maintain real competition.[52]

The independent authorities are composed of few members – usually five – and selected from persons with specific and ascertained professional qualifications and experience. The President of the Republic (following the proposal of the Prime Minister and after a deliberation by the Cabinet) usually nominates the members of the Authorities. Sometimes the Parliament takes part in the nomination through the power of designation held by the Presidents of both Houses.

52 For a general comprehensive overview see Clarich (2005).

The first independent authority, established in 1974 with Law n. 216, was the '*Commissione nazionale per le società e la borsa*'-CONSOB: a kind of watchdog of the Stock Exchange and related markets. The CONSOB is entrusted with the delicate and extremely important mission of overseeing the complete fairness and accuracy of shares, stocks and bonds and the activity of the companies whose securities are traded on the Stock Exchange. The CONSOB can take all the measures deemed necessary to guarantee the transparency of the information and the fairness of the transactions on the markets.

The number of independent authorities in the economic sector has increased since the early 1990s. At the beginning of 1990s, a strong policy aimed to privatize public undertakings was implemented. The prevailing need for public finance led to significant changes in the public management of the economy. The growth of the independent authorities has been based on several economic and political factors:

- the lack of competition in several industrial fields;
- the need to avoid remaking private monopoly situations in the process of privatization;
- the need to safeguard the quality of services and the level of tariffs in public utilities;
- the necessity to fully comply with the general principle based in the Italian legal system to ensure a distinction between the political sphere and concrete economic affairs;
- the impact of European laws.

Thus, the institution of regulatory authorities has been tied to the transformation of state-run companies and producers of goods and services into private companies. In the early 1990s, the distinction between policy making and business management began to be considered a general principle in the entire sector of public powers. In theory, the former should only create guidelines of public action, but not make concrete decisions. However, it was necessary to ensure that markets not suffer from changes due to political affairs so impartial and independent bodies were created.

This led to the creation of the '*Autorità Garante della concorrenza e del mercato*' – also known as the 'Antitrust Commission.'[53] As its name suggests, the main duty of the Commission is to control the enterprises operating in the market in order to prevent any company or economic entity from gaining and exploiting a monopolistic position, or even a dominant position, in the market. To this end, the Commission, which has gained a strong role and a remarkable reputation, has the power to prohibit certain conduct, issue fines and offer its professional opinion on questions of market concentration.

As far as the public utilities field is concerned, the first proposals for providing independent authorities were put forward in 1992. The 'decree-law', n. 333

[53] Created by law n. 287 of 1990.

of 1992,[54] carried out the transformation of state run economic bodies to private concerns. Moreover, law n. 537 of 1993, delegated the Government to set up bodies to regulate utilities of special public interest. The 'decree-law', n. 332 of 1994,[55] further allowed the transfer of transformed-companies' shares in the fields of transport, telecommunications, energy and defence, on condition that independent bodies having regulatory power and quality control were already set up. Regulatory authorities in Italy were, therefore, provided by law in conjunction with the political decision to privatize large sectors of the economy in order to obtain public funds.

Thus, several regulatory authorities have been created in the past four years. Among these, the 'Authority for the Electrical Energy and Natural Gas' ('*Autorità per l'energia elettrica e il gas*') and the 'Authority for the Telecommunications Sector,' ('*Autorità per le garanzie nelle comunicazioni*') have been entrusted with the task to supervising the industry and protecting users and consumers during the privatization process of very important sectors of the national economy.

3.4 The Regulatory Powers of Independent Authorities: Rule Making, Administrative, Quasi-Judicial

The regulatory authorities have been given effective powers to perform the difficult task entrusted to them. These powers are related both to fact-finding and decision-making. As to the former, the authority is normally provided with all the data it needs to be able to do its work, particularly when it is required to set tariffs using the price-capping system. Thus it has to know the production costs to the company in question. Another very important instrument is transparent accounting and the possibility that the regulator may set accounting and management rules. The authority can acquire this data, if necessary, by imposing penalties.

The example of one authority in particular, the authority for energy and gas allows for a better understanding of how the authorities work in Italy. The authority for energy and gas has powers of active administration in the fields of energy and gas, which do not differ from those of ordinary government departments. In other words, while not part of the Government, they perform many governmental functions.

The Public Utilities Law is the general law regulating energy and gas sectors[56] and entrusts the Authority for energy and gas with the protection of fundamental interests, such as:

- to guarantee promotion of competition and efficiency in the field of public utilities;
- to guarantee suitable levels of quality in the utilities, in a context of profitability and financial balance;

---

54 Converted by law n. 359 of 1992.

55 Then converted by law n. 474 of 1994.

56 N. 481 of 1995.

- to guarantee accessibility and diffusion of utilities over the whole country;
- to implement a clear, dependable system based upon prior criteria tariffs;
- to promote the defence of customers' interests.

The regulatory authority, therefore, works as a sector authority. It is an authority vested with the power of controlling an industry by making rules (tariffs and, to certain extent, regulations), administration (the proposals of permit schemes to the minister, quality control, requests of documents, inspections and sanctions) and finally, holding quasi-jurisdiction (conciliation and arbitration procedures between service providers and customers).

The rule-setting and law-making functions relate to the procedures for providing the service, particularly the quality of management ('it shall define and monitor quality standards') and the economic aspects (tariffs). The Authority is also empowered to submit proposals to the Government and Parliament on the statutory regime of the utilities.[57]

Administrative functions include putting forward plans to the Ministry of Industry for concessions depending upon the structure of the public utilities market. The force of these proposals lies in the fact that the Minister of Industry has little control over the decisions of the authority. The ministry may request the Authority to re-examine their plans. However, if the authority confirms these plans, they may only be overturned by a ruling of the entire Cabinet and then only if there are substantial grounds for doing so in the general public interest.[58] The regulatory authority may also impose penalties.

As far as the quasi-judicial powers for settling disputes are concerned, the Authority may hold reconciliation and arbitration hearings between users and service-providers.

3.5 Accountability and the Regulatory Authorities

The presence of independent regulatory authorities with wide-ranging powers means that the exercise of these powers is no longer directly referable to government, and thus cannot be responsible towards the Parliament, as it normally is.

However, controls do exist--if indirectly. According to the principle of ministerial autonomy set forth by art. 95, par. 2, of the Italian Constitution, ministers are responsible for the acts adopted within the exercise of their respective ministries. This provision must be read together with the principle of distinction between administration and politics, according to which, ministers define policy and strategy, assess results, and appoint general directors, but have no further direct involvement in administration. However, the Parliament conditions the tenor of the authority in a number of ways. Parliament most often appoints the members of the authority and receives the regular annual report the authorities

[57] See article 2, par. 12, letter a.

[58] Article 2, par. 12, and 13 of law n. 481 of 1995.

are obliged to present. It can also convene hearings of an Authority. Ultimately, within the appointment mechanisms themselves, the Parliament seeks to insure the highest level of independence and impartiality with respect to the status of members of authorities.

Regarding these procedures, the system is not always the same. The regulatory authorities' members are sometimes appointed by Parliament (that is the case for the *Autorità garante della concorrenza e del mercato*, the Antitrust commission). In other cases, competence is shared between Government and Parliament, as the former has the power to appoint, but only on the basis of a positive vote of the relevant Parliamentary committees. Sometimes a mixed system has been provided, as is the case for the recently appointed *Autorità per le comunicazioni*.

There is no single provision for the private status of members of authorities, but generally they cannot take up any other job or undertaking as long as they are in office. In the case of the more recent authorities, the members are obliged to not have any relationship with the relevant sector for four years from the end of their service (*Autorità per l'energia elettrica e il gas and Autorità per le comunicazioni*). Also, for more recent authorities, the reappointment of members at the end of their term is not allowed (as for the *Autorità Antitrust, Autorità per l'energia elettrica e il gas, Autorità per le comunicazioni*). The law does not provide for an authority member's removal, but is reasonable to think that they can be removed in case of very serious events that disqualify them from office.

Autonomy helps to ensure that regulators are free to satisfy their stated objectives transparently and neutrally. In accordance with European directives, Italian regulatory authorities enjoy substantial autonomy in staffing and budget policies. The tenure of the commissioners is usually longer than the frame of a legislature, (usually five years or seven years in the case of the Antitrust Commission) thus increasing the political neutrality of the appointments over the medium term. It must be stressed that independence from political power appears to be the consequence of a distinction between politics and management of concrete affairs, which has been provided for the common public administration as well.[59] Distinguishing administration from politics is one of the most important reform guidelines law n. 29 of 1993 introduced. In principle, politicians (ministers, mayors, etc.) are responsible for policies, and public managers for administration management and direction.

The staffing procedure for the authorities has also undergone reforms that seek to reinforce the fairness and impartiality in the system. Administrations' and agencies' managers and employees must respect laws and regulations, must accomplish the program established by government authority, must comply with the constitutional principle of P.A. impartiality and fairness, and must be protected from politicians' interferences in the management of the administration. They are selected, with few exceptions, through public competitions. Objective mechanisms for measuring their performance allow the coexistence

59 Under law n. 29 of 1993, article 14.

and the coherence between the political strategic guidance and the autonomy and responsibilities of public managers in the administrations' direction.

The so-called civil service's privatization introduced by law n. 29 of 1993 may be considered one of the most radical changes introduced by the Italian reform system. Moving from the customary continental European public law regime, still in force 15 years ago, Italy now has a Civil Service regulation mostly similar to the Anglo-Saxon regime.

With regards to civil law for civil servants, the public administration now has roughly the same powers and obligations as private sector employers and public managers and employees have almost the same rights and duties as the private companies' managers and workers. In the regulation of their rights and duties, laws and decrees are now replaced by contracts for about 80% of public managers and employees.[60] The national labour contracts, agreed through collective bargaining, replaced the law in determining employment conditions and general frames for salaries and tasks. In this context, integrative and individual contracts fix the individual salaries and tasks and should be used for promoting efficiency and professionalism.

Thus, the government not only influences the choice of the members but may also condition their work by laying down general provisions. The Authority must exercise its powers in accordance with general policy guidelines as well as with those issued for the industry by the Government. It is also the Government that is required to put forward to the Authority, in the Economic and Financial Programming Document, the demands for the development of public utilities and services designed to meet the overall interests of the country.

Further accountability mechanisms have been sought in the Authorities decision-making process. All the proceedings must apply the principle of *auditur et altera pars* which provides for the presence of all the parties involved including those in the weakest position such as services users. For instance, law n. 481 of 1995 provides specific procedural guarantees in this regard[61] and requires the regulatory authority to hold regular hearings with environmental associations and trade unions, and to monitor the efficiency and effectiveness of the services and the consumer demand. These constraints are binding on the authority, because any interested party may appeal against any action that is in contrast with these instructions. Furthermore, the Administrative Courts may overturn all acts of the regulator, as well as the acts of administrative bodies.

[60] Public law is still in force for the Army, the Courts, the diplomats and the prefects.

[61] See, article 2, par. 24.

Bibliography

ANGIOLINI (1998)

V. Angiolini, *'Le braci del diritto costituzionale ed i confini della responsabilità politica'*, in *Rivista di Diritto Costituzionale* (1998) 57 ff.

ANGIOLINI (2001)

V. Angiolini, 'La difficile convivenza tra responsabilità politica e responsabilità giuridica', in N. Zanon and F. Biondi (a cura di), *Percorsi e vicende attuali della rappresentanza e della responsabilità politica* (Milano 2001).

ARMAROLI (1983)

P. Armaroli, *L'ultima crisi della legislatura* (Quad. Cost. 1983).

AZZARITI (2004)

G. Azzariti, *Politica e processi* (Giur. Cost. 2004).

BASSANINI (2000)

F. Bassanini, 'Overview of Administrative Reform and Implementation in Italy: Organization, Personnel, Pocedures and Delivery of Public Services' (2000) *International Journal of Public Administration 229 ff.*

BIN & PITRUZZELLA (2005)

R. Bin & G. Pitruzzella, *Diritto pubblico* (Padova 2005).

CALANDRA (1985)

P. Calandra, *La crisi rientrata del governo Craxi* (Quad. Cost. 1985).

CARETTI (YEAR)

P. Caretti, *'Responsabilità politica'*, in *Enc. giur. Treccani.*

CARETTI & DE SIERVO(2004)

P. Caretti & U. De Siervo, *Istituzioni di diritto pubblico* (Torino 2004).

CARLASSARE (2001)

L. Carlassare, *Governo, parlamento, Presiedente della Repubblica*, report on the national convention AIC, Palermo, 8-10 novembre 2001.

DE CARO BONELLA (1985)

C. De Caro Bonella, *Cronaca di una crisi annunciata* (Quad. Cost. 1985).

DE CARO BONELLA (1996)

C. De Caro Bonella, *I gruppi parlamentari nella XII legislatura* (Rass. parlam. 1996).

CATELANI & LABRIOLA (2001)

A. Catelani & S. Labriola, *La Costituzione materiale. Percorsi culturali e attualità di un'idea* (Milano 2001).

CLARICH (2005)

M. Clarich, *Autorità indipendenti. Bilancio e prospettive di un modello* (Bologna 2005).

CURRERI (2001)

S. Curreri, 'Rappresentanza politica e mobilità parlamentare', in N. Zanon & F. Biondi (a cura di), *Percorsi e vicende attuali della rappresentanza e della responsabilità politica* (Milano 2001) 189 ff.

FERRARA (2005)
G. Ferrara, 'Sulla responsabilità politica', in G. Azzariti (a cura di), *La responsabilità politica nell'era del maggioritario e nella crisi della statualità* (Torino 2005) 35 ff.

GROTTANELLI DE SANTI (2006)
G. Grottanelli De Santi, 'The Italian Variant of Federalism', in J. Fedke and B.S. Markesinis (ed.), *Patterns of Regionalism and Federalism* (Oxford and Portland 2006) 3 ff.

GROTTANELLI DE SANTI (1990)
G. Grottanelli De Santi, 'Indirizzo politico', in *Enc. giur. Treccani* (Roma 1990) vol. XVI.

HINE (1993)
D. Hine, *Governing Italy* (Oxford 1993).

LUPO (2004)
N. Lupo, 'Alcuni dati e qualche considerazione sulle procedure (tradizionali e nuove) di controllo parlamentare', in E. Rossi (ed.), *Maggioranza e opposizioni nelle procedure parlamentari* (Padova 2004) 125 ff.

MANZELLA (1969)
A. Manzella, *Note sulla questione di fiducia. Ancora sui rapporti fra maggioranza e opposizione* (St. parlam. e di pol. cost. 1969) n. 5-6.

MORTATI (1962)
C. Mortati, *Costituzion della Repubblica Italiana*, Enc. dir. XI (Milano 1962).

MUSSARI (1997)
R. Mussari, 'Autonomy, responsibility and New Public management in Italy', in L.R. Jones, K. Schedler and S.W. Wade (eds.), *International Perspectives on the new public management* (Greenwich 1997).

PACE (1979)
A. Pace, 'Il potere di inchiesta tra maggioranza e minoranza', in F. Cosentino, *Il parlamento nella Costituzione e nella realtà* (Milano 1979) 272 ff.

PEZZINI (1985)
B. Pezzini, 'La questione del voto segreto in parlamento', in *Dir. e soc.* (1985) 181 ff.

PITRUZZELLA (1998)
G. Pitruzzella, *Responsabilità politica*, Dig. Disc. Pubbl. (Torino 1998).

RESCIGNO (1977)
G.U. Rescigno, *Dal governo delle astensioni al governo senza fiducia e senza programma* (St. parlam. e di pol. cost. 1977).

RESCIGNO (1988)
G.U. Rescigno, 'Responsabilità (diritto costituzionale)', in *Enciclopedia del diritto* (Milano 1988) vol. XXXIX 1351 ff.

RESCIGNO (2005)
G.U. Rescigno, 'Trasformazioni e problemi della responsabilità politica oggi', in G. Azzariti (a cura di), *La responsabilità politica nell'era del maggioritario e nella crisi della statualità* (Torino 2005) 13 ff.
SARTORI (1987)
G. Sartori, *Elementi di teoria politica* (Bologna 1987).
SICARDI (2004)
S. Sicardi, 'Il problematico rapporto tra controllo parlamentare e ruolo dell'opposizione nell'esperienza repubblicana', in E. Rossi (ed.), *Maggioranza e opposizioni nelle procedure parlamentari* (Padova 2004) 139 ff.
TRAVERSA (1992)
S. Traversa, *I rapporti parlamento-governo con particolare riferimento alla parlamentarizzazione delle crisi e alla sfiducia individuale* (Rass. parlam. 1992).
VOLPI (2003)
M. Volpi, 'Responsabilità e immunità degli organi titolari di poteri politici. Un'analisi comparata', in L. Carlassarre, *Diritti e responsabilità dei soggetti investiti di potere* (Padova 2003) 24 ff.

CHAPTER 8

Political Accountability in the Netherlands

Hansko Broeksteeg

1 Introduction

Article 42, par. 2 of the Dutch Constitution provides: 'The King is inviolable, the ministers are accountable'. This article is seen as the constitutional basis for political accountability. The provision is, however, vague. It does not specify what 'accountable' exactly means, or to whom and for what ministers are accountable.

In this contribution, we would like to elucidate political accountability in the Netherlands. First, the context of political accountability, the parliamentary system, will be described. The main actors, government and parliament, will be introduced (par. 1.1). Then the history and origin of political accountability will be sketched (par. 1.2). Subsequently the questions of who is accountable (par. 2) and what for (par. 3) will be answered. The meaning and function of political accountability will be elucidated (par. 4). Furthermore, we will introduce other types and forms of accountability (par. 5). Then the role of parliament when activating political accountability will be explored (par. 6). Finally, the consequences (or sanctions) of political accountability will be described (par. 7).

1.1 Government, Parliament and Parliamentary System

The Dutch system of central government is a parliamentary system within a constitutional monarchy. In this paragraph, the actors within this system will be introduced: first the government and ministers, then parliament and finally their relationship. The link between the government and ministers can be explained by describing the constitutional doctrines of political accountability and the vote of no-confidence.

Executive powers mainly belong to the government. The ministers and the King form the government. Though the King is, according to the Constitution, part of the government, he is not involved in making, executing or implementing policy. That is a task of the ministers. The King is inviolable, or in other words immune, and ministers are politically accountable to parliament.[1] The Council of Ministers (*ministerraad*) is composed of ministers, chaired by the prime minister. The Council discusses matters of general government policy and promotes consistency of that policy.[2] The ministers (apart from the prime minister, there are in the present cabinet 15 ministers) and secretaries of State (in all 11) form the cabinet.

Ministers head a ministry. In addition, there are 'ministers without portfolio' which means that they do not head a ministry. A minister without portfolio is only made accountable for certain tasks, such as development cooperation, immigration or constitutional reform. At the moment (2007), there are three ministers without portfolio. In most departments, there are secretaries of State. A secretary of State is subordinate to the minister. He is not a member of the

---

1 Article 42 Constitution.

2 Article 45 Constitution.

Council of Ministers. He does the same job as ministers, as far as their portfolio reaches, and he has, according to the Constitution, the same powers as ministers.[3]

As we can see, the terminology concerning the government is rather confusing. The words 'government', 'cabinet' and 'Council of Ministers' have been used. To summarize the preceding: the government is comprised of the King and the ministers; the cabinet is formed by the ministers and the secretaries of State; the Council of Ministers consists of the ministers. When referring to a specific government, one usually refers to the prime minister, for example 'the second Balkenende cabinet'. The prime minister is *primus inter pares*. He has, by and large, the same legal powers as other ministers, but in practice, his position has become more and more important. He is seen as the leader of the cabinet, due to his position within the EU as a member of the European Council. Besides, the prime minister is responsible for the coordination of the cabinet policy and is the first minister to be accountable for the King and the Royal House.

The Dutch parliament, the States-General (*Staten-Generaal*), consists of two Houses: the Lower House (*Tweede Kamer der Staten-Generaal*: translated literally as Second Chamber) and the Upper House (*Eerste Kamer der Staten-Generaal*: translated literally as First Chamber). This bicameral system was instigated by the Belgians in 1815, when the Netherlands and Belgium were united. Nowadays, the Lower House is directly elected; the Upper House is indirectly elected by the members of the provincial councils.

Both Houses have, legally speaking, the same tasks and functions. Both are involved in the process of legislation; the Upper House, however, does not have the powers to initiate or amend bills. The Upper House has the right of veto on bills. They have the same parliamentary powers, such as the right to ask questions, the right of interpellation and the right of parliamentary enquiry. There are, however, some major differences between the Houses, which have grown during the parliamentary history. The Lower House has a political primacy in comparison to the Upper House. The Lower House is the first House to be consulted in the procedure of legislation and, as was mentioned before, is directly elected by the people. In addition, the Upper House is not involved in the process of cabinet formation. The Upper House has often been seen as a House of reconsideration. It is assumed that it has a special task in the process of legislation: it will guard against unconstitutional or hasty legislation.[4]

A system of proportionate representation is provided for both Houses of the States-General.[5] One of the consequences of this system is that many parties are represented in parliament. After the elections of 2006, ten political parties are represented in the Lower House; also, in the Upper House ten political parties are represented. As a consequence of the large amount of political parties repre-

---

3 Article 46 Constitution. See further par. 2.1.4.

4 Kortmann, Bovend'Eert (1993) 67.

5 Article 53, par. 1, Constitution.

sented in parliament, the formation of a new cabinet is a very complicated and lengthy procedure. This process of cabinet formation is unwritten.

The Dutch system of government is a parliamentary system. Political accountability and the *vertrouwensregel* (to be translated literally as 'confidence rule', also known as vote of no-confidence) form the cornerstones of this system. Ministers and secretaries of State are politically accountable to both Houses of parliament. This accountability is provided in article 42, par. 2 of the Dutch constitution. This provision is, as has been said, vague on questions as to what this accountability exactly means or to whom ministers are politically accountable.

Along with the vote of no-confidence, the system of checks and balances allows the government to dissolve the Houses of the States-General.[6] Dissolution of parliament, however, means in practice also the resignation of the cabinet: since 1922, it is customary that the cabinet will tender its resignation just before elections.

1.2 A Short History of Political Accountability

In the preceding paragraph, the unification of the Netherlands and Belgium in 1815 was mentioned. It did not last very long. The separation of the two countries in 1830 was laid down in a Treaty in 1839. A new Dutch constitution was necessary. The constitution of 1840 was a sign for a modern parliamentary system. A criminal accountability of ministers was introduced: ministers were made accountable under criminal law for their duty of care to ensure the correct implementation of the constitution and other laws.

The introduction of criminal accountability in 1840 did not primarily have the purpose to prosecute ministers. This can be illustrated by the so-called *contraseign* (or: contra signature). The aim of the *contraseign* was to force the King to involve ministers in his resolutions and decrees. This was possible by obliging the King to let the ministers sign his resolutions and decrees and making ministers criminally accountable for these resolutions and decrees. In this way, the powers of the King could be restricted, as these powers were made dependent on the signature of ministers. This could also have been made possible by introducing political accountability, but in 1840, the time was not ripe yet.[7] From an historical point of view, criminal accountability can thus be seen as a stepping stone to political accountability as introduced in 1848.[8]

The most important constitutional reform in Dutch constitutional history is the reform of 1848. Political accountability was introduced, as well as the possibility for the government to dissolve both Houses of the States-General. Parliament acquired important powers, such as the right of interpellation. As a result of the introduction of political accountability, ministers became account-

6 Article 64 Constitution.

7 Broeksteeg (2004) 166-169.

8 See comprehensive: Broeksteeg (2004) 125-128.

able for the government policy and they had to render account to parliament directly.[9] In practice, the changes did not, however, weaken the role and position of the King. Even when he had to share his rule-making powers with ministers, he had still autonomous powers. The position of parliament was not very strong, as there were no political parties and there was, by absence of a vote of no-confidence, no parliamentary system yet. An important component of the parliamentary system, the vote of no-confidence, was lacking. In 1866 and 1868, some major conflicts occurred between the government and the Lower House. Since these years, it is clear that a minister or a cabinet must resign when losing the confidence of a House of the States-General, unless the government dissolves this House. It is, however, not possible to dissolve the House twice for the same issue. Since 1866/1868, the parliamentary system was definitively established.[10]

Political accountability nowadays operates as the crucial link between government and parliament. It can be regarded as a keystone of the Dutch parliamentary system. Political accountability for the King is not a major constitutional issue any more. As we shall see in the paragraphs hereafter, political accountability at present is a method that allows parliament to control the government and the government departments, the civil service.

2 Accountability: The Actors

2.1 Who is Accountable?

2.1.1 Ministers

Article 42, par. 2, of the Dutch Constitution provides that ministers are accountable. They are, together with the Secretaries of State (see par. 2.1.4.), the only persons who are politically accountable towards parliament. Because the King is inviolable, he is not politically accountable. In addition, neither civil servants nor agencies are politically accountable. They cannot be obliged by parliament to render account.

There are some exceptions to this rule. Civil servants may have to render account to parliament in the case of a parliamentary enquiry. Civil servants are, on the basis of the Law on the Parliamentary Enquiry, obliged to appear before the parliamentary enquiry commission and are obliged to answer to the enquiry commission.[11] Another exception is the possibility of article 69, par. 3 Constitution: a minister may be assisted by civil servants in parliament.

9 Elzinga, Warmelink (1993) 17-18.

10 Kortmann, Bovend'Eert (1993) 2-3.

11 See for the political accountability of a minister for the declarations of civil servants towards a parliamentary enquiry commission: Tuurenhout (1992) 49.

2.1.2 Collective Political Accountability

Ministers are above all politically accountable on an individual basis. In Dutch constitutional literature, there is a discussion whether the ministers as a collective can be held accountable. Some authors argue that a collective political accountability evolves from an individual one.[12] These authors argue that the basis for collective accountability can be found in the rule of homogeneity, meaning that ministers have to act as a unit and that they commit (or bind) themselves to the decisions made in the council of ministers. The rule of homogeneity is necessary for the cabinet to form a front towards parliament and to prevent ministers from deviating from the government policy. A minister may not act contrary to decisions of the council of ministers.[13] A minister who does not want to be politically accountable for a decision of the council has to resign. That does, however, not occur often. In 1978 minister of Defence Kruisinga resigned, because he could not support a decision of the council of ministers concerning the introduction of neutron shells in Western Europe. A breach of the rule of homogeneity occurred in 2006. The Third Balkenende cabinet, consisting of CDA and VVD ministers, had already tendered its resignation, because of elections. The newly elected Lower House took a decision on the asylum policy, which acted counter to the cabinet policy. A political crisis arose: the CDA ministers in the cabinet could support the new policy concerning asylum seekers, but the VVD ministers declared that they could not support this decision. Finally, the VVD ministers were staying on, but the breach of the rule of homogeneity was a fact. This incident seemed to be dictated by the special circumstances in which the cabinet tendered its resignation and the newly elected Lower House changed sides. The incident has to be seen as a once-only event and it has been criticized in newspapers and by constitutional lawyers.

The council of ministers is, according to article 45, par. 3, of the Constitution and article 4, par. 1 of the Rules of procedure of the council of ministers, competent to deliberate and to decide on the general government's policy and it has to take care of the unity of that policy. The council of ministers is, from a constitutional point of view, only to be seen as an institute with no external relations. It has no legal relationship to other organs of government or parliament.[14] Referring to political accountability: the council of ministers as such has no relationship to the Houses of parliament and renders no account to them. The Houses of the States-General only have to deal with the individual ministers, not with the council of ministers as such.[15] Most authors state, therefore, that the council of ministers is only an intern structure (a meeting of ministers) and a

[12] See for example: Bovend'Eert (1988) 134. See for a survey, with further references: Engels (1994) 59-63.

[13] See article 12, par. 2, Rules of procedure of the council of ministers. When a minister considers that a decision of the council is incompatible to his accountability, he has, according to article 12, par. 1, to inform the council.

[14] Bovend'Eert (2002) 63.

[15] Kortmann (1987) 179-180.

collective political accountability should not be assumed. The conclusion must be that ministers are individually accountable for decisions that are taken in the council of ministers.[16]

2.1.3 Secretaries of State

Secretaries of State are, as a sort of under-ministers, in the same way politically accountable as are ministers. They are, however, only accountable for the policy fields and tasks that have been allocated to them.[17] At the same time, the minister remains accountable for the portfolio of a secretary of State (article 46, par. 2, Constitution). Parliament has the opportunity to call the minister as well as the secretary of State to account on the same subject. Van der Linden, for example, secretary of State of Foreign Affairs, had to resign when the Lower House no longer had confidence in him. When the Lower House also tended to accept a vote of no-confidence towards minister of Foreign Affairs Van den Broek, prime minister Lubbers had to threaten them with a cabinet crisis. The coalition parties then scrambled backwards (1988).[18] A secretary of State not only needs the confidence of parliament, but also the confidence of the minister. Though a minister can not dismiss a secretary of State, the latter has no other way than to resign when the first loses confidence. In 't Veld, secretary of State of Education had to resign when minister of Education Ritzen lost his confidence in In 't Veld (1993). Secretary of State of Justice Glastra van Loon had to resign after a difference of opinion with minister of Justice Van Agt (1975).

2.2 And to Whom?

Article 42, par. 2, of the Constitution is not clear as to whom accountability has to be rendered; it only states that ministers are accountable. Article 68 of the Constitution clarifies the forum to which information must be provided: the Houses of the States-General, either separately or in joint session. In Dutch constitutional literature, it has been maintained that this is a convincing indication for the question of to whom accountability has to be rendered.[19] The Dutch constitution does not distinguish in rendering accountability towards the Lower House and towards the Upper House. It endows both Houses with the powers to call ministers into account. This means that also the Upper House has these powers and that ministers are obliged to render account to the Upper House. In practice, however, parliamentary control by the Upper House is not

[16] See also: Engels (1994) 59.

[17] See article 3 of the Law of 25 January 1951 (*Wet houdende nadere voorzieningen in verband met de invoering van de ambten van minister zonder portefeuille en staatssecretaris*).

[18] See comprehensive: Groeneveld (1988) 430-439.

[19] See for example: Postma (1985) 63 and 103; Munneke (2006) 76-87.

very intensive. On the ground of its political relationship towards the Lower House, the Upper House uses its powers restrictively.[20]

3 The Object and Scope of Accountability

The Dutch constitution is not clear about the object and scope of political accountability. The Constitution gives some indication. In the first place, in article 42, par. 2: the actions and omissions of the King are attributed to ministers. In the second place, in article 44, par. 1: ministries and departments shall be headed by a minister. As a consequence, the (functioning of the) civil service is also attributed to ministers. In the Dutch literature on political accountability, there seems to be consensus that political accountability exists for: 1) the King; 2) the actions and omissions of the minister himself; 3) the civil service/the ministry. Firstly, we will introduce the constitutional adage 'no accountability without legal competences'.

3.1 Accountability and Competences: The Scope of Political Accountability

'No accountability without legal competences' is a well-known adage in Dutch constitutional law.[21] The adage provides for a limitation of political accountability. It means that when a minister has full competences on a certain object, he can be held fully accountable. When he has limited legal competences on a certain object, he can only be held accountable for the use of these competences. When he does not have legal competences on a certain topic, he can not be held accountable. We can elucidate this with an example: a minister is accountable for agencies, but only to a certain extent. This depends on the law that establishes the agency. The minister is accountable as far as he disposes of legal competences that have been provided in the law concerned. If he does not dispose of legal competences on the agency in question, he can not be held accountable.

An example is the market competition rules. In the Market Competition Law (*Mededingingswet*), the Dutch market competition authority has been established. This authority is made responsible for the execution of the Market Competition Law. The minister of Economic Affairs has some legal competences with regard to the authority. He can, for example, appoint and dismiss the managers of the authority, decide on their salary or provide lines of policy with regard to the activities of the authority. It is for the use of these legal competences that he is politically accountable. He can not, however, be held account-

[20] De Vries (2000) 165-166 and 174-175. The question whether the Upper House can apply a vote of no-confidence towards a minister, will be answered in par. 7.3.

[21] Steekhoudend ministerschap, Rapport van de externe commissie Ministeriële verantwoordelijkheid, 's-Gravenhage 1993, *TK* 1992-1993, 21 427, nrs. 40-41, 9.

able, for example, for the heading for the staff of the authority, simply because he has no legal competences with regard to the staff, or for decisions made in individual cases, again because the concerning law does not provide for ministerial competences.

3.2 Object

3.2.1 The Minister

A minister is politically accountable for his own actions and omissions. The political accountability is limited by his portfolio. The political accountability is made 'visible' by the contra signature (*contraseign*): the ministerial signature of acts and Royal decrees. A minister is accountable for the policy-making as well as for the implementation of laws, at least as far as his competences reach.

3.2.2 The Civil Service

Article 44, par. 1, of the Constitution provides that ministries are conducted by a minister. From this article can be deduced that a ministry is a hierarchical organisation and that the minister has the competence to give instructions to the civil servants in his ministry. Civil servants use their competences in the name and on authority of the minister. In the Netherlands, ministers do not have a political cabinet.

3.2.2.1 Civil Servants, Fundamental Rights and Political Accountability

A civil servant is, for the exercise of his duties, only accountable towards his minister. This also has consequences for the fundamental rights of civil servants. Civil servants have these rights, but the exercise of these rights can be limited. These limits have been laid down in article 125a of the Civil Servants Act: the exercise of the freedom of speech, the right to assemble and the right to demonstrate is limited when the 'good performance of the function of civil servant' or 'the good functioning of the civil service' can not be guaranteed.

In Dutch constitutional literature, however, a discussion is carried on the freedom of speech of civil servants. Some authors state that the freedom of speech of civil servants is wide-ranging. A civil servant should have the right to express his opinion, also when this opinion differs from that of his minister.[22] This is, however, contrary to fundamental principles as loyalty, objectivity and impartiality. As we argued before, civil servants do have a serving task. Furthermore – and according to the prevailing doctrine – when their opinion differs from the opinion of the government, the authority of the minister will be under-

[22] De Winter (1999) 1691; Peters, De Vré (2005) 348-352.

mined. The exercise of the freedom of speech has its consequences for the political accountability of a minister.[23] Therefore, we must accept that the freedom of expression of civil servants is limited.

Since 2003, there are legal provisions on the issue of whistleblowers.[24] A whistleblower is a civil servant that reveals incriminating information (in general about the department or civil servants), without an instruction or permission of the minister.[25] In that case, it concerns not the personal opinion of a civil servant, but information of serious facts, such as abuse of integrity, insufficient supervision on expenses, unsafe working situations or the bad treatment of the staff. Article 125, par. 1, Civil Servants Act provides that such a civil servant has to follow an internal procedure within the department. He has to contact his supervisor, who has to give his opinion. When this procedure does not come to a satisfactory result, the civil servant has to turn to an independent commission (Commission Integrity National Government) that will investigate the abuse. This internal procedure provides for legal protection of civil servants. It is not meant for criticism on the minister's policy or for conflicts concerning the legal position of civil servants.

3.2.2.2 The Fiction of Political Accountability and the Doctrine of Reproach

Some authors in Dutch constitutional literature have stated that political accountability is a fiction and that a so-called 'doctrine of reproach' has to be adopted.[26] What do these notions of fiction and doctrine of reproach mean? A department is a big and complex organisation. It is, in practice, impossible, that a minister can give instructions to all the civil servants and can control them personally. In that sense, ministerial control can be seen as a 'fiction'. The question is then, whether a minister can be held accountable for something he can, in practice, not influence. Following these authors, there is a fiction of political accountability: political accountability is not a realistic, workable doctrine, because the minister can not control all his civil servants.

To resolve this problem, a doctrine of reproach has been proposed as a limitation of political accountability. This doctrine runs as follows. A mistake of a civil servant can not be reproached to a minister, when he can not have knowledge of mistakes of civil servants. In such a case, it would not be fair to force the minister to resign, because of mistakes by civil servants. This illustrates, though, that the doctrine of reproach is more a matter of censure, than of political accountability. This can also be illustrated by an example in practice. In 1987, the question raised whether minister of Fishery Braks was accountable for his civil service, when it concerned actions of that civil service of which he

---

[23] Cliteur (2000) 94; Warmelink (1999) 1891-1892; Verhey (2001) 24.

[24] *Stb.* 3003, 60.

[25] See comprehensive: Bovens (2000b) 61-62.

[26] See for example: Lubberdink (1992) 12; Scheltema, Lubberdink (1980) 13; Tuurenhout (1992) 39.

did not know. Prime minister Lubbers called in the theory of reproach. During the parliamentary debate, it became evident that prime minister Lubbers had not intended to limit political accountability, but merely the possibilities for parliament to pass a vote of no-confidence. This was also the case with regard to secretary of State of Public Housing Brokx. The secretary of State stated that the actions of the civil service could not be reproached against him. However, he had to resign.[27]

3.2.2.3 Political Accountability by Civil Servants

There has been a discussion whether it is desirable that civil servants can give information to parliament directly, thus independent from the minister. Some authors state that the parliament should obtain information directly from civil servants. Parliament could obtain more information, if also civil servants were competent to supply it.[28] Several arguments have been used against this.[29] In the first place, the hierarchical relationship between minister and civil servant would no longer exist when civil servants can act independent from their minister. The advantage of this hierarchical relationship is that the information, requested by the Houses of parliament, is given by one person, i.e. the minister.[30] Parliamentary control can become very diffuse when several or a lot of civil servants can be called into account – and not only one minister. Indeed, parliament may obtain more information, but as a consequence of the large number of persons parliament can call into account, the civil service will become 'intangible'.

Furthermore, minister and civil servants can be played off against each other. The relationship and the atmosphere between minister and civil servant can deteriorate. Consequently, the authority of the minister can erode, not only the authority towards the civil servant, but also towards parliament. It is difficult for a minister to act firmly in parliament when a civil servant from his ministry gives other information than the minister himself. In addition, ministers can pass problems to their civil servants, just to keep themselves out of harm's way. It can be very practical and convenient for a minister to shift important problems to civil servants.

In other words, accountability by civil servants will interfere within the heart of parliamentary control and its effectiveness. Parliament may obtain more information, but the powers of parliament will erode. Because there could be

---

27 Broeksteeg (2004) 57-58. In this context Dutch constitutional literature sometimes mentions the Carrington-doctrine: a minister has to resign because of problems within or due to his ministry, also when it can not be reproached to him. See for example: De Ridder (1998) 123.

28 Van Maarseveen (1987) 1516; Tuurenhout (1992) 198-201; Bovens (2000a).

29 See comprehensive: Verhey (2001).

30 Warmelink (1994) 111-112.

many persons to address for information, the civil service will not longer be controllable.[31]

3.3 Agencies

Some governmental tasks, mostly policy-executing, -implementing and operating tasks, are organised within private or public agencies. These agencies are not hierarchical subordinate to the minister. They have been set up for several reasons. In the first place, an agency can be established, because the fulfilment of tasks needs to be independent. An example is the electoral council (*Kiesraad*) that enacts the election results. In the second place, a minister or a department can have their own interests in the fulfilment of tasks. Therefore, an institution as the Central Office for National Statistics is an independent agency. In the third place, it can be desirable that some governmental tasks will be fulfilled in a businesslike fashion, to operate more efficiently. In the last place, some agencies are established to confer participation of others, i.e. people of organisations outside the department. An example is some councils in the field of social security that grant the 'consumers' a say in the policy concerning social security.[32] In the Netherlands, there are more than 400 agencies.[33]

A minister is only politically accountability on matters so far as he has competences. These competences are limited when it concerns agencies; thus, the accountability of a minister is also limited. In the law that establishes agencies, the legal competences of a minister are provided. In this way, the political accountability of ministers can be determined exactly.

Because all agencies are different from each other, the legal competences of a minister do also differ and therefore also political accountability for each agency is different. There are agencies for which there is hardly any political accountability, because legal competences of ministers are lacking. An example is the electoral council that we mentioned earlier. Any concern or interference of a minister is undesirable, because of political interests of the minister in the tasks of the council. Another possibility is that there is only political accountability for the main features, the outlines of policy making. An example is the agency that operates study grants, the *Informatie Beheer Groep*. The minister has only a say with regard to some main points of the policy, such as the level of the grants. In this respect, a difference between policy and execution/operation is often made in literature. Policy should be under parliamentary control; agencies should operate the policy. In this opinion, agencies cannot formulate policy and should only have technical or organisational competences. The difference between policy and operation has, however, been criticised in literature. It can be vague what policy is and what operation is.[34]

---

31 Verhey (2001); Warmelink (1994) 111-112.

32 Boxum (1994) 259-263.

33 <www.zboregister.nl> gives a survey of agencies.

34 Zijlstra (1997) 124.

It may be clear that when political accountability for agencies is limited, this will have consequences for the parliamentary control. When political accountability lacks for certain matters, parliament cannot control these matters. As a result, parliamentary control concerning agencies is limited as well.[35] We must realise that such a lack in political accountability and by that in parliamentary control can be intended. It can be necessary that there are authorities that need to maintain distance to politics, to guarantee an independent or professional operating of tasks.

The lack of parliamentary control is also the reason that agencies have been criticised and discussed in parliament as well as in constitutional literature. This discussion can be summarised as follows. According to some authors, some operating tasks have to return into a department. Also the powers of a minister towards agencies should be strengthened and improved.[36] Recently, a government commission on agencies has proposed to abolish all agencies, except the agencies that need to be independent of political influences.[37] By returning their tasks into a department, a minister is in any case accountable. In this way, parliamentary control on the executive can be increased. Some authors state, however, on the other hand, that setting up agencies can improve parliamentary control. Parliament can concentrate on the main features of governmental policy and ministers would not render accountability on details. A minister should only prepare and determine policy. Then parliament will only control these tasks of the minister. As a result, control on incidents will decrease.[38]

Because of the number and the different forms of agencies, a bill containing general rules on agencies recently is promulgated.[39] This bill provides for many objects, such as the competences of ministers, the appointment of the members of the board, control systems, financial supervision, et cetera. It will, however, take a while before this bill can realise that agencies will be more uniform.

There are also other proposals to solve the lack of parliamentary control. Agencies should inform the minister more than nowadays, agencies should provide for annual reports, they should be more transparent. Furthermore there are proposals for supervision councils, limited terms for appointment, more financial control and provisions with respect to neglect of tasks.[40]

---

35 Bovens (2000a) 10 ff.; Zijlstra (1997) 117-119. See also: Steekhoudend ministerschap, Rapport van de externe commissie Ministeriële verantwoordelijkheid, 's-Gravenhage 1993, *TK* 1992-1993, 21 427, nrs. 40-41, 48.

36 Kummeling (2000) 32-38; Zijlstra (2004) 1980 ff.

37 Werkgroep Verzelfstandige Organisaties op Rijksniveau (Werkgroep-Kohnstamm), Een herkenbare staat: investeren in de overheid, Den Haag 2004.

38 Steekhoudend ministerschap, Rapport van de externe commissie Ministeriële verantwoordelijkheid, 's-Gravenhage 1993, *TK* 1992-1993, 21 427, nrs. 40-41, 40.

39 *Stb.* 2006, 587.

40 See for example: Steekhoudend ministerschap, Rapport van de externe commissie Ministeriële verantwoordelijkheid, 's-Gravenhage 1993, *TK* 1992-1993, 21 427, nrs. 40-41, 49-51; Werkgroep Verzelfstan-

4 Obligations Resulting from Accountability

Now, after describing the scope and object of political accountability, we can deduce obligations resulting from accountability. The Dutch statesman and founding father of the Dutch 1848-Constitution, Johan Rudolf Thorbecke, stated that being accountable primarily means to answer questions posed by (members of) parliament.[41] More Dutch authors, such as Lagemans, Buijs and Van Maarseveen, defined political accountability as the obligation to give answers to parliament.[42] This view of political accountability corresponds to article 68 of the Constitution: 'Ministers and Secretaries of State shall provide orally or in writing the Houses either separately or in joint session, with any information requested by one or more members, provided that the provision of such information does not conflict with the interests of the State.'

Also in modern constitutional literature, the meaning of political accountability as answering and giving inquiries to parliament has often been described, but also extended. For example a commission on constitutional reform, the commission-Scheltema, defined being accountable as being responsible, being answerable as well as elucidating, explaining, justifying and defending policy decisions.[43]

Furthermore, being accountable means the obligation to appear in parliament. When parliament – the Lower House as well as the Upper House – wants a minister to appear in parliament, a minister is obliged to. Although the Constitution does not provide for this obligation, the threatening of the motion of no-confidence implies this.

5 Other Forms of Public Accountability

Some authors state that the concept of political accountability loses significance. Political accountability would not satisfy in modern times. In the first place, it seems that the civil service exercises its competences fairly independent. The civil service has been professionalized in the last decades. In addition, political accountability should, as has already been mentioned, be a fiction: the civil service has grown that much, that it cannot be held fully in control by the minister. As a consequence, parliament cannot control adequately the quality of the (fulfilment of tasks of the) civil service. This means that the purpose of political accountability, making parliamentary control on the civil service

dige Organisaties op Rijksniveau (Werkgroep-Kohnstamm), Een herkenbare staat: investeren in de overheid, Den Haag 2004, 8-9 and 39.

41 Thorbecke (1841) 253.

42 Lagemans (1855) 30; Buijs (1883) 361; Van Maarseveen (1965) 498.

43 Steekhoudend ministerschap, Rapport van de externe commissie Ministeriële verantwoordelijkheid, 's-Gravenhage 1993, *TK* 1992-1993, 21 427, nrs. 40-41, 8.

possible, can not be achieved sufficiently nowadays.[44] In the second place, it is the opinion of Bovens that political accountability is a too vertical and hierarchical concept that needs to horizontalise.[45] This opinion follows from the idea that the government is not longer an essential participant in making policy, but only a partner that makes its policy together with other social participants. We can refer to the idea of the civil society and the development from 'government' to 'governance'. There are lots of institutions outside the ministerial departments that pursue their public policy. The development of the number of agencies impairs the concept of political accountability as ministers lose their grip on these agencies. Besides, this concept loses significance as a result of EU-decision making: ministers cannot be held fully to account for decisions that have been taken in the First Pillar of the EU. Because of this development, other forms of public (and not political) accountability would be necessary. Some forms that have been discussed in Dutch legal literature are mentioned here.[46]

In the first place we can follow the discussion as has been mentioned in par. 3.3.: several means can complete political accountability for (for example) agencies. This can be internal control within the agency. We have mentioned annual reports, supervision councils, financial control and provisions with respect to neglect of tasks. These means can make more public control on agencies possible. They can create more transparency on the fulfilment of tasks by agencies.

In the second place there can be accountability through new public institutions. Scheltema argues that a new independent supervisor (A Quality Chamber) has to be established, supervising the quality of the operating by the government. This Quality Chamber could test independently the functioning of the civil service. An independent institute can act as an alternative or as an addition to political accountability.[47] A proposal as such, would, according to other authors, make the functioning of the governmental department more complicated. New control mechanisms can result in more bureaucracy. The question rises why there is not more attention to an improvement of parliamentary control as the panacea for the lack of accountability. Furthermore, there is already an institution that acts like a Quality Chamber, namely the National Audit Office. This Office can investigate the efficiency and effectiveness of the operation of policy. This includes for example agencies.[48]

In the third place, there is discussion on accountability towards persons or parties such as councils of participants or clients. It concerns people that are the 'consumers' of the governmental policy, the interested parties. This form is often seen as horizontal accountability, as mentioned before. There are different forms of accountability to interested parties: participation, public inquiry procedures, complaints committees or departments or consumer councils. Verhey

44 Scheltema (2000) 1862-1863.

45 Bovens (1998); Bovens (2000a) 15.

46 Verhey, Verheij (2005) 236-237.

47 Scheltema (2000) 1866-1867.

48 Heringa (2001) 155 ff.; Verhey (2001) 30.

and Verheij warn, though, that these forms of horizontal accountability may not lead to regulatory capture. The institution can be imprisoned by interest and lobby groups.[49]

In the fourth place, transparency is a theme is Dutch legal literature. Institutions with governmental tasks clarify how they fulfil their tasks by annual reports, on websites, et cetera. Clear procedure rules and transparency standards are, however, lacking. Governmental information can be claimed with an appeal on the Law publicity of administration.[50]

The question is whether these forms of public accountability can be seen as a (full) alternative to political accountability. We have seen that these forms of public accountability have their disadvantages. Besides, these themes are an object of discussion, as their importance and value is not clear yet. Moreover, these forms of public accountability do not guarantee democratic legitimacy of policy-making, for example by democratic influence in the procedure of by policy-making or parliamentary control. Therefore, we have to conclude that these interesting forms of public accountability can be useful as complementary to political accountability, but not as an alternative or a substitute.

6 Activating Accountability: Parliamentary Control and the Process of Rendering Account

6.1 Parliamentary Control

Political accountability is directly related to political control. Political accountability can be activated by political control by parliament. When parliament uses its possibility to control, ministers are obliged to render account. The States-General can use several instruments of political control: the right to pose questions, the right of interpellation and the right of parliamentary inquiry. Article 68 of the Constitution is the basis of the right to pose questions and the right of interpellation.[51] In this article, it is provided that 'Ministers and State Secretaries shall provide orally or in writing the Houses either separately or in joint session, with any information requested by one or more members, provided that the provision of such information does not conflict with the interests of the State'. Article 70 Constitution is the basis of the parliamentary enquiry: 'The two Houses shall jointly and separately have the right of inquiry to be regulated by Act of Parliament'. The rights to pose questions, of interpellation and of parliamentary inquiry have been elaborated in the Law on the Parliamentary Inquiry and the Rules of Procedure of the Lower House and the Upper

49 Verhey, Verheij (2005) 251.

50 See for example: Damen (2000) 1813 ff.

51 See for these rights: Postma (1985).

House.[52] Not only the Lower House of the States-General, but also the Upper House, has these rights, though they do not call in these rights as frequently as the Lower House does. The Upper House has never executed a parliamentary enquiry and calls in the right of interpellation on average of only once every several years.

The right to be informed is passive as well as active. This means, according to the government, that ministers are required, of their own accord, to give information to parliament when parliament needs the information for fulfilling its tasks properly.[53]

As article 68 provides, information may not conflict with the 'interests of the State'.[54] This is the only limitation of article 68. Information can be refused with an appeal to the interest of the State. Within the 'interest of the State' comes the unity of the government, the safety of the State, trade secrets, the protection of private life, information on criminal investigation or information that can not be published because of a legal obligation of secrecy.[55] The 'interest of the State' is thus a large concept. It can contain different meanings.

Finally, the obligation to give information and the obligation to render account have to be distinguished. Article 68 Constitution provides that a minister has to give information to parliament, when parliament so requires. A minister is, however, not obliged to render account, when the subject of accountability is not within his competences (or portfolio). He has to give information to parliament, but he may desist from rendering account.[56]

6.2 The Process of Rendering Account

In Dutch literature, it has been stated that the process of rendering account can, in theory, be divided in three stages.[57] The first stage is the information stage. Members of parliament can pose questions or call in the right of interpellation. Ministers are obliged to give the information required by (the member of) parliament. The second stage is the debate stage. In this stage parliament and ministers will, on the basis of the information that has been given, debate. This means arguing and criticizing by parliament and explaining, justifying and defending policy decisions by ministers. The third stage is the sanctioning stage. This stage will be explained in paragraph 7.1. In practice, it will not always be necessary to pass through all stages. Parliament can hold the view that giving information or having a debate will satisfy. Moreover, all stages can be mixed.

---

[52] Articles 133-150 Rules of Procedure of the Lower House; articles 128-140 Rules of Procedure of the Upper House.

[53] *TK* 1985-1986, 19 014, nr. 5, 6.

[54] *TK* 1976-1977, 14 225 (R 1051), nr. 3; Munneke (2006).

[55] Bovend'Eert (2002) 88.

[56] See also: Munneke (2006) 76-87.

[57] Elzinga (1994b) 42-44.

7 Consequences

7.1 Sanctioning Stage

In the preceding paragraph the sanctioning stage is mentioned. It is the last stage in the process of rendering account. The ultimate sanction is a dismissal of a minister, after passing a motion of censure by parliament. This is called the *vertrouwensregel* (confidence rule, or vote of no-confidence): when one of the Houses of the States-General does not have sufficient confidence in a minister, the minister has to resign. As a matter of course, a motion of censure as such is seldom tabled.

The consequences of rendering account are broader than only the vote of no-confidence. Other consequences of the process of political accountability can be the amendment or rejection of a bill, the acceptance a motion, the amendment of a budgetary bill, et cetera. In addition, political sanctions can be imposed, such as not returning in a new cabinet, no promotion from secretary of State to minister or a lower position on the election lists.

7.2 Vote of No-confidence

The vote of no-confidence, from which the historical background has been described in par. 1.2, provides that a minister who no longer has the confidence of one of the Houses of the States-General has to resign. The vote of no-confidence can be applied to an individual minister, an individual secretary of State and to the cabinet as a whole.[58] Parliament can call in the vote of no-confidence at any time. The calling in of the vote is not limited by procedural rules. It is a political and not a legal issue whether the vote will be called in. The calling in of the vote of no-confidence is a subjective assessment by parliament. Also party political motives can play a role when calling in a vote of no-confidence. Van Aardenne, for example, minister of Economic Affairs in the First Lubbers Cabinet, had to render account in a parliamentary enquiry. The enquiry commission was of the opinion that Van Aardenne deluded parliament. A motion of censure seemed unavoidable. Yet, Van Aardenne was vice prime minister on behalf of the VVD. The VVD threatened a cabinet crisis, if the other party in the cabinet coalition, the CDA, would support a vote of no-confidence. Van Aardenne could serve out his time as a minister, but was not appointed in the Second Lubbers Cabinet. This makes clear that the passing of a vote of no-confidence is, to a large extent, dominated by political motives and that it is not a legal issue.

In the Netherlands, the vote is (usually) formulated negatively: no minister can maintain his position against the will of the majority of the Lower House. Confidence in a minister is assumed, until a vote of no-confidence has been

58 The prime minister does not have a special role when parliament applies the vote of no-confidence. In practice, he will debate on behalf of the cabinet with the parliament.

passed. This is also the reason that a procedure of investiture is unknown in Dutch parliamentary law. In addition, it is not usual for a minister to ask confidence of parliament. Only once has there been a minister, minister Sorgdrager of Justice in 1995, that asked for the confidence of parliament. This request did not lead to a vote of confidence, but the chairmen of the coalition parties in the Lower House declared explicitly that they did not have no-confidence.

The vote of no-confidence can be seen as a sanction on political accountability, but the vote is a constitutional doctrine, apart from the doctrine of political accountability.[59] Ministers can be accountable, though the vote of no-confidence is not at issue. Parliament can dismiss a minister, though he has rendered account sufficiently. In addition, it is possible to call in the vote, when a minister is not accountable any more for a certain topic, but when he is assigned to another portfolio in the mean time. This means that parliament can pass a vote of no-confidence, even when a minister is, in the meanwhile, accountable for another department. In 1988, for example, the Lower House passed a vote of no-confidence against minister of Defence Van Eekelen, because of an issue concerning him as a minister of Foreign Affairs in an earlier cabinet period. In 2002 minister of Defence Korthals resigned, because of an issue concerning him as a minister of Justice in an earlier cabinet.[60] Political accountability and the vote of no-confidence do thus have a relationship to one another, but they have to be distinguished; they have their own role in the parliamentary system.[61] There is a possibility to call in the vote of no-confidence, but whether parliament will is a political question.

No-confidence can appear by accepting a vote of disapproval by parliament. The main alternative is the lack of support of the adherent political party in parliament. In the parliamentary practice, there are several examples of resigning ministers, due to this lack of support. See for example the dismissal of secretary of State Brokx (1986), minister Van Eekelen (1988), secretary of State Van der Linden (1988), secretary of State Ter Veld (1993) and secretary of State Nijs (2004).

In the period 1945-2006, ten cabinets have had to resign, of which five were due to a lack of confidence. Five cabinets had to resign, due to internal conflicts. In the same period, 52 ministers and secretaries of State resigned, of which 13 were because there was a lack of confidence of parliament, a coalition party in parliament or the adherent party of the minister. The other 39 ministers resigned because of an appointment elsewhere, health reasons or a difference of opinion within the cabinet or the department.[62]

---

59 Bovend'Eert (2002) 33-34; Broeksteeg (2004) 24-30 and 352-359.

60 Broeksteeg (2004) 25.

61 Steekhoudend ministerschap, Rapport van de externe commissie Ministeriële verantwoordelijkheid, 's-Gravenhage 1993, *TK* 1992-1993, 21 427, nrs. 40-41, 12.

62 Broeksteeg (2004) 27-30.

7.3 The Vote of No-confidence and the Upper House

In paragraph 2.2, it has been explained that ministers are accountable towards the Lower House and the Upper House. However, constitutional lawyers discuss the question whether the Upper House can apply the vote of no-confidence. The Upper House has a reticent position, compared to the Lower House that is far more political than the Upper House. In the past, the Upper House has applied the vote of no-confidence several times, but since 1875, only in 1958. In 1958 secretary of State Kranenburg had to resign after the so-called Helmet affair. Kranenburg was secretary of State of Defence and bought inferior helmets for the armed forces. In recent years, however, the Upper House caused some cabinet crises. The Second Kok Cabinet tended to resign in 1999 when the Upper House rejected a bill concerning the introduction of a referendum. The cabinet breach could be healed. In 2005, De Graaf, minister for constitutional reform, resigned when the Upper House rejected a bill that would introduce directly elected mayors.

According to some authors, the Upper House has left the application of the vote to the Lower House. It would not be a task of the senate, in its reticent position, to apply the vote of no-confidence.[63] Kummeling has argued that a vote of no-confidence may only be tabled by the cabinet, not by the Upper House.[64] Most authors however, maintain that the vote of no-confidence can fully be applied between Upper House and cabinet. There is a distinction between the appliance of the vote and the reticent use of it. In addition, there are no constitutional written or unwritten rules, which provide that there would be no vote of no-confidence. Furthermore, the government has affirmed the existence of the vote of no-confidence at the constitutional revision in 1983. Besides, the Upper House is co-legislator and controls the government. Then, it has to have legal powers towards government. The Upper House would however not dispose of significant powers, when this House could not apply the vote of no-confidence.[65]

8 Summary and Conclusions

By calling ministers to account, the parliament can control the government's office and influence the policy-making of the minister. The minister has to give information to parliament. Being accountable is, however, more than giving information. It means the obligation to answer and explain, justify and defend policy decisions. Political accountability and the vote of no-confidence are the central elements in the Dutch parliamentary system.

In 1848, when political accountability was introduced, the importance of political accountability concerned the relationship between King and ministers.

---

63 Oud (1967) 303; Van Zanen (1985) 376.

64 Kummeling (1992) 23.

65 Kortmann (2001) 295-296; Postma (1987) 91; De Vries (2000) 368-371.

Nowadays it mainly concerns the relationship between ministers and parliament. The government's administration has been attributed to a minister. Parliament can control the administration via the minister. The preceding means that political accountability has to be seen as a key issue of the parliamentary democracy. Political accountability is indispensable for parliamentary democracy. It forms the essence of the parliamentary democracy.

Bibliography

BOVEND'EERT (1988)

P.P.T. Bovend'Eert, *Regeerakkoorden en regeringsprograms*, diss. Nijmegen ('s-Gravenhage 1988).

BOVEND'EERT (2001)

P.P.T. Bovend'Eert e.a. (eds.), *Grensverleggend staatsrecht (Kortmann-bundel)* (Deventer 2001).

BOVEND'EERT (2002)

P.P.T. Bovend'Eert, *Ministeriële verantwoordelijkheid* (Nijmegen 2002).

BOVENS (1998)

M.A.P. Bovens, *The quest for responsibility: accountability and citizenship in complex organisations* (Cambridge 1998).

BOVENS (2000A)

M.A.P. Bovens, *De vierde macht revisited* (Utrecht 2000).

BOVENS (2000B)

M.A.P. Bovens, 'Bij de duivel te biecht? Kanttekeningen bij de voorstellen voor klokkenluidersvoorzieningen' (2000) *Bestuurswetenschappen*, 61 ff.

BOVENS (2006)

M. Bovens, 'Analysing and Assessing Public Accountability, A Conceptual Framework, European Governance Papers', <www.connex-network.org>.

BOXUM (1994)

J.L. Boxum, 'Ministeriële verantwoordelijkheid en zelfstandige bestuursorganen', in D.J. Elzinga (ed.), *Ministeriële verantwoordelijkheid in Nederland* (Zwolle 1994) 259-263.

BROEKSTEEG (2004)

J.L.W. Broeksteeg, *Verantwoordelijkheid en aansprakelijkheid in het staatsrecht* (Deventer 2004).

BUIJS (1883)

J.T. Buijs, *De Grondwet, deel 1* (Arnhem 1883).

CLITEUR (2000)

P.B. Cliteur, 'Vrijheid van meningsuiting voor ambtenaren in Nederland' (2000) *TBP* 94 ff.

DAMEN (2000)

L.J.A. Damen, 'Openbaarheid van bestuur in discussie', (2000) *NJB* 1813 ff.

ELZINGA (1994A)

D.J. Elzinga (ed.), *Ministeriële verantwoordelijkheid in Nederland* (Zwolle 1994).

ELZINGA (1994B)

D.J. Elzinga, 'De politieke ministeriële verantwoordelijkheid' in D.J. Elzinga (ed.), *Ministeriële verantwoordelijkheid in Nederland* (Zwolle 1994) 31-49.

ELZINGA, WARMELINK (1993)
D.J. Elzinga, H.G. Warmelink, *Het Nederlandse parlementaire stelsel* (Nijmegen 1993).

ENGELS (1994)
J.W.M. Engels, 'De collectieve ministeriële verantwoordelijkheid', in D.J. Elzinga (ed.), *Ministeriële verantwoordelijkheid in Nederland* (Zwolle 1994) 59-63.

GROENEVELD (1988)
H.A. Groeneveld, *De staatssecretaris in Nederland 1948-1988*, diss. Amsterdam (Deventer 1988).

HERINGA (2001)
A.W. Heringa, 'Ministeriële verantwoordelijkheid en parlementaire controle', in P.P.T. Bovend'Eert, J.W.A. Fleuren, H.R.B.M. Kummeling, *Grensverleggend staatsrecht (Kortmann-bundel)* (Deventer 2001) 155 ff.

KORTMANN (1987)
C.A.J.M. Kortmann, *De Grondwetsherzieningen 1983 en 1987* (Deventer 1987).

KORTMANN (2001)
C.A.J.M. Kortmann, Constitutioneel recht (Deventer 2001).

KORTMANN, BOVEND'EERT (1993)
C.A.J.M. Kortmann, P.P.T. Bovend'Eert, *The Kingdom of the Netherlands, An Introduction to Dutch Constitutional Law* (Deventer/ Boston 1993).

KUMMELING (1992)
H.R.B.M. Kummeling, *De Nederlandse Eerste Kamer, preadvies voor de vereniging van de vergelijkende studie van het recht in België en Nederland* (Zwolle 1992).

LAGEMANS (1855)
H.G. Lagemans, *De leer der ministeriële verantwoordelijkheid en hare toepassing in het Nederlandsche staatsregt* (Leiden 1855).

LUBBERDINK (1992)
H.G. Lubberdink, *De betekenis van de ministeriële verantwoordelijkheid voor de organisatie van het openbaar bestuur* (Arnhem 1992).

VAN MAARSEVEEN (1965)
H.Th.J.F. van Maarseveen, 'Ministeriële verantwoordelijkheid' (1965) *NJB* 495 ff.

VAN MAARSEVEEN (1978)
H.Th.J.F. van Maarseveen, 'Reidans der niet-verantwoordelijken' (1978) *NJB* 1516.

MUNNEKE (2006)
S.A.J. Munneke, *Inlichtingenplichten en verschoningsgronden in het staatsrecht* (Deventer 2006).

OUD (1967)
P.J. Oud, *Het constitutioneel recht van het Koninkrijk der Nederlanden* (Zwolle 1967).

PETERS, DE VRÉ (2005)
J. Peters, I. de Vré, 'Vrijheid van meningsuiting van ambtenaren bedreigd' (2005) *NJB* 348ff.

POSTMA (1985)
A. Postma, *Het interpellatie- en vragenrecht van de Eerste en Tweede Kamer* (Groningen 1985).

POSTMA (1987)
A. Postma, 'De Eerste Kamer timmert aan de weg', (1987) *Namens* 91 ff.

DE RIDDER (1998)
J. de Ridder, 'Verzelfstandiging en het primaat van de politiek' (1998) *Beleid en Maatschappij* 123 ff.

VAN ROSSEM, VERHEY, VERHEIJ (2005)
A.A. van Rossem, L.F.M. Verhey, N. Verheij, *Toezicht, Preadviezen voor de NJV* (Deventer 2005).

SCHELTEMA (2000)
M. Scheltema, 'Voldoet de ministeriële verantwoordelijkheid nog bij een professionele overheidsorganisatie?' (2000) *NJB* 1861 ff.

SCHELTEMA, LUBBERDINK (1980)
M. Scheltema, H.G. Lubberdink, *Ministeriële verantwoordelijkheid en parlementaire controle, in: Parlementaire controle en democratie in de verzorgingsstaat* (Nijmegen 1980).

THORBECKE (1841)
J.R. Thorbecke, *Aanteekening op de Grondwet, deel I* (Den Haag 1841).

TUURENHOUT (1992)
M.E. Tuurenhout, *Parlementaire controle en ambtelijke verantwoordelijkheid* (Arnhem 1992).

VERHEY (2001)
L.F.M. Verhey, *De zwoegers uit het vooronder, Over ambtelijke taakuitoefening, ministeriële verantwoordelijkheid en parlementaire controle* (Deventer 2001).

VERHEY, VERHEIJ (2005)
L.F.M. Verhey, N. Verheij, 'De macht van de marktmeesters', in A.A. van Rossem, L.F.M. Verhey, N. Verheij, *Toezicht, Preadviezen voor de Nederlandse Juristenvereniging* (Deventer 2005) 251 ff.

DE VRIES (2000)
F. de Vries, *De staatsrechtelijke positie van de Eerste Kamer* (Groningen 2000).

WARMELINK (1999)
H.G. Warmelink, 'Vrijheid van meningsuiting voor ambtenaren!' (1999) *NJB* 1891-1892.

DE WINTER (1999)
R.E. de Winter, 'Vrijheid van meningsuiting voor ambtenaren!' (1999) *NJB* 1691.

WITTEVEEN, KUMMELING, STROINK (2000)
W.J. Witteveen, H.R.B.M. Kummeling, F.A.M. Stroink, *Het primaat van de politiek, Publikaties van de staatsrechtkring, Staatsrechtconferenties* (Deventer 2000).

ZANEN VAN (1985)
J.H.C. van Zanen, 'De Eerste Kamer en de vertrouwensregel, of je weet maar nooit hoe een koe een haas vangt' (1985) *Ars Aequi* 372 ff.

ZIJLSTRA (1997)
S.E. Zijlstra, *Zelfstandige bestuursorganen in een democratische rechtsstaat* ('s-Gravenhage 1997).

ZIJLSTRA (2004)
S.E. Zijlstra, 'Weg met de zelfstandige bestuursorganen?' (2004) *NJB* 1980 ff.

CHAPTER 9

Political Accountability in Poland

Ryszard Piotrowski

1 Constitutional Framework

According to the 1997 Constitution, the Republic of Poland is a democratic state ruled by law. The system of power rests on the principle of the separation and balance of powers. The Constitution recognizes the inherent, inalienable and inviolable dignity of people as a source of rights and freedoms. The fulfilment of those values and principles makes indispensable a democratically elected Parliament and politically accountable Government.[1]

The Constitution vests legislative power in the Sejm and the Senate, executive power in the President and Council of Ministers, and judicial power – in courts and tribunals. Thus the Sejm shares its legislative function with the Senate.

The Sejm is composed of 460 deputies, elected in universal, equal, direct and proportional elections, conducted by secret ballot. The Senate consists of 100 senators, elected in universal and direct elections, by secret ballot. According to the Constitution, the deputies and the senators are representatives of the Nation and are not bound by the instructions of their electorate. The term of office, that is the term during which the mandate of the Sejm remains valid, amounts to 4 years and commences on the day the Sejm assembles for the first sitting after the election. It ends on the day preceding the assembly of the Sejm of the succeeding term of office. There is no interim period. The Sejm works in accordance with the principle of permanence – there is no division of the term of office into sessions and periods between sessions. The mandate of the Senate begins and expires together with the mandate of the Sejm. The Sejm may shorten its term of office by a resolution passed by a majority of at least two-thirds of the votes of the statutory number of deputies (i.e. the resolution must be adopted by no less than 307 deputies). This means a simultaneous shortening of the term of office of the Senate.

The legislative competence of both Chambers is not symmetrical. The Constitution provides the Sejm with a dominant role in the legislative process. The inequality of the two Chambers of the Polish Parliament is also expressed in the fact that only the Sejm is vested with the right to control the Council of Ministers.

The Constitution shapes a delicate system of balance between powers of the state, which is described as a parliamentary-cabinet system with a slight inclination towards the presidential system. Only the Parliament can pass statutes to which the constitution grants a special role in the system of sources of law as regards the determination of the legal position of the citizens.

Neither the President nor the government has the authority to proclaim acts, which would have the force of statute (excluding regulations which have the force of statute proclaimed by the President during martial law). The activity of Parliament is submitted to the control of the Constitutional Tribunal.

---

1 This paragraph is based upon my descriptive remarks in Piotrowski (1999).

According to the Constitution the President is the supreme representative of the Republic and the guarantor of the continuity of state authority. He is elected for a five-year term of office in universal, equal, and direct elections, conducted by secret ballot. The President does not bear political responsibility towards the Parliament nor either of the two Chambers. The National Assembly, formed by the Sejm and the Senate sitting together, has the power (by a majority of at least two-thirds of the statutory number of members) to bring an indictment against the President for and infringement of the Constitution or statute, as well as for the commission of an offence. The President is held accountable to the Tribunal of State. On the day on which the National Assembly adopts the respective resolution, he is suspended from discharging all functions of his office.

The Sejm's confidence (expressed by an absolute majority vote in the presence of at least half of the statutory number of deputies) forms an indispensable premise for the existence of government appointed by the President.

The President may shorten the term of office of the Sejm only in instances specified in the Constitution. The President is obliged to make such a decision if, during the creation of the government it should become clear that the Sejm is not in a position to grant a vote of confidence even with a simple majority vote, in the presence of at least half of statutory number of deputies. The President may also decide to shorten the Sejm's term of office (he has the power but not the obligation to do so) if, after 4 months from the day of the submission of the budget to the Sejm, it has not been presented to the President for signature.

2 The Notion of Political Accountability in Polish Constitutional Law

The terms 'political accountability' and 'political responsibility' are subsumed in Polish constitutional law in the notion of 'parliamentary accountability', i.e. the accountability of the Cabinet (Council of Ministers) and its individual members to the Parliament or, to be more precise, to its lower house, the Sejm. As put by L. Garlicki, 'the essence of political (parliamentary) accountability lies in its dependence on the Sejm's political discretion.' This accountability 'may be invoked for any reason and at any time, provided that a majority capable to pass an appropriate resolution emerges at the Sejm.'[2]

Article 157 of the Polish Constitution reads:

1) the members of the Council of Ministers shall be collectively responsible to the Sejm for the activities of the Council of Ministers;
2) the members of the Council of Ministers shall be individually responsible to the Sejm for those matters falling within their competence or assigned to them by the Prime Minister.[3]

---

[2] Garlicki (2006) 288.

[3] *The Constitution of the Republic of Poland* (1999).

This accountability of the Cabinet – which involves the penalty of removal from office – extends to the policies pursued and to the manner in which power is exercised. When the Cabinet is held to account politically, this means that a new majority has emerged at the Sejm, capable of forming a government that has a new composition and pursues a basically new agenda. Under the Constitution, political accountability may apply to individual Cabinet ministers (the Sejm may pass a vote of no confidence in a single minister) and the Cabinet *in corpore* (the Sejm may pass a constructive vote of no confidence in the Cabinet, i.e., appoint a new Prime Minister and a new Cabinet, its makeup indicated by the new Prime Minister, by a majority of 231 out of the 460 Deputies). To describe this kind of accountability, the constitutional analyses published in Poland apply the terms 'parliamentary accountability'[4] and 'political responsibility,'[5] which in the present paper will be equated with the notion of 'political accountability,' as most appropriate for the purpose of comparative studies.

Individual ministers are also politically accountable to the Prime Minister, who may request their resignation at any time and for any reason. If such request remains unheeded, the Prime Minister approaches the President who changes the composition of the Cabinet in accordance with the Prime Minister's request.

In addition to the political accountability, there is also constitutional accountability, understood as being answerable for a breach of law.

Article 156 of the Polish Constitution reads:

1) the members of the Council of Ministers shall be accountable to the Tribunal of State for an infringement of the Constitution or statutes, as well as for the commission of an offence connected with the duties of his office.
2) on the motion of the President of the Republic or at least 115 Deputies, resolution to bring a member of the Council of Ministers to account before the Tribunal of State shall be passed by the Sejm by a majority of three-fifths of the statutory number of Deputies.

English-language constitutional analyses published in Poland describe this answerability with the term 'constitutional accountability,'[6] to which are held – before the Tribunal of State – Cabinet members, the Polish President, the Governor of the Nation Bank of Poland, the Head of the Supreme Audit Chamber, members of the National Council for Radio and Television, as well as persons appointed by the Prime Minister to run a ministry and the Commander-in-Chief. Appointed by the Sejm from among its Deputies and Senators, the Tribunal of State is an organ of the judiciary; in addition to removal from office, it may also impose other sanctions specified in statutes. As with political account-

[4] Sarnecki, Szmyt, Witkowski (1999) 167 ff.

[5] Piotrowski (1999) 10.

[6] Sarnecki, Szmyt, Witkowski (1999), *ibidem*.

ability, the exercise of constitutional accountability is premised on a political decision of the Sejm.

Cabinet members bear both political and constitutional accountability. In addition to this differentiation, the notion of 'political accountability' happens to be used in public debate in a broader meaning – as political accountability of, e.g., Sejm deputies or political parties towards voters, who may refuse their support and thus express disapproval of political elites' performance. In that particular meaning, as the elites' answerability for the shape of Poland's post-communist systemic transformation, the notion of political accountability has been at centre stage of public debate since the latest parliamentary election (September 2005).

On the other hand, the Cabinet's political accountability *to Parliament* has failed to attract any wider interest among the public. This, however, cannot be said of subjecting to the Sejm's control the Governor of the National Bank of Poland, by means of summoning him to appear before a Sejm investigative committee. The Sejm has adopted a resolution to that effect, but it was subsequently appealed by the opposition to the Constitutional Tribunal, which struck down the resolution as violating the central bank's autonomy and, in consequence, being unconstitutional.

Under the present Constitution of 1997, the mechanism of the Cabinet's political accountability has not been effectively used in even a single case so far. Ten motions to hold ministers politically accountable were presented during the third Sejm (1997-2000), and 18 during the fourth Sejm (2001-2005). None received the required majority support, which, according to L. Garlicki, exposes them as being part of a political game.[7] Neither was any Cabinet change effected in the period via a constructive vote of no confidence.

The existing constitutional arrangements are so effective in obstructing the exercise of political accountability as to enable a relatively long operation of minority Cabinets (in situations where no majority emerges at the Sejm that would be capable of appointing a new government). The system of proportional representation is conducive to the Sejm's political diversification, and this renders it more difficult to assemble a constitutionally required number of votes needed to appoint a new Cabinet. A minority government has a limited capacity to attend to the country's problems, only seeking to make it to the end of the Parliament's term – and the Constitution favours that. The existing systemic arrangements foster not so much the efficiency of government as its stability. According to the opinion expressed in the report on the basic problems referring to the application of the Polish Constitution 'practice has confirmed the usefulness of constructive vote of no confidence as a factor for stabilizing the government's functioning. This results from the experiences of the minority governments'.[8]

---

7 *Op.cit.*, 291.

8 Cf. Działocha (2006) 86.

This state of affairs, however, is not without influence upon society's attitude towards the authorities. Asked in a 2003 poll about who rules Poland, respondents pointed to the Cabinet (24%), Parliament (17%), corruption-prone cabals (14%), the President (13%), financial elites (12%), and 9% said the country was ruled by no one.[9] In 2005, 52% of those questioned believed that non-democratic regime might be better than democracy.[10] Coming as a related development was a low turnout at the recent parliamentary election, in 2005, which enabled a party with a relatively small backing (as a proportion of all those eligible to vote) to form the government. Initially, it operated as a single-party minority Cabinet (protected by the constitutional requirement of a constructive vote of no confidence, which the bickering opposition found exceedingly difficult to meet). In May 2006, a coalition was formed to provide majority support for the Cabinet.

3 Government and its Accountability

The Polish Constitution of 1997 vests the power to form the Cabinet (Council of Ministers) with the President and a parliamentary majority – and if the Sejm (the lower house of the bicameral legislature) fails either to support the Presidential initiative or appoint the government on its own, the parliament's term is cut short. This is a parliamentary system, with its typical duality of the executive branch and the government's dependence on a parliamentary majority,[11] although under the present Constitution it contains a number of important modifications, such as: presidential elections by general ballot; no role whatever for the Senate in forming the government and overseeing its activity; a mechanism of 'constructive vote of no confidence' to make frequent changes of the Cabinet more difficult (the government cannot be brought down without simultaneously indicating a new Prime Minister).

The Constitution provides for three stages of the government formation processes, which is set in motion by the resignation of the previous Cabinet (this is occasioned by one of these occurrences: the first sitting of a newly elected Sejm; the tendering of resignation by the Prime Minister; the defeat at the Sejm of a motion of confidence in a newly formed government; a successful vote of no confidence).

Involved in the government-formation process are usually more parties than one, because under proportional representation none of the rival parties manages to win a Sejm majority sufficient to rule on its own. Negotiations between the parties intending to form the Cabinet are sealed with a coalition agreement (after the latest parliamentary election in 2005, the talks held by the two winning parties – which, incidentally, failed to produce a new Cabinet – were broadcast live on TV).

---

9 Cf. CBOS opinion-poll centre release, October 2003.

10 Cf. CBOS opinion-poll centre release, November 2005.

11 Cf. Grzybowski (1999) 151; Sartori (1994).

The content of the Prime Minister's inaugural address ('expose') is determined by the PM himself, who consults the government programme with his political party and the leaders of coalition partners. In subsequent actual practice the lines of government activity are usually corrected, and it is only the opposition that invokes the promises made in the inaugural address, just to demonstrate that they are not being kept.

In the first stage of government formation (referred to in literature as a Sejm-over-President stage[12]), the President names the Prime Minister-designate who proposes members of the Council of Ministers. The Prime Minister and other members of his Cabinet are appointed by the President within 14 days of either the Sejm's inaugural sitting or acceptance of the previous government's resignation. Within 14 days of appointment by the President, the Prime Minister submits to the Sejm the programme of his government with a request for a vote of confidence. The Sejm passes the vote of confidence by absolute majority, in the presence of at least half the statutory number of Deputies.

If the government is not appointed by this procedure, the second, Sejm-only stage begins, at which the Prime Minister and the Council of Ministers of his choice are approved by the Sejm by absolute majority of the votes cast, in the presence of at least half the statutory number of Deputies. The Council of Ministers, so elected, is then appointed by the President.

At the second stage of government formation, known as the Sejm-only stage, the right to put PM candidates is vested with groups of at least 46 Deputies. If a candidate wins an absolute majority of votes in the presence of at least half the statutory number of Deputies (such statutory number being 460), he is appointed Prime Minister and then proceeds to present to Parliament his Cabinet's programme and composition. No Cabinet has been formed to date under this procedure.

If the second stage fails to produce a government, the third one is set in motion, where it is the President who appoints the Prime Minister and, at the latter's request, the remaining members of the Council of Ministers (it can be described as a President-over-Sejm stage). The Sejm passes a motion of confidence in the Cabinet within 14 days of the latter's appointment by the President, in the presence of at least half the statutory number of Deputies. If the vote of confidence is defeated, the President must cut short the Sejm's term and order a new election.

At the third stage, referred to as the President-over-Sejm stage, the decisions on government formation are made exclusively by the President and the Prime Minister. The President first appoints the Prime Minister, and that, at the letter's request, he appoints the remaining Cabinet members. Obviously, the President may consult the political parties represented in the Sejm.

Each Cabinet minister may lose their post individually through a vote of no confidence at the Sejm, passed by a majority of votes of the statutory number of Sejm Deputies, on a motion proposed by at least 69 Deputies. The minister

[12] So in Garlicki (2002) 121.

is then dismissed by the President, who may do that at the Prime Minister's request, too. Cabinet ministers may also tender their own resignations. After dismissing a minister, the President appoints a new one on the Prime Minister's motion, without a formal participation of the Sejm.

As previously mentioned, the Sejm may remove the Prime Minister only together with the entire cabinet, after passing a motion of no confidence by a majority of votes of the statutory number of Deputies. Such a motion must be proposed by at least 46 Deputies and must indicate by name the candidate Prime Minister ('constructive motion of no confidence'). Following its passage by the Sejm, the President accepts the Cabinet's resignation, appoints the Sejm-elected new Prime Minister and, on his advice, the remaining members of the Council of Ministers.

In addition to that, a Cabinet minister (including the Prime Minister) may be referred to the State Tribunal for violation of the Constitution or statutes and for crimes committed in connection with their office – on a motion proposed by either the President or a group of at least 115 Deputies. The Sejm Resolution is then passed by a majority of three-fifths of the statutory number of Deputies, which is equivalent to suspension from office.

These constitutional arrangements were tested in practice during two four-year parliamentary terms: 1997-2001 and 2001-2005. The years 1997-2001 saw a cohabitation[13] between a President, elected by general ballot in 1995, and a government formed after the 1997 election by a parliamentary majority of various political groups. The coalition broke up, though – not least because of centrifugal tendencies within its backbone, the Solidarity Elections Action – and was succeeded by a minority government. Criticised for ineffectiveness and scoring low in opinion polls, that Cabinet nevertheless survived till the end of the term – in the absence of a Sejm majority capable of proposing a joint candidate for the Prime Minister. Major laws were being passed, each time enlisting the support of an ad hoc majority. In particular, care was taken to avoid a situation where failure to pass the annual budget within the constitutional time limit would authorise the President to shorten the parliamentary term.

In the 2001-2005 term, the President (chosen by general ballot in 2000) and the Sejm majority (elected in 2001) were of a similar political persuasion. Yet the government, initially seen as coherent and dynamic, was weakened by the need to form coalitions (of three parties initially, then of two). Moreover, it was incapacitated by a set factors which included conflicts between the Prime Minister and his political party on the one hand and the President on the other, social policy decisions perceived the public as reneging on election promises, and corruption scandals revealed by the media – which led to the resignation of the Prime Minister himself. The new Cabinet was formed only at the third stage of the previously described procedure, which means that the Sejm was not capable of passing a vote of confidence in the Presidential candidate in the first stage, did not reach agreement on its own candidate in the second stage (even despite

[13] Cf. Garlicki (2002) 118.

the prolongation of a deadline for entering candidates) – and it was only under the threat of dissolution that it backed in the final stage the previously rejected Presidential candidate, by simple majority. The Prime Minister so chosen later quit the party that provided the political backbone for his government, and joined an opposition grouping on whose ticket he later run – unsuccessfully – for the Sejm. Scoring dismally low at opinion polls, that Cabinet stayed in office till the end of the term, there being no candidate for the Prime Minister acceptable to the opposition. Nor was the opposition able to push through a motion of no confidence in individual ministers of the Cabinet which, although formally assured of support in the Sejm, actually operated as a minority government.

The almost-simultaneous Presidential and parliamentary elections of the fall of 2005 led to a situation where the new head of state and the leader of a grouping than won a plurality are not only members of the same party – actually, they are twin brothers. Their party (Law and Justice), after failed attempts to form a coalition, managed to get its own cabinet appointed (at the first stage of the constitutional process), enlisting the support of parties that stay outside the government. Formally, this is a minority cabinet, but it enjoys a level of support at the Sejm that suffices to operate as a majority government.

The Constitutional procedure for cabinet formation and reshuffle greatly influences the concept and practice of political accountability. With the bar set at a high level this mechanism renders possible the operation of a cabinet that gets poor marks from the public and is inept in tackling problems of major importance for the electorate. Abandoning electoral promises right after the election goes unpunished. Under a 1996 ruling by the Supreme Court, claims of failure to fulfil electoral promises (made during the presidential campaign) are not actionable in courts.[14]

All this encourages distrust in the political class and low election turnout, which in turn leads to a situation where political parties have no incentive to prove their effectiveness in governing. Rather, they can relay on the support of their hardcore constituency, who go by ideology rather than a rational appraisal of the facts. As in other democracies, the election outcome in Poland is largely contingent on the intensity of media campaigns. The proportional representation regime in elections to the Sejm has the effect of favouring political parties. As L. Garlicki points out, 'in practice, one could hardly imagine any chances for a candidate not proposed or backed by the existing political parties, and in the case of elections to the Sejm, involving proportional representation and minimum thresholds, this is outright impossible.'[15] These questions, analysed as they are by constitutionalists, sociologists and political scientists,[16] rank among the classical dilemmas facing democracies in the contemporary world.[17] Political

---

14 Cf. Garlicki (2002) 263.

15 So in Garlicki (2002) 169.

16 Cf., e.g. Garlicki, *ibidem*; Krzemi ski (2005) 497. Cf. also, Piotrowski (2005) 53.

17 Cf., e.g. Sartori (1993) 327.

accountability, however, is not a 'hot issue' in discussions at the national level. Academic debates are focused rather on the constitutional accountability.[18]

Article 157 of the Constitution states unequivocally that members of the Council of Ministers are jointly accountable to the Sejm for the activities of the Council of Ministers, and that they are individually accountable to the Sejm for matters in their competence or matters assigned them by the Prime Minister. Thus the way the Constitution defines Cabinet members' political accountability to the Sejm is in line with the rules of the parliamentary system, were accountability is exercised not only by the Cabinet as a whole, but also its individual ministers.

Although the Constitution does not speak of *political* accountability, theorists agree that such accountability does take place, given the phrase 'to the Sejm'.[19] The Constitution does not formulate any criteria for evaluation of government activity, nor does it require the government to be guided by a programme that is subject to evaluation. What matters is the political criteria, i.e., convergence with the political preferences of the Sejm majority. Therefore, the Constitution presents political accountability as a right of the Sejm – in its capacity as representation of the governed – to evaluate the activity of the government and of its individual ministers, and also the Sejm's right to change the makeup of the Cabinet, bring down the existing government and appoint a new one.

The Constitution introduces a degree of ministers' political accountability to the Prime Minister, who can, by his discretion, request the President to change the composition of the cabinet – and the President has to oblige.

The Constitution differentiates between accountability to the Sejm, being of a political character and referred to in doctrine as parliamentary, and accountability to the State Tribunal, which is of a legal character and termed constitutional. However, constitutional accountability is enforced by a decision of the Sejm, which brings it closer to political accountability. According to the scholarly report concerning the basic problems referring to the application of the 1997 Constitution, 'the principle that 3/5 of votes of the statutory number of Deputies are required for the Sejm to take a resolution to bring a member of the Council of Ministers to accountability before the Tribunal of State prevents the opposition .from pursue charges against member of the current cabinet. This is a barrier that protects the majority against the threat of constitutional accountability with the result that an attempt to use it may be efficient in case of a certain change of the distribution of political forces. A sanction for infringing the Constitution or statutes is 'postponed' until the then opposition becomes the majority'.[20]

Political accountability is of an objective nature, and does not necessarily have to involve any degree of blame. Cabinet ministers may be taken to account at any time and for any reason. According to the dominant view in doctrine,

---

18 Cf. Działocha (2006) 92 as an example of the above mentioned tendency.

19 So in Sokolewicz (2001) 7.

20 Cf. Działocha (2006) 93.

political accountability is enforced not so much for reasons that have made the Sejm pass a no-confidence motion, but rather due to the fact that the Cabinet has lost the Deputies' trust.[21]

In accordance with this opinion, it is possible for a vote of no confidence to be passed exclusively for political reasons. The Cabinet, or its individual ministers, are then forced to resign for no dereliction of duty, but because a parliamentary majority has emerged that is capable of effecting change.

Under the Council of Ministers Act, a change of Cabinet entails the tendering of resignation by secretaries and undersecretaries of state, voivodes (unelected provincial governors) and deputy voivodes. Whether or not the resignations are accepted is decided by the new Prime Minister within three months of appointment of the new Council of Ministers. In practice, as already noted, the changes are more sweeping. The office holders removed from their posts are, in a way, held to account for having been linked to the previous government (or to the previous 'ruling establishment', as the notion has recently been termed in public debate).

Given the remote chances of success, in practice the political-accountability instrument is resorted to by the opposition in order to exert moral pressure on the government. This enables the negative emotions and tensions accompanying the governing process to be defused, thus strengthening representative democracy. At the same time, however, the ineffectiveness of opposition initiatives results in a declining support for democratic institutions, social frustration, and a yearning for new constitutional arrangements.

In a broader sense of the notion, political accountability also includes the responsibility borne by representatives of individual parties standing for re-election. The voters may deny them support, thus giving the thumbs-down on their respective parties' activity so far, including their activity in government.

Accountable to the voters is a President running for re-election (the Constitution restricting the number of his terms in office to two). The voters may deny him support, thus expressing a negative assessment of his activity so far. When a new President takes over, this also translates into personnel changes at the Presidential Chancellery.

The change of government represents some kind of a taking to account – politically – of major officials in government administration, voivodes (regional governors) with associates, heads of government agencies, some ambassadors with their aids, government representatives on boards of companies with a Treasury shareholding, chief executives in companies that are still wholly state-owned, and the police and secret service officers believed to be associated with the government of a party that has been voted out.

It may happen that due to a coincidence of parliamentary and presidential elections, political accountability is exercised by a person not accountable politically under law. In 2005, such was the case with the governor of the central bank (National Bank of Poland). He is not made accountable politically under

[21] Cf. Sokolewicz, *ibidem.*

the law, and yet the newly elected President announced he would not propose the present governor for re-election by parliament when the latter's current term expires. The Governor of the National Bank of Poland is only constitutionally accountable to the Tribunal of State, but is not politically accountable to the Sejm.

These changes, where political accountability often comes as an expression of political interests, tend to be presented by the new authorities as an element of the promised renewal of the state. Election losers, on the other hand, tend to view this as an indication of state capture by political parties. This view is dominant in debates on the condition of the state, but without exerting any influence on actual practice. The winning political party in the 2005 parliamentary election has purged many state-office holders, citing the need to improve the operation of the state. The losing parties treat these changes as signs of state capture by political parties, and criticise the winner-takes-all practices.

Political accountability is the subject of academic pursuits and accompanying doctrinal controversies over the interpretation of Constitutional provisions. They centre, in particular, on the question of whether the President is bound by the Prime Minister's request to remove a Cabinet minister. The opinion that the President might refuse to oblige has emerged in doctrine, but the prevailing view is that unless the Prime Minister's request is formally correct, the president has no choice left.[22]

A major theme in the public debate in recent years has been the blurring of accountability in the Polish state system. Critics point out that the existing systemic arrangements enable the Parliament and the President to shift the buck to the Cabinet, and the latter to shift it back to the Parliament and the President. This has led to demands for major systemic reforms, such as introducing the presidential system, greatly strengthening the presidential powers, and replacing proportional representation with a majoritarian system with first-past-the post elections in single-member constituency.[23]

The notion of the blurring of accountability means that those who – from the constitutional viewpoint – are responsible for a poor condition of, e.g., health care or labour-market situation may get off the hook. This is because the government is the creation of political parties, which call the shots when it comes to the exercise of political accountability in respect of the Cabinet and its members, or the exercise of constitutional accountability. Those in power may also convince voters that the poor state of public affairs is no fault of theirs but of someone else, e.g., the opposition that has obstructed the government's efforts, or the existing procedural constraints preventing the government from acting effectively – sometimes referred to as insurmountable 'impossibilism'.

---

[22] Cf. Sokolewicz, *ibidem*.

[23] Cf. Piotrowski (2005) 153.

4 Accountability: The Government and its Obligations

Under the Polish Constitution, the Cabinet (Council of Ministers) as a whole is politically accountable to the Sejm (the Senate is not mentioned as part of the process). The Constitution describes this as a joint accountability, but it also provides that Cabinet ministers are accountable to the Sejm individually.

Under a rationalised parliamentary model adopted in the Constitution, the entire Cabinet can only be subjected to a 'constructive' motion of no confidence, where a Prime Minister candidate must be indicated, with the support of at least 231 out of 460 Deputies.

The Prime Minister is not individually accountable to the Sejm. He can be removed only by constructive motion of no confidence in the whole Cabinet. But the Constitution provides room for the Prime Minister's resignation (this, indeed, already took place in practice), as a stepping stone to the resignation of the Cabinet – which however may, or may not, be accepted by the President. This means that, to a certain extent, the Prime Minister is also politically accountable to the President. The Prime Minister is accountable to the Sejm for the President's official acts which he countersigns. This constitutional arrangement means that the Sejm, when rejecting a presidential official act countersigned by the Prime Minister, actually passes a constructive motion of no confidence in a government that enjoys the support of a parliamentary majority. No such instance, however, has so far taken place in practice.

Under the Constitution, the Prime Minister may at any time propose that the Sejm pass a motion of confidence in his Cabinet. For the government to win under this procedure, a simple majority will suffice, in the presence of at last half the statutory number of Deputies. The proposal may only be submitted by the Prime Minister.

Ministries are formed, and their structures laid out, by Council of Ministers regulation. Secretaries and undersecretaries of state are politically accountable to the minister at whose request they are appointed (and removed) by the Prime Minister – but it may happen that the latter acts in this respect on his initiative.[24] Pursuant to Article 38 of the Council of Ministers Act, upon acceptance by the President of the Cabinet's resignation, the secretaries and undersecretaries of state, voivodes and deputy voivodes follow suit – but acceptance of their resignations is left to the new Prime Minister, who has for this three months after the appointment of his Cabinet.

If the motion of no confidence towards the Cabinet can be proposed on any grounds, it then follows that its extent covers the activity of all entities subordinated to the government, including government agencies and the tenured civil servants reporting 'within statutory bounds' to the Head of the Civil Service who, in turn, reports to the Prime Minister. Both the Cabinet as a whole and its individual ministers are politically accountable for the operation of govern-

24 Cf. Garlicki (2005) 316.

ment administration, including, e.g., the agencies in charge of EU-sponsored agricultural programmes or pharmaceutical oversight (the health minister cited an improper performance of the pharmaceutical supervision inspectorate as the reason for his resignation in November 2006, which was rejected by the Prime Minister).

On the other hand, ministers' individual accountability extends only to matters within their competence and matters assigned to them by the Prime Minister.

Tenured civil servants are hired and fired according to a fixed procedure set out statutorily and eliminating any political arbitrariness. But under this procedure, the service contract may be terminated in the event of a 'loss of unimpeachable opinion', which may set in motion dismissals in the nature of political accountability. One cannot rule out that the notion of 'loss of unimpeachable opinion' may be interpreted in a way that extends it to encompass collaboration in pursuing the programme of a government that has been called to account politically by the Sejm or brought down in the wake of a lost parliamentary election.

Starting from September 2005, heads of central state administrative offices, state agencies and state special-purpose funds are appointed under competitive selection procedure for the duration of their tenure. The procedure basically eliminates room for ahead-of-time dismissals for political reasons (political accountability). But the State Cadres Pool and Senior State Positions Act of August 2006 provides that a removal 'may take place at any time', i.e. also prior to the expiry of one's tenure. With the adoption of this Act the competitive selection procedure has been abolished.

The heads of the Internal Security Agency and the Intelligence Agency are politically accountable to the Prime Minister. Appraisals of their performance may also be formulated by the Sejm's Special Services Committee.

Political accountability is both collegial (or, as the Constitution puts it, 'joint') when it applies to the Cabinet as a whole, and individual, in respect of particular ministers. The Prime Minister may be taken to account on political grounds together with the entire Cabinet. The notion of joint accountability means a lawful obligation to resign upon passage of an appropriate Sejm resolution, whether or not there are any objective, rational reasons for such resignation.

5 The Scope of Accountability

The political responsibilities of ministers and the whole Cabinet include the formulation and implementation of government policies. Under the Council of Ministers Act, ministers take part in 'formulating state policies, and are accountable for the contents and pursuit of Government activities' (Article 7.1), almost the same as implementation of government policies.

Ministers bear political accountability for the exercise of their statutory powers. They are also accountable for the activity of the entire Cabinet and the Prime Minister – so it is not inconceivable for them to be taken to account for something on which they have had no influence, when a given aspect of government activity lies outside their respective remits. A detailed brief for a minister is set out by the head of government in a regulation, which also specifies – if the minister is assigned to head a department of government administration – the list of subordinated or overseen organs. A minister may also be granted oversight and control powers in respect of certain organs and entities on the strength of statutes or in accordance with procedures laid down in statutes. The term 'department of government administration' is not confined to a single office, but usually represents a vast branch of the administration. The Government Administration Departments Act lists these branches and assigns them to particular ministers.

Pursuant to Article 13 of the Council of Minister Act, the Cabinet 'in consultation with the interested institution or group of the public may appoint joint commissions comprising representatives of the government and the said institution or group of the public'. The commissions would work towards reaching common ground on 'matters of importance for Government policy and interests of the institution or group of the public represented on the commission'. The Cabinet, the Prime Minister and individual ministers may be taken to account for the operation of the commissions in the same manner as they bear overall political responsibility. One example of such a body is the Joint Commission of Central and Local Government, which operates pursuant to a specific statutory act describing its formation and operating rules. The Commission expresses the common opinion of central and local government which must be agreed by both parties. In the absence of agreement, both parties announce their own positions. The commission is something more than an advisor to the Cabinet, its aim is to engage in dialogue and, where possible, develop common positions. This is especially true of passing opinions on draft normative acts and government action plans.

A government minister is assisted by his political aides, who form his private political office, known as the political cabinet (resembling a *cabinet ministériel* in France). Given that ministers may be taken to account politically for any reason resulting in the loss of the Sejm's trust in them, the activity of members of such private political offices may also be a reason behind the Sejm's passing a motion of no confidence in a minister.

Under the Council of Ministers Act, ministers are accountable for government activity, including the activity of the respective departments subordinated to them. But they are also accountable jointly with the entire Cabinet for the operation of departments within other minister's remits. 'With a view to adjusting the operating modes and activities of the subordinated or overseen central organs of State administration and other offices or organisational units to the policy laid down by the Council of Ministers', a minister may issue 'binding instructions and orders' to heads of these institutions and, in this way, also to the officials reporting to these heads. Such commands, however, must not apply to decisions 'regarding the substance of a matter processed by means of administrative decision' (Article 34a of the Council of Ministers Act). Those ministers who run state administrative departments (so-called departmental ministers) exercise their powers on their own behalf, while the ministers handling matters assigned them by the Prime Minister (so-called ministers without portfolio) act by the Prime Minister's authorisation. The Council of Ministers Act stipulates that the ministers in charge of specific organs oversee and control these organs. On the strength of specific statutory authorisations, ministers in charge of government administrative departments issue generally binding regulations. They may also issue ordinances that only bind the organisational units subordinated to them. At the Prime Minister's request, the Cabinet may rescind a ministerial regulation or ordinance.

The organisational units going by the name of government agencies enjoy diverse legal status. Some of them are central organs of state administration, other ones are state legal persons and state organisational units (as opposed to organs of state administration), and still other ones are commercial law companies. Vested with the right to dispose of state assets, these entities have been established to perform specific tasks of public administration.[25] Not independent of the government, they are subordinated to, or overseen by, the Prime Minister or individual ministers, even though most agency heads are appointed under competitive selection procedure. The Cabinet and individual ministers are politically accountable for the operation of these agencies: the Sejm may pass a motion of no confidence in a minister or the entire Cabinet (in this case, it must be a 'constructive' motion) for any reason whatever, which means also due to dissatisfaction with the performance of an agency.

6 Activating Accountability: Parliamentary Control and Transparency

Comparing the reality with a representation of how one thinks it should be like, and formulating conclusions from such juxtaposition is the essence of any act of control. The notion involves testing, reviewing, scrutinising, examining, investigating, overseeing and looking into. In this sense, the control activity is closely linked with the nature of parliamentary proceedings. Control is not about directing or managing. Especially in a system of checks and balances, Parliament must not transcend the constitutional limits of its control function.

But legislative activity will be ineffective unless the lawmakers are apprised of the reality. Lawmaking is strictly linked to learning about the subject of regulation – which is coessential with parliamentary control in the area to be

[25] Cf. Jagielski (2003) 188.

regulated. And legislative activity requires that lawmakers take incessant care of the law's conformity with the Constitution, which is also a kind of control or, to be more precise, self-control.

Under a democratic state's checks and balances, the control of the executive is the Parliament's essential job, on a par with lawmaking. Important and unique roles in the control process are played by the Sejm, its committees and the Deputies.

In the light of the Constitution passed by the National Assembly on 2 April 1977, a distinction should be made between parliamentary control *sensu stricto* and *sensu largo*.

And so the Sejm's control function[26] in the strict sense of the notion applies to 'the Council of Ministers' activity within the scope defined by the Constitution and statutes' (Article 95). The control activity covers the operation of the government (the Cabinet and government administration) with respect to the State's internal and foreign policy, to an extent not reserved 'for other organs of the State and local government' (Article 146). The Constitution also authorises the Sejm to control local government (Article 171), either indirectly, by controlling the Council of Ministers' oversight of local government, or directly, by checking if a local government legislature 'glaringly violates the Constitution or statues'.

Two key elements flesh out the Sejm's powers to control government activity: the budgetary process and the Sejm's examination of the Cabinet's budget implementation report and memorandum on State debt. Based on this examination, the Cabinet's record for prior year is either approved or rejected (Article 226 of the Constitution). The Sejm also considers a report on the attainment monetary policy targets by the Monetary Policy Council (an organ of the central bank, the National Bank of Poland). These targets are notified to the Sejm by Council simultaneously with the government's submission of the draft budget.

The Sejm examines the budget implementation report jointly with the opinion of the Supreme Audit Chamber (NIK), whose operation provides an institutional guarantee of the discharge of the Sejm's control function. The Sejm and its organs, especially committees, may request the NIK to conduct an inspection.

The Sejm's control powers towards the government stem from the constitutional provisions on the Council of Ministers' accountability to the Sejm. They also extend to all of the President's 'official acts' subject to countersignature by the Prime Minister – where the latter, 'upon signing the act, becomes accountable to the Sejm' (Article 144.2). In addition to that, given the Sejm's participation in fleshing out the President's constitutional accountability, its control may extent to check the legality of presidential activity.

It follows then that the constitutionally defined extent of the Sejm's control functions is fairly wide. It is further widened by Article 111 of the Constitution, which authorises the Sejm to appoint ad hoc investigating committees to 'examine a particular issue'. Such a committee comes as an instrument of the

26 Cf. Piotrowski (1999) 39 ff.

Sejm's controlling activity, but because of the wording of Article 111, it may take interest in matters outside the purview of the executive branch and local government. Consequently, while staying within the bounds of law and especially the Constitution, the Sejm may find itself competent to control 'particular issues', if only that does not encroach on the constitutional powers of the executive and judiciary branches, and does not transcend the nature of the control function, by turning into directing or binding inspiration.

Under the Sejm Investigating Committee Act, each and every person subpoenaed by the committee must turn up and testify. In practice, this applies not just to officials subordinated to the government, but also to individuals outside the administration, such as journalists or businessmen. The immoderation which investigating committees[27] shown in this respect has provoked critical comments by experts and politicians. Most notably, the question was whether an investigating committee may hold a hearing of the incumbent President. With experts' opinions divided,[28] the President refused to testify before a committee.

The proceedings of the investigating committees – which were criticised by some as abusing the procedure of parliamentary investigation for current political gain[29] – proved devastating for the ruling party in the 2001-2005 term (the Democratic Left Alliance, or the SLD). The committees were among factors that prodded some SLD members, including the incumbent Sejm Speaker, to form a new party (it did not make it to the new Parliament). The debilitated SLD lost the parliamentary election, although it retained presence in the newly chosen 5th Sejm. One committee had its fair share in the withdrawal from the presidential race by an SLD-backed contender. Committee proceedings were open, but some sittings were closed – which, however, did not stop some members from passing information to the media. This openness was conducive to the transformation of committee debates into a forum for political confrontation.[30]

Under the Constitution, the Sejm is vested with control of government activities, but it may also control entities other than the executive branch. This holds in particular for those aspects of control that are coessential with the passage of statutes governing matters outside the sphere of the executive branch.

To some extent, the Sejm controls the correctness of suing Deputies in court, in cases where a Deputy's activity 'within the scope of his mandate' violates

27 In the 4th Sejm, committees investigating corruption dealt with an amendment to the Radio and Television Act, state authorities' action towards a domestic petroleum corporation, and the privatisation of the PZU national insurer.

28 For the possibility of the incumbent President's being questioned by a Sejm investigating committee, cf. *Przegl d Sejmowy*, 2004(1) 65. For the President's being subpoenaed by a Sejm investigation committee, cf. *Studia Iuridica* 2004(XLIII) 191.

29 So in Garlicki (2005) 261.

30 These experiences seem to bear out this observation by J. Dunna: 'The best of regimes of freedom of information would always be open to infinite manipulation and largely at the mercy of fluent hypocrisy'; Cf. Dunn (1999) 340.

third parties' rights. In such cases, they can be taken to court only 'by consent of the Sejm' (Article 105.1 of the Constitution). The Sejm's nod is also needed to remand or arrest a Deputy. Thus the Sejm, and sometimes its Speaker, retain control of measures aimed to enforce a Deputy's criminal liability. The Sejm also decides whether or not a Deputy can be taken to the State Tribunal, for violation of the ban on business operations, imposed by Article 107 of the Constitution. Before adopting the relevant resolution, the Sejm examines if there are sufficient grounds to institute proceedings that may lead to loss of the Deputy's status.

The Sejm's control powers also extend, albeit in a varying degree, to the operation of State control and law enforcement organs. The powers towards the Supreme Audit Chamber actually transcend the control functions, given the constitutional provision on the Chamber's subordination to the Sejm. Pursuant to Article 204 of the Constitution, the Supreme Audit Chamber 'submits to the Sejm annual reports on its activity'. But the President of the Chamber is not politically accountable to the Sejm, even if he is constitutionally accountable to the State Tribunal (which entails the Sejm's participation in fleshing out this accountability). Under the Constitution, the President of the Supreme Audit Chamber must not be held criminally liable without the Sejm's consent.

The Sejm relations with the Ombudsman are of a slightly different nature. The latter remains 'independent' and 'autonomous', but he 'is accountable only to the Sejm, as defined in a statute' (Article 210 of the Constitution). Under the Constitution, the Ombudsman must annually apprise the Sejm of 'his activity', and the Ombudsman Act allows for his removal where he has 'broken his oath' – a norm so general as to permit the Ombudsman's removal for political reasons.

As for the National Radio and TV Council, counted by the Constitution among State control and law enforcement organs, the Radio and Television Act stipulates that the Sejm co-participates in controlling the institution. The Council submits to the Sejm annual reports on its operations, which may be rejected by the house. If the Senate does the same, this is equivalent to the expiry of the Councils' term, subject to consent by the President.

The Sejm's committees have an important role to play in the exercise of the house's control functions. Already mentioned has been the select investigating committee, a dedicated instrument of control, vested with special powers. Each Sejm committee operates in accordance with the Sejm Rules, providing that the committees 'in particular' examine the reports and information memorandums from ministers and heads of central organs of State administration, and also 'heads of other State offices and institutions' (Article 156.1 of the Sejm Rules). The committees also 'analyse the operation of individual departments of State administration and economy'. The Sejm Rules place ministers and other state officials under the obligation to submit reports and convey information 'on demand by the Presidium of the committee', and to take part in committee sessions where matters related to their respective terms of reference are taken up. The Presidium of a committee and its chairman may also invite to sessions persons other than State administration officials 'to present information and explanation about matters taken up at the session or investigated by the committee' (Article 153.2 of the Rules). This authorisation may be used where the committee transcends the control of the executive branch in the strict sense of the notion.

Wide room for control activity by Sejm committees is provided under the Sejm Deputy and Senator Mandate Act, where Article 16.2 stipulates that such control may be exercised in respect of matters within the committees' remit. The committees are authorised to demand 'information and explanation' from a range of entities which include local government organs and institutions, NGOs, central and local government-owned companies, incorporated companies with a state shareholding and municipal legal persons. The act does not specify the extent of the information, and therefore great care must be taken to ensure that a commission's control activity stays within the Parliament's constitutional responsibilities. Control activity is also taken up in Article 167 of the Sejm Rules, where committees are granted the right to visit and examine the operation of companies with a Treasury shareholding, State-owned enterprises and other State institutions. The information so obtained may influence such assessments and actions as the committee may find appropriate and compliant with the Constitution, statutes and the Sejm Rules.

Also within this line of activity is the submission to the house of draft resolutions, which under Article 158 of the Sejm Rules, may take the form of a resolution proper (call for a certain State organ to take one-off action indicated in the resolution), a declaration (commitment to a certain behaviour), appeal (call for a certain behaviour to be followed, or for an initiative or project to be launched), or a statement (position on a certain matter).

A committee may also pass a desideratum or an opinion. Under Article 159 of the Sejm Rules, the desideratum contains the committee's demands regarding 'particular issues', and may be addressed to the Council of Ministers or individual ministers, the President of Supreme Audit Chamber, the Governor of the National Bank of Poland, the Attorney General, and the Chief Inspector for Labour. The addressees may – but do not have to – comply with the committee's requests, and it is their duty to reply and notify in writing the Speaker of the Sejm about the 'position taken' on the matter within 30 days of receipt of the desideratum, unless the Speaker of the Sejm sets another time limit at the request of the addressee and in consultation with the Presidium of the committee. The Rules vest the Sejm Speaker with considerable competences as to how committees use the desideratum as an instrument of control and inspiration. It is the Sejm Speaker who conveys the commissions' desiderata to the 'relevant organs'. And the Rules authorise him to 'return to the committee its desideratum with a substantiated request to reconsider the matter', where he does not share the committee's position. But the latter may upheld its point of view and pass the desideratum again, which then must be delivered to the addressee.

This internal procedure for the handling of desiderata at the Sejm demonstrates how difficult and complex it may be to set the limits which the committee must not transcend while performing its parliamentary control function. Where a committee does not receive a reply on time or finds the reply unsatisfactory, it may repeat the desideratum, 'ask the Sejm speaker to return the reply as unsatisfactory', or 'submit to the Sejm the draft of the relevant resolution'.

Another instrument at the committees' disposal, which slightly differs from the desideratum, is the formulation of an opinion. According to Article 160 of the Sejm Rules, the opinion 'presents the position on a particular issue'. The committee may 'present the opinion' to the same organs to which desiderata are sent, plus 'other central offices and institutions of the State'. The opinion is more about inspiring than controlling, although the committee may ask the addressees to 'present their position on issues raised in the opinion, and a memorandum on how the conclusions from the opinion are being implemented' – within the time limits and on terms defined in the Sejm Rules for the handling of desiderata. Thus the powers at the Sejm Speaker's disposal are equivalent to those enjoyed in respect of desiderata. The addressee of an opinion is required under the Sejm Rules to present position 'at the committee's request'.

Some of the Sejm committees play a truly special role in performing the house's control function. Ad hoc investigating committees were mentioned earlier in this paper, and there is also the Secret Services Committee, which under Article 140 of the Rules 'participates, in respect of maters related to secret services, in the proceedings involving draft annual budgets and other financial plans of the State, and in the examination of reports on implementation thereof, and it presents its opinion to the relevant committees'. This confirms the controlling character of the committee's activity. Its members have access to state secrets 'of special importance for the defence, armed forces and security of the State'. The committee's remit includes, in particular, the examination of annual reports by heads of secret services and the handling of complaints about the operation of these services.

Elements of the exercise of the control function can also be seen in the proceedings of the Constitutional Accountability Committee, especially where it studies the validity of initial requests for taking someone to account on constitutional grounds. The Constitutional Accountability Committee plays an important role in the Polish legal system. Its position is decisive in determining whether or not the most senior office holders will be brought to the Tribunal of State. It is to this committee that the Sejm Speaker sends a preliminary request to hold a person accountable constitutionally. The Commission produces a report for the Sejm, thus providing the basis on which the House develops its own decision on the matter. Under the Tribunal of State Act, the Constitutional Accountability Committee may hear witnesses and experts, and demand any records and documents from state institutions and nongovernmental organisations. The person indicated in the request is authorised to produce explanations.

The Disciplinary Committee is engaged in control activity, too, especially where it handles the Sejm's consent to take a Deputy to account or to have them remanded or arrested, and where it exercises its powers to oversee the operation of the Sejm's Chancellery.

Among control prerogatives of the Parliamentary Ethics Committee are those dealing with analysis of Deputies' assets statements submitted to the Sejm Speaker. The findings of the analysis are presented to the Sejm Presidium. We thus have a body to perform the control function in respect of Deputies' wealth. Work is currently underway on establishing at the central government level an Anti-corruption Office that will operate in the same manner as secret services, and whose terms of reference will include verifying the veracity of Deputies' assets statements.

But it is the Members of Parliament themselves who play the most important part in the discharge of the Sejm's control function. Under the Constitution, the Sejm Deputy and Senator Mandate Act, and the Sejm Rules, the position of the Deputies determines the final wording of resolutions which the house or committees adopt in exercising their previously discussed control powers.

In addition to the fundamental right of casting a vote, the MPs enjoy a statutory right to 'express their position' and 'propose motions', whether at plenary or committee debates; in particular, they may make statements according to procedures set out in both houses' rules. The Sejm Deputy and Senator Mandate Act authorises them to propose to the presidium of either house that a particular issue be considered by the house or its committee, and also to ask a committee to take up a given matter (articles 14 and 15).

Each Sejm Deputy enjoys a constitutional right to ask an interpellation question to the Prime Minister and other Cabinet ministers. Under the Sejm Rules, they may also ask interpellation questions to the President of the Supreme Audit Chamber and Governor of the National Bank of Poland. The Sejm Rules require such questions to concern 'issues of fundamental significance' and be submitted in writing to the Sejm Speaker (Article 192). It is important that a Deputy's interpellation question contain a brief presentation of the factual state of affairs and actual queries, resulting form such presentation and being in line with the addressee's competences. The Rules authorise the Sejm Presidium do evaluate whether these conditions are met by a particular interpellation question, and to refuse accepting a question that fails to comply. The Presidium may also demand that 'expressions offending the Deputies' ethics be crossed out from the interpellation question'. The question is conveyed by the Sejm Speaker to the addressee, who has to reply 'through the offices of the Sejm Speaker' within 21 days of receipt of the question. The Speaker sends a copy of the reply to the interpellant, and publishes it in an appendix to the Sejm Minutes. Where the interpellant does not receive a reply on time or finds the reply unsatisfactory, he may ask the Speaker to demand additional explanation or 'to put the interpellation question on the agenda of the sitting', which translates into presenting the contents of the question, getting a reply from the addressee and also other possible explanations in response to the interpellant's queries, plus a discussion 'about the interpellation question and the reply given'. Importantly, the Sejm may ask the questioned party to supplement the reply. At any rate, the replay to an interpellation question 'constitutes a binding position' of the addressee.

Of a slightly different nature are Deputies' queries. Under Article 115 of the Constitution, such queries to the Prime Minister and Cabinet ministers should be answered 'within 21 days'. The Sejm Rules broaden the group of addressees to include the President of the Supreme Audit Chamber and the Governor of the National Bank of Poland. The query's purpose is to 'obtain information about current questions related to State policies'. While interpellation questions must be in writing, at least at the early stages, the Deputies' queries are 'formulated orally' and must be followed by 'direct reply'. But spontaneity is eliminated by the specific character of parliamentary proceedings and concern for the effectiveness of the procedures followed. The Sejm Rules require the Deputy to advise the Presidium of the subject and the addressee of the query at least 12 hours prior to the commencement of a sitting. And it is the Sejm Presidium that, after consulting the Convention of Senior Deputies, defines the order of queries for each sitting. The Rules do not leave much for arbitrariness here, requiring that the Presidium should be guided by 'the relevance and special importance of the queries, the sequence in which readiness to ask queries have been signalled, and the intention to provide the chance of asking queries' to Deputies in accordance with the size of their respective caucuses. In contrast to interpellation questions, no discussion is held over the queries and the reply given. But additional queries and additional replies are allowed. The reply to a query is a binding position of the entity to which it has been asked.

The Constitution requires that the Prime Minister and ministers, in addition to replying to interpellation questions and queries, also provided 'replies concerning current affairs' at each sitting of the Sejm (Article 115). The provision is of considerable importance for the discharge of the Sejm's control function, for the information so obtained may provide a point of departure for further proceedings of the house.

It is also the Deputies' task to inspire the Constitutional Tribunal to control the compliance of regulations 'issued by central organs of the State', i.e. notably the Council of Ministers and government administration, with the Constitution, ratified international agreements and statutes. A motion to the Tribunal to that effect may be proposed by the Sejm Speaker or a group of 50 Deputies (Article 191 of the Constitution).

Apart from the control instruments and procedures available at the Sejm, the Sejm Deputy and Senator Mandate Act opens wide room for Members of Parliament's control activity outside the house. In the first instance, it gives them the right to 'information and explanations', to be obtained from 'Cabinet ministers and representatives of the relevant organs and institutions of the State and local government' in respect of all matters connected with the performance of their duties as Members of Parliament (Article 16). The Deputies and Senators are also authorised to 'obtain information and materials from, and inspect the operation of, organs of State administration and local government, and also companies with a State Treasury shareholding and State- and local government-owned companies' (Article 19). This right is restricted by the Act's requirement that there must be a linkage between obtaining the information and inspecting on the one hand and the discharge of the mandate on the other. Deputies' activities must not do harm to 'other parties' personal interests', and must comply with the 'regulations on statutorily protected secrets'. Under the Confidential Information Protection Act, one can get access to such information only after going through check-up proceedings conducted by State security services; such proceedings are not applied to Deputies and Senators, unless the information is classified as 'top secret'. The right to inspection seems particularly important, authorising the Deputy to acquaint himself with the actual state of affairs personally, directly and with his own eyes.

The Act provides an opportunity for Deputies and Senators to control the course of their intervention with 'an organ of government administration or local government, a state-owned company, an NGO, and a non-State business entity'. The ID of a Member of Parliament 'gives the MP the right to enter' these entities, whose heads are required to admit the visitor 'in connection with a matter related to the discharge of his mandate', and also to 'provide information and explanations concerning the said matter' (Article 20). A Deputy or a Senator may also take part in sessions of the local assembly covering the constituency from which they are elected, and in sessions of district and municipality councils.

Alongside lawmaking, the discharge of the control function is the essence of parliamentary proceedings in a democratic state. In this respect, the Sejm has a definite advantage over the Senate, reflecting both the Constitution's bi-cameral design and Poland's traditions.

It is not possible for Parliament to exercise its control functions without proper institutional and procedural instruments. There seems to be no shortage of such instruments in Polish systemic law. To what extent and how effectively they are used in practice depends on the MPs themselves.

7 Consequences

The Sejm's control powers towards the government also stem from those provisions of the Constitution which deal with the Council of Ministers' accountability to the Sejm. As already noted in this article, the Sejm may pass a motion of no confidence or (if asked by the Prime Minister) a motion of confidence in the Cabinet and in individual ministers. The passage of a motion of no confidence and defeat of a motion of confidence in the Council of Ministers are among constitutional conditions for the Cabinet's dismissal (Article 162).

The motion of no confidence is a highly effective means of the Sejm's control activity, one that is very troublesome for the government. The Constitution does not specify the reasons for which the Deputies pass such a resolution with a critical assessment of the whole Council of Ministers. Article 158 of the Constitution details the rules of procedures in such cases, providing that a motion of no confidence is passed by a majority of the statutory number of Deputies. The motion, to be proposed by a group of at least 46 Deputies, must indicate the candidate for the new Prime Minister. Consequently its passage is equivalent to a simultaneous election of a new Prime Minister – hence its 'constructive' character. The house's resort to this means of control activity appears to be co-essential with the discharge of the creation function. The Constitution seeks to ensure that a motion of no confidence is proposed after mature consideration and with adequate support. It must be put to the vote 'not earlier than seven days after its proposal'; and for a repeat motion this is 'not earlier than three months after the proposal of the previous motion', unless at least 115 Deputies subscribe to the motion.

With regards to individual ministers, a no-confidence motion must be proposed by at least 69 Deputies, and is passed by a majority of votes of the statutory number of Deputies. The procedural guarantees here are similar to those which the Constitution provides for a vote of no confidence in the Cabinet. But no linkage is imposed regarding the appointment of a censured minister's successor.

As for the motion of confidence in the Cabinet proposed by the Prime Minister, it is passed by a majority of votes in the presence of at least half the statutory number of Deputies. Pursuant to articles 154 and 155 of the Constitution, a motion of confidence in the government is also voted as part of the Cabinet appointment process.

Apart from possibly being the target of a no-confidence motion, a Cabinet minister may be dismissed by the Prime Minister, who submits the relevant proposal to the President. The Constitution states that the President makes changes in the composition of the Cabinet on a motion of the Prime Minister, which means he must not act against that motion.

8 In Conclusion

1. The version of a rationalised parliamentary system, adopted in the Polish Constitution, tends to produce results not always intended by its authors. In the light of to-date practice, the Sejm has proved incapable of effectively using the instrument of no-confidence motion. The practice of Deputies' involvement in government and party activity is conducive to blurring the difference between the legislative and executive branches, as well as rendering political accountability less effective – which is further fostered by Deputies' use of the instruments at their disposal for control and inspiration of the executive

branch,. The lawmaking process, too, offers a host of opportunities for obscuring the boundaries between Parliament and government, and for watering down political accountability.

2. The existing constitutional arrangements are conducive to Cabinets' staying long in office, even where their effectiveness in handling social problems is questioned by the public. As a result, every four years, the ruling parties are taken to account politically by voters (turning out in low numbers as they are), which results in major personal reshuffles at the centres of political and, partly, economic authority. This encourages state capture by political parties and deepens distrust in politicians, thus further affecting the electorate's readiness to go to the polls.

3. When mechanisms of political accountability get jammed, this has the effect of weakening the effectiveness of public authorities and adding to disenchantment with the existing forms of the democratic system – all of which emboldens the seekers of new solutions.

Bibliography

DUNN (1999)

J. Dunn, 'Situating Political Accountability', in A. Przeworski, S.C. Stokes, B. Manin, *Democracy, Accountability, and Representation* (Cambridge 1999), 340 ff.

DZIAŁOCHA (2006)

K. Działocha (ed.), *Basic Problems of Applying the Constitution of the Republic of Poland. Final Research Report* (Warsaw 2006).

GARLICKI (2002)

L. Garlicki, 'Rada Ministrów: powoływanie-kontrola-odpowiedzialność', in A. Bałaban (ed.), *Rada Ministrów. Organizacja i funkcjonowanie* (Kraków 2002), 121 ff.

GARLICKY (2005)

L. Garlicki, *Polskie prawo konstytucyjne* (Warszawa 2005).

GARLICKY (2006)

L. Garlicki, *Polskie prawo konstytucyjne* (Warsaw 2006).

GRZYBOWSKI (1999)

M. Grzybowski, 'The System of Government in the Constitution of the Republic of Poland of 2nd April 1997', in P. Sarnecki, A. Szmyt, Z. Witkowski, *The Principles of Basic Institutions of the System of Government in Poland* (Warsaw 1999), 151 ff.

JAGIELSKI (2003)

J. Jagielski, 'Administracja centralna', in M. Wierzbowski (ed.), *Prawo administracyjne* (Warszawa 2003), 188 ff.

KRZEMIŃSKI (2005)

I. Krzemiński, 'IV RP – rozczarowanie i nadzieja', in *Ius et Lex* (2005(1)), 497 ff.

PIOTROWSKI (1999)

R. Piotrowski, *Sejm of the Republic of Poland. Structure. Procedures. Functions* (Warsaw 1999).

PIOTROWSKI (2005)

R. Piotrowski, 'Inventing a new Republic: proposals for constitutional reform in Poland compared', in, *Venice Commission: Evaluation of fifteen years of constitutional practice in central and eastern Europe* (Strasbourg 2005), 53 ff.

PIOTROWSKI (2005)

R. Piotrowski, 'Koncepcje nowego ustroju pa stwa w projektach zmian konstytucyjnych', in *Ius et Lex* (2005(1)), 153 ff.

SARNECKI, SZMYT, WITKOWSKI (1999)

P. Sarnecki, A. Szmyt, Z. Witkowski (eds.), *The Principles of Basic Institutions of the System of Government in Poland* (Warsaw 1999).

SARTORI (1993)

G. Sartori, *Democrazia. Cosa e* (Milano 1993).

SARTORI (1994)

G. Sartori, *Comparative Constitutional Engineering* (London 1994).

SOKOLEWICZ (2001)
W. Sokolewicz, 'Uwagi do art. 157', in L. Garlicki (ed.), *Konstytucja RP. Komentarz*, vol. II (Warszawa 2001), 7 ff.

CHAPTER 10

Political Accountability in Spain

Enoch Alberti

1 Scope of the Study

This paper basically restricts itself to the issues addressed by the 'Political Accountability in European Perspective' questionnaire. However, this does not preclude the possibility of extended treatment of other aspects of political accountability in Spain if necessary in order to explain or better understand the main issue.

There is no clearly delimited legal definition of 'political accountability' in Spain; indeed in legal doctrine the term can even be the subject of debate and lacks clear-cut definition. It can, however, be used without giving rise to excessive difficulties in referring in general to the consequences that may derive from the actions of public bodies which, by a process of elimination, are deemed not to be criminal, disciplinary, patrimonial or legal in general, and which are the result of a control action carried out by political authorities, especially Parliament, on the basis of criteria of appropriateness, convenience or efficacy. In this sense, the 'Political accountability' concept may be referred to in Spain as the control of persons and bodies activities, according with those *political* criteria, and also to the result of this control. In common language, not strictly in legal sense, when somebody demands the *political responsibility* of an authority or, in general, a person in a public office, he is clearly requiring his removal or resignation, and not only putting him under supervision or control.

The consequence par excellence of this accountability is resignation or removal from public office of the person concerned. However, removal is not the unique possible effect of this responsibility: the result of the accountability process may be expressed in terms of approval or disapproval, without carrying necessarily, in this last case, the obligation of resignation. The essence of this accountability lies with the control itself, with the fact of putting some activities under an external control, which will be exercised on the basis of political, not legal criteria. Moreover, this control leads to a public debate, between the arguments that justify the action submitted to control and those that question this action on the basis on its appropriateness, convenience or efficacy. Political accountability must lead to this public debate, and from this debate must be deduced consequences in terms of approval or disapproval of the action and the person submitted to control.

It is also important to note that accountability may be autonomous (due to actions which do not entail any other consequence in criminal, civil or administrative law) or may exist alongside other forms of accountability, as a complementary result of actions which involve also another types of responsibilities or effects, in the criminal, civil or administrative fields. The separation of both types of responsibility has been controversial in Spain. Sometimes it has been argued that the political responsibility, with the consequences that it entails, must follow the juridical responsibility, especially in the criminal field. In this way, the removal or resignation must occur only after a judicial sentence, which determines the facts and their juridical (criminal, civil or administrative) effects. This position, in my opinion, does not realize the different nature of both types of responsibility, which operate with two different control parameters. Moreover, I think it is possible to say that it is just because of the limited scope of the juridical control that the political accountability exists, to reach the fields where the juridical responsibility can not reach, and enable the control of actions which are proper from a legal point of view, but they are not appropriate, or, at least, they can be questioned from another point of view of appropriateness. Hanging the political responsibility on the juridical (and judicial) responsibility leads, in my opinion, to a serious limitation of the first one, which entails the risk of making it lose its sense.

In addition, the last general remark. The consideration of political accountability in this paper will mainly concern it as affecting the central state government of Spain. It should be borne in mind that the Spanish State comprises two territorial levels of government: central and autonomous community, plus the local level. Both systems are based on the same representative principle and their government is organised on the same parliamentary model. This paper then shall basically focus on the level of central government, although occasional reference may be made to autonomous government.

The paper will address the following issues:

i) the system of parliamentary government established by the Spanish Constitution of 1978 as the general framework for political accountability;
ii) the actors in accountability: accountable persons and instances in which accountability may be demanded;
iii) the scope of accountability;
iv) mechanisms of accountability;
v) the consequences of enforcement of accountability.

2 Political Accountability Within the General Framework of the System of Parliamentary Government Established by the Spanish Constitution of 1978

2.1 Rationalised Parliamentarism and Government Stability

The Spanish Constitution of 1978 (SC hereafter) established a rationalised parliamentary system of government, clearly setting out the parliamentary mechanisms for formation of Government and enforcement of its political accountability. The basic aim of this explicit provision for mechanisms and procedures whereby the Parliament may express its confidence in the Government was to ensure stable government, as was clear from the constituent debate. The underlying aim of the regulation governing the Spanish system of parliamentary government was to establish a Government which was accountable to Parliament, yet relations between both bodies were designed in such a way as to safeguard the Government from possible fluctuations and contingencies occurring within Parliament itself. Essentially, this was a matter of ensuring that the Government had solid parliamentary support, facilitating formation of the Government and regulating censure so as to ensure that its parliamentary defeat would at least lead to replacement by another with a more solid parliamentary majority. To this end, should it prove impossible to achieve an absolute majority on the first vote, parliamentary investiture of the Government can take place with a simple majority of the lower house (the Congress of Deputies); in contrast, however, a motion of censure, which is constructive in nature and which must include proposal of an alternative Presidential candidate who is automatically invested should the motion prosper, can only succeed if obtaining the support of an absolute majority of the Chamber.

Formation of a Government can only take place by means of the two mechanisms established by the Constitution: either parliamentary investiture in the aftermath of elections or alternatively in cases of death or resignation of the President of the Government (art. 99 SC), or secondly, through successful presentation of a motion of censure against the Government, which entails automatic investiture of the alternative candidate (art. 113 SC). It is to say that, until now, all Governments in Spain have been formed through the way of art. 99 SC. There have been only two motions of censure (presented in 1980 and in 1987), and none of them has been successful.

2.2 The Central Role of the President of the Government

In both cases, the President of the Government plays a determinant role. In the investiture session, it is the President who must present his or her programme to Congress and obtain Congress's confidence (either by absolute majority in a first vote, or by simple majority in a second round 48 hours later). There is no obligation on the President to present the proposed cabinet team. In the motion of censure, it is also the presidential candidate who plays the main role, more so indeed than the Government being censured, since the main issue of discussion is the programme for government presented by the alternative presidential candidate and whether he or she obtains a sufficient parliamentary majority for a change of government. The extremely important role played by the President is further reinforced by the authority invested in him or her by the Constitution to, firstly, designate or remove ministers from office (although formally these roles fall to the King, the latter has in fact no real substantive power to intervene, art. 100 SC) and secondly, to direct and coordinate Government action (art. 98.1 SC). Therefore, the President is clearly accorded a pre-eminent position within the Government vis-à-vis the other ministers, so much so that at times the Spanish government system has been termed a Chancellor or Prime Ministerial system.

This explains why it is the President who embodies Parliament's confidence in the Government, and why the President is the centre of imputation and demands for enforcement of the Government's political accountability by Parliament.

There are also other mechanisms of political accountability which do not necessarily involve the President (such as, parliamentary questions and interpellations, the work of investigative committees, scrutiny and debate of communications, plans and programmes and informative appearances and sessions, all of which will be addressed in section 4). What all these mechanisms share is that they are planned to inform and account to Parliament on the management of public affairs by the concerned institutions and bodies and their authorities and directors. They also share the fact that in none of them does accountability lead to obligatory resignation from office. Accountability mechanisms entailing forced resignation or removal from public office are reserved to the President and their effects channelled through him or her.

2.3 The Power to Dissolve Parliament

As a counterbalance to the political accountability of the Government, which can lead to its fall, the Constitution also grants the President the power to dissolve both houses of Parliament, as a form of resolving any possible disputes which may occur between both institutions, by going to the people and calling an early election. The President's power to dissolve Parliament (art. 115 SC) is subject to certain constraints (it cannot be exercised to coincide with a motion of censure nor within a year of the last such motion) and is in addition to the Constitutional provision (art. 99.5) for dissolution of Parliament and the calling of elections when no presidential candidate obtains sufficient support for investiture within two months of the first investiture vote. The President of the Government also plays an extremely important role in this process, he or she having exclusive responsibility for exercise of this authority, although the decision must first be submitted to the Council of Ministers for deliberation.

2.4 Criminal Accountability

In addition to political accountability, the Constitution also establishes the criminal accountability of members of the Government and its President. This accountability derives from offences typified as such in the Criminal Code and is subject to two particularities (art. 102 SC): (i) provision of a special personal privilege for processing and judging members of the Government, whereby their criminal accountability may only be tried before the Supreme Court for the duration of their status as members of the Government (and not before the ordinary judges according to ordinary rules of proceeding competence); and (ii) provision for a special procedure for their trial for certain offences (treason and offences against the State), which may only take place in cases of accusations brought on the initiative of one-quarter of the members of the Congress of Deputies and approved by a majority of the chamber (and not on the initiative of the Public Prosecutor, the victim or the citizens, through a public action when admissible). Appraisal then falls to the Supreme Court.

3 The Actors in Accountability: Accountable Persons and Instances in Which Accountability May be Demanded

3.1 The President and Joint Government Accountability

For the reasons set out above, there is no doubt that the main figure of political accountability in the Spanish system established by the 1978 Constitution is the President of the Government. In addition to assuming accountability to the Congress for his or her own actions, including directing and coordinating the Government and designating its members, the President embodies what is termed joint Government accountability, i.e., accountability for actions of the Government as a whole and for those of its individual members (art. 108 SC and 113 SC). Only the President may sack ministers, and therefore, their political accountability, if the purpose is to remove them from office, must be sought via the President. Likewise, the President's personal accountability also affects all members of his or her Government, and resignation or removal from office of the President will also entail resignation of all members of the cabinet.

These mechanisms are all expressly set out in the Constitution. While those that include the possibility of the Government's fall are directed towards the President (motion of censure) or only can be activated by him or her (vote of confidence), those that are directed at individual ministers or occupants of other positions do not involve provision for forced resignation from office.

3.2 Ministers

The ministers are individually accountable to Parliament for management of their Departments and are also jointly accountable for the performance of the Government as a whole (art. 98.2 SC and art. 108 SC). This individual accountability is channelled through various instruments (infra 4); however, under no circumstances do they include provision for forced resignation from office.

3.3 Senior Officials and Civil Servants

Under the Spanish system (formed at this point by the provisions of the Constitution, on one hand, and, on the other, by the Government Act – *Ley 50/1997, de 27 noviembre, de Organización, Competencia y Funcionamiento del Gobierno* – and the Organisation and Functioning of the General State Administration Act – *Ley 6/1997, de 14 abril, de Organización y Funcionamiento de la Administración General del Estado* – both containing the general regulation of Government and State Administration, under the constitutional rules), there is no provision for (a) specific political accountability for senior officials and managerial staff of the Government or Administration of the State (Secretaries of State, General Secretaries, Sub-Secretaries, General Technical Secretaries, Directors General and General Sub-Directors). Their accountability must be channelled through the Minister under whom they serve, since it is with the ministers that authority to appoint these officers lies (on agreement of the Council of Ministers), and correspondingly they also have the authority to remove them from office. This authority to appoint and remove from office means that in practice Ministers are accountable for the actions of their subordinates.

Therefore, senior officials and managerial staff assume individual criminal accountability for their actions (i.e., for acts which are offences) and patrimonial accountability (i.e., for economic injuries to individuals due to malevolent intent or grave negligence, art. 145 & ff. of the Public Administrations Act – *Ley 30/1992, de 26 de noviembre, de Régimen Jurídico de las Administraciones Públicas y del Procedimiento Administrativo Común*; it is to say that the patrimonial responsibility of this staff is produced in front of the Administration, because the economic injuries to individuals due to the activity of the Administration must be compensated directly by the Administration, and then it can require the damage compensation to the senior official or the civil servant who is responsible). However, they themselves are not directly politically accountable. Nevertheless, managerial staff, and also civil servants, may be called to appear before Committees of the Congress of Deputies to report on matters in which they are competent (art. 44.3 Rules of Procedure of the Congress). Such appearances are merely informative in nature and cannot lead to direct demands for resignation. Political accountability for their actions, and the corresponding consequences, including forced resignation/removal from office, when possible (especially in case of managerial staff) must be channelled via the Minister under whom they serve.

Civil servants, who are not political appointees, have criminal, patrimonial and disciplinary accountability. The first two forms are similar to those described for senior political appointees. Disciplinary accountability, on the other hand, takes the place of the (indirect) political accountability of politically appointed staff, since civil servants cannot be discretionally removed from office by the corresponding Departmental Minister. Political accountability for their action falls to the Minister, they themselves however only being liable to disciplinary action for actions constituting administrative infractions.

3.4 Directors of Independent Governmental Agencies

Directors (Presidents, General Directors) of independent governmental agencies (such as the National Stock Market Commission, the Nuclear Safety Council, the Data Protection Agency, the Bank of Spain, the Telecommunications Market Commission, the Restrictive Practices Court and the National Energy Commission, among others), in addition to criminal and patrimonial accountability for their actions, are also politically accountable. However, there is no general provision for enforcement of this accountability (in the sense that these independent authorities have not yet been the subject of general regulation) and this accountability is channelled through the mechanisms provided by their particular set up legislation and the Rules of Procedure of Parliament, as we will see later.

The Government assumes political accountability for the actions of the independent agencies in accordance with its powers to intervene and its authority over the agencies. This varies from case to case, in line with the respective legislation, all of which to date takes the form of specific, individual legislation. In general, however, it can be said that the Government can appoint the board members (at least in part) and intervene, removing them from office in cases of grave failure to fulfil their legal obligations or in cases of seriously prejudicial action. In this area, the Government must assume political accountability deriving from such actions. However, the Government does not on the other hand in general have authority to intervene regarding the day-to-day management or functioning of the agencies, unless the specific law attributes it this authority. Thus, political accountability lies mainly with the boards of the agency themselves. Here the problem lies with the lack of appropriate mechanisms to channel and enforce this accountability, or perhaps better to say, with the weakness of such mechanisms.

The individual laws creating and regulating each agency can establish certain provisions in this respect, such as the obligation to provide periodic (usually annual) reports to Parliament, which may be examined and lead to a call to appear before Parliament (such is the case of the National Stock Market Commission, the Nuclear Safety Council, the Data Protection Agency, the Bank of Spain, the Telecommunications Market Commission and the National Energy Commission). The Rules of Procedure of the Congress make general provision for appearances by authorities and civil servants, as mentioned above, which also includes directors of the independent agencies. However, both general parliamentary appearances and those that are specifically provided for in the individual legislation regulating the agencies are merely informative in function, and it is difficult to say that they constitute a form of effective political control leading to binding or obligatory consequences.

Therefore, unlike criminal and patrimonial accountability, the political accountability of these agency directors is highly limited, since the Government can only act within the range of its generally restricted powers, and there are no adequate mechanisms to make these scanty powers of intervention effective with regard to day-to-day management.

A different case, at least in part, is the new type of agencies regulated by the new State Agencies for the Improvement of Public Services Act – *Ley 28/2006, de 18 de julio, de Agencias estatales para la mejora de los servicios públicos* – which introduce new formulas providing for higher levels of political control (i.e., effective exercise of the legally attributed functions). These new formulas, to be applied to executive agencies (i.e., agencies with executive functions which take charge of management of certain public programs and are linked to certain Ministries) include, as a main mechanism, the programme-contract. These programme-contracts, or management-contracts, are to be signed by the Government and the agencies and have to contain the objectives to reach, the management plan and the indicators to assess the results. They will enable the Government to demand accountability regarding the accomplishment of the established objectives, with consequences for non-accomplishment as established by the programme-contract itself. This approach would appear to increase the agencies' accountability to the Government, by setting up report and control formulas, their performance having a bearing on certain other aspects as well (for example, salary and incentive payments). It is necessary to note, however, that these new formulas (which are in fact new mechanisms of relationship between Government and its bodies, replacing hierarchy for autonomy plus accountability) do not avoid the political accountability of Government for the agencies' action. It is even to say that they increase the possibilities of political control of Government, because they offer new control parameters and new relationship channels between Government and agencies which can be submitted to the control activity of Parliament.

The new Agencies Act also provides a general relationship between agencies and Parliament, through annual reports which are to be sent to Chambers and callings to appear of Agencies' Presidents and Directors before Parliament committees. This provision must be seen not only as a general possibility to act so (general possibility which is already contemplated in the Procedural Rules of both Chambers of Parliament, as said before), but rather as a general requirement to establish a permanent and ordinary relationship between these agencies and Parliament.

3.5 The Congress of Deputies as an Instance of Demands for Enforcement of Accountability

In the two-chamber Spanish parliamentary system, the Congress of Deputies is the setting for enforcement of the Government's political accountability. It is the only scenario in which the main mechanisms of political control can be exercised, such as the motion of censure and votes of confidence. On the other hand, the ordinary control procedures, such as parliamentary questions, interpellations and appearances, also take place in the Senate, although this chamber's role is very much a secondary one in the exercise of these functions. This is in keeping with the fact that investiture of the Government takes place solely and exclusively in the Congress. In this way, it can be said that the confidence required between Parliament and Government, and on which the

Government's political accountability to Parliament is based, is in reality a confidence between Government and the Congress of Deputies.

The main instruments of political control and enforcement of political accountability are exercised in the Plenary Assembly of Congress (the motion of censure, vote of confidence, general debates, and weekly tabling of Government questions). The committees also play an important role in parliamentary control of the Government (questions, interpellations, informative sessions, appearances, investigative committees), yet they are marginal to the control-sanction instruments which may lead to the fall of the Government.

4 The Scope of Accountability

4.1 Subjective Scope

As outlined in the previous section, the President of the Government and the Ministers are the basic channels for imputation of political accountability not only for their performance (individual or that of the Government as a whole) but also for the actions of the authorities, civil servants and organisms working under their authority. The essential component for determining the subjective scope of each Minister's political accountability (and by extension, that of the President of the Government, and the Government as a whole) is his or her authority to designate and remove from office the relevant persons. This enables one to establish an equation between authority to designate-remove persons from office and political accountability for their actions. Although there do exist some mechanisms providing for direct political accountability (basically parliamentary appearances), political accountability for the actions of subordinates falls to the person who appoints them. In the individual sphere, these persons have personal responsibility for their actions (i.e., criminal, patrimonial and, where appropriate, administrative disciplinary accountability).

4.2 Objective Scope

Political accountability covers all actions carried out by the person him or herself or by the person to whom they can be imputed. Given that the Spanish system entails an upward transfer of political accountability towards the person who has the authority to appoint and remove from office the individual performing the action, then accountability *in eligendo* (i.e., for appointment in office) and *in vigilando* (i.e., for performance of duties of office, when authority to control and supervise is also attributed) is extremely important in practice.

In the case of directors of independent governmental agencies, although there is no general regulation of this area, it seems that Ministers, and by extension, the Government and its President, can only be politically accountable for actions carried out under their authority, and the nature of such actions varies from case to case, depending on the specific legislation. The Government cannot be made accountable for actions carried out by the agencies independently of the Government, which is precisely what is sought in most cases and what justifies the existence of such bodies. In these cases, which normally concern the day-to-day management of the agencies, there is a considerable vacuum with regard to possibility to establish political accountability, which must be sought on the grounds of appropriateness, convenience and efficacy. It is precisely this independent evaluation of these (non-legal) appropriateness criteria that lies at essence of such organisms, and any external control (by the Government or Parliament) could be considered as illicit intervention in their functions and a breach of their statutes. Nevertheless, it would be possible to increase the accountability of such called *independent authorities* by appearing before Parliament. The only fact of appearing, reporting and discussing the affairs they deal with, it is a good exercise of accountability, and its regular practice should increase it in a notable way.

Related to executive agencies, as indicated above (supra 2), the new Agencies' Act introduces objective-driven programme-contracts to establish parameters for evaluating the efficacy of these agencies in reaching their objectives and performing their functions. However, so far as these agencies are linked to certain Ministries, the final responsibility for their action rests with them.

5 Mechanisms of Accountability

Political accountability in Spain is fundamentally concentrated in the Government and channelled via Parliament, by means of a range of instruments, which may either lead to forced resignation of the Government (motion of censure and vote of confidence) or not (ordinary instruments for control of the Government). There are also certain parliamentary procedures for control of certain types of Government action, which are also channelled through Parliament.

5.1 Motion of Censure

The Constitution makes explicit provision for the motion of censure (art. 113) as the most potent instrument for enforcing the Government's political accountability. Through the motion of censure, Parliament can force the Government to resign and replace it with another one with a stronger majority. This is a constructive motion of censure, designed along the lines of the German *Grundgesetz* model, which seeks to avoid the maximum mechanism of Parliamentary control of the Government leading to situations of instability. Therefore, to prosper, the motion of censure, which must have the backing of one-tenth of the deputies on proposal and must include an alternative candidate for the Presidency of the Government, needs the support of an absolute majority of the Congress, in which case the Government leaves office and the alternative candidate is automatically invested. In this way, a negative majority becomes a positive one, making it extremely difficult for motions of censure to prosper, even in cases where Governments have weak Parliamentary majorities. This explains why this mechanism has been so rarely exercised since 1978 (on only three occasions), and why it has never succeeded.

As regulated in the SC, the motion of censure seeks to determine whether a stronger Government majority than the present one could be formed in Parliament, in which case, a change of Government occurs. This is why scrutiny of the alternative candidate takes precedence over criticism of the government. It is in fact an opposition attempt to invest an alternative President.

5.2 Vote of Confidence

The vote of confidence, also expressly set out in the SC (art. 112), is a mechanism for explicit reflection of Parliament's confidence in the Government, and the initiative lies exclusively with the President of the Government subject to preliminary deliberation with the Ministers Council. To prosper, a vote of confidence only requires a simple majority of the Deputies. Should the vote fail, the President must resign, and the ordinary investiture procedure to designate a new President of the Government begins (art. 99 SC). It is important to note that a vote of confidence can only be proposed on the Government programme or on a general policy statement, not on specific bills or a draft State Budget; in other words, it cannot serve to put pressure on Parliament to pass certain laws.

5.3 Ordinary Mechanisms for Political Control

The Spanish parliamentary system also includes other instruments for political control of Government, which serve to demand and enforce its political accountability to Parliament, although they do not lead to enforced removal from office or resignation of either the President, when directed at this office, nor the other members of the Government, individually, who can only be removed from office by the President, as we have seen. Since these mechanisms are the usual means by which the Government's political accountability is sought, they may be termed ordinary mechanisms for political control.

They are the traditional instruments in this area, and are as follows:

- Parliamentary questions to the Government, which are presented in writing and may be answered orally or in writing, either in the Plenary Assembly or in Committee. Parliamentary questions, like the other ordinary instruments for political control, can take place both in the Congress of Deputies and the Senate, unlike the motion of censure and the vote of confidence, which may not be exercised in the higher chamber, as nor indeed may investiture of the President. The weekly oral question session for the Government in the Plenary Assembly of the Congress of Deputies, which takes place every Wednesday afternoon, is especially important;

- interpellations, by means of which Members of Parliament question the reasons or purposes behind Government action. These must also be presented in writing and lead to Plenary debate in the corresponding chamber. The outcome may be a motion on which a vote is taken, expressing the Chamber's position on the relevant issue;
- investigative committees, which the Chambers may establish (on the initiative of two parliamentary groups or one-fifth of the deputies in the Congress, or 25 members of the Senate, representing at least two groups, or on the initiative of the Government itself) to examine any issue of public interest. Investigative committees may call on any individual to appear before them and conclude with presentation of findings to the Plenary Assembly of the relevant chamber for a vote. The resulting report may be sent to the Director of Public Prosecutions for initiation of appropriate action should there be evidence of a penal offence. However, the conclusions of Investigative Committees are not binding for the courts nor do they have any bearing on case outcomes;
- requests for information to the Government, requiring data, reports or documents on any issue (art. 109 SC and 7 RCD). In the case of classified data (as defined by the Official Secrets Act), the Government may facilitate the required data to a restricted number of deputies (those designated for this purpose by each parliamentary group, the spokesperson for each group, the President of the Chamber or the relevant committee, depending on the sensitivity of the information). These may not disclose the contents of the data. Classified documents may not be reproduced or copied, and the Government may request that the session be declared secret (rules established in the Resolution of the Presidency of the Congress of Deputies, 2 June 1992). There is also a special procedure for control of reserved funds (Law 11/1995, of 11th May), exercised by means of a special committee, presided over by the President of Congress and composed of the designated deputies with access to the classified data. The Government must report to this committee every six months, sessions are secret and committee members are not permitted to disclose the contents of the classified information;
- appearances by members of the Government (art. 110.1 SC), public authorities and civil servants, reporting to the chambers on matters within their competence (art. 44 RCD, art. 202 RS). These appearances, which may take the format of informative sessions before committees, may be requested either by the Government or by the chambers, but do not lead to adoption of resolutions;
- and, finally, parliamentary control of Government action takes place by means of the general debates arising from presentation of Government

statements or plans. These general debates conclude with a vote on the relevant resolution (art. 196 - 198 RCD). Especially important in this respect is the annual state of the Nation debate in the Congress of Deputies.

5.4 Specific Procedures involving Control of Government Action

The Spanish parliamentary system also includes a number of other procedures which involve parliamentary control of certain Government actions. These are also exercised in Parliament, and are:

- Parliamentary intervention during emergencies (art. 116 SC): Government must inform Congress of the declaration of a state of alarm, which does not entail suspension of fundamental rights; previous authorisation from Congress is required for declaration of a state of emergency and declaration of a state of siege or war can only be made by Congress itself. It has never been applied;
- previous approval by the Senate is required for measures proposed by the Government to force an Autonomous Community to fulfil its constitutional and legal obligations (art. 155 CE). It has never been applied;
- Congress may validate or repeal decree-laws passed by the Government in cases of extraordinary and urgent need (art. 86 SC);
- the Houses of Parliament may control the legislative decrees passed by the Government by parliamentary delegation, under the terms of the law of delegation (art. 82.6 SC).

6 The Consequences of Enforcement of Accountability

The idea that political accountability leads to resignation or removal from office is widespread in Spain. This is indeed the maximum expression of the obligation to make good the political consequences of a given action; however, it cannot be the only form. In reality, the instruments for political accountability which make provision for a legal obligation to resign are limited in number and exceptional in nature (the motion of censure and the vote of confidence, as outlined above, supra. 4). In contrast, the ordinary mechanisms for enforcing political accountability of the Government and other executive agents which channel political control do not lead, at least not necessarily, to resignation or removal from office; rather they seek clarification of facts and rectification (or orientation, should the check be carried out *ex ante*) of actions. This means that firstly, the possibility of extending provision for obligatory resignation to instruments which do not at present include this, should be considered, and secondly, that the consequences arising from political accountability and the forms of political atonement for actions subject to this accountability should be reconsidered. Unfortunately, however, debate on this issue in Spain at present is practically non-existent. If removal or forced resignation are in fact the exception of political accountability processes, but at the same time are the consequences par excellence of this type of responsibility, it should be considered that the main weight of political accountability should move from the result to the path itself, as a way to supply wide and good quality information and to open a transparent discussion on public affairs. On the other hand, it should be very important to separate political responsibility from other types of responsibility, especially criminal ones. This is perhaps the main problem on this point in Spain: the link between both different types of responsibility makes ineffective on quite a lot of occasions the political accountability, because this mechanism is not launched until the juridical responsibilities have been set. And at this moment, the facts are old and the public interest for them has been usually reduced in a notable way.

CHAPTER II

Political Accountability in Sweden

Joakim Nergelius

1 General Aspects and Constitutional Framework[1]

Sweden is a parliamentary democracy based on popular sovereignty and rule of law at the same time, as follows from chapter 1, article 1 of the Constitution (Instrument of Government) of 1974, which entered into force 1 January 1975. The independence of the respective executive, legislative and judicial powers is guaranteed through various provisions of the Constitution, but the idea of separation of powers was not present when the Constitution, replacing an ancient and partly obsolete Constitution from 1809, was elaborated in the 1960s and –70s. The whole political atmosphere in Sweden at that time, like in the other Nordic countries, was permeated with the idea of popular sovereignty, which was seen as the ideological basis or foundation of the successful welfare state. Later on and in particular after 1 January 1995, when Sweden joined the European Union, the idea of separation of powers has gradually become more influential.

The Parliament (*Riksdag, riksdagen*) consists of 349 members, all sitting in the same chamber. National elections take place every fourth year in September and, at the same time, municipal elections take place to the 285 municipalities. The election system is strictly proportional. Each party which gains at least 4% of the votes in the country will be represented in Parliament.[2] At the moment, seven parties are represented there.

Sweden is still a monarchy, though the tasks of the King are mainly representative. The political power rests with the Parliament and in particular the government. Within the government, the prime minister has a very strong position. In fact, the parliament only votes on his nomination and he is then free to choose any members that he wishes of the government.

The most important of the constitutional acts, *Regeringsformen* (The Instrument of Government) was enacted in 1974 and then entered into force on 1 January 1975. Apart from that, the Act of Succession from 1809, regulating the heritage to the throne, and the Freedom of Press Act from 1949 (but tracing its origins back to 1766) are both important parts of the Swedish constitutional heritage. Due to the quick technical development, a new, special Freedom of Speech Act was introduced in 1991 in order to bring TV, radio, video and other "modern" media in line with newspapers and books, covered since before by the Freedom of Press Act.

Apart from that, a number of important basic human rights are covered both by the 2nd chapter of the Instrument of Government and by the European Convention, which has applied as domestic Swedish law since 1 January 1995. However, generally speaking, the constitutional tradition in Sweden must be described as weak, and it is only in the last ten years that an increased interest

---

1 All translations from the Swedish Constitution are taken from the official publication The Constitution of Sweden – The Fundamental Laws and the Riksdag Act, Stockholm – *Sveriges Riksdag* 2003.

2 Apart from that, a party which receives 12 % of the votes in one of the 24 constituencies will gain an MP coming from that particular area; see IG 3:7 sect. 2.

in constitutional issues from scholars and the media has been visible. This has a lot to do with the fact that the Constitution from 1809 gradually became obsolete; it stated for instance that the King governed and ruled the state alone and that the knights, the clergymen, the merchants and the farmers had their own chambers in the Parliament (until 1866). When democracy prevailed, around 1920, Sweden in reality did not have a valid constitution until 1974. Nevertheless, the country was successful during this time. Thus, the general feeling that the constitution and its text is tremendously important for the development within the society, so common in many other states with more dramatic historical backgrounds, has never really been felt throughout Sweden. One scholar has even described the period from 1920-1974 as "the unconstitutional half-century".[3]

As mentioned above, as far as the formation of the Government is concerned, the Swedish Constitution only regulates the appointment of the Prime Minister, who is then, once appointed, free to choose any other ministers that he wants to include in the Government. This fact undoubtedly reflects the generally very strong position of the Prime Minister in the Swedish Constitution and political life, as will be further explained below. In a corresponding way, parliamentary votes on the dismissal of ministers also distinguish between the Prime Minister and other ministers; while the latter ones may be dismissed individually, a vote of lack of confidence in relation to the Prime Minister (PM) would affect the government as a whole and normally lead to its resignation. According to chapter 6, article 5 of the Instrument of Government (IG), both kinds of dismissals are in fact quite possible, but the legal and political consequences are thus quite different in the two situations; see also chapter 6 articles 6-7.

Those points must be explained a little bit more in detail. According to chapter 6, article 1 of the Instrument of Government, the government consists of the PM and other ministers. The PM is appointed according to the procedure envisaged in chapter 6, articles 2-4, while it is clearly stated in chapter 6, article 1 that the PM, once appointed, appoints the other ministers himself, according to his free choice. (Naturally, if the government should consist of more than one party, it seems more natural that the other party or parties, to which the PM does not belong, will nominate its or their members of the government autonomously, but this part of the process, including some political bargaining, is not covered or regulated by the Constitution.) The importance of those rules and the concentration of power that it entails for the PM should actually be underlined and seen in the perspective of a general lack of shift of the political power, where one and the same party – the Social Democrats – has held governmental power from 1932-76, 1982-91 and since 1994, acting in coalition with other parties only in 1939-45 and 1951-57. This seems to be unprecedented in other European countries.

How, then, is the procedure for appointing the PM regulated? It takes place normally after elections, if the government is changing (like in 1991 or 1994),

[3] Cfr F. Sterzel (1998).

but also if the PM has died (like in 1986) or resigned for personal reasons (like in 1996). However, after an election when the Government does not resign, like in 1998 or 2002, the procedure is not used.

The Speaker of the Parliament, who does also have a very crucial position in this respect, summons representatives from each party group represented in the Parliament for consultations. The procedure is then largely informal, but the idea behind the rules is that the Speaker shall be more or less convinced that his proposal will not be turned down by the *Riksdag* when he places it before that Chamber (after consultations also with the deputy speakers). It may thus be necessary that the Speaker, at least in politically tricky moments (which have hitherto not been so frequent but might occur after the next Parliamentary election in September 2006), can show some political sensitivity or "*Fingerspitzgefühl*" in this respect.

Sweden does normally have governments that possess only a minority of the places in the Parliament. In fact, the latest majority government resigned in May 1981. This is due partly to the proportional electoral system, but also to the fact that when the vote on the proposed PM will take place, he or she is rejected only if more than half the Members of the *Riksdag*, i.e. 175 ones, vote against the proposal (IG 6:2). Thus, there is no requirement that the PM and the Government shall be supported by a majority within the Parliament as long as it may expect support for its proposals, in terms of budget, legislation and other matters, from a majority of the MP's. Undoubtedly, this rule has made the task easier for the normally governing Social Democrats, skilful at obtaining support from other left-leaning parties.[4] In fact, it happened in 1978 that the leader of the liberal party was appointed PM with the support only of his own group (with 38 places), when the Social Democrats decided not to vote against him for tactical reasons.

Should the proposal for a new PM after all be rejected by the *Riksdag* (which has so far never happened), the procedure is repeated. But if the proposal should be rejected four times, the procedure is abolished in order to be resumed when a new parliamentary election has been held (IG 6:3). However, once appointed, as mentioned above, the PM appoints the other ministers and informs the Parliament of his choices (6:4).

As indicated, this clear difference between the appointment of the PM and the other ministers is reflected also in their respective positions as far as political accountability is concerned. The rules will be dealt with more in detail below, but the main difference is that ordinary ministers may be discharged for different reasons (of their own free will, by the decision of the PM or by a vote of no confidence from the Parliament), while the Speaker has to discharge all the other ministers if the PM is discharged or dies (IG chapter 6, articles 6-7). Thus, it is fair to conclude that the difference in the procedure of appointment

4 Still, the rule does of course not explain that party's dominance from 1932-1974, before the new Constitution entered into force.

corresponds to a difference in political accountability between the PM and the other ministers, who are on the other hand all treated equally.

The concept of political accountability exists within the doctrine(s) of constitutional law and above all political science, but it must be explained that the doctrine of constitutional law was for a long time very limited. It is only in the last ten years that it has actually started to grow and discuss important issues of this kind in a critical manner. In political science, on the other hand, there has been a vivid debate in the last ten years not least on this topic, which is due above all to the current mechanism(s) of regular co-operation between the government and one or more parties (the Farmers from 1995-98 and the leftist, former Communist as well as the Green Party since 1998). This system is allegedly detrimental to the very idea of political accountability in the traditional Swedish sense of the word, since the legal and constitutional mechanisms that exist for supervision do only relate to the government as such, but not to the parties who support the government (in exchange of various political favours). Thus, those latter parties are able to exert a huge political influence without being subject to scrutiny or being held politically accountable. It must also be mentioned that political accountability as such is not mentioned within the Constitution (IG), that talks instead of "Parliamentary Control", which is dealt with in chapter 12 as explained below. Thus, the concept of political accountability is clearly more important in the general political and constitutional discussion than in the constitutional law, where it is in fact not distinctly defined and has no specific legal meaning.

Apart from the political accountability, there is also a legal accountability. According to chapter 12, article 3, an acting or former minister may be held accountable for a criminal act committed in the performance of his ministerial duties only if he has grossly neglected his official duty. A decision to institute criminal proceedings is then taken by the Committee on the Constitution and the case will be tried by the Supreme Court. But outside the area of the official duties, the ministers will thus not enjoy any immunity from criminal procedures. Nor can he expect any special procedures to take place should he be accused of having committed a crime.

2 The Actors

The basic rule in the Swedish constitution is that the government is accountable or responsible as a whole, or as a collective as it is sometimes expressed, for its actions. As will be explained below, the individual responsibility and accountability is legally and formally limited (e.g. IG chapter 7, article 3 and chapter 11, article 7). Nevertheless, such accountability may be established, since the real scope of action of the individual minister is undoubtedly greater than those rules do indicate.[5] Individual ministers may of course also be held accountable for their political statements, comments, points of view etc, which may set the more specified rules on their accountability into motion. Thus, such a thing as an individual accountability before the Parliament does exist, as follows clearly from the rules on the parliamentary vote of no-confidence.

Except for the strictly legal accountability mentioned above, the ministers are accountable only to the Parliament, whereas the civil servants are not, as may have been expected, legally accountable to the Parliament or the Government. Instead, they may be subject to the control conducted by the well-known Ombudsman (cfr IG chapter 12, article 6), an original Swedish invention which is however legally speaking not extremely forceful. On the other hand, the civil servants have full legal responsibility for their actions and may be prosecuted at any time for any irregularities conducted within their professional activities. In other words, they have no immunity at all. Also, the general transparency within the public administration and the accessibility of documents is likely to contribute to the supervision of their activities, also by the media.

Legally speaking, the collective accountability means that the government as a whole is legally accountable and responsible for the Government's decisions, which are made at meetings where at least five ministers must be present (IG chapter 7, article 4). Obviously, illegalities or other irregularities are extremely rare in those kinds of decisions, but the only possibility to avoid such accountability is for the individual minister to have his or her dissenting opinion entered into the record from the Government meeting (IG 7:6). Should that actually happen – which is rare but not unique – the dissenting minister will not be held legally accountable for the decision. In the eyes of the public, he or she will probably also avoid political responsibility (but is on the other hand likely to see his influence within the government reduced).

3 The Scope of Accountability

The basic features of the Swedish Constitution, as outlined above, also mean that ministers as individuals or the government as a whole is accountable mainly for policy-making, but not for the execution or implementation of its own decisions. This is a fact that has to do with the traditionally high level of autonomy of the Swedish public administration and its bodies.[6] According to IG chapter 11, article 7, no public authority, including the *Riksdag* and

---

[5] This is also underlined in one of the leading constitutional comments, E. Holmberg, N. Stjernquist (2003) 132.

[6] For various reasons, the concept of "agencies" does not seem to fit well with the Swedish system and terminology as far as the public administration is concerned, since the Swedish system knows only the concept of Public Authority (*"myndighet"* or *"förvaltningsmyndighet"*). Such administrative authority may be delegated to companies, associations, foundations etc (IG chapter 11, article 6, sect. 3), but the scope

the Government, may determine how an administrative authority shall decide in a particular case relating to the exercise of public authority vis-à-vis a private subject or a local authority, or relating to the application of law. In the constitutional doctrine and in the settled practice of the political bodies, this has for a long time been interpreted to mean that the ministers may not interfere in the concrete, specific activities of the administrative bodies.[7] An interesting case in order to illustrate this may be the events following the assassination of Prime Minister Olof Palme in 1986. In 1988, it was revealed that the Minister of Justice Ms Anna-Greta Leijon had written a letter of recommendation to a private friend, Mr Ebbe Carlsson, in order to help him conduct certain private investigations related to the murder, on the cause of which he had certain theories. While co-operating with a few policemen who shared his views, his actions and investigations, which included some illegal acts, were not sanctioned by the responsible police authorities or the officers in charge of the official murder investigation. Thus, the way in which the Minister of Justice had supported his private activities, without informing the police authorities, provoked harsh protests from the police and was seen as an illegal and unconstitutional involvement in police affairs from the Minister, who later had to resign as will be explained below.

Thus, ministers do normally not have the power to interfere in the work of public authorities or give detailed instructions to civil servants, though general political guidelines are of course allowed. At the same time, however, ministers are normally not accountable for the actions of public authorities. Once again, a discussion on the role of the Minister of Justice may illustrate the situation. In the summer of 2004, a number of heavily guarded prisoners escaped from different Swedish prisons. The right-wing opposition then asked for the resignation of the Minister of Justice, but since he could not be held accountable or responsible for the errors or mistakes made by responsible civil servants in the relevant public bodies, those demands had no legal or constitutional base. Only if the minister has known for some time about problems in specific bodies without reacting or doing anything about them (something that was actually discussed in relation to those events) may the minister be held legally or politically accountable.[8]

In this way, there may thus be said to exist a clear relation between the scope of accountability of the ministers, which is very limited as far as the actions and decisions of the public authorities for which they are politically responsible is

---

of such delegation is limited. A study from 1989 that deals with administration outside the traditional realm of public authorities is L. Marcusson, *Offentlig förvaltning utanför myndighetsområdet*.

7 It may be noted that IG 11:7 does not apply to the Government itself, since that is not an administrative authority.

8 Yet another Minister of Justice, Mr Wickbom, was forced to resign when a convicted spy managed to escape in 1987, but this was contrary to how the system normally works and actually mainly reflected his weak position within the Government. Due to discussion on his general competence and ability, the PM after the escape decided to replace him with Ms Leijon, who was then forced to resign less than a year later for quite different reasons.

concerned, and their legal powers, which are also limited in relation to those authorities. It should be noted that a Parliamentary Committee appointed in 2003, the so-called *Ansvarskommittén*, has been told to look into the effects of this traditional autonomy and independence of the public authorities. From the government, it was then argued that this independence does not work well in relation to the EU, e.g. whenever EU ministerial or committee meetings are held. However, it looks unlikely that this committee will propose any changes in this area.

It should also be added here that almost all public authorities work under the Government, unless the Constitution or a law expressly state that they work under the Parliament (IG chapter 11, article 6). Ministers are also accountable for the actions of their political advisors. The work of those advisors does often form a most important part of the political decision-making of the minister, of which however he or she must be fully accountable. Thus, the role of the advisors is not regulated as such by the constitution or by other laws.

Methods such as "co-regulation" or "open method of coordination" are unheard of in the Swedish constitutional context, while there is a substantial scope for the Government to regulate through delegated legislation, as follows from chapter 8 IG, in particular articles 7-13. But this issue on the division of legislative authority between the Parliament and the Government appears to fall outside the scope of this study. In fact, it seems slightly difficult to imagine the equivalents of such legislative concepts as the open method of co-ordination at the Swedish national legislative level, though that issue will not be developed here.

What could be mentioned once again, however, is the current unclear situation concerning the co-operation between the Social Democratic Government and two supporting parties, the Left and the Green Party. The latter ones do not form part of the Government and are thus formally not accountable for its decisions, but at the same time they have advisors working in some Ministries and major political decisions, including budgetary ones, are made after negotiations between the Government and those parties. As mentioned above, this state of affairs is increasingly criticised for the very fact that it undermines political accountability in the traditional sense.

4 Activating Accountability: Parliamentary Control and Transparency

According to rules on financial power in chapter 9 IG, state funds may not be used other than as determined by the *Riksdag*. This reflects an old tradition, and the *Riksdag* also determines the principles for the administration and disposition of State property. But at the same time, funds and other assets of the State are at the disposal of the Government (9:8). So how do those rules fit?

The simple answer is that the Government submits a proposal for an annual budget to the *Riksdag* (chapter 9, article 6), who then decides on whether to approve the budget or not. Normally, certain modifications are made after negotiations in the various parliamentary committees, but the *Riksdag* does after this procedure approve the budget (the opposite has never happened).[9] And in the next step, the Government implements by its own decisions the budget which is formally decided by the *Riksdag*. In this way, at least formally, the *Riksdag* maintains control of the state assets.

Furthermore, both decisions in relation to the budget and other political decisions are subject to parliamentary control. In fact, and as mentioned above, a special chapter in the IG, chapter 12, is devoted to this topic. As will be explained below, the possibility to declare a lack of confidence in a Minister is probably the most important part of the instruments at the Parliament's disposal in this respect (IG chapter 12, article 4). Apart from that, any member of the *Riksdag* may submit an interpellation or put a question to a minister on any matter concerning the minister's performance of his official duties (12:5). More detailed rules on those institutes are to be found in chapter 6 of the *Riksdag* Act. A permission from the Speaker is necessary in order for the interpellation to be addressed to the Minister,[10] who is formally not obliged to answer. However, should an answer not be given within two weeks, an explanation for this is required.

The role of the Constitutional Committee, which is regulated in chapter 12, articles 1-2, is very important in this respect. The rules on the possibility for parliamentary committees to call or summon civil servants to questioning, in order to examine whether the government or individual ministers may have acted incorrectly in relation to public authorities or otherwise, are to be found in chapter 4, article 11 of the Riksdag Act. Those rules were enacted after the above-mentioned affair in 1988 concerning a private person, Mr Ebbe Carlsson, who had initiated his own investigations into the murder of the former PM and was supported in his actions by the Minister of Justice. The majority of the Constitutional Committee then found that open hearings could take place and that also civil servants should be called to those. Such meetings, where civil servants are asked to provide information, may be open to the public or not depending on the circumstances (Riksdag Act 4:13). It is however only a matter of providing information. Such persons are for instance never heard under oath. Civil servants working for authorities under the Government – i.e. the vast majority of the public bodies, as explained above – who doubt the wisdom of passing information to one of the different parliamentary committees, of which there are totally sixteen, may refer the request from the committee to the

9 Like most other parliamentary decisions, including legislative ones, such decisions are made by a simple majority of the voting MP's, as stated by IG chapter 4, article 5.

10 Should the Speaker and the majority of the *Riksdag* not agree on whether the question may be put forward, the Constitutional Committee will have to decide the issue.

Government for a final decision on whether to occur before the committee or not (Riksdag Act 4:11).

Debates in the chamber of the Swedish Parliament are normally open to the public. Apart from debates and "hearings" within the Committees, the Parliament may organise special hearings with experts. Such a hearing on the increased scope of separation of power in the traditional sense and the role of the courts was e.g. organised in March 2000 and, interestingly enough, the issue of accountability and control was discussed in the same way recently, i.e. through a general discussion at a public hearing where no decisions were made (15 November 2005). Also the new Committee drafting constitutional amendments (*Grundlagsutredningen*), which is supposed to deliver proposals before the election in 2010, has organised two similar events.

The other ways of exercising control, i.e. through votes on lack of confidence and the control exercised by the Constitutional Committee (*Konstitutionsutskottet*, KU) will be dealt with in the next section.

5 Consequences

According to IG chapter 12, article 4, the *Riksdag* may at any time declare that a minister no longer enjoys its confidence, though such a declaration requires support of more than half the total membership of the *Riksdag* (i.e. 175 members). The motion calling for such a declaration must however be supported by at least one tenth of its members (i.e. 35). Such questions against individual members have been raised at various times, e.g. 1985 when the Foreign Minister was accused of not supporting an official Swedish position against the Soviet Union. However, such a motion has never been supported by the majority, but when the Minister of Justice Ms Leijon resigned in 1988, this was a direct consequence of the fact that the majority, consisting of right-wing parties and the Communist Party, had declared its will to vote against her.

The same procedure applies in relation to the PM, but as mentioned above, the difference is that if he or she should resign, the other ministers must also be discharged by the Speaker (IG 6:7). This could thus be described as a kind of "collective dismissal". However, it must be noted that, in a situation where the Parliament has declared its lack of confidence in a minister – the PM or another one – he or she does actually not have to resign if the Government may call for an extraordinary election within one week from the declaration. Such elections may never be called within three months from the date when a newly elected *Riksdag* is convened (IG chapter 3, article 4), but otherwise this possibility remains open for the Government in such a situation.[11]

[11] In June 1988, when Ms Leijon was forced to resign, this option was not interesting for the Government should she have chosen to face the vote of confidence, since an election was going to take place in September that year anyway.

As mentioned above, the PM may also in other situations dismiss Ministers at any time. In fact, the current PM has since March 1996, when he took office, disposed of over a total of 51 Ministers, although only some twenty are sitting in the Government simultaneously. This also reflects the increasingly strong position of the PM, which is now starting to be criticised by the doctrine and even sometimes described as "presidential" in its nature.

It must also be mentioned that every year, the Constitutional Committee exercises an examination of the ministers' individual performance of their official duties, as well as the handling of Government business in general. The Committee writes an annual report to the Parliament on its observations, which is quite often a matter of political controversy. However, the party representation in the various parliamentary committees, including this one, corresponds to the situation in the Parliament as a whole, which makes open criticism against the Government somewhat less likely and unusual. The President of the Constitutional Committee does however always represent the opposition. And should the majority of the Committee reach the conclusion that criticism against a minister is required, it will state so in its report (a so-called "*prickning*", which may be politically sensitive but lacks formal legal significance).

In order for the Committee to fulfil its duties, it is entitled to have access to the records of decisions taken in Government matters and all the documents pertaining to such matters. It may also act upon the observations of other committees.[12]

In relation not least to EU matters and, albeit indirectly, the resignation of the Commission in March 1999, also the birth of the new National Audit Office, which is since 2002 regulated in IG chapter 12, article 7, is of great interest. This new public authority resides under the Parliament and has replaced both the old National Audit Office, which worked under the Government, and the so-called Parliamentary Accountants, who were politicians and acting MP's![13] It may be of a certain interest to know that this new office was in a way born out of a huge and highly public conflict in 1999 between the former Managing Director of the Old National Audit Office (*Riksrevisionsverket*) Ms Inga-Britt Ahlenius, and the former Minister of Finance Mr Ringholm. Ms Ahlenius, who was also a member of the Group of Experts whose report in March 1999 led the EU Commission to resign (and who does now hold a very high position as a kind of "super-accountant" within the UN), advocated strongly in favour of creating this new, independent auditing office and did thus, finally, "win" this battle with the Government.

This new office is under the direction of three Auditors General, who are elected by the *Riksdag* and decide independently what activities that shall be audited. When conclusions from the audit are drawn, the Board of the office

[12] Those rules on the Constitutional Committee are to be found in chapter 12, articles 1-2 IG, as mentioned above.

[13] The new agency is called, in Swedish, *Riksrevisionen*. It has thus replaced both the former bodies *Riksrevisionsverket* and *Riksdagens revisorer*.

puts forward to the *Riksdag* the proposals and reports which result, as well as the official audit statements.

To summarise, the vote on lack of confidence for a certain minister and the annual reports of the Constitutional Committee are the two main instruments for the Swedish Parliament to exercise its control over the Government. In the future, the reports of the National Audit Office may also come to be very important, though that remains to be seen. Further reform proposals are from time to time suggested in the debate and it is very likely that the newly appointed Committee for Constitutional Reform will also look into this area. Thus, the topic is a "living" one within the doctrine.[14] However, it should be noted that *Grundlagsutredningen*, the newly appointed committee dealing with constitutional reform, has not been instructed to look into this particular issue.[15]

6 A Case Study: The Tsunami Report

In relation to Sweden, it should be noted that the system of political accountability for the government was vividly discussed in the first week of December 2005, as a result of the report from the special Commission on the responsibility for mishandling of the consequences of the tsunami in south-east Asia on 26 December 2004, in which some 600 Swedish citizens died.[16] The report was clear in placing the main responsibility for things that had not functioned during and after the catastrophe on the government and the Prime Minister in particular. The main criticism was that a national alert system in times of catastrophes and urgent crisis had never been installed. Thus, the public authorities had no real instructions and simply did not know exactly how to act in this totally unexpected and unforeseen situation.

In the aftermath of the report, it has been much discussed whether the opposition parties should have called for a vote on lack of confidence against the Prime Minister, in line with IG chapter 12, article 4, and thus against the whole government. Finally, on the 6th December 2005, they decided not to do so but to wait instead for the inquiry that the Constitutional Committee was going to start. In view of the very sharp criticism in the report, together with the previous situations e.g. in 1980, 1985 or 1996, when such votes have been called for what seems to be less severe errors, this decision does not seem to be entirely logical. It shall thus be viewed in light of the fact that a new Parliamentary election will take place in September 2006, which means that the opposition has had an obvious political interest in keeping the issue "alive" as much as possible until then, rather than seeing it formally settled by such a vote almost a year in advance. In particular, this was the case since it seemed clear that the Govern-

---

14 See, among others, Höök, Lundin (2001) 117-128 and Ekroth (1999) 189-235. Among political scientists, see among others Lewin (1999).

15 Its instructions are to be found in *Kommittédirektiv* 2004:96.

16 The full title of the report is *Sverige och tsunamin – granskning och förslag*, SOU 2005:104.

ment's supporting parties, i.e. the Left and the Green Party, would not have voted against the Prime Minister should such a vote have taken place. Still, from a legal and constitutional point of view, the decision not to ask for such a vote here was hardly justified.

Instead, the Constitutional Committee of the Parliament came to examine the behaviour of the Government during and after the tsunami quite thoroughly, as a part of its regular supervision of the Government. In fact, the opposition parties placed some lawyers and other MP's, who are legal experts within the Committee for those particular hearings, which somehow seemed to be intended to underline their legal and not exclusively political nature. The findings of the Committee are to be found in the report KU 2005/06:8,[17] presented in March 2006, in which sharp formal criticism was raised against a number of ministers, including the Prime Minister and the Foreign Minister. However, the Foreign Minister, Ms Freivalds, choose to resign in March 2006 before the report was published, allegedly for mishandling of issues related to the so-called Muhammed crisis but in reality acting as a scapegoat for the whole government. After that, the opposition parties decided not to raise a vote of confidence against the PM or any other minister.

7 Analysis

Without criticising the existing Swedish rules in this field as such, which would be futile when they have actually existed for quite a long time and will obviously not be subject to revision in quite a long time – partly because they are considered to be a part of the existing constitutional tradition – a few distinctive features, that are in fact slightly problematic – may after all be identified.

One such feature is the important but quite puzzling role of the Constitutional Committee, KU. As mentioned above, the parliamentary examination of how the government has conducted its activities in the past year is done mainly through the works of this body. As far as the political examination is concerned, the main problem here seems to be that the party representation within the committee is the same as for the parliament as a whole, a fact which reduces the possibility of the opposition to criticise the government for mismanagement of certain issues. But even more puzzling, perhaps, is the tendency clearly shown through the hearings on the Tsunami aftermath, namely that the work of the Constitutional Committee also tends to be of a legal character. This is a kind of examination, then, the legal basis of which is unclear and does not follow clearly from the IG (where the rules in chapter 12, articles 1-2 do actually not distinguish between different kinds of control in this way). However, from the accountability point of view, it seems clear that the supervision exercised by

---

[17] The full official title of which is *Granskning av regeringens krisberedskap och krishantering I samband med flodvågskatastrofen* 2004, vol. 1-3.

the Constitutional Committee must above all be a political one (which does not exclude that clear violations of law, like the one made by Ms Leijon in 1988, may be subject to political criticism, since a minister who violates the law is not likely to be handling the job very well).

Another clear feature is of course the very strong emphasis on parliamentarianism and popular sovereignty within the whole Swedish constitutional system. From the accountability point of view, perhaps the absence of any control as such of the activities of the Parliament, the legislative branch, is the clearest example of this. "Parliamentary control" in the sense of chapter 12 IG does obviously only refer to the control exercised by the Parliament over the other branches of Government.

From a practical point of view, apart from the absence of a strong system of judicial review and the relatively weak general position of the courts, the judicial branch, this is perhaps most visible through the model of so-called "negative parliamentarianism" that is used when a new PM and thus a new government is being appointed. The fact that this can – and does in fact regularly – take place with the support of only a minority of the MP's does obviously lead to a tradition of weak governments. At the same time, another interesting feature or pattern that Sweden seems to share with the UK is that a strong formal emphasis on parliamentarianism does actually lead to a situation where the government is the stronger actor, that regularly takes initiatives and has the ability to force the Parliament to obey its wishes. A detailed analysis of this topic clearly falls outside the scope of this article, but it could at least be said that a strong parliamentarianism does not automatically lead to efficient modes of political accountability. On the contrary, a situation where the government is supported by a majority of the Parliament without actually comprising or representing parties that possess such a majority, may actually be described as the worst possible as far as political accountability is concerned.

Finally, the independence of the public authorities (or "agencies") and the prohibition against any governmental interference in their handling of specific cases may on the other hand be described as a positive element of the Swedish constitution, notably from the accountability perspective since any violation of this principle (which is constitutionally protected by IG chapter 11, articles 2 and 7) is easily discernible, as shown once again through the example of Ms Leijon in 1988. Together with the right of access to documents and the transparency principle that is still governing the public administration, this is also the most likely explanation for the still rather low degree of corruption in Sweden, which could otherwise be surprising in a country where the same political party has kept the governmental power for almost 70 years.

Bibliography

EKROTH (1999)

J. Ekroth, 'Några reflektioner angående Konstitutionsutskottets granskning av regeringen' in N. Berggren, N. Karlson, J. Nergelius (ed.), *Makt utan motvikt – Om demokrati och konstitutionalism* (Stockholm 1999) 189-235.

HOLMBERG, STJERNQUIST (2003)

E. Holmberg, N. Stjernquist, *Vår författning* 13th ed. (Stockholm 2003).

HOOK, LUNDIN (2001)

J. Höök, O. Lundin, 'Kontroll och ansvarsutkrävande i svensk offentlig förvaltning' (2001) *Nordiskt Administrativt Tidsskrift* 117-128.

LEWIN (1999)

L. Lewin, *Bråka inte! – Om vår tids demokratisyn* (Stockholm 1999).

MARCUSSON (1989)

L. Marcusson, *Offentlig förvaltning utanför myndighetsområdet (Uppsala 1989).*

STERZEL (1998)

F. Sterzel, *Författning i utveckling* (Uppsala 1998).

CHAPTER 12

Political Accountability in the United Kingdom

Adam Tomkins*

1 Introduction: British Parliamentary Government

The United Kingdom of Great Britain and Northern Ireland ('Britain') is a constitutional monarchy with a parliamentary government. The head of state is the monarch and the head of the government is the Prime Minister. While the monarch retains a number of important legal powers, which should not be under-estimated, the monarchy's role is now largely formal and, in particular, its executive role is largely consultative.[1] It is accordingly with the political accountability of the Prime Minister and the government that this chapter is concerned, and not with the accountability of the monarchy. The United Kingdom Parliament is composed of two Houses: the House of Lords and the House of Commons. The House of Lords remains an entirely unelected House. Since the House of Lords Act 1999 removed the majority of the hereditary peers from the Lords, almost all its members are appointed for life. The government published plans in early 2007 to effect further reforms to the composition of the House of Lords, but these have not yet been brought into force. The House of Commons is elected at least every five years under the 'first-past-the-post' electoral system (that is to say, not under any system of proportional representation). As we shall see, every government minister is a member of one or other of the two Houses of Parliament, the large majority coming from the Commons.

Since 1999, there has in Britain been a new level of devolved government in Scotland, Wales and Northern Ireland. For reasons of space, this chapter is concerned with political accountability only at the UK level: the devolved administrations are not considered. Practices of political accountability in the devolved administrations have emerged as being in several respects different from UK-level practices, not least because in Scotland, Wales and Northern Ireland different (proportional) electoral systems are employed, resulting in hung parliaments and either coalition or minority governments.[2]

1.1 Composition and Structure of British Government

As stated above, the head of the British government is the Prime Minister. There is no *legal* requirement that there be a prime minister. As with much of the British constitution, the office of Prime Minister was not created out of constitutional principle. Rather, it emerged out of political convenience. It is often remarked that the first Prime Minister was Sir Robert Walpole (who held office from 1721 until 1742) and that there has continuously been a Prime Minister since William Pitt the Younger (who became Prime Minister in 1783). Today the Prime Minister is the leader of the political party which, for the time being, is able to command majority support in the House of Commons.

---

* Parts of this essay draw on two earlier publications: Tomkins (2003) Chap. 5 and Tomkins (2006) Chap. 1.

1 See Tomkins (2003) 62-72.

2 For Scotland, see Winetrobe (2006) Chap. 7; for Wales, see Rawlings (2003) Chaps 6-7.

He or (once)[3] she is appointed by the Queen. However, if the Queen were to appoint someone other than the leader of the majority party in the Commons to the office, or indeed if she were to appoint no one to the office, she would not be acting illegally. Improperly, perhaps, but not illegally.

The fact that the Prime Minister is now the person who leads the party with majority support in the Commons is a rule of constitutional politics, not a rule of law. Most commentators employ the term 'constitutional convention' to describe such rules. The very office of Prime Minister is a creation of constitutional convention, not of law. The status of constitutional conventions is contested. Some commentators insist that they are descriptive only and that to ignore or flout them means not that the constitution has been breached but that it has been changed. Others take a more prescriptive approach and hold that if someone refuses to follow a convention they are acting unconstitutionally ('acting unconstitutionally' being something different from 'acting illegally'). Even if this second view is preferred,[4] the arbiter of whether or not behaviour contrary to a convention is unconstitutional is not a court of law but is, in this case, Parliament. All commentators agree that to the extent that conventions may properly be described as rules, they are rules that may not be judicially enforced: they are enforced by political institutions such as the House of Commons. Thus, if the Queen refused to appoint a Prime Minister she would not be acting illegally but she may well be acting unconstitutionally, albeit that the judge of her actions would be Parliament – and in particular the House of Commons – rather than the courts of law. The principal rules of government accountability in Britain – rules which are known as the doctrines of collective and individual ministerial responsibility – are constitutional conventions.

While the head of government is the Prime Minister, the most common constitutional description of British government, in the twentieth century at least, was that it was an example of 'Cabinet government'.[5] Like the Prime Minister, the Cabinet is a creature of convention rather than of constitutional law, emerging in its modern form during the course of the eighteenth century. Members of the Cabinet are appointed by the Queen on the advice of the Prime Minister. The Prime Minister determines who sits in his Cabinet and which Cabinet ministers are responsible for which areas of government policy. The Cabinet usually comprises about 20-24 senior government ministers, although the number is not fixed. It generally consists of the most senior minister from each government department. The total number of ministers is normally about 110, the majority of whom are junior ministers who do not sit in the Cabinet. All ministers are members of one of the two Houses of Parliament. In most administrations about 90 will be MPs in the House of Commons and about 20 will be peers in the House of Lords.

---

3 Margaret Thatcher, Conservative Prime Minister from 1979-1990 is, to date, the only woman to have held the office.

4 Which, in my view, it should be: see Tomkins (2003) Chap. 1.

5 See, e.g., Sir Ivor Jennings' pioneering study (1936).

Most government departments are headed by a minister known as a Secretary of State. In legal terms, the major unit of executive power in Britain is the government department. When modern statutes confer powers on the executive, they tend to do so by empowering 'the Secretary of State'. In British constitutional law, 'government is ministerial government. Powers and duties are laid on ministers, not on the Prime Minister' and not on the executive at large.[6] In law, if not in practice, the responsibility of a Secretary of State for the policies pursued in his (or, more rarely, her) department rests with the Secretary of State alone. No other minister, not even the Prime Minister, has the legal power to override him. The Prime Minister and the Cabinet may encourage or discourage, but technically, they cannot instruct individual ministers in the exercise of their powers.

Such may be the legal position but the political reality is quite different. Ministers who fail to carry the support of the Prime Minister will quickly find themselves shuffled out of office. Moreover, while ministers cannot formally be told by the Prime Minister or the Cabinet to exercise their powers in a certain way, they are bound by what the Prime Minister and/or the Cabinet decide is government policy. As we shall see below, it is a constitutional convention that all ministers in the government (whether members of the Cabinet or not) must take collective responsibility for all government policy. This gives the Prime Minister considerable strength (or, at least, it does for as long as the Prime Minister retains effective control over his government's policy-making), as any minister who finds himself unable to support and defend government policy in Parliament and in public will be expected to resign immediately from office.

Before we leave questions of the composition and structure of the executive there is one further aspect to be noted: the civil service. More than 450,000 civil servants are employed to assist ministerial government in the development of policy and in the delivery of public services.[7] The civil service is not party-political. The same civil servants serve ministers of all political persuasions. Civil servants are recruited, appointed and promoted professionally on merit, on the basis of open competition. Civil service positions are not political appointments for ministers. This has been the case in Britain since the middle of the nineteenth century.

The vast majority of civil servants are concerned with service delivery rather than with policy development. In the most radical and important reform of the civil service in more than a century, the Thatcher governments of the 1980s reorganized the service, in effect splitting it into two. Those who were concerned with service delivery rather than with policy development were 'hived off' into so-called 'executive' or 'next steps' agencies. These agencies remained attached to their parent departments but were given chief executives, budgets, and

6 Jones (1987) 64.

7 This number excludes those employed by the National Health Service, those employed to teach in state (public) schools and those employed as local government officers. It also excludes the military and the police. In this sense the 'civil service' comprises only one part of the public sector.

performance targets of their own. The aim was to find ways of streamlining the civil service, to bring the famously Thatcherite values of economy, effectiveness and efficiency – the so-called 'three Es' of value-for-money audit – into the heart of the civil service. The reform, which was not reversed by the Labour government that came into power in 1997, was controversial among constitutional commentators mainly for its apparent undermining of the traditional lines of accountability of government to Parliament. As we shall see, the constitution imagines that ministers are accountable to Parliament for everything that happens within their departments. How the semi-autonomous next steps agencies would be made to fit within this paradigm was a matter that caused considerable difficulties.[8]

2 Political Accountability and Parliament

By far the most important aspect of political accountability in the British context is the doctrines and practices of ministerial responsibility to Parliament. It is with a detailed consideration of these that this part of the chapter is concerned. Part three of this chapter will then, more briefly, consider extra-parliamentary forms of political accountability. Our examination of parliamentary accountability is divided into several sections: we start by outlining the nature of collective and individual responsibility, before moving on to consider the assault that was made on ministerial responsibility during the 1990s and the response that Parliament has offered since 1997. We close with an overview of the mechanisms of parliamentary accountability.

2.1 Collective Responsibility

The constitutional conventions of collective and individual ministerial responsibility provide that all ministers are responsible to Parliament for the policies, decisions, and actions of the government. The convention of collective responsibility means that all ministers in the government must accept responsibility for the policies, decisions, and actions of the government, even if they did not personally develop or take them, and even if they personally disagree with them. Despite the fact that the convention is sometimes (and wrongly) referred to as collective Cabinet responsibility, it applies equally to Cabinet and to junior ministers.

Collective responsibility means that all ministers must be prepared to defend government policy in Parliament. If the government takes a decision or adopts a policy with which a minister personally disagrees, and that minister is not prepared to support the government's position in Parliament (both in terms of his voting and of his speaking), then the minister must resign from the government. Resignations due to breakdowns of collective responsibility are infrequent

8 See further, below.

but, when they do occur, are often dramatic. Among notable examples are the resignations of Nigel Lawson (as Chancellor of the Exchequer) and Geoffrey Howe (as Deputy Prime Minister) in 1989 and 1990 respectively, over European and economic policy. It was these resignations that effectively triggered the end of Mrs Thatcher's Prime Ministership and, indeed, of her political career. Further examples are the resignations of Cabinet ministers Robin Cook and Clare Short over the Iraq war in 2003.

Notions of collective responsibility emerged in British government in the early eighteenth century. The first use of collective responsibility was to protect Cabinet ministers from the monarch. Until as late as the reign of Queen Anne (1702-1714), the monarch him- or herself generally attended meetings of the Cabinet. This practice ceased with the accession in 1714 of George I (who spoke no English). After this point, because of the absence of the monarch from Cabinet meetings, the Cabinet became more likely to arrive at decisions at odds with the monarch's personal view. Angry or disappointed monarchs might consequently seek to dismiss the individual ministers that were responsible for promoting in Cabinet policies with which the monarch subsequently disagreed. To prevent the monarch from acting in this way, the Prime Minister and Cabinet would present the monarch with a united front, making it impossible for him to take action against particular ministers: if the king disliked government policy, he would have to dismiss the government as a whole, rather than pick off individual ministers.

This early use of collective responsibility, however, has little to do with its modern function. Ministerial responsibility (both collective and individual) is now understood as being an obligation that ministers owe *to Parliament*: it is not concerned with the relationship between ministers and the monarch. The modern sense of collective responsibility did not emerge until rather later in the eighteenth century: the dates 1780-1832 are usually given as the period in which collective ministerial responsibility to Parliament developed as a constitutional convention.

The purpose behind the modern convention of collective responsibility is to enable Parliament to identify what the government's position is on any given issue. Parliament would not be able to hold the government to account if it did not first know what the government's policy or decision-making on a given matter was. If one minister tells Parliament that the government's policy is one thing, and a second minister tells Parliament that it is another, it would be impossible for Parliament effectively to pin the government down. Further, the doctrine of collective responsibility also disables ministers from evading responsibility by stating that a certain policy or decision was not their domain, but was that of some other minister.

Enabling ready parliamentary identification of government policy, and preventing ministers from evading responsibility for policy by pointing the finger at each other, can be seen as the positive aspects of collective responsibility. There are some more troubling aspects of the convention, however, that arguably detract from its value. Two such aspects stand out: the practice of unanimity, and that of confidentiality. Government decisions are presented to Parliament and to the public as if they are all unanimous. The only formal exception is the 'agreement to differ'. This is a rare device that the Prime Minister may deploy, which effectively suspends the rules of collective responsibility for a certain prescribed time over a certain discrete matter. It was employed only three times in the twentieth century, most famously in 1975 when Labour ministers were split over the result they desired of the referendum that was held to determine whether the United Kingdom would remain a Member State of the European Community.

While the agreement to differ is the only formal exception to the practice of unanimity, there are many informal exceptions. Keen observers of British politics are able quickly to learn of disagreements between ministers over a range of policy issues. Stories emerge in the newspapers and elsewhere of such disagreements because the political system accommodates a number of 'safety valves'[9] that allow disgruntled or impassioned ministers to blow off steam where they disagree with one another but are not prepared to resign over their disagreements. Leaks, unattributed briefings, semi-on-the-record conversations with lobby correspondents, and so forth, are the means by which such steam is released.

How far ministers will be allowed to go in such matters will be a matter for the judgement of the Prime Minister, a judgement which will be considerably shaped by the political climate in Westminster. In the most extreme case the Prime Minister may even feel that he himself has to resign, rather than dismiss those of his ministers that are briefing against him. Such a display of Prime Ministerial vulnerability, however, is rare, and the more usual consequence of the practice of unanimity is to strengthen, rather than to undermine, the position of the Prime Minister. This is because it is the Prime Minister that will have the last word in determining what the policy is which his ministers must then unanimously support. It is also the Prime Minister that decides whether to employ the agreement to differ, just as it is the Prime Minister who decides exactly how much leaking and unattributable briefing he will tolerate. The practice of unanimity therefore contributes significantly to the power of the Prime Minister in being able to secure obedience from his ministers.

The second aspect of collective responsibility which may give rise to cause for concern is the practice of confidentiality. All discussion among ministers, or between ministers and civil servants, contributing to the development of government policy is confidential. This practice is strictly complied with – or at least it is while ministers remain in office. (Once they leave office it has now become commonplace for former ministers to publish diaries or memoirs of their time in government.) The difficulty with confidentiality is that it severely limits openness. How can government be held effectively to account if it is closed, private, and protected by both the convention and the law of confidence?

---

[9] This is the phrase that Rodney Brazier has used in this context (1999) at 145.

Does Parliament not first need to know what government is doing before it can successfully hold the government to account? Well, perhaps not: it could be argued that as long as Parliament knows what it is that government has decided, it does not additionally need to know a great deal about the internal processes by which government arrived at its decision. There is a strong counter-argument, however. It will sometimes be important, for political accountability to be effective, for Parliament to be able to investigate not only the decisions of the government, but also the internal decision-making processes, yet it is just such processes that may be protected under the practice of confidentiality.

2.2 Individual Responsibility

The convention of individual ministerial responsibility provides that ministers are individually responsible to Parliament for their policies, decisions, and actions, and for the policies, decisions, and actions of their departments. 'Responsible' in this context has a rather stronger meaning than in the context of collective responsibility. In that context it amounts to little more than an obligation to defend and support government policy. In the context of individual responsibility, however, it means that, in addition to having to defend their policies, ministers are personally liable to Parliament for the quality and success of their policies. Such liability is political, not legal, and as such it attracts political, rather than legal, sanctions. We are not talking here about litigation and damages, but about explanation, apology, and, in the most serious cases, resignation.

Resignation from office is the ultimate sanction that Parliament can force on a minister who breaches the convention of individual responsibility. There has been much confusion in recent times about the relationship between resignation and responsibility, with some commentators suggesting that resignations are required in order to show that ministers are responsible – that is, that unless there is a resignation whenever anything goes wrong, the convention of individual responsibility has somehow failed. Such analysis, however, is flawed. Resignation and responsibility are not synonymous. Of course, it will sometimes be the case that the minister's behaviour is so gravely in error that only a resignation will suffice, but in other instances it will be perfectly possible for a minister to accept responsibility without having to resign. A minister who inadvertently misleads Parliament, for example, because he misremembers a statistic, and who later returns to Parliament to correct his mistake and to apologize for having made it, is unlikely to have to resign over the matter: yet in returning to Parliament to rectify his earlier error he is taking, not evading, responsibility.

2.2.1 Responsibility to Whom?

The definition of individual ministerial responsibility we have used up to this point (namely, that ministers are individually responsible to

Parliament for their policies, decisions, and actions, and for the policies, decisions, and actions of their departments), requires clarification in two important respects. First, to whom is it that the obligation of responsibility is owed? And secondly, what exactly is it that ministers are responsible for? The first question is easier to answer than the second. The obligation of individual ministerial responsibility, like that of collective responsibility, is owed to Parliament. If the minister concerned is an MP, then his or her obligation of individual responsibility will be owed to the House of Commons; if the minister is a peer his or her responsibility will be to the House of Lords. This is, at any rate, the theory. As a matter fact, however, a number of other parties intervene, and the practical operation of individual responsibility is a less straightforward matter than the simple interaction of minister and Parliament alone. Political parties, political leaders (and especially the Prime Minister), and the media may all, in addition to Parliament, play important roles in determining a minister's fate in cases of individual responsibility. If a minister finds herself under vigorous parliamentary attack, but has strong support from the Prime Minister, from her own political party (either on the backbenches or in her own constituency), or from the media, then she may well be able to ride out the storm relatively unscathed. Conversely, a minister may find that he has no realistic option other than to resign from office, even if Parliament is not urging him to step down (perhaps because it is in recess), where he lacks support from the Prime Minister or from his party, or where he is being constantly pilloried in the media.[10]

2.2.2 Responsibility for What?

The second respect in which our basic definition of individual responsibility requires further clarification concerns what it is, exactly, that ministers are constitutionally responsible for. Perhaps the best approach to this problem is to divide the issues for which ministers may be constitutionally responsible into three categories: first, the minister's own policies and political decisions and actions; secondly, the minister's private life and personal conduct; and thirdly, the actions of, and the decisions taken within, the minister's department. To start with the first category, which is the easiest, ministers are clearly individually responsible for their own policies and for their own political decisions and actions.

The second category is slightly more troublesome: to what extent are ministers constitutionally responsible to Parliament in respect of their private behaviour, as opposed to their public policy-making? Should a minister who finds himself embroiled in a sex or financial scandal resign? A frequent pattern in this context is for ministers initially to resist calls for resignation, but for such resistance sooner or later to prove futile. It is sometimes argued that ministers' personal conduct should have no bearing on their public accountability, and that a distinction should be drawn between the political issues with respect to which

[10] For examples, see Tomkins (2003) 142-44.

ministers are responsible to Parliament, and more personal issues with respect to which they are not. However, current practice does not appear to reflect this view, fitness for office being seen as a public and constitutional issue which can be affected by ministers' personal conduct as well as by their public policy-making.[11]

The category that has proved most difficult is the third: namely, political errors which are the fault of the minister's department, but not of the minister him- or herself. Are ministers individually responsible to Parliament for *everything* that happens in their departments? There was considerable controversy about this issue in the 1950s, in the so-called Crichel Down affair. Crichel Down was a piece of farmland purchased by the government in 1938 for military use. The scandal in the 1950s concerned the extent of ministerial responsibility for promises that were apparently made by various civil servants to the land's former owners as to the government's preparedness to sell it back to them. When the Conservative minister, Thomas Dugdale, announced that it had been decided not to resell the land to its former owners, he was compelled to resign.

For more than thirty years Dugdale's resignation was routinely cited by commentators as the perfect example of a minister honourably accepting individual responsibility for political misjudgements that were made, without his personal knowledge, by civil servants working in his department. Since the government's records of the Crichel Down affair became available in the mid-1980s, however, this interpretation – dominant as it was – has been exposed as myth.[12] Dugdale did not sacrifice himself on the altar of constitutional convention: he resigned because the policy of keeping farms under state control that he had inherited from the Labour government of 1945-51, and that he had sought to continue, was hated by Conservative backbench MPs to such an extent that Dugdale eventually lost support in Cabinet: that is, he resigned due to the obligations of collective, not individual, ministerial responsibility.

At the time of Crichel Down there was much political concern, particularly in the Conservative party, about the exponential growth in the size (and power?) of the civil service. Spurred on by two world wars and by the advent of larger, more interventionist government, the fear was that the civil service had become a force unto itself, and moreover, was one which Parliament could not effectively hold to account. As it was put during parliamentary debates on the Crichel Down affair, 'there has been criticism that the principle [of ministerial responsibility] operates so as to oblige ministers to extend total protection to their officials and to endorse their acts, and to cause the position that civil servants cannot be called to account and are effectively responsible to no-one'.[13]

Addressing these concerns, the Home Secretary, Sir David Maxwell-Fyfe, gave an important speech in the House of Commons in which he sought to outline the way in which the convention of individual ministerial responsibil-

---

[11] For a cogent and valuable discussion, see Brazier (1994) 431.

[12] See Nicolson (1986) and Griffith (1987) 35.

[13] Sir David Maxwell-Fyfe, Home Secretary, HC Deb., Vol. 530, col. 1285 (20 July 1954).

ity would operate in the context of the relationship between ministers and their civil servants. Maxwell-Fyfe distinguished between four different situations. First, 'in the case where there is an explicit order by a minister, the minister must protect the civil servant who has carried out his order'. Secondly, 'equally, where the civil servant acts properly in accordance with policy laid down by the minister, the minister must protect and defend him'. Thirdly, 'where an official makes a mistake or causes some delay, but not on an important issue of policy and not where a claim to individual rights is seriously involved, the minister acknowledges the mistake and he accepts the responsibility, although he is not personally involved. He states that he will take corrective action in the department ... [but] he would not ... expose the official to public criticism'. Finally, 'where action has been taken by a civil servant of which the minister disapproves and has no prior knowledge, and the conduct of the official is reprehensible, then there is no obligation on the part of the minister to endorse what he believes to be wrong or to defend what are clearly shown to be errors of his officers,' but even in this situation, Maxwell-Fyfe continued, the minister will 'of course' remain 'constitutionally responsible to Parliament for the fact that something has gone wrong, and he alone can tell Parliament what had occurred and render an account of his stewardship'.[14]

This is a strong and powerful reassertion of the principles of individual ministerial responsibility, and makes it clear that ministers will be individually responsible to Parliament not only for their own policies and political decisions and actions, but also for those of officials working in their departments. This is as it should be. Civil servants are not themselves accountable to Parliament, although they may under certain limited circumstances be called to give evidence before a select committee.[15] Civil servants are accountable to their ministers, not to Parliament, and ministers are in turn accountable to Parliament, on the terms set out in the Maxwell-Fyfe speech.

2.2.3 Individual Responsibility and the Major Government (1991-97)

Having in the previous sections set out the established rules of individual responsibility, we can now proceed to examine their operation in practice in recent times. Principles of individual ministerial responsibility came under considerable strain in the 1990s, particularly during the premiership of John Major. The first challenge arose in 1994. The Cabinet Secretary,[16] Sir Robin Butler, was called to give evidence to the Scott inquiry[17] and to the House of Commons Select Committee on the Treasury and Civil Service, both of which were investigating matters relating to the political accountability of ministers

---

[14] *Ibid.*, cols. 1285-87.

[15] The powers of select committees are considered further, below.

[16] That is, the head of the civil service.

[17] For the Scott inquiry, see below.

and civil servants. In his evidence, Butler argued that a distinction ought to be drawn between ministerial accountability and ministerial responsibility. Ministerial accountability to Parliament, he argued, consisted of a minister's ultimate duty to account to Parliament for the work of his department. Ministerial responsibility, on the other hand, arises only where a minister is directly and personally involved in an action or decision and implies that the minister carries personal credit or blame for that action or decision. In its report, the Treasury and Civil Service Committee criticized Butler's position, describing it as 'unconvincing'.[18]

The government argued that Butler's position was not an original one, but was based on the constitutional precedent of Crichel Down, and in particular on Maxwell-Fyfe's speech. The select committee disagreed, describing the government's position as being 'more novel than its advocates are prepared to admit'.[19] On analysis, the select committee is correct: Maxwell-Fyfe's 1954 speech is an extremely weak precedent for the position adopted forty years later by John Major's government. As we saw, the purpose of Maxwell-Fyfe's speech was to indicate that, contrary to popular fears at the time, ministers were fully responsible to Parliament for the actions and failures of civil servants. Maxwell-Fyfe was attempting to bring the decisions and actions of civil servants within the framework of ministerial responsibility. The Butler distinction between responsibility and accountability, on the other hand, is a device designed to limit the scope of ministers' obligations to Parliament. Nowhere in Maxwell-Fyfe's speech is there any indication that there might be a constitutionally recognized distinction between responsibility and accountability. On the contrary, the essence of his speech is that ministers are both responsible and accountable to Parliament in all four of the situations he outlined: in all four examples, it will be recalled, a minister has to 'render an account of his stewardship' and at all times ministers remain 'of course ... constitutionally responsible'.

The second challenge to individual responsibility that was made during John Major's time as Prime Minister was the policy/operations distinction. The architect of this challenge was Michael Howard MP, the incumbent Home Secretary. Howard argued that ministers were individually responsible to Parliament only for their policies. In Howard's view, operational failures, as opposed to failings in policy, fell outside the scope of ministerial responsibility to Parliament. The circumstances in which this argument arose were as follows. After a series of high profile prison escapes in 1994-95 Michael Howard appointed Sir John Learmont to chair an independent inquiry into prison security. The inquiry's report was highly critical of the Prison Service (a next steps agency within the Home Office) and of the entire system of prison management, from the level of prison governors and more junior staff all the way up to the chief executive of the Prison Service and to the Home Office and its ministerial team itself.[20]

---

[18] Treasury and Civil Service Committee, *The Role of the Civil Service*, HC 27 of 1993-94, para. 132.

[19] *Ibid.*, para. 122.

[20] *Review of Prison Service Security*, Cm. 3020, October 1995.

The report was replete with examples of how the problems in the Prison Service were not self-contained, but implicated the Home Office and, indeed, the Home Secretary himself.

When the Learmont report was published, a political storm broke out, and the opposition called for Michael Howard's resignation. He refused to resign, however, and instead called for the resignation of Derek Lewis, the chief executive of the Prison Service. When Mr Lewis refused to resign, Mr Howard dismissed him. Why was it Mr Lewis who was held to be responsible in this way, and not the minister? Michael Howard claimed that he as Secretary of State was responsible only for policy matters, and the problems which had been identified in the Learmont report were operational concerns, not matters of policy. The person responsible for operational matters was the chief executive, not the Secretary of State, and therefore Derek Lewis was responsible, not Michael Howard. The Secretary of State would naturally have to come to the House of Commons and explain – or give an account of – what had happened (he was in that sense constitutionally accountable to Parliament) but he was neither personally nor constitutionally responsible, in his view. The purported distinction between policy and operations is controversial. It is extremely difficult to know how to classify something as either policy or operational: for example, is a decision to reduce prisoners' visiting time a policy or an operational decision? What about over-crowding, or the re-introduction of slopping out, or staff shortages, or deciding to keep a set of prisoners confined in their cells for 23 hours per day – are these policy matters or operational matters, and how can we tell?

The final challenge that John Major's ministers made to the doctrine of individual responsibility concerned the provision to Parliament of government information. It has always been clear – and uncontroversial – that ministers who lie to Parliament will have to resign once their lies are revealed as such. What, however, of the situation in which a minister misleads Parliament, but does not at the time realize that he is doing so? Do ministers have to resign whenever they mislead Parliament, or only when they knowingly mislead Parliament? If the latter, does it make any difference whether the minister ought to have realized that he was misleading Parliament?

These questions arose out of the findings of the Scott report. Lord (formerly Sir Richard) Scott was appointed in 1992 to chair an inquiry into claims that the government had misled Parliament over its covert encouragement of British defence exporters to trade with Saddam Hussein's Iraq in the 1980s, and had subsequently attempted to cover up its earlier deception in such a way as to risk the wrongful criminal conviction and imprisonment of a number of British exporters. The report of the Scott inquiry was published in 1996. On the core claim that a number of ministers had misled Parliament as to the content of government policy with regard to permitting defence exports to Iraq, the Scott report found that ministers had repeatedly answered parliamentary questions in such a way as was 'inaccurate and misleading', that a variety of government statements had been 'designedly uninformative', that ministers had 'failed to inform Parliament of the current state of government policy on ... arms sales to Iraq', and that such failure had been 'deliberate'.[21] This may seem clear, but the matter was clouded by a further set of findings to the effect that the ministers concerned had acted without 'duplicitous intention'.[22]

There had been a number of ministers involved, but by the time the Scott report was published, only one remained in office: William Waldegrave MP. The 'without duplicitous intent' conclusion may be difficult to reconcile with the 'designedly uninformative' and 'deliberate failure to inform' conclusions, but it nonetheless enabled the government to present the findings of the Scott report as if the inquiry had found that to the extent that ministers had misled Parliament they had done so only unknowingly. In the government's view, while ministers were responsible to Parliament if they knowingly misled it, they did not have to take individual responsibility where they had unknowingly misled it. Relying on this distinction, Waldegrave was rescued from having to resign: like Michael Howard before him, he was saved by the government's rewriting of the rules.

As with the policy/operations distinction, the knowingly/unknowingly distinction was unheard of before the government invented it in order to save Mr Waldegrave. Indeed, in the articulation of the obligations of individual responsibility in the Major government's own rule book, there was no mention of the distinction. Since 1945 all Prime Ministers have issued to their ministers a document that was until 1997 known as Questions of Procedure for Ministers, or QPM. Since 1997 it has become known simply as the Ministerial Code. John Major's version of QPM made provision for individual ministerial responsibility as follows:

> Ministers are accountable to Parliament, in the sense that they have a duty to explain in Parliament the exercise of their powers and duties and to give an account to Parliament of what is done by them in their capacity as ministers or by their departments. This includes the duty to give Parliament, including its select committees, and the public as full information as possible about the policies, decisions and actions of the government, and not to deceive or mislead Parliament and the public.

As can be seen, there is no mention in this passage – which comes from the Prime Minister himself – of any of the three distinctions that the Major government sought to introduce. Even his own version of QPM failed to provide authority for the responsibility/accountability distinction, for the policy/operations distinction, or for the knowingly/unknowingly distinction. And yet both Michael Howard and William Waldegrave managed to evade responsibility. They managed to do so because the government itself was able to rewrite the

[21] *Report of the Inquiry into the Export of Defence Equipment and Dual-Use Goods to Iraq and Related Prosecutions*, HC 115 of 1995-96, paras. D3.107, D4.28-D4.30 and D4.42.

[22] *Ibid.*, para. D3.124.

rules. Until 1997 the authors of the rules governing ministerial responsibility were government ministers. Maxwell-Fyfe was a government minister (he was Home Secretary) when he gave his authoritative interpretation in 1954. So too in the 1990s were the responsibility/accountability distinction, the policy/operations distinction, and the knowingly/unknowingly distinction introduced by the government itself.

2.2.4 Parliament's Response

There were many in Parliament, on both sides of the House of Commons, who considered that what the government had done was improper. In the light of the political controversy that surrounded these issues, the Public Service Committee, an all-party select committee in the House of Commons, embarked in 1996 on a detailed inquiry into the use and abuse of the conventions of ministerial responsibility. Its report was unanimous, and constitutes a highly significant step in Parliament's response to the challenges which the Major administration had posed for it.

The Committee's report was deeply critical of the responsibility/accountability distinction that Sir Robin Butler had sought to introduce in 1994. The report strongly disagreed with the approach that Butler had adopted, stating that:

> It is not possible absolutely to distinguish an area in which a minister is personally responsible, and liable to take blame, from one in which he is constitutionally accountable. Ministerial responsibility is not composed of two elements with a clear break between the two. Ministers have an obligation to Parliament which consists in ensuring that government explains its actions. Ministers also have an obligation to respond to criticism made in Parliament in a way that seems likely to satisfy it – which may include, if necessary, resignation.[23]

In addition to its rejection of the responsibility/accountability distinction, the Committee also rejected Michael Howard's purported distinction between policy and operational failures. The Committee stated in its report that a broad 'pattern of incompetence' leading to a series of operational failures is a matter for which a minister ought to be held individually responsible. The Committee further stated that if even a single operational failure was serious enough, and was closely connected to the minister's responsibility for the overall organization of his department, it might well be appropriate for the minister to resign.[24] The Committee was clear that 'what ministers must never do is to put the blame onto civil servants for the effects of unworkable policies and their setting of unrealistic targets'.[25]

---

[23] Public Service Committee, *Ministerial Accountability and Responsibility*, HC 313 of 1995-96, para. 21.

[24] *Ibid.*, para. 19.

[25] *Ibid.*, para. 20.

Having explained what it did not consider ministerial responsibility to be, the Committee then set out what it did consider ministerial responsibility to consist of, and to require. The terms that the Committee adopted are important, and it is worth setting them out at length:

> Ministers owe a fundamental duty to account to Parliament. This has, essentially, two meanings. First, that the executive is obliged to give an account – to provide full information about and explain its actions in Parliament so that they are subject to proper democratic scrutiny. This obligation is central to the proper functioning of Parliament, and therefore any minister who has been found to have knowingly misled Parliament should resign. ... Second, a minister's duty to account to Parliament means that the executive is liable to be held to account: it must respond to concerns and criticism raised in Parliament about its actions because Members of Parliament are democratically-elected representatives of the people. A minister's effective performance of his functions depends on his having the confidence of the House of Commons (or the House of Lords, for those ministers who sit in the upper House). A minister has to conduct himself, and direct the work of his department in a manner likely to ensure that he retains the confidence both of his own party and of the House...[26]

From this passage it can be seen that the government found more support in Parliament for its insistence that ministers need not resign if they have been found to have misled Parliament unknowingly than it found for the responsibility/ accountability distinction or for the policy/operations distinction. However, the Committee was not entirely supportive of the government's position even on this point. On the issue of the provision of information to Parliament, the Committee attempted to shift attention away from ministerial resignation and towards a focus on the quality of the account that ministers should provide. In 1994 the government had introduced a Code of Practice on Access to Government Information. This Code required government departments to make available to Parliament and to the public a number of categories of government information. The Code has now been replaced by the Freedom of Information Act 2000, which came fully into force in 2005. As is usual in the realm of freedom of information, duties to disclose are not absolute, but are limited by a series of exemptions, which are listed in the Act. The Public Service Committee, in its consideration of individual responsibility and ministers' provision to Parliament of government information (whether in debate, in evidence before a select committee, or in answering a parliamentary question) concluded that whenever ministers refuse to make information available to Parliament, they must explain (1) that they are doing so, (2) why they are doing so, and (3) which exemption provision of the Code (now the Act) they are seeking to rely on to justify the refusal to disclose.[27]

---

[26] *Ibid.*, para. 32.

[27] Public Service Committee, n. 23 above, para. 154.

This outcome represents a considerable victory for the select committee, and indeed for Parliament generally. In none of the three respects in which it had sought to alter the rules of individual responsibility was the Major government ultimately successful. Both the responsibility/accountability distinction and the policy/operations distinction were unambiguously rejected by Parliament, a fact that was recognized and acknowledged by the government which, from the autumn of 1996 onwards, dropped its former insistence on them. The distinction between knowingly and unknowingly misleading Parliament was accepted by Parliament, but only in the context of ministerial resignations. As far as the routine of accountability is concerned, the effect of the reforms that followed the Public Service Committee's report was significantly to sharpen ministers' obligations to report fully and accurately to Parliament.

Such an achievement would have marked out the work of the Public Service Committee as being of considerable constitutional significance of itself. As it was however, this achievement was crowned by a greater one. This is because, in addition to its work in battling against the substance of the Major government's attempted refinements to the rules on individual responsibility, the Public Service Committee also agreed that the means by which the government had sought to make its refinements ought no longer to be available to it, or indeed to any future government. As we saw above, the government was able to attempt to rewrite the rules because, as the position then stood, these were rules the most authoritative articulation of which was contained in the document Questions of Procedure for Ministers (QPM) – a document that the government itself wrote.

The Public Service Committee recommended, and Parliament agreed, that Parliament should take ownership of these rules, and that they should be enshrined in a way that rendered them beyond unilateral government amendment. The mechanism chosen to put this recommendation into effect was that each House of Parliament would pass a Resolution setting out the rules and expectations of individual responsibility. No longer would self-serving amendments to QPM or the Ministerial Code suffice to alter the rules of political accountability. Only the Houses of Parliament themselves may modify or rescind their Resolutions. The government acting alone will no longer be able to effect changes to the rules of ministerial responsibility.

The text of the Resolutions passed by the two Houses of Parliament incorporates the substance of the interpretation of individual responsibility that was offered by the Public Service Committee. The full text of the Resolution of the House of Commons is as follows:

> (1) Ministers have a duty to Parliament to account, and be held to account, for the policies, decisions and actions of their departments and next steps agencies;
>
> (2) It is of paramount importance that ministers give accurate and truthful information to Parliament, correcting any inadvertent error at the earliest opportunity. Ministers who knowingly mislead Parliament will be expected to offer their resignation to the Prime Minister;

(3) Ministers should be as open as possible with Parliament, refusing to provide information only when disclosure would not be in the public interest, which should be decided in accordance with relevant statute and the government's Code of Practice on Access to Government Information;

(4) Similarly, ministers should require civil servants who give evidence before parliamentary committees on their behalf and under their directions to be as helpful as possible in providing accurate, truthful and full information in accordance with the duties and responsibilities of civil servants as set out in the Civil Service Code.[28]

The Resolutions were passed immediately before Parliament was dissolved in preparation for the 1997 general election. After that election, the new Prime Minister, Tony Blair, issued to all ministers a new Ministerial Code. Blair's Code reproduced the text of the parliamentary Resolutions, and specifically drew ministers' attention to those Resolutions, making it clear that as far as the government was concerned, it is Parliament that now sets the parameters of individual responsibility. Gordon Brown's Code, issued when he replaced Tony Blair as Prime Minister in 2007, proceeds on the same basis.

2.3 The Mechanisms of Parliamentary Accountability

Parliament has three main ways of holding the executive to account: debate, parliamentary questions, and select committees. Of these, debate is probably the least penetrating. Debate is important for discussing general issues and broad principle, and big set-piece debates on topical issues can attract significant media attention. Through debate ministers can be forced to come to Parliament to set out government policy and to defend it, and opposition and backbench MPs (or peers) will have the opportunity to point out defects with, alternatives to, and inconsistencies within, government policy, but this is about as far as debate can go. Scrutiny by debate is painting with a broad brush. It can be a useful starting point, but it does not generally allow Parliament to get to the detailed points that more rigorous scrutiny will frequently need to focus on.

Parliamentary questions take two forms: oral and written. Oral questions are put during question time – there will normally be about an hour of question time during each parliamentary day. All ministers have to attend a period of question time every four weeks or so, but probably the best known aspect of question time is Prime Minister's question time, which occurs weekly when Parliament is in session, and lasts for thirty minutes each week. Oral questions are an effective means of putting ministers on the spot, and of testing their

[28] HC Deb., Vol. 292, cols. 1046-7 (19 March 1997). For the House of Lords Resolution, which is in identical substantive terms, see HL Deb., Vol. 579, col. 1057 (20 March 1997).

parliamentary skills, but whether the cut and thrust of question time really amounts to effective political accountability is perhaps doubtful.[29]

Written questions, on the other hand, are a vital ingredient of contemporary parliamentary practice, and contribute a great deal to the system of political accountability. Answers to written questions are not delivered in the Chamber, and so they receive no air time, but they are printed in the daily parliamentary record, Hansard, and they constitute one of the foremost means by which MPs (and peers) may obtain information from ministers. As we saw in the previous section, one of the central allegations investigated by the Scott inquiry was that ministers had repeatedly misled Parliament by providing incomplete or inaccurate answers to parliamentary questions, and in particular to written questions. As a result of the findings of the Scott report on this matter, a number of reforms were made to the guidance that is issued to government departments concerning the drafting of answers to parliamentary questions. Not only were the guidelines strengthened, but so too was the monitoring of departments' compliance with the guidelines. Since 1997 the House of Commons Select Committee on Public Administration has conducted an annual inquiry into ministers' answers to parliamentary questions. Every year the Committee publishes a report, analysing improvements that have been made and highlighting the issues with regard to which further improvement is still required. The Committee has identified good practice, and has named and shamed those departments that continue only haphazardly to abide by the guidelines. As well as valuably maintaining the high profile of this issue throughout Parliament, the Committee's work has kept up significant pressure on the government, forcing it to promise that the poorer departments improve and reform their practices. The Committee's work in this area has made a valuable contribution. Its persistence has helped to make parliamentary questions a more reliable and more potent mechanism by which parliamentarians may force information out of government departments that would frequently prefer, if they had their way, not to have to release it. It is the constancy and tenacity of the Committee's work that is its real value.

The third mechanism Parliament has at its disposal to enable it to hold the executive to account is the select committee system. Select committees are important to both Houses, but since 1979 the departmental select committees of the House of Commons have been especially influential. These committees were restructured in 1979 so that there would be one select committee for every government department. Thus the Home Affairs Committee monitors the Home Office, and the Education Committee monitors the Department for Education, and so on. In addition, there are a number of cross-cutting commit-

29 Prime Minister's question time remains the best known way in which the Prime Minister is routinely made personally to account to Parliament, but it is no longer the only way. Since 2002 the Prime Minister has, every six months, given detailed evidence on government policy to the Liaison Committee of the House of Commons. The Liaison Committee is composed of the MPs who chair the various select committees of the House of Commons. On select committees see further below.

tees, of which the two most important, in terms of scrutiny, are the Public Administration Committee and the Public Accounts Committee. The Standing Orders of the House of Commons provide that the role of departmental select committees is 'to examine the expenditure, administration, and policy' of government departments. In order to carry out these tasks select committees have the power to send for persons, papers, and records. They have their own small staff, and they may appoint specialist advisers. Once appointed committees decide for themselves which aspects of departmental administration and policy they should investigate. Departmental select committees are the unique preserve of backbench MPs: no ministers may serve as members. Each committee has between 11 and 17 members, the political complexion of whom will reflect that of the Commons as a whole. Thus, if sixty per cent of MPs are from the Labour party, sixty per cent of the membership of each committee will be composed of Labour party MPs. Committees are appointed at the beginning of each Parliament (that is, following a general election) for the duration of the Parliament (that is, until the next general election).

Select committees allow groups of MPs to develop detailed knowledge on discrete areas of policy. Under an active and enthusiastic chair, select committees are able to embark on four or five major investigations in each session (that is, each year). As well as giving otherwise generalist MPs particular areas of expertise, select committees enable the House of Commons to launch in-depth inquiries into particularly problematic or controversial aspects of government policy, allowing Parliament to probe more systematically and more deeply into government decision-making than is possible in debates or though parliamentary questions. Complex matters that have been the subject of valuable select committee investigations in recent years include the child support agency, rail privatization, arms exports, the role of the private sector in the NHS, and the Bank of England's monetary policy committee, among many others.[30]

Which MPs will serve on, and who will chair, each committee are matters for the party managers – the whips – to resolve at the beginning of a new Parliament. This is an issue which is capable of generating considerable political controversy. Following the 2001 election, government whips sought to make a number of alterations to the membership, and chairmanship, of select committees. Most notoriously, the government sought to oust two Labour MPs, Gwyneth Dunwoody and Donald Anderson, from the chairs of the Transport and of the Foreign Affairs Committees, respectively. Parliament – and in particular the parliamentary Labour party – revolted, and in an unusual show of defiance voted down the government's proposed membership. The whips had to think again, and Mrs Dunwoody and Mr Anderson were re-instated as the chairs of their committees.

Both positive and negative conclusions can be drawn from this story. On the plus side, it suggests that select committees are sufficiently powerful, prestigious and effective to be taken seriously by the government and its whips. If

[30] On select committees, see further Tomkins (2003a).

select committees were worthless, or ineffective, why go through the bother of seeking to manipulate their membership and direction? But on the minus side, of course, these committees are supposed to be rigorous and independent committees of inquiry. If the whips can so easily remove thorns from the government's flesh, will that not discourage rigour? If the whips have control over membership, does that not dilute the extent to which the committees can truly be said to be independent of government?

We know that the government is defined as those politicians who can command majority support in the House of Commons. We know also that since the mid nineteenth century the device that has been employed to generate and to maintain such support is the political party. Since the 1870s it has been the case that when there is a Tory majority in the Commons, there will be a Tory (or Conservative) government, and when there is a Whig, Liberal or Labour majority, there will be a Whig, Liberal or Labour government. Thus, what we have come to mean when we say that the government is accountable to Parliament, is that the government is accountable to a group of politicians the majority of whom are members of the same political party as that which forms the government.

With mass democracy has come the modern, centralized organization of the political party, and with party has come the greatest single challenge that the system of parliamentary accountability has yet had to face. The challenge is formidable, but we should take care nonetheless not to exaggerate it. We have encountered in this chapter numerous instances where party has not been the obstacle to effective political accountability that it might have been. Several ministers have been forced to resign from office because backbenchers from their own party have lost confidence in them. Indeed, Mrs Thatcher herself fell from office not because of opposition from the Labour party, but because she lost the support of her own party in Parliament. Just as MPs can sometimes turn against their own ministers, so too are parliamentarians able to transcend the party divide to work together on a variety of issues that concern Parliament as a whole. We have seen several examples of this in what we have considered here: the unanimous reports of all-party committees such as that of the Public Service Committee on ministerial responsibility in 1996, or those of the Public Administration Committee on parliamentary questions since 1997 are impressive examples. Indeed, it is very much the norm, not the exception, for select committee reports to be unanimous: only rarely are they split along party lines.

Nonetheless, that party has the potential to disrupt the system of political accountability is amply demonstrated by the actions of the Labour whips in 2001. Potential is not always realized, however, and what was notable about the events of July 2001 was not so much that the whips tried it on, but that Parliament stood up to them, and won. Just as the Major government found that it was unable to secure the changes to individual responsibility that it had sought in the 1990s, so too did the Labour whips find that, even with an overwhelming majority of MPs, and even in the euphoria of a second successive election victory, Parliament was not so easy to manipulate when it came to fiddling with the ways in which it holds the government to account.

3 Political Accountability Outside Parliament

Ministerial responsibility to Parliament is the most important form of political accountability in the British constitutional system, but it is not its only form. Indeed, the modern British state encompasses a bewildering array of institutions and mechanisms designed to hold government to some form of account. Financial accountability is the responsibility of the public auditors: the National Audit Office, headed by the Comptroller and Auditor General, which reports to Parliament through the powerful Public Accounts Committee of the House of Commons. Forms of legal accountability arise through the law of judicial review and through the tens of thousands of cases heard each year by tribunals in fields such as immigration, tax and social security. The Parliamentary Ombudsmen handles complaints of maladministration. As with the National Audit Office, the ombudsman reports regularly to Parliament through a House of Commons Committee: in the ombudsman's case, the influential and widely respected Public Administration Committee. The National Audit Office and the Parliamentary Ombudsmen are but two of the many institutions of government scrutiny that report regularly to Parliament. Altogether there are several dozen, ranging from the Civil Aviation Authority to the Law Commission and from the Electoral Commission to the Food Standards Agency. One of the most significant challenges for effective political accountability lies in the extent to which Parliament and its committees are able to use the expert and often extremely detailed data contained in the reports of bodies such as these. There is no shortage of scrutiny. But what is required is co-ordination and effective channelling of scrutiny. This is now regarded as a key task of Parliament's select committees.[31]

The most high-profile form of political accountability outside Parliament comes not from any of these permanent bodies of regulation or scrutiny, but from *ad hoc* public inquiries. In the previous section we encountered the Scott inquiry into arms-to-Iraq. During Tony Blair's time in office there were several very high profile and politically controversial public inquiries. These include the following:

- the Saville inquiry into 'Bloody Sunday' (30 January 1972), when the British Army shot and killed fourteen people in Northern Ireland and injured many more. This inquiry, chaired by a Law Lord, was established by the Prime Minister in 1998, completed its hearings in 2005 and, at the time

[31] See Hansard Society (2001) Chap. 8. There is also of course the question of holding the scrutineers and regulators of government accountable, on which see House of Lords Constitution Committee, *The Regulatory State: Ensuring its Accountability*, HL 68 of 2003-04.

of writing, has still to publish its report;[32]

- the Hutton inquiry, ostensibly into the death of the government scientist Dr David Kelly, but ranging also into the truth (or otherwise) of the government's claims about the state of its intelligence with regard to Iraqi weapons of mass destruction in the lead-up to the Iraq War of 2003. The BBC reported that the government had 'sexed-up' (i.e., heavily spun) the dossier outlining its intelligence and knew that some of the most headline-grabbing claims made in it were unreliable (David Kelly, it turned out, was the BBC's source). The Hutton inquiry largely exonerated the government (resulting in several senior resignations at the BBC) but, the Hutton report being widely seen as something of a 'white-wash', it failed to achieve closure, the Iraq issue continuing to dog the Blair government throughout its remaining years in office;[33]
- the Butler review which, following on from the Hutton inquiry, looked in more detail at the ways in which intelligence advice was used by the government in the lead-up to the Iraq War.[34]

The large number of such inquiries to be held under the Blair government prompted a range of concerns.[35] It is ministers (usually the Prime Minister) who decide whether or not to establish an inquiry: how may ministers be held to account for their decisions to establish – or not to establish – such inquiries? No public inquiry was established, for example, in the aftermath of the terrorist attacks on London's public transport on 7 July 2005. How may the terms of reference or the choice of chairman be effectively scrutinised? Is one function of the public inquiry to remove an issue of political controversy from Parliament: do public inquiries supplement, or sometimes supplant, Parliament's role in securing accountability? Public inquiries are sometimes extremely expensive (most notably the Saville inquiry): do they present good value for money? Where judges are chosen to chair public inquiries (as in the cases of the Scott, Saville and Hutton inquiries, for example), are the constitutional principles of the separation of powers and the independence of the judiciary threatened? Many of these questions are now addressed in legislation – the Inquiries Act 2005 – which was passed in part to allay fears that public inquiries were becoming so central to political accountability in Britain that they were themselves in need of careful regulation. Whether the 2005 Act will succeed in this regard it is too soon to tell.

---

[32] See <www.bloody-sunday-inquiry.org>.

[33] See <www.the-hutton-inquiry.org.uk>, Danchev (2004) 436 and Coole (2005) 465.

[34] See <www.butlerreview.org.uk> and Danchev, *ibid.*

[35] See House of Commons Public Administration Committee, *Government by Inquiry*, HC 51 of 2004-05.

4 Conclusion: The Reputation and Future of Political Accountability

As this chapter has shown, political accountability, both within Parliament and beyond it, is absolutely central to the contemporary constitutional order and to political practice in Britain. No account of British government, or of the British constitution, would be complete (or even satisfactory) without taking it fully into consideration. Yet, in recent years, the practices and norms of political accountability have come under sustained criticism in Britain – most notably among constitutional lawyers. In 2000, for example, the editors of a widely read collection of essays on constitutional law removed from the volume an essay on ministerial responsibility that had been included in earlier editions on the ground, they stated, that 'the doctrine of individual ministerial responsibility has been significantly weakened over the last ten years or so, so that it can no longer be said, in our view, that it is a fundamental doctrine of the constitution.'[36] As we saw above, the practice of individual ministerial responsibility did indeed take a number of knocks in the 1990s, but what this verdict overlooks is the way in which Parliament responded to these knocks not only to re-state the doctrine of individual ministerial responsibility, but to do so in a manner which actually *strengthened* it as a constitutional doctrine.

There are, perhaps, two main reasons why a number of constitutional lawyers have undervalued the ongoing importance, and under-estimated the continuing centrality, of political accountability. The first concerns the way in which political party is held to contribute to an undermining of political accountability in practice. We outlined the nature of this problem above. John Major's ministers, Michael Howard and William Waldegrave, were able, in the short-term, to get away with their re-writing of the rules of ministerial responsibility because the institution to which they were accountable – the House of Commons – was composed of a majority of MPs loyal to the same political party (the Conservative Party) as at the time composed the government. In contemporary British politics this is always the way: the government is always composed of the party able to command majority support in the House of Commons. Ministerial responsibility to Parliament in effect therefore means ministerial responsibility to an institution the majority of whose members are liable to be politically sympathetic – and loyal – to the government.

While there is some force in this argument, we should be careful not to exaggerate it. Party is of course a powerful force in modern politics. But even in Britain's adversarial, first-past-the-post, two-party system with clear govern-

---

[36] Jowell & Oliver (2000) viii. The essay on ministerial responsibility was not re-instated in the fifth edition (2004). Professors Jowell and Oliver are not alone in this view: compare E. Barendt's (in my view wholly unsustainable) observation that it is now 'rare for the House of Commons to hold an individual minister to account' (1998) 116). It may be rare for the House of Commons to compel a minister to resign when he or she continues to enjoy the support of the Prime Minister and the Cabinet, but Parliament continues to hold ministers to account every day it sits.

ment majorities, party is not always in practice the force it may appear to be on paper. For one thing, party loyalty is not an especially strong characteristic of select committees. As we saw above, the various select committee inquiries and reports that have played such a key role in Parliament's re-assertion of the principles of political accountability since 1996 have been cross-party and unanimous: i.e., not split along party lines. Furthermore, however, the recent and extremely important work of the political scientist Philip Cowley has shown that, even when it comes to legislative debates in the chamber of House of Commons (where party loyalty is normally thought to be a stronger force than it is in select committees) rebellion *against* the party line has been a striking feature of modern parliamentary government.[37] Loyalty to party, it seems, is less a threat to systems of political accountability than might at first have been thought.

The second factor contributing to the undervaluing in some quarters of political accountability concerns the relative rise of legal forms of accountability. Since the seventeenth century the courts in Britain have played a relatively minor role in seeking to hold central government to constitutional account. While there has throughout this period been a principle of legality in our constitutional law, it has been a principle with a weak content: insisting only that the government act in accordance with legal authority and steering clear (on the whole) of imposing substantive limitations on the range of measures that the government may lawfully adopt.[38] The same constitutional commentators who have tended to undervalue political accountability have, at the same time, been active in campaigning for a greater judicial role in British constitutional law. Subjecting the government to judicial review is, indeed, a feature of British constitutional law and government that has grown enormously in importance in the last twenty to thirty years. In more recent years human rights law has also been used to bolster this aspect of the constitution.[39] A significant part of the argument in favour of such moves has been to advocate their necessity in the face of the alleged failings and limitations of political accountability.

From the point of view of the constitutional lawyer, this is perhaps the greatest challenge now posed to Britain's traditions of political accountability: namely, how to sustain their continued vitality in what is, for us, the still new era of judicial review and human rights law. Will the primary institution of government accountability continue to be Parliament, or will the courts now begin to assume that role? The balance or, in more confrontational times, perhaps the tension, between these two is likely to be one of the most considerable and persistent constitutional challenges of the twenty-first century.

---

37 See Cowley (2005).

38 The classic authority is *Entick v Carrington* (1765) 19 St. Tr. 1029: see Tomkins (2003) 78-80.

39 See Tomkins, *ibid.*, Chap. 6.

Bibliography

BARENDT (1998)

E. Barendt, *An Introduction to Constitutional Law* (Oxford 1998).

BRAZIER (1999)

R. Brazier, *Constitutional Practice* (Oxford 3rd edn. 1999).

COOLE (2005)

D. Coole, 'Agency, Truth and Meaning: Judging the Hutton Report' (2005/35) *British Journal of Political Science* 465 ff.

COWLEY (2005)

P. Cowley, *The Rebels: How Blair Mislaid his Majority* (London 2005).

DANCHEV (2004)

A. Danchev, 'The Reckoning: Official Inquiries and the Iraq War' (2004/19) *Intelligence and National Security* 436 ff

GRIFFITH (1987)

J. Griffith, 'Crichel Down: The Most Famous Farm in British Constitutional History' (1987/1) *Contemporary Record* 35 ff.

HANSARD SOCIETY (2001)

Hansard Society, *The Challenge for Parliament* (London 2001).

JENNINGS (1936)

Sir Ivor Jennings, *Cabinet Government* (Cambridge 1936).

JONES (1987)

G.W. Jones, 'The United Kingdom', in W. Plowden (ed.), *Advising the Rulers* (Oxford 1987) 185-215.

JOWELL & OLIVER (2000)

J. Jowell & D. Oliver (eds.), *The Changing Constitution* (Oxford 4th edn 2000).

NICOLSON (1986)

I. Nicolson, *The Mystery of Crichel Down* (Oxford 1986).

RAWLINGS (2003)

R. Rawlings, *Delineating Wales* (Cardiff 2003).

TOMKINS (2003)

A. Tomkins, *Public Law* (Oxford 2003).

TOMKINS (2003A)

A. Tomkins, 'What is Parliament for?', in N. Bamforth & P. Leyland (eds.), *Public Law in a Multi-Layered Constitution* (Oxford 2003) 70 ff.

TOMKINS (2006)

A. Tomkins, 'The Struggle to Delimit Executive Power in Britain', in P. Craig & A. Tomkins (eds.), *The Executive and Public Law: Power and Accountability in Comparative Perspective* (Oxford 2006) 16 ff.

WINETROBE (2006)

B. Winetrobe, 'Public Accountability in Scotland', in A. McHarg & T. Mullen (eds.), *Public Law in Scotland* (Edinburgh 2006).

CHAPTER 13

Political Accountability in the EU Member States: Different Concepts and Practical Implications

Hansko Broeksteeg, Ilse Van den Driessche and Luc Verhey

1 Introduction

As was said in the introductory chapter, this research tries to answer the question of how political accountability can be further developed in the future European Union. In trying to find an answer, we have asked ourselves to what extent constitutional principles and practices on political accountability at the national level could be relevant for the European Union. Before we go deeper into the EU in the next chapter, we will first examine the national systems in a comparative perspective. Are there any common principles and practices in the EU Member States as meant above and if yes, what are they?

2 Limitations on Comparative Research

The foundation of the comparison made below can be found in part II of this book. In this part, political accountability has been described and analyzed separately for eleven EU-Member States. Before we go into the main features of the national concepts and the most important similarities and differences between them as they come forward from the national reports, we first have to make a comment of a more general nature. A real accurate comparison of the concepts of political accountability is for various reasons extremely difficult if not almost impossible to make. While comparing the various concepts, one has to realize time and again that the historical, cultural and political context varies widely in each and every Member State. This variety has substantial implications: it makes comparative research on key issues of constitutional and political systems, as for example on the concept of political accountability, extremely complicated.[1]

What is especially difficult in the comparative research upon which this book is based is to precisely know and understand what is meant by the constitutional concept or a particular aspect thereof. Because of the differences in historical, cultural and political context, it can easily happen that in Member States A and B one uses the same words for what, if one looks more carefully, appears to be different or, conversely, that one uses different terms for what is basically the same. This is especially the case with a general and abstract concept, like political accountability. The question of what one precisely means with 'accountability' or similar concepts, like 'responsibility' and 'control' in a specific national context, can easily lead to misunderstandings.

Moreover, one has to put in mind that constitutional theory can substantially differ from daily practice. What is described as a rule, a principle or a convention in the national constitution or in constitutional doctrine perhaps has never become real practice, or if it ever was in the past, has gradually drifted away from daily practice. Constitutional theory could have gradually become incomplete or gone out of date or could otherwise have changed in practice over

[1] Legrand (2002) 225-257. See also Koopmans (2003) 4 ff.; Claes (2006) 187 ff.

the years. These differences between theory and practice can cause difficulties whilst interpreting research results. It can for example not be excluded that behind fundamentally different theories in Member States A and B, there is in fact a daily practice which in both states is more or less the same or at least far less different than it originally seemed. But also the opposite could occur; while the constitutional principles in Member States A and B are still the same on paper, both states could have developed themselves in opposite directions as a result of which daily practices have become fundamentally different.

For these reasons, one has to be very cautious while comparing the national systems and concepts as described in part II of this book. Even if one could assume that the terms, which are used to define the concept of 'political accountability', or parts thereof, are sufficiently clear to make a sound comparison, one cannot be exactly sure about the political practice behind the constitutional theory of political accountability. A more in-depth, empirical study would be needed. Therefore, the results of the comparative research in this book are to a large extent tentative; they give a relatively clear but provisional and non-exhaustive picture of the concept of political accountability in eleven Member States which should be tested and further elaborated upon in future research. However, given these limitations, the national reports as included in part II of this book already give a rich and instructive insight in national concepts of political accountability in a variety of EU Member States. They give cause for some general observations in a short comparative chapter.

The order of this chapter is as follows. Firstly, we will examine to what extent political accountability in the described countries resembles or differs and to what extent a common concept of political accountability can be deduced from the analysis in part II of this book (par. 3). We will further examine if and to what extent the scope and the content of political accountability as a concept are dependent on or linked to the scope of ministerial or governmental powers[2] (par. 4). Next, we focus on the differences between and the consequences of collective and individual political accountability (par. 5). The practical implications of the concept of political accountability, for example, for the civil service and for agencies are described in the following paragraphs (par. 6 and 7). Finally, the process of rendering account (par. 8) and the consequences that may result from political accountability, in particular, the parliamentary power to pass a motion of no-confidence, are examined (par. 9). We end with some concluding remarks in which we look ahead to the question we deal with in the last chapter of this book: could the constitutional principles and practices on political accountability at the national level be relevant for constitutional developments in the European Union and, if yes, how (par. 10).

---

[2] By competences is meant the legal powers that are attributed to the ministers.

3 Concepts of Political Accountability

3.1 Different Concepts

First and foremost, we have to deal with the question of how to define political accountability. If we want to find the common denominators of the concept of political accountability at the national level and learn from its benefits and shortcomings to the benefit of the EU, we need to know more precisely what we are talking about. Although at first sight we seem to know what is meant by political accountability, the concept is difficult to define and can easily give cause to misunderstandings.

In our introductory chapter, we mentioned the different elements of (political) accountability as defined by for example Oliver and Bovens.[3] On the basis of which we have distinguished, the following elements of political accountability are:

- the accountor fulfilling his obligation to inform the forum and to explain and justify his conduct;
- the forum interrogating the accountor and debating the adequacy of the explanation of its conduct;
- the forum passing judgment and the accountor facing the consequences.

Although these elements seem to exist and at least implicitly be part of or linked to the concept of political accountability in all the Member States, the preceding chapters show that the answer to the question of what political accountability exactly is, differs considerably in each country. Not only is the concept of political accountability in itself notoriously difficult to describe with precision, it also has to be understood within the history and the political and legal culture in each and every Member State.

If we look at the concept of political accountability from a theoretical perspective, we in fact can distinguish two divergent approaches. In the large majority of the Member States involved in this research, one seems to focus on the parliamentary power to appoint and dismiss the ministers. One concentrates on the parliament passing judgment on the governments policy and more specifically on its ultimate power to decide on the government's future. However, although this parliamentary power also exists in the Netherlands, the United Kingdom, Denmark and Germany, the concept of political accountability in these countries seems to be defined otherwise; it is defined from the point of view of the accountor, the ministers, being obliged to give information and to explain and justify how they have used their powers. This difference in perspective has, as we will see, direct consequences for the issues being discussed under the heading of 'political accountability'. Before going into these issues, let us first elaborate on the difference in theoretical perspective.

---

3 See Verhey, Claes (2008) chapter 1, par. 2.2.

3.2 The 'Parliament-oriented' Model of Political Accountability

In the large majority of the Member States[4] involved in this research, the key element of political accountability is the confidence the parliamentary majority must have in the government. Political accountability as a term is often used in the same breath with the confidence parliament has or has lost in a minister or in the government as a whole. Therefore, this model of political accountability focuses mainly on the role of parliament: it is a 'parliament-oriented' model. Democratic legitimacy can be seen as the underlying principle of this model. The confidence of the parliamentary majority in the government as a *'conditio sine qua non'* expresses the fact that the government must be democratically legitimized by the parliament being the representative of the people.

Most of the time parliamentary attention is merely focused on the negative side of political accountability: ministers can be blamed for something for which they can be held to account. So, if the parliament judges that a minister is 'accountable', this means he has to take the blame for something that has gone wrong and therefore has to face the consequences. Alberti, for example illustrates this clearly with regard to Spain where political accountability has been described as:

> 'the consequences that may derive from the actions of the public bodies'.[5]

The term 'consequences' first and foremost means parliament sending away the government or an individual minister.

Although one often seems to be focused on the negative consequences for the government, more particularly the dismissal of ministers, the concept of political accountability also includes positive consequences. Political accountability in the 'parliament-oriented' model also means that the government has to receive and maintain the confidence of the parliamentary majority. So according to Ziller, political accountability in France:

> 'means that members of government need the approval/acceptance of the President in order to be appointed and the acceptance of the National Assembly to keep their function'.[6]

As a result, the government often explicitly has to obtain a vote of confidence by the parliament[7] when it takes office. To retain this confidence the ministers give account on their policy: they explain and justify what they have or have not done

---

4 Belgium, the Czech Republic, France, Italy, Poland, Spain and Sweden.

5 Alberti (2008) chapter 10, par. 1.

6 Ziller (2008) chapter 5, par. 2.

7 Or, as is the case in France, the government needs the confidence of the (elected) president.

as a minister. Parliament then assesses the achievements of the government and the government has to accept the consequences thereof. Government can often also initiate a vote of confidence itself to assure that it still has a sound majority in parliament.

The foregoing implies that political accountability in the 'parliament-oriented' model is not only about maintaining or losing the confidence of the parliamentary majority. If one speaks of political accountability, often attention has also been paid to what happens before the final parliamentary judgment. So the fact that ministers have to give account to parliament can at least implicitly be considered part of the concept as well. In Belgium, for example, when defining political accountability, the obligation to render account is mentioned right next to the parliamentary power to send away ministers. In Poland, the concept of political accountability primarily means the parliamentary power to appoint and dismiss the government, but this by implication means that it permits the government to be called into account for its actions.

3.3 The 'Government-oriented' Model of Political Accountability

The 'parliament-oriented' model of political accountability is not accepted in all countries. What comes forward in part II of this book is that, especially in the Netherlands, Denmark and the United Kingdom, the confidence that parliament must have in the government is indeed a central element of the parliamentary model as such, yet not of the concept of political accountability. In these Member States, one departs from a theoretically different starting point; political accountability is focused on what the individual minister or the government can be held accountable for. It is a 'government-oriented' model.

So, in this model the object of the accountability of the individual minister or the government is a key issue. In trying to define this object, one needs to find criteria to determine for which objects ministers or the government is precisely accountable. Here one can take different views. One can choose a strictly legal approach by making the scope of the political accountability dependent on the minister's or the government's legal competences. Presumably, the Netherlands is the strongest example of this.[8] However, one can also take another, perhaps more empirical, perspective. The scope of the political accountability of a minister can also be determined by the portfolio he has obtained at the time he was appointed. Generally speaking, the minister is then accountable for the policy areas within his portfolio.

In trying to identify the object of accountability in the 'government-oriented' model it is essential that the concept of accountability does not only imply that ministers are accountable for their own conduct, but also for the conduct of others, especially for civil servants. However, in this model it is not self-evident that the government is politically accountable for the executive as a whole. The

[8] Broeksteeg (2008) chapter 8, par. 3.

accountability of the ministers could be limited due to a legal provision or a political agreement. Especially with regard to certain types of executive agencies, it is generally accepted that the political accountability can be limited in so far as ministers have legal competences with regard to agencies or can otherwise influence their conduct.

While the 'parliament-oriented' model of political accountability focuses mainly on the forum to which ministers are accountable (the parliament), the 'government-oriented' model is rather fixed on the accountor: the government itself. In fact, the confidence the parliamentary majority must have is regarded as a consequence of political accountability, not as part of the concept itself. This notion is perhaps most clearly present in the Netherlands. Broeksteeg states that in Dutch doctrine the vote of no-confidence 'is a constitutional doctrine, apart from the doctrine of political accountability'.[9] Also Tomkins,[10] in his analysis of the British system, clearly distinguishes between political accountability on the one hand and parliamentary confidence; apparently they are not synonyms. In Denmark the parliamentary power to pass a motion of no-confidence can be seen as a consequence of the government being accountable as well; the power itself is however not the key issue in the concept of political accountability.[11]

3.4 Germany: A Mixed System

None of the countries' structures or approaches to political accountability is alike, as we shall see. However we were able to classify them in two main models of political accountability. In Germany the situation seems somewhat different. In the German system, political accountability is seen as a concept that is closely linked to the so-called 'chain of legitimacy'. This chain implies that all powers and competences follow from the people. Originally, only the Prime Minister ('*Bundeskanzler*') was regarded as being politically accountable, because a motion of no-confidence can only be tabled by the parliament against him. Seen from this perspective, there is thus a theoretical link between the appointment and dismissal of the prime minister by parliament and his political accountability.

However, this is not the whole story. Although individual ministers cannot be forced by parliament to resign, they have to render account to parliament because of article 65 of the German Constitution. This article provides:

> 'The Chancellor determines and is responsible for the general policy guidelines. Within the limits set by these guidelines, each Minister conducts the affairs of his department independently and on his own responsibility. (...)'

---

9 Broeksteeg (2008) chapter 8, par. 7.2.

10 Tomkins (2008) chapter 12, par. 2.

11 Jensen (2008) chapter 4, par. 6.

As a result every individual minister must directly give an account to parliament on how he has 'conducted the affairs of his department'.

So we conclude that in Germany there are in fact two views on political accountability at the same time. Firstly it has been used to make clear that the parliament can force the government to take the consequences for what went wrong in a particular case ('to blame the government'). This part first and foremost focuses on the *Bundeskanzler*. However, in the process of giving an account, the role which individual ministers play with regard to his or her department is seen as essential. In Germany, we have to conclude, elements of both models as distinguished above, seem to be accepted at the same time.

4 The Scope of Political Accountability

4.1 Governmental Powers

In line with the 'government-oriented' model the legal adage 'no accountability without competences' is in fact the core of political accountability theories in the Netherlands. This means that a minister is only accountable in so far he has legal competences to achieve his policy.

However, in most of the other Member States involved in this research, such a strong legal approach does not seem to be accepted; so, in most countries there does not seem to be a direct relationship between the legal competences of a minister and his political accountability. It is true that adages such as 'Accountability follows powers' and '*Pas de pouvoir sans responsabilité*' seem to have a certain relevance in, for example, Spain, France, Germany, Sweden, Poland, Belgium and Italy, but this apparently has, at least in most of these countries, a meaning different from the Netherlands. In these systems the concept of 'power' seems to refer to the non-legal term 'influence'. With the exception of France,[12] where according to Ziller the political accountability of a minister corresponds with his competences, the term 'competences' is often interpreted as 'influence' or 'power'. So for example in Germany, accountability is, according to Mehde, 'restricted to matters the minister can influence'.[13] And in Denmark, as Jensen has described, 'a minister is responsible for the actions within the framework of the ministry to the extent that he can actually influence the actions in question'.[14]

With regard to Italy, Violini, Ninatti and Tiberi mention the adage 'accountability follows powers' as apparently being relevant as well.[15] In Italy ministers are accountable for '*il indirizzo politico*', which refers to the general governmental policy, the political agenda as it may. The concept of '*indirizzo politico*' seems

12 Ziller (2008) chapter 5, par. 5.

13 Mehde (2008) chapter 6, par. 4.

14 Jensen (2008) chapter 4, par. 4.

15 Violini, Ninatti, Tiberi (2008) chapter 7, par. 1.3.

to give rise to discussion on what it exactly means; what is precisely meant by 'general governmental policy'? Because the concept of '*indirizzo politico*' until now has remained vague, it also seems to be unclear what the ministers are precisely accountable for.

In the Member States, where any link has been recognized between the powers of a minister and his accountability, this seems to be particularly relevant for certain types of agencies.[16] In fact this link can directly or indirectly be found in the majority of national systems involved in this research. In (among others) Sweden, the Netherlands and Spain the general accepted assumption is that in so far as the ministerial powers towards agencies have weakened, the ministerial accountability has become restricted as well. However, in most of the analyses of the national systems in part II of this book it remains open whether the concept of 'power' is meant in a legal ('competence') or in a non-legal ('influence') sense.

4.2 Political Accountability for Policy-making

In an ideal world governmental policy is not only made; it should also be executed. This raises the question of whether the government or the ministers are only accountable for their policy-making or for the execution and implementation of this policy as well. In most countries involved in this research, like the Netherlands, Belgium, France, Germany and Poland, ministers are accountable for both.

However, as we also shall see below,[17] political reality is more complicated. In several countries ministers have sometimes been inclined to evade their accountability by saying that they cannot, at the end of the day, be held responsible for what went wrong in the farthest corners of their department. For example in France, although ministers are theoretically fully accountable for both the policy and the implementation thereof, ministers usually do not resign for grave mistakes in operational matters. In practice such mistakes regularly leads to the forced resignation of the officials or political advisers concerned.

The only Member State involved in this research where the political accountability is also restricted in a constitutional sense is Sweden. In Sweden, the Constitution explicitly provides that political accountability only concerns the policy-making. As a result ministers are not accountable whatsoever for the execution or implementation of their policy. So the Swedish public service disposes of a high level of autonomy. This even includes ministerial departments: ministers may not meddle in the concrete, specific activities of their department. Therefore ministers departments can, to a certain extent, be compared to agencies which have a strong position in Sweden as well. Instead of political accountability Sweden uses alternative forms of accountability like legal provisions to enhance transparency and the Ombudsman.[18]

16 See par. 7.1.

17 See par. 6.2.

18 Ziller (2001) 102-119.

5 Collective or Individual Accountability

5.1 Introduction

As we have seen in most chapters in part II of this book a distinction can be made between individual and collective political accountability. The content of these two types of accountability varies per national system; it depends on how political accountability is defined in general. Moreover, as we will see below, which type of accountability, collective or individual, is predominant varies as well. This again has to be seen in the context of which model of political accountability ('parliament-oriented' or 'government-oriented') the Member State concerned adheres to.

5.2 Primarily a Collective Accountability

In most countries involved in this research, collective accountability is accepted as a notion being that the government as a whole can be dismissed by parliament. Individual accountability then only exists, when ministers can be dismissed individually. We find this reasoning in for example Belgium, France, Italy, Poland, Sweden and the Czech Republic. In all these countries accountability is primarily a collective one.

However, within this group of countries some variations can be identified. In France and in the Czech Republic, there is in fact no room for individual accountability, since parliament cannot dismiss individual ministers. Only the government as a whole and the prime minister are, in this sense, politically accountable. When a motion of censure is tabled, it concerns the whole government. It is the President and the prime minister – and not parliament – who can dismiss an individual minister.[19] In the Czech Republic all individual accountability is excluded; the Czech government is a collective public body. It takes its decisions as a whole and therefore it is accountable as a whole.[20]

In Spain, Belgium, Italy and Sweden individual accountability does exist to a certain extent, but is derived from the collective one. It means that individual ministers render account to the parliament on behalf of the whole government. The Spanish constitution provides that only the government as a whole is accountable. A motion of no confidence, addressed to the prime minister, implies an expression of a lack of confidence in the government as a whole. However, in Spain also an individual accountability is assumed, because parliament can call individual ministers to account. Yet, a motion of no confidence against an individual minister is not possible. So the parliament cannot dismiss individual ministers; the only way to achieve this is by trying to force the prime minister to dismiss an individual minister.[21]

---

19 Ziller (2008) chapter 5, par. 8.

20 Hofmann, Kopal (2008) chapter 3, par. 3.3.

21 Alberti (2008) chapter 10, par. 3 and 5.

The latter is also the case in Belgium and Italy: a motion of no confidence is addressed to the whole government. Until the constitutional reform in 1993 the Belgian parliament could force individual ministers to resign, though this proved to be rather difficult in practice. The dismissal of an individual minister in practice meant the resignation of the whole government.[22] Nowadays parliament can accept a motion of no confidence, but ministers are not constitutionally obliged to resign. In practice it will however be unacceptable if one stays in office after parliament has expressed its lack of confidence. In Italy, the prime minister is accountable for the '*indirizzo politico*', while individual ministers are accountable for their departments. Here, an individual accountability of ministers is deduced from the collective accountability as well, though parliament cannot dismiss individual ministers. In Italy individual accountability is however seen as problematic, because it:[23]

> 'does not include any suitable instrument for sanctioning a minister'.

The strongest individual accountability, within the group of countries mentioned above, exists in Sweden. In Sweden individual ministers can be dismissed by parliament; here an individual accountability exists apart and independent from the collective one. As Nergelius states in his analysis of the Swedish system:[24]

> 'Thus, such a thing as an individual accountability before the Parliament does exist, as follows clearly from the rules on the parliamentary vote of no-confidence'.

5.3 A Pivotal Role of the Prime Minister

In the Member States that primarily focus on collective political accountability, there is a pivotal role for the prime minister. Within the government he is primarily accountable; he is the 'figurehead' of the government as a collective body. In this sense a predominant role for the prime minister seems to exist in for example Belgium, the Czech Republic, Germany, France,[25] Italy, Poland, Spain and Sweden.[26]

How this can work in practice can be illustrated by the Spanish system. As Alberti has described, the Spanish prime minister (*Presidente del Gobierno*) 'embodies Parliament's confidence in the Government'. Parliament can only

[22] Van den Driessche (2008) chapter 2, par. 5.

[23] Violini, Ninatti, Tiberi (2008) chapter 7, par. 2.4.

[24] Nergelius (2008) chapter 11, par. 2.

[25] In France, the President should dismiss the prime minister on request of the House of Representatives. If the majority of the House of Representatives is backing the President, he can, however, also decide to dismiss the prime minister autonomously, which he does by expressing the wish that the prime minister resigns himself.

[26] Nergelius (2008) chapter 11, par. 1.

dismiss the government as a whole by passing a motion of no-confidence against the prime minister. The resignation of an individual minister can only be prompted via the prime minister. Because the parliament cannot send away an individual minister, it only can try to persuade the prime minister to enhance the resignation of the minister concerned. This seems to be more or less the same in the Czech Republic, France, Italy, Spain, Belgium and Germany.

In the last three countries, a motion of no confidence must be a 'constructive' one. This means that the parliamentary majority, who wants to send away the government, also has to mention the name of a new prime minister. This procedure intends to prevent that the parliament would too easily pass a motion of no confidence. In Poland the Constitution explicitly provides that only a motion of no-confidence in the government as a whole needs to be constructive; it does not apply if parliament wants to dismiss an individual minister.[27]

As we have seen before,[28] Germany has a mixed model of political accountability. On the one hand it is focused on the prime minister (the *Bundeskanzler)* as being the only minister against whom a motion of no confidence can be passed. On the other hand the role of individual ministers has been seen as essential in the light of article 65 of the German Constitution as they are obliged to give an account to parliament on how he has 'conducted the affairs of his department'. As a result it can be concluded that Germany has both collective and individual accountability. However, Mehde makes clear that in practice:[29]

> 'collective accountability does not feature prominently in the German constitutional system' and that 'the main focus lies with the accountability of individual ministers'.

In Germany, like for example in the Netherlands, collective accountability is only assumed for decisions of the council of ministers. We will come back to this below.

5.4 Primarily an Individual Accountability

In a 'government-oriented' model the picture is rather different. Seen from the perspective of this model, a collective political accountability will often be accepted only in so far as the government as a whole has legal competences or powers at its disposal. This seldom is the case; competences most of the time are granted to individual ministers. So in 'government-oriented' models like the Netherlands, United Kingdom and Denmark political accountability has been regarded as primarily individual.

In the Netherlands there is a very strong emphasis on individual accountability. There is even a debate among constitutionalists whether, next to individual

---

27 Piotrowski (2008) chapter 9, par. 3.

28 See par. 3.4.

29 Mehde (2008) chapter 6, par. 3.

accountability, there is a collective accountability at all. Most Dutch authors take on the view that there is not because the council of ministers as a collective has no legal competences as such. Despite the fact that the council of ministers is very powerful if we look at daily practice, in constitutional terms it is just an internal body that is only competent to regulate its own internal affairs. Decisions with external effect are only taken by the government[30] or by an individual minister.[31]

In the United Kingdom political accountability is primarily individual as well. Accountability in British constitutional law as well as in political practice means that account is given by individual ministers in the first place. However, here, the concept of collective accountability is generally accepted. It is even seen as the derivative of the individual one. It means that ministers have to support the government policy. In the words of Tomkins:[32]

> 'all ministers in the government must accept responsibility for the policies, decisions, and actions of the government, even if they did not personally develop or take them, and even if they personally disagree with them'.

They are bound by what the government decides is government policy:

> 'All ministers must be prepared to defend government policy in Parliament'.

If a minister fundamentally disagrees with his colleagues and is not prepared to accept the consequences of the government policy, he has to resign. The purpose behind collective accountability in the British system is that parliament must be able to identify what the government's position is on a given issue. Moreover, it prevents a minister from evading his accountability by saying that a certain decision was not his, but was taken by another minister. For this reasons homogeneity of government policy is necessary, as well as confidentiality of what has been discussed in the council of ministers.

6 Political Accountability for the Civil Service

6.1 Democratic Control on the Civil Service

Most ministers are the head of a department. The logical result of this is that ministers are accountable for the conduct of the civil servants who work at their department. This places the civil service under parliamentary control. In most Member States involved in this research, political accountability is

30 In the Netherlands the council of minister differs from the government. The government consists of the King and the ministers together, while the King is not part of the council of ministers.

31 Broeksteeg (2008) chapter 8, par. 2.

32 Tomkins (2008) chapter 12, par. 2.1.

seen as a way to give democratic legitimacy to the civil service via the minister. By way of calling the minister into account, the directly elected parliament can control the civil service.

The latter is also the underlying principle of the so-called 'unbroken chain of legitimacy' in Germany. This chain of democratic legitimacy starts with the people democratically legitimizing the parliament through elections. A parliamentary majority then in turn legitimizes the government by giving the government its support. And to conclude the chain, the civil servants are under control of the government via the individual ministers. There is therefore an unbroken chain between the civil servants and the parliament via the ministers. As Mehde says in Germany:[33]

> 'ministerial accountability is the instrument enabling Parliament to control the executive as a whole'.

6.2 Limiting Accountability?

In the United Kingdom as well as in the Netherlands a discussion was brought up regarding the question of whether a minister is accountable for everything that occurs in his department or only for those issues for which he can be personally blamed. The underlying idea of a more restricted accountability is that, considering the complexity of a department, it is impossible for the minister to adequately control the whole civil service. The minister can not know and control everything that is taking place within his department. In the view of some, political accountability has become a 'fiction'. In theory the minister has to account to parliament for everything his civil servants have or have not done, but if we look at daily practice it would not be reasonable to hold him responsible for matters that he could not know or influence.

In British literature one sometimes refers in this context to the term 'causal responsibility'. This 'implies that the minister carries personal credit or blame for that action or decision'.[34] In this view a minister is always *accountable* for what has happened within his department, but not necessarily *responsible*. This means that a minister always can be called into account by the parliament and always has to answer parliamentary questions on what went wrong, but he should not always be obliged to carry personal credit or blame. It can however, in such a case, be 'appropriate' to resign. Yet, this doctrine of causal responsibility is not uncontested in British legal literature or in parliament. On the contrary, the House of Commons has explicitly rejected this attempt to limit political accountability.[35] This is the same in the Netherlands, where the 'rule of blameworthiness', comparable with the British concept of 'causal responsibility', is not accepted in constitutional literature, nor in politics.[36]

[33] Mehde (2008) chapter 6, par. 4.

[34] Tomkins (2008) chapter 12, par. 2.2.3.

[35] Tomkins (2008) chapter 12, par. 2.

[36] Broeksteeg (2008) chapter 8, par. 3.

However, in Denmark such a doctrine of causal accountability does seem to exist. According to art. 15, Danish Constitution, there is no limit as to what ministers can be held accountable for and therefore ministers are, as a principle, accountable for everything that takes place within their department. In practice however, they are only accountable for subject matters that they can influence. As Jensen stated in Denmark:[37]

> 'in practice a minister will only be held accountable for actions that can reasonably be attributed to his own conduct (or lack of conduct)'.

The Act on Ministerial Responsibility which limits the legal responsibility of ministers is also used as a 'fairly accurate description of actual limits of political responsibility', which means that no vote of no confidence will be approved unless it falls within the realm of art. 3 Act on Ministerial Responsibility.[38]

In the other Member States, relying on what has said in part II of this book, the question of limiting political accountability is not much of an issue. In general, the following reasoning seems to be generally accepted: the minister is at the top of the departmental hierarchy and therefore is politically accountable in the sense that he can be called into account and can be held responsible for the departmental civil service. Whether the minister personally can be blamed in a specific case is not relevant. Or, as is said in the Polish report:[39]

> 'Political accountability is of an objective nature, and does not necessarily have to involve any degree of blame'.

6.3 Rendering Account by Civil Servants

In all the Member States involved in this research, it is not customary that civil servants are (directly) accountable to parliament. As a rule they are not obliged to give information or explain or justify their conduct to parliament. This of course does not mean that they are not accountable at all. They are however solely accountable to their minister, not to other institutions.

A common exception to this rule is that civil servants sometimes have to render account or to give information to a parliamentary committee of inquiry. Examples can be found in the Netherlands, the United Kingdom and Sweden.[40] Moreover, in some Member States, some very specific types of civil servants are, to a limited extent, accountable to parliament as well. These civil servants are for example the head of the National Bank, the president of a National Audit Office, the Ombudsman, or some chief executives of agencies, for example in the Czech

---

37 Jensen (2008) chapter 4, par. 3.

38 Jensen (2008) chapter 4, par. 3.

39 Piotrowski (2008) chapter 9, par. 3.

40 Broeksteeg (2008) chapter 8, par. 6.1; Tomkins (2008) chapter 12, par. 2.2.3; Nergelius (2008) chapter 11, par. 6.

Republic, Poland and Spain.[41] It is however unclear whether and to what extent this accountability is a controversial issue.

In France the accountability of civil servants seems to go even further. Ziller describes that parliament has the right to scrutinize civil servants within departments as well as civil servants employed in independent agencies. Legislation prescribes which civil servants have to give an account to parliament.[42]

7 Political Accountability for Agencies

7.1 Introduction

In almost all of the Member States involved in this research it seems as if the political accountability for agencies is a controversial topic. The main issue here is their democratic legitimacy. More specifically the presumption is that at least in some cases the mechanisms to keep agencies under democratic control are too weak.

The political accountability for agencies varies from country to country. Although it sometimes has remained unclear as to what extent the government or individual ministers can be held accountable for the conduct of agencies, it seems as if one can divide the Member States involved in this research into three categories:

1) ministers are not politically accountable for agencies (see par. 6.2);
2) ministers are fully politically accountable for agencies (see par. 6.3);
3) ministers are politically accountable for agencies in so far as they have legal competences with regard to agencies or can otherwise influence their conduct (see par. 6.4).

7.2 No Accountability

We have seen before[43] that ministers in Sweden are only accountable for the policy-making of the government and not for the execution thereof. The main rule is that a minister is not (fully) accountable for 'public authorities'. These authorities include agencies. Nergelius points out that only in exceptional cases can this be otherwise:

> 'Only if the minister has known for some time about problems in specific bodies without reaching or doing anything about them (...) may the minister be held legally or politically accountable.'[44]

---

[41] Hofmann, Kopal (2008) chapter 3, par. 4.5; Piotrowski (2008) chapter 9, par. 6; Alberti (2008) chapter 10, par. 3.4.

[42] Ziller (2008) chapter 5, par. 5.

[43] See par. 4.2.

[44] Nergelius (2008) chapter 11, par. 3.

In practice a minister sometimes even refuses to give an account to parliament. This means that there is by and large no political accountability for agencies in Sweden.

In this category we can to some extent also place France and the Czech Republic.[45] Here ministers in most cases do not seem to be politically accountable for agencies either. However, a distinction is made between agencies that belong to the 'central administration of the State' and other agencies. With regard to agencies in the first category, ministers cannot give orders, although they have some specific legal competences. Because of these competences one can say that there is a limited political accountability. However, for all other agencies there is no political accountability. The government has only influence by means of its power to appoint the members of the executive and/or the supervisory board of an agency. This situation can only be changed if the legislator would reverse the independence of the agency.

7.3 Full Accountability

In the second category of the Member States involved in this research ministers are fully accountable for agencies. This is for example the case in Poland and Belgium.[46] The underlying idea here is the need for overall democratic control over the executive. Even though ministers might not have full control over the policy and decision-making of the agency in the pure legal sense, ministers are nevertheless considered to be accountable towards parliament for the whole executive, therefore including the agencies. In these Member States it is thought to be constitutionally unacceptable if one or more parts of the executive would operate outside the scope of parliamentary control. However, daily practice can be different. It sometimes occurs that ministers, although formally accountable, refuse to give an account in so far as it concerns agencies .[47]

In the United Kingdom, the so-called 'next steps agencies' have been established. Their amount has grown enormously over the years. Most civil servants now are employed in a next steps agency. Next steps agencies are, from a legal point of view, part of the department, but have in practice an autonomous position. The establishment of next steps agencies does not have any consequences for the political accountability of the ministers. They remain fully accountable. However, in practice, next steps agencies are considered to be responsible for the implementation of policy.[48]

Since, according to German constitutional theory, agencies interrupt the chain of legitimacy, in Germany there is no tradition of transferring powers to independent agencies. An interruption of the chain of legitimacy, by providing organizations or civil servants with specific competences while they fall outside

45 Ziller (2008) chapter 5, par. 5.

46 Piotrowski (2008) chapter 9, par. 4; Van den Driessche (2008) chapter 2, par. 4.4.

47 Van den Driessche (2008) chapter 2, par 4.

48 Tomkins (2008) chapter 12, par. 1.

the hierarchical civil service, needs a particular justification and can only be accepted in exceptional, unusual cases.[49] Not many executive tasks have therefore been transferred to agencies in Germany. In so far as agencies have been established, a minister still remains fully accountable for the agencies within his portfolio. Mehde states with regard to accountability and agencies:[50]

> 'Political accountability of ministers in relation to the administrations they are in charge of is taken for granted'.

7.4 Limited Accountability

In most Member States involved in this research ministers seem accountable for an agency only insofar as they can actually influence the actions and decisions of the agency concerned. However, the extent to which ministers are considered to be accountable in daily practice is less clear. Taking into account the limited amount of legal competences which a minister often has over an agency, one can imagine that also the practical influence on the decision making of the agency is limited. If a minister is only empowered to control the budget or to appoint the members of the board, to what extent can he then also influence the decisions that should be made by the agency? And to what extent can the parliament hold a minister accountable for decisions of independent agencies which he cannot have control over? These questions seem to be the object of an ongoing discussion in at least some of these countries.

In the Netherlands[51] for example, the official doctrine is that a minister can only be held to account for an agency, as far as he has legal competences: no accountability without legal competences. These competences are provided for in legislation that establishes the agency and usually concern the control over the budget, the appointment and the dismissal of members of the management board, the power to quash decisions of the agency and, eventually, the power to give general policy guidelines. So, officially parliament can control agencies only to a limited extent by means of a limited ministerial accountability. However, what this means in practice is often unclear. Because of the large number of agencies in the Netherlands (about 400) and the fact that at least until now[52] the legislation substantially varies per agency, it is at times not clear to what extent the minister is accountable. Moreover, political reality shows that, if there is a real political problem due to serious failures within an executive agency, parliament does not accept that a minister is not accountable, although from a legal

49 For this reason Germany often raises objection against the large amount of agencies and the establishing of new agencies on EU-level.

50 Mehde (2008) chapter 6, par. 2.

51 Broeksteeg (2008) chapter 8, par. 3.3.

52 Recently introduced general legislation on agencies should bring more clarity and unity in the present chaos of legal rules. See Kaderwet (2006), nr. 587 and Kaderwet <http://www.minbzk.nl/actueel?ActItmIdt=108141> (November 2007).

point of view the minister is not competent and although at an earlier stage the same parliament has accepted the legislation in which the ministerial competences have been restricted.

In Spain the heads of agencies have to render account directly to parliament. Parliament can call them into account orally as well as in writing. They can be forced to appear in parliament. Parliament cannot, however, send the heads of agencies away. For this reason, some authors call this a limited accountability.[53] In Italy political accountability is considered limited as well, because the influence of the Italian government on agencies has decreased over the years.[54]

7.5 Conclusion

To summarize we can conclude that in the majority of the Member States involved in this research a weakening of legal competences or influence of the government towards agencies leads at least in theory to a weakening of its political accountability. This seems to be the case in the Netherlands, Italy and Spain. In some of these countries this is highly controversial because of the inherent weakening of the role of parliament. In Germany, Poland, Belgium and, with regard to the next step agencies, the United Kingdom, political accountability for agencies is not limited: ministers are accountable for the executive as a whole, so including agencies. Finally in Sweden there is as a rule no political accountability for agencies whatsoever. In this category we can also place France and the Czech Republic, although with some exceptions.

8 The Process of Rendering Account

8.1 Obligations Following from Accountability

All countries involved in this research have, by and large, similar procedures of parliamentary scrutiny. These procedures concern submitting questions and interpellations, as well as the right of inquiries. In some countries the right of budget is also explicitly mentioned as an instrument of parliament to scrutinize the government.

The process of rendering account seems essential in both concepts of political accountability as described above.[55] This process includes various elements. It regards the obligation to give information when parliament so requires, in the first place. In the Netherlands this obligation is provided for in the Constitution.[56] In Denmark there exists a constitutional obligation to reply to questions

53 Alberti (2008) chapter 10, par. 3.4.

54 Violini, Ninatti, Tiberi (2008) chapter 7, par. 3.1.

55 See paragraphs 2.2. and 2.3.

56 Broeksteeg (2008) chapter 8, par. 6.

in debates that concern matters of public interest, as stated in art. 53 Danish Constitution.[57]

There is a broad consensus in the Member States that giving information to parliament alone is not enough. Political accountability also means that the minister must respond to criticism by the parliament, explain and justify governmental policy or decisions and put matters right if it should appear that errors have been made. In all the Member States this process seems more or less the same.

Some differences between the Member States can be identified regarding the obligation of ministers to appear in parliament. Most authors participating in this research explicitly mention that in their country ministers can be requested to attend a meeting of parliament. In Belgium, the House of Representatives can request the presence of the members of government. This obligation is provided for in the Constitution. Some Belgian scholars even consider this obligation to be the legal basis for political accountability, as well as the basis for the parliamentary rights to submit interpellations and questions.[58] In the Czech Republic the personal appearance of ministers in meetings of parliament is seen as a constitutional duty that is derived directly from political accountability.[59] The German Bundestag, however, can also demand the presence of members of the government, though it is 'certainly not the most important element of the system of political accountability in Germany'.[60] Also in France, there is no strict obligation of ministers to appear in parliament. The personal appearance in parliament has a 'minor function'.[61]

8.2 Refusal to Answer

Finally, it can be noted that the constitutional order of most countries involved in this research allows ministers to refuse answering parliamentary questions only to a limited extent. Openness of the government to the democratically elected representatives of the people has been, at least in theory, regarded as essential. However, there are exceptions. Generally accepted grounds for refusing information could be e.g. the protection of the safety of the state and the prevention of or the combat against crime. Other grounds for the refusal of information can be the external relations of the state, the protection of privacy or matters that are *sub iudice.*

Differences between the Member States can be identified regarding the extent to which reasons for refusing of information to parliament are prescribed by written law. Belgian constitutional law for example does not provide for any

57 Jensen (2008) chapter 4, par. 5.

58 Van den Driessche (2008) chapter 2, par. 3.2.

59 Hofmann, Kopal (2008) chapter 3, par. 5.2.

60 Mehde (2008) chapter 6, par. 5.

61 Ziller (2008) chapter 5, par. 6.

legal rules.[62] Nor does the Danish Constitution, but, according to Jensen, Danish ministers do have 'a near-duty to answer questions in the parliamentary question time',[63] which follows from article 20 of the Order of Business of the parliament. A minister can refuse to answer questions during question time, but in practice he will have to justify his refusal and abuses could easily be sanctioned by a vote of no-confidence. In addition, according to the Act on Ministerial Responsibility, legal responsibility can be incurred if a minister gives information to Parliament that is incorrect or misleading or withholds relevant information. British ministers have to justify a refusal to answer by means of a reference to the Freedom of Information Act. This implies that British ministers have to inform parliament that they refuse to give information, have to explain why they refuse to do so and have to indicate on which provision in the mentioned Act the refusal is based.[64] In the Netherlands the Constitution provides for a governmental power to refuse information to parliament 'in the interest of the state'.[65]

9 Facing Consequences

9.1 Positive and Negative Vote of Confidence

As seen before one can, roughly speaking, distinguish two concepts of political accountability: the 'parliament-oriented' and the 'government-oriented' model.[66] Although their theoretical orientation is different these are both concepts which fit into and are inherent to a parliamentary system. This means that in both concepts parliament can ultimately pass a judgment regarding the extent to which they have confidence in the government.

As far as the character of this judgment is concerned the Member States involved in this research show quite some variation. Generally speaking such a judgment can be positive (approving or confirming confidence) or negative (disapprove confidence), but these options do not exist in all the Member States at the same time and in the same way. All Member States involved in this research know, as inherent to a parliamentary system, the parliamentary power to pass a vote of no-confidence, but not all of them also know a vote of confidence. As far as Member States do have the option of a vote of confidence, the legal basis and the procedure that can lead to such a vote, can differ remarkably in each country.

In most countries the formal installation of the government includes an investiture by the parliament in the form of a vote of confidence. We find this procedure in Poland, Belgium, Italy, Spain, Germany and the Czech Republic.

62 Van den Driessche (2008) chapter 2, par. 3.2.1.

63 Jensen (2008) chapter 4, par. 5.

64 Tomkins (2008) chapter 12, par. 2.2.4.

65 Broeksteeg (2008) chapter 8, par. 6.1.

66 See paragraphs 3.2. and 3.3.

In Belgium, for example, a new government is installed by the Head of State, but the government refrains from acting as long as it does not have an explicit vote of confidence by the House of Representatives.[67] In these countries, including France,[68] the government can also ask for a vote of confidence at each and very moment after its installation. The underlying idea is that the government must always be sure that it can rely on the support of the democratically elected parliament. As we already have seen above,[69] in these countries, the confidence that a parliamentary majority must have in the government is the key element of the concept of political accountability ('parliament-oriented' model).

In the Netherlands, Denmark and United Kingdom, which all have a 'government-oriented' concept of political accountability, only a negative vote – a vote of no confidence – exists. In these Member States parliament cannot pass a motion of confidence, nor can the government explicitly ask for confidence. The assumption is that parliament has confidence in a minister or in the government, until proven otherwise, by passing a motion of no confidence by the majority. As a result these countries also do not have a procedure of investiture.

9.2 Procedures

A vote of no confidence must sometimes be 'constructive' in nature. This means that if parliament wants to pass a motion of no confidence, the motion also must contain the name of the new (prime) minister. The object of this condition is that the parliamentary system becomes more stable. The parliament is less inclined to send away the government, if it at the same time has to propose a solution to the problem by naming a new prime minister who can count on the approval of a parliamentary majority. The constructive vote of (no-)confidence is known in Poland, Spain, Belgium and Germany.[70]

In the Netherlands and the United Kingdom the procedure of the motion of no-confidence is unwritten. In the other countries, the Constitution provides for the procedure either briefly (Denmark, Sweden) or extensively. The latter is especially the case in the countries with a constructive motion of no confidence. Additional conditions for accepting such a motion can for example be a cooling-off period between the handing in of the motion and the actual vote. In France and Belgium, parliament may vote on the motion only after a period of at least 48 hours. In Italy this period is even three days.

---

67 Van den Driessche (2008) chapter 2, par. 4.1.

68 Ziller (2008) chapter 5, par. 3.

69 See paragraph 3.2.

70 Piotrowski (2008) chapter 9, par. 2; Van den Driessche (2008) chapter 2, par. 5; Alberti (2008) chapter 10, par. 2.1; Mehde (2008) chapter 6, par. 6.

9.3 The Role of the Prime Minister

We already mentioned the pivotal role of the prime minister in some Member States involved in this research.[71] In most Member States a motion of no confidence can only be directed at the government as a whole. This means that parliament itself cannot send away an individual minister. If it wants an individual minister to be sent away, it has to pressure the prime minister to dismiss the minister concerned. For example with regard to Germany, Mehde states in this context:[72]

> 'The position of ministers is tied to the one of the Chancellor'.

Individual ministers can only be dismissed by the federal president at the request of the Chancellor. The latter is also the case in for example the Czech Republic.[73]

In Belgium it is accepted that the House can express that it no longer has confidence in an individual minister. However, according to the Constitution it still cannot dismiss an individual minister. However, if the loss of confidence would be expressed in a single minister, it would not be unusual for the prime minister to force the minister in question to resign. In France, the House of Representatives can only pass a motion of no confidence towards the prime minister. If this happens the whole government resigns.

Summarizing the parliament cannot pass a motion of no-confidence against an individual minister in the Czech Republic, France, Spain, Belgium, Italy and Germany. In these countries the prime minister has a central role in the government, compared to for example in the Netherlands and Denmark. In the United Kingdom, the prime minister has also a pivotal role as head of the majority party, but parliament can at least in theory dismiss individual ministers. In the United Kingdom political accountability is, as we have seen, primarily individual.

9.4 Summary

Again, here we find a remarkable distinction between the Netherlands, the United Kingdom and Denmark on the one hand and the other Member States involved in this research on the other. In the Netherlands, the United Kingdom and Denmark parliamentary confidence in the government is assumed, until a parliamentary majority passes a motion of no confidence. In the other countries it is more or less the other way round; parliament can (or in some countries: must) explicitly express its confidence in the government. In most of the latter countries some form of investiture procedure exists: parlia-

---

71 See par. 5.3.

72 Mehde (2008) chapter 6, par. 6.

73 Hofmann, Kopal (2008) chapter 3, par. 4.3.

ment has to explicitly express its confidence in a newly formed government. In some of these countries the vote of no confidence can be 'constructive' in nature. This means that if the parliament wants to send away the government, the motion of no confidence must contain the name of the new prime minister who should form a new government.

10 Concluding Remarks: A *Ius Commune*?

What does political accountability precisely mean if we compare the concepts as they exist in the eleven Member States of the EU involved in this research? Is there an *ius commune* on the concept of political accountability and if yes, what does it look like? The answer to these questions is far from easy. As we have said at the beginning of this chapter,[74] one has to realize time and again that the historical, cultural and political context varies widely in each and every Member State.

This variety in context has substantial implications: it makes comparative research on key issues of constitutional and political systems, as for example on the concept of political accountability, extremely complicated. It therefore is also very difficult to detect a precisely defined '*ius commune*' on political accountability. Our research only delivers a provisional and non-exhaustive picture that should be tested and further elaborated in a more in-depth research. Nevertheless it can be maintained that our research gives insight into at least the main features of the national concepts of political accountability. It is worthwhile to see what these main features are and what they could mean for the future of the European Union.

If we try to summarize the essence of this research it can be concluded that at first sight the differences between the Member States involved in this research seem fundamental. The constitutional theories underlying the 'parliament-oriented' and 'government-oriented' concepts of political accountability, as we have distinguished in this chapter, seem to be quite different.[75] However, assuming that these concepts indeed depart from a different theoretical perspective, one runs the risk to overestimate the importance of these differences. After all the Member States involved in this research all[76] have a parliamentary system. In such a system the concept of political accountability plays a vital role. In all the Member States political accountability is in fact the essential mechanism for the parliament to hold a grip on the government and its members.

If we, from this general perspective, try to look behind the apparently different constitutional theories, it is possible to detect an '*ius commune*' in general terms. Although the emphasis varies from Member State to Member State, it

[74] See par. 2.

[75] See paragraph 3.2. and 3.3.

[76] Except maybe for France that is often referred to as a semi-presidential system. Ziller however also defines France in essence as a parliamentary system.

seems that in every system at least three basic elements of political accountability can be distinguished:[77]

- *being accountable:* the guarantee of the government being accountable to the parliament for the use of its executive powers.
- *calling to account*: the right of the parliament to call the government to account which results in the obligation of the government to inform the parliament and to explain and justify its conduct;
- *holding to account*: the right of the parliament to make a judgment on the conduct of the government which results in the obligation of the government to accept the consequences; this could ultimately mean resignation.

In this chapter we have elaborated on some details of each of these elements from a comparative perspective. In the next chapter we will see what these elements could mean for the further development of accountability mechanisms in the European Union.

[77] A rather similar division of political accountability into three basic elements was introduced by Elzinga in the Netherlands. See Elzinga (1994) 31 ff.

Bibliography

ALBERTI (2008)

E. Alberti, 'The Political Accountability of the Government in Spain', in L. Verhey, H. Broeksteeg, I. Van den Driessche (eds.), *Political Accountability in Europe: Which Way Forward? A Traditional Concept of Parliamentary Democracy in an EU Context* (Groningen 2008).

BROEKSTEEG (2008)

H. Broeksteeg, 'Political accountability in the Netherlands', in L. Verhey, H. Broeksteeg, I. Van den Driessche (eds.), *Political Accountability in Europe: Which Way Forward? A Traditional Concept of Parliamentary Democracy in an EU Context* (Groningen 2008).

CLAES (2006)

M. Claes, 'Constitutional law', in J.M. Smits (ed.), *Elgar Encyclopedia of Comparative Law* (Cheltenham 2006) 187-199.

VAN DEN DRIESSCHE (2008)

I. Van den Driessche, 'Political Accountability in Belgium', in L. Verhey, H. Broeksteeg, I. Van den Driessche (eds.), *Political Accountability in Europe: Which Way Forward? A Traditional Concept of Parliamentary Democracy in an EU Context* (Groningen 2008).

ELZINGA (1994)

D.J. Elzinga, 'De politieke ministeriële verantwoordelijkheid', in D.J. Elzinga (ed.), *Ministeriële verantwoordelijkheid in Nederland* (Zwolle 1994) 31-49.

HOFMANN, KOPAL (2008)

M. Hofmann, J. Kopal, 'Political Accountability in the Czech Republic', in L. Verhey, H. Broeksteeg, I. Van den Driessche (eds.), *Political Accountability in Europe: Which Way Forward? A Traditional Concept of Parliamentary Democracy in an EU Context* (Groningen 2008).

JENSEN (2008)

J.A. Jensen, 'Political Accountability in Denmark', in L. Verhey, H. Broeksteeg, I. Van den Driessche (eds.), *Political Accountability in Europe: Which Way Forward? A Traditional Concept of Parliamentary Democracy in an EU Context* (Groningen 2008).

KADERWET (2006)

'Kaderwet zbo's', *Staatsblad* 2006, nr. 587.

KADERWET (2007)

'ZBO's binnen kaders, Rapportage op hoofdlijnen van het Begeleidingsteam Kaderwet zbo's', 2007 <http://www.minbzk.nl/actueel?ActItmIdt=108141> (november 2007).

KOOPMANS (2003)

T. Koopmans, *Courts and Political Institutions. A Comparative View* (Cambridge 2003).

LEGRAND (2002)
P. Legrand, 'Public Law, Europeanisation and Convergence: Can Comparatists Contribute?', in P. Beaumont, C. Lyons and N. Walker (eds.) *Convergence and Divergence in European Public Law* (Oxford 2002).

MEHDE (2008)
V. Mehde, 'Political Accountability in Germany', in L. Verhey, H. Broeksteeg, I. Van den Driessche (eds.), *Political Accountability in Europe: Which Way Forward? A Traditional Concept of Parliamentary Democracy in an EU Context* (Groningen 2008).

NERGELIUS (2008)
J. Nergelius, 'Political Accountability in Sweden', in L. Verhey, H. Broeksteeg, I. Van den Driessche (eds.), *Political Accountability in Europe: Which Way Forward? A Traditional Concept of Parliamentary Democracy in an EU Context* (Groningen 2008).

PIOTROWSKI (2008)
R. Piotrowski, 'Political Accountability in a Polish Perspective', in L. Verhey, H. Broeksteeg, I. Van den Driessche (eds.), *Political Accountability in Europe: Which Way Forward? A Traditional Concept of Parliamentary Democracy in an EU Context* (Groningen 2008).

TOMKINS (2008)
A. Tomkins, 'Political Accountability and British Government, in L. Verhey, H. Broeksteeg, I. Van den Driessche (eds.), *Political Accountability in Europe: Which Way Forward? A Traditional Concept of Parliamentary Democracy in an EU Context* (Groningen 2008).

VIOLINI, NINATTI, TIBERI (2008)
L. Violini, S. Ninatti, G. Tiberi, 'Political accountability in Italy', in L. Verhey, H. Broeksteeg, I. Van den Driessche (eds.), *Political Accountability in Europe: Which Way Forward? A Traditional Concept of Parliamentary Democracy in an EU Context* (Groningen 2008).

ZILLER (2001)
J. Ziller, 'European Models of Government: Towards a Patchwork with Missing Pieces' (2001) *Parliamentary Affairs* 54 102-119.

ZILLER (2008)
J. Ziller, 'Political Accountability in a European Perspective – France', in L. Verhey, H. Broeksteeg, I. Van den Driessche (eds.), *Political Accountability in Europe: Which Way Forward? A Traditional Concept of Parliamentary Democracy in an EU Context* (Groningen 2008).

CHAPTER 14

Political Accountability in the European Union: Conceptual Analysis and Future Prospects

Luc Verhey, Monica Claes and Hansko Broeksteeg

1 Introduction

This book seeks to ascertain whether and how political accountability can be further developed in the future European Union, building on national constitutional concepts, principles and practices on political accountability. Article 6 EU states that the European Union is founded on the principles of freedom, democracy, human rights and the rule of law principles which 'the Member States have in common'. These national constitutional foundations may be relevant also in the context of political accountability.[1]

Consequently, comparative research is central in this book.[2] The aim was to identify common principles (*'ius commune'*) and practices which have been developed in various national systems over many years or sometimes even centuries with regard to political accountability and to see to what extent these principles and practices are or could be relevant for the future development of the constitutional system of the European Union. To what extent could national constitutional concepts and principles in this field be a source of inspiration for the European Union?

In the following sections we will first give a brief outline of the current debate on political accountability in the European Union (par. 2) and then summarize the concept of political accountability as it exists at present (par. 3). We will deal in more detail with the question of whether such a concept is in place at the European level and if yes, what it looks like. As said in the introduction we mainly concentrate on the political accountability of the Commission towards the European Parliament. The description of this relationship will not be exhaustive; we will only describe the key points that are relevant for our research. After this we will go into the question of to what extent, taking into account the particular features of the European Union, the national principles and practices on political accountability in the Member States, as analysed in chapter 13 of this book, could be relevant for the European Union (par. 4). We will end this chapter with a few concluding remarks (par. 5).

2 Political Accountability in the European Union: A Brief Outline

2.1 Towards a Parliamentary System?

For the first time in the history of European integration, the European Parliament in the fall of 2004 came close to refusing the first line up of the Barroso Commission. This was only prevented because the President chose not to submit his proposed Commission to a vote, since in his opinion, a negative vote would not be positive for the European institutions or for the Euro-

1 See for further details chapter 1.

2 See for a comparative research in the same field Craig, Tomkins (2006).

pean project. Yet the *de facto* rejection of the Commission by the Parliament, along with the debate preceding the nomination of Barroso, claiming that the President, and the composition of the entire Commission for that matter, should reflect the composition of Parliament, may mark the development of a new constitutional practice in the formation of a Commission as well as the introduction at the European level of a regime more akin to a parliamentary regime.[3]

This is confirmed by article 9D TEU, as supposed to be amended by the Reform Treaty. It provides that taking into account the elections to the European Parliament, the European Council shall propose to the Parliament a candidate for President of the Commission. The Parliament shall then elect the President as proposed by the European Council. The events surrounding the nomination of the Barroso Commission and the way institutional relationships have been developed since were generally perceived to reflect an important step forward in the reinforcement of the European Parliament and the development in the direction of a parliamentary system at EU level.

These events are reminiscent of the fall of the Santer Commission in 1999, when the European Parliament asked a Committee of Independent Experts to examine 'the way in which the Commission detects and deals with fraud, mismanagement and nepotism' and 'to establish to what extent the Commission, as a body, or Commissioners individually, bear specific responsibility'. The first report of the Committee, containing the much quoted statement that 'it is becoming difficult to find anyone who has even the slightest sense of responsibility', finally lead to the collective resignation of the Santer Commission, before the Parliament could come to a vote. The events were marked as the coming of age of the Parliament, and as the confirmation of the Parliament as 'the only Union institution able and willing to hold the Commission to account for its conduct as an administration'.[4] The motion of censure, which had long been considered as a nuclear option, too devastating in its consequences ever to be resorted to, now appeared to be a real option, one that could even transform into a method to hold individual Commissioners to account: the threat may suffice to convince individual Commissioners to step down, or to force the President to ask his or her resignation. 'The thread of responsibility linking the Commission to the Parliament, which once seemed so tenuous, has become a rope of steel'.[5]

Chapter 7 of the second report of the Committee of Independent Experts[6] attempted to analyse issues of accountability and responsibility of the Commission in particular and other EU institutions in general, by focusing on three subjects including 'institutional accountability of the Commission, commissioners and officials *vis-à-vis* the democratic institutions of the European Union, notably the European Parliament, both positively (giving account) and negatively

---

3 So Editorial Comments (2004) 1478.

4 So Editorial Comments (1999) 271.

5 So Editorial Comments (1999) 271.

6 The report is available on the Parliament's website: <http://www.europarl.eu.int/experts/default_en.htm>.

(being held to account)'.[7] While the report dealt mostly with questions of ethical and legal responsibility, it was also highly critical of the Commission on the issue of political accountability, holding that:

> 'The Commission must now come to terms with both the Council and the Parliament where these share legislative competence, but more importantly, it must familiarise itself with a more stringent notion of accountability inherent in parliamentary control. Recent events have highlighted that the Commission can no longer consider itself immune either from intense parliamentary scrutiny or its consequences. The end result should not only be a stronger European Parliament, but also a stronger Commission, provided that the new Commission draws the right lessons from past experiences. It must opt unreservedly for openness and transparency, for responsibility and accountability in its relations towards the other institutions and towards those over whom it exercises power (...)'.[8]

The report concluded that the concepts of political responsibility and accountability remained unclear and that mechanisms for their practical application remained inadequate. It added to its report a list of recommendations including the establishment of clear codes of conduct for commissioners, of organisational rules for cabinets, of guidelines to ensure openness and transparency and including proposals for Treaty reform relating to political responsibility mechanisms to be laid down in the Treaty.

The report also highlighted the issue of the role of the European Parliament in its relation to the Commission. It drew on the relationship between Parliament and the executive branch in parliamentary democracies,[9] which it held to be of a dual nature:

1) Parliament has a right to be informed by the Executive, which gives account of its action (which it defined as 'accountability') and
2) Parliament also judges the ultimate political responsibility of the Executive and draws the political consequences (defined as 'political responsibility').

It recognised that there are important differences in the constitutional systems of the EU Member States as to the precise form of ministerial accountability and responsibility, and that the position of the European Parliament could not be assimilated entirely with that of a national parliament. Yet, this did not prevent 'national parliaments from serving as a model, insofar as they reveal constitutional characteristics which may increasingly also shape the role of the European Parliament'.[10] This point was further developed by Walter van Gerven,

---

7 Committee of Independent Experts (1999b) 110-111, marginal number 7.1.5.

8 Committee of Independent Experts (1999b) 112, marginal number 7.2.5.

9 In this context, it left aside the legislative competences of the Commission.

10 Committee of Independent Experts (1999b) 129, marginal number 7.14.2. Given the abundant academic literature on the 'democratic deficit' within the EU the opinion of the Committee does not

member of the Committee of Independent Experts, in a guest editorial in the *Common Market Law Review*, when he wrote:

> 'It will be obvious that many of the issues touched upon in the first and the second report, (..), raise constitutional questions which the legal orders of the Member States have in common. This is therefore an area where comparative research would be particularly helpful in uncovering common principles, which would in turn help in designing constitutional rules for the European Union – with account being taken, of course, of the peculiarities of the Union's legal order. The committee has tried as far as possible to base its assessments on such common principles, both in the first and (especially) in the second report'.[11]

There thus appears to be an assumption in the reports of the Committee that accountability and responsibility of the Commission and of the Union as a whole should, as far as possible, reflect the common constitutional principles of the Member States. However, the Committee itself still remained vague about what the precise content of concepts like 'accountability' and 'responsibility' in the EU context should be.

2.2 The Accountability of the EU Executive

What exactly are these 'peculiarities' of the Union's legal order referred to by Van Gerven? It is difficult to characterize the EU in general terms. Whatever the EU's precise nature between a State and an international organisation,[12] one could say that it is a multi-level polity with a complex interweaving of executive tasks at the Union and Member State levels. Institutions such as the European Council, the Council and the Commission have no parallel in national States or international organisations both exercising executive functions. One cannot simply identify one of these institutions as 'the' EU executive.[13]

Concentrating ourselves on the Commission as was explained above,[14] the Commission combines administrative, executive and legislative functions.[15] The Commission is accountable to the Parliament in the sense that it can be censured by it, it must give account to it, but at the same time, it is under the Treaty bound to be independent. Or to put it in a provocative manner: the Commission is not about government, it is about governance; it is politically neutral, it does not make political choices, but merely technocratic decisions, it is merely functional and must first and foremost be independent and efficient. It represents the general interest of the Union while democratic representation

seem to be uncontroversial. Critical about the Committee is for example Harlow (2002) 56.

11 Van Gerven (2000b) 6.

12 There is abundant literature on this issue. See for example Craig (1999) Ch. 1.

13 Curtin (2004). See also Craig (2006) 315 ff.

14 See chapter 1, par. 1.5.

15 Chalmers, Hadjiemmanuil, Monti, Tomkins (2006) 87 ff.

is guaranteed through the European Council, the Council (both indirectly) and Parliament (directly).[16]

While these statements may be correct in theory, the day-to-day practice demonstrates that most of them no longer hold true. The Commission may not be a 'government' in common parlance that does not imply that it should escape political accountability. It is difficult to maintain that the Commission does not make political choices, that it merely takes technocratic decisions. 'Independence' as required by the Treaties does not equal 'political neutrality', and it cannot be used to limit responsibility and accountability.[17]

The need for accountability of the Commission seems to have been recognised by the Commission itself. After the resignation of the Santer Commission, the incoming Commission Prodi presented itself as a force of change.[18] In his first major address to the European Parliament, Romano Prodi emphasised that he would not hesitate to ask for the resignation of an individual Commissioner should this prove necessary. The new commissioners accepted their portfolios on this understanding, even if individual responsibility was not provided for in the text of the Treaties.

In addition, a new Code of Conduct was produced, and the Rules of Procedure were revised.[19] A Task Force for Administrative Reform (TFRA) was set up under the lead of Vice President Neil Kinnock, which produced a White Paper on Administrative Reform in March 2000.[20] The overall aim of the White Paper was, so it claimed, to provide the strong Commission which a strong Europe needed. This means a Commission which should be 'independent, accountable, efficient and transparent, and guided by the highest standards of responsibility'.[21] The White Paper demonstrated the desire to guarantee a strong, independent and effective Commission, concentrating on its core business, and able to fulfil its institutional role as the motor of European integration. Nevertheless, it remained a rather limited exercise of internal administrative reform, 'revealing an administration desperately trying to pull itself up by its bootstraps'.[22]

It was soon followed by a more encompassing White Paper on European Governance, released in July 2001.[23] This White Paper was drafted by a Governance Team within the Commission, after extensive consultation outside the

16 These statements are intentionally provocative, but the vision of the EU and the Commission underlying the White Paper on European Governance does reflect some of these ideas. See for instance the box defining 'the Community method', White Paper on European Governance, COM (2001) 428 final, p. 8. For a critical appraisal of the underlying vision of European integration and the role of the Commission therein, see Weiler (2001), <http://www.jeanmonnetprogram.org/papers/01/013401.html>.

17 See Follesdal, Hix (2005) 20.

18 So Mehde (2001) 423.

19 Discussed in Craig (2000) 98 ff.

20 *Reforming the Commission*, COM (2000) 200.

21 *Ibid.*, 3.

22 So Curtin (2001).

23 COM (2001) 428 final.

Commission and debate within it. It moved the reform beyond the issue of internal administrative reform into the much wider, and vaguer, issue of EU governance in general and the role of the Commission in it. 'Governance' itself was defined as the 'rules, processes and behaviour that affect the way in which powers are exercised at European level, particularly as regards openness, participation, accountability, effectiveness and coherence'.[24] It set out five principles underpinning good governance: openness, participation, accountability, effectiveness and coherence, each of them 'important for establishing more democratic governance'.

The Commission cautioned that this White Paper could not be seen as a magic cure for everything, presumably referring to the legitimacy crisis of the Commission specifically and the Union in general, the alleged democratic deficit[25] and/or the sense of alienation of many European people described in the White Paper's introduction. However, the explanation of 'accountability' as a principle of good governance was vague and added nothing. It merely stated that:

> 'Roles in the legislative and executive process need to be clearer. Each of the EU institutions must explain and take responsibility for what it does in Europe. But there is also a need for greater clarity and responsibility from member States and all those involved in developing and implementing EU policy at whatever level'.[26]

The White Paper contained a set of proposals for change, divided in four sections. These included involvement, quality and enforcement of EU policy, a stronger link between European governance and the role of the Union in the world, and finally, a refocusing of the Union in general and the institutions in particular. It called for a return to the Community method, in which each institution should refocus on its core tasks. In this model, the Commission would be the institution representing the general interest. Roughly stated, the Commission should focus on its executive role, under new general conditions to be laid down by the Council. The Council and the Parliament should then make the political judgment on how well the executive process was working, thus improving accountability.

The context of the White Paper is perhaps even more interesting than its actual content. The Paper must be placed in the context of a wider reform process, both internally to the Commission and externally.[27] The White Paper

[24] On 'governance' there is an abundant amount of literature. A summary of the relevant issues can be found in Craig, de Búrca (2007) 144 ff. See further De Schutter, Lebessis, Paterson (2001), De Búrca (2003) 814 ff., Curtin, Wessel (2005) and Möllers (2006) 313 ff.

[25] Which the Commission did not share: 'These results have been achieved by democratic means' and 'The Union (..) has a double democratic mandate though a Parliament representing EU citizens and a Council representing elected governments of the Member States'. See *White Paper* 7.

[26] See *White Paper* 10.

[27] Walker (2001) 22.

project proceeded in parallel with the IGC leading to the Treaty of Nice, which in turn launched a deeper and wider debate about the future development of the European Union, leading to the Laeken Declaration and the Convention. Especially in that context, the absence of any explicit constitutional discourse and the one-sided focus on governance is striking.

Subsequently the Reform Treaty reflects a choice for the 'separate hats' view concerning executive power, more particularly with regard to the Presidency of the Union as a whole. It means that there should be a President of the Commission and a President of the European Council, and that the executive power would be exercised by both the Commission and the European Council (c.q. the Council of Ministers).[28] When it comes to the Commission-Parliament relationship, further steps seemed to be taken in the direction of accountable government as in parliamentary systems. According to art. 9A TEU (as supposed to be amended by the Reform Treaty) the European Parliament shall elect the President of the Commission. This is further elaborated in the provisions on the Commission. While the Commission, in carrying out its responsibilities shall be completely independent (art. 9D (3) TEU, as supposed to be amended by the Reform Treaty), it shall:

> 'as a body, be responsible to the European Parliament. In accordance with Article 201 of the Treaty on the Functioning of the European Union, the European Parliament may vote on a censure motion on the Commission. If such a motion is carried, the members of the Commission shall resign as a body and the High Representative of the Union for Foreign Affairs and Security Policy shall resign from the duties that he or she carries out in the Commission'.

In addition, and this is new, according to art. 9D TEU the European Council should take into account the elections to the European Parliament when proposing a candidate for President of the Commission. The president, the High Representative of the Union for Foreign Affairs and Security Policy and the other members of the Commission shall be subject as a body to a vote of consent by the European Parliament, and subsequently be appointed by the European Council. As under the existing Treaty, a member of the Commission shall resign if the President so requests (art. 9D (6) TEU, as supposed to be amended by the Reform Treaty).

3 The Concept of Political Accountability

3.1 Introduction

This section attempts to formulate the concept of political accountability, as it currently exists in the European Union. To make this analy-

[28] Craig, De Búrca (2007) 141.

sis useful in terms of a comparison with the national systems that are involved in our research, the same key questions as contained in the questionnaire for the national reports in part II of this book. These questions are as follows:

1) Who is accountable?
2) To whom is one accountable?
3) For what is one accountable?
4) How is one made accountable?
5) What are the possible consequences of being accountable?

As has often been done in the national reports in part II of this book, the question as to who is accountable to whom are addressed jointly.

3.2 Accountability: The Actors

3.2.1 Who is Accountable and to Whom?

Within the European Union there is no clear concept according to which political accountability is centralized in a 'government'. The EU has no 'government' in the traditional sense. The EU has a 'dual executive': the executive power is shared by the Council (or the European Council) and the Commission.[29] Neither the Council (c.q. the European Council), nor the Commission can be compared with a regular parliamentary government.

Nevertheless, many of the functions exercised by the Commission can be described as being 'governmental' in nature. The Commission's task is to oversee the application of EU-law, to execute the budget and managing programmes and to exercise coordinating, executive and managing functions.[30] It shares some of these functions with national authorities administering and executing EU law, and with the Council, which has original executive power but normally delegates it under its conditions, while it may retain the implementing powers rather than delegating them to the Commission.[31] On the other hand, the Commission also participates in the legislative function. Traditional conceptions of separation of powers, both institutionally and functionally, do not apply to the institutional triangle in the EU.[32] Yet, mechanisms for the exercise of political accountability are in the Treaties provided for the Commission *vis-à-vis* the European Parliament, while political accountability of the members of the Council is deviated via the national governments to the national parliaments.[33]

---

[29] See par. 2.2.

[30] See also art. 9D (1) EU (as supposed to be amended by the Reform Treaty).

[31] Art. 202 EC.

[32] Of course, a strict separation of powers does not apply in any system, but in the EU the relationships may be even more complex or atypical by the existence of unusual institutions such as the Commission, the Council and the European Council.

[33] This will now for the first time be made explicit in art. 8A EU (as supposed to be amended by the Reform Treaty).

Article 197 EC states that the Commission shall reply to questions put to it by the European Parliament or by its members and that members of the Commission may attend all meetings of the European Parliament. They shall, at their request, be heard on behalf of the Commission. Furthermore, the annual general report submitted by the Commission shall be discussed by the European Parliament in open session. The Reform Treaty stipulates in general terms that the Commission, as a body, 'shall be responsible to the European Parliament'.[34] In addition, there are general obligations of the Commission as well as other EU-bodies with regard to public consultation and transparency.[35]

European public officials are not politically accountable. They are under no legal duty to give account to the European Parliament or to the Council (c.q. the European Council), in the sense of explaining and defending decisions that have been taken.[36] Nevertheless, they do bear what is called ethical responsibility.[37] They are subject to written rules of conduct. The van Buitenen-incident has demonstrated that the accountability of public officials sometimes goes beyond the boundaries of hierarchical control. This incident shows what whistle blowing is like in many Member States, one of the issues.

Other bodies like executive agencies are not always politically accountable themselves either, though they are considered to be subject to general principles of good governance.[38] Most of the agencies are accountable to the Commission in the first place. However, some agencies are also accountable to the European Parliament and/or the Council.[39] At least in some Member States similar developments have taken place. National agencies and related bodies do sometimes give account directly to national parliaments. The question of how this relates to the traditional political accountability of national governments will be left aside here; we will touch upon this issue later in this chapter.[40]

The Commission is considered to be *politically* accountable to the European Parliament in the first place. The Constitutional Treaty stipulates this explicitly. In addition, in many cases the Commission is controlled[41] by the Council by means of the complex system of Comitology. Finally, there is also accountability

---

34 Art. 9D (8) EU (as supposed to be amended by the Reform Treaty).

35 Art. 8B EU and art. 21 EC (as supposed to be amended by the Reform Treaty).

36 Of course officials who work under the responsibility of the Parliament or the Council itself, are obliged to give account, but this does fall outside the scope of 'political' responsibility.

37 Committee of Independent Experts (1999b) par. 7.6 and further.

38 See art. 16A EC (as supposed to be amended by the Reform Treaty).

39 European Commission (2002) 718.

40 See in particular par. 4.7.6.

41 It is doubtful whether one could speak of 'accountability' here. In the context of the Comitology system the Commission does not give an account in the sense of explaining and justifying its conduct in the first place. It is more like a mechanism by which the Council can influence (or sometimes even determine) decisions which are being prepared by the Commission.

in a much broader sense to society as a whole. This accountability closely relates to other principles of good governance such as transparency and participation.[42]

3.2.2 Collective or Individual Accountability?

The Commission is only as a body politically accountable. Under art. 201 EC the Members of the Commission resign as a body if a motion of censure is carried by Parliament. It is the Commission as a college that takes decisions, not its individual Members: all decisions are taken in the name of the Commission.[43] The Commissioners are not appointed individually but collectively as a body. Collegiality was introduced to prevent a dominating loyalty of the Commissioners to their Member States of origin. A long-time collective decision-making has to guarantee the exercise of powers in accordance with the general European interest.

Collective political accountability has been translated into obligations of individual Commissioners as laid down in a Code of Conduct.[44] For example Commissioners may not make allegations out of the policy line of the Commission or make public what has been said in meetings of the Commission. The Committee of Independent Experts proposed to re-define the principle of collective accountability in the EC-Treaty and to define it as accountability of the Commission as a whole and of individual Commissioners for decisions, taken as a collective.[45] As can be derived from part II of this book, similar concepts of collective accountability can be found in some Member States.

Although strictly speaking political accountability of the Commission is collective, there has been a development towards individually assigned portfolios (see also par. 4.2 below). In addition, even though Commissioners act on behalf of the Commission, they do in practice render account individually to the European Parliament. In this respect it could be argued that in addition to collective accountability, at least in practical effect, a form of individual accountability of Commissioners has developed. The Treaty of Nice has formally introduced the possibility for the President of the Commission to ask an individual Member of the Commission to resign, and the obligation for the Members to resign if the President so requests, after obtaining the approval of the College (art. 217 (4) EC).[46]

---

42 See European Commission (2001).

43 The Commission can, however, authorise its members to adopt certain decisions in its name. See Case 5/85 (*AKZO Chemie BV and AKZO Chemie UK Ltd.* v. *Commission*) 1986, 223.

44 European Commission (2004).

45 Committee of Independent Experts (1999b) par. 7.5.3. See also Van Gerven (2005) 87-88.

46 This is confirmed by the European Commission (2004) at marginal number 1.2.1.

3.2.3 The President of the Commission

Formally speaking, individual accountability is internal in the Commission. Within the Commission, the President can call the individual Members to account. The President has a task to 'activate' the individual political accountability.[47] In this respect the role of the President has been strengthened: he plays an important role in selecting candidates for the Commission, he allocates the portfolios and can reshuffle portfolios during his term of office.[48] Finally, a Member of the Commission shall resign if the President so requests (art. 217 EC).[49]

The strengthening of the President's role raises the question whether he is still merely a 'primus inter pares'. Shaw has argued that in this respect a more presidential system has been created.[50] On the other hand, his room for manoeuvre is restricted by the demands of the Member States. Member States will continue to put pressure on the President in order for their Commissioners to receive the most significant portfolios.

The Dehaene report on the enlargement of the European Union (1999) stated that it is essential *'de délimiter clairement la responsabilité individuelles des Commissaires'*. The events in the van Buitenen-incident *'posent la question de la responsabilité individuelle des Commissaires et de son articulation per rapport à la responsabilité collective de la Commission'*.[51] These questions relate to the issue of individual accountability. Is it desirable to introduce individual political accountability to the European Parliament? What should be the role of the President of the Commission? As shown in chapter 13 of this book at least in some Member States similar questions have arisen in the past with regard to the accountability of individual ministers and their relation to the Prime Minister.

3.3 Accountable for What?

3.3.1 Introduction

The next question is: accountable for what? The problem is that at the EU-level all sorts of activities take place within more or less obscure bodies like networks, agencies and committees. These activities are sometimes executed by the Member States, by the Council, by the Commission or a mixture of it. It concerns policy-making as well as different types of administration. On the whole, the analysis beneath relates to the Commission and its Members, as well as the cabinets, the administration and including bodies for which the

---

47 See also article 217 EC and art. 9D (6) EU (as supposed to be amended by the Reform Treaty). See further Van Gerven (2000a) 98.

48 Shaw (2000) 112-113.

49 See also art. 9D (6) EU (as supposed to be amended by the Reform Treaty).

50 Shaw (2000) 110.

51 Rapport-Dehaene (1999).

Commission can be held accountable. This includes participation of the Commission in other bodies like networks and committees.

3.3.2 Policy-making and Execution

All Commissioners are assigned a portfolio.[52] These portfolios contain a particular area of accountability. The distribution of portfolios is largely a matter of negotiation and political balance between the Member States. This means that in practice the President of the Commission can only to a certain extent allocate the portfolios in accordance with his own preferences. Reshuffles do usually not occur during the session of a Commission.[53] President Barroso did however re-shuffle his Commission when his first line-up threatened to be rejected by the European Parliament.

The Committee of Independent Experts observed that Members of the Commission are not only accountable for policy-making within their portfolio, but also for the execution thereof.[54] Van Gerven has pointed out that a division between policy-making and execution makes sense, since it relates to the essential tasks of the Commission. However, the Commission is, according to Van Gerven, also accountable for the implementation of policy and laws. This is a task which they have in common with the DG's.[55] Besides, if the Commission should not be accountable for the execution of their policy, who can then be held accountable for it? Nevertheless, there seems to be no agreement on the exact extent of the Commission's accountability.

In addition, the scope of accountability for policy-making is not entirely clear. New policy instruments used by the Commission, like 'co-regulation' and the so-called 'open method of co-ordination', are very confusing in terms of accountability. What these instruments have in common is that the Commission shares its policy-making powers with 'those most affected', 'stakeholders' at the European and the national level. Although the Commission itself has stated in its White Paper on European Governance that the use of the open method of co-ordination 'must not dilute .... the political responsibility of the Institutions' and that 'it should ensure overall accountability' amongst other things by reporting to the European Parliament,[56] it is not clear what impact the use of such instruments has on political accountability.

3.3.3 Accountability for Civil Servants

Another issue is whether the Commission can only be held accountable for its own actions and of its Members or also for actions of other

[52] See Nugent (2001) 101-109.

[53] Nugent (2003) 117.

[54] Committee of Independent Experts (1999b), par. 7.9.1.

[55] Van Gerven (2000a) 99.

[56] *White Paper* 22.

persons, such as civil servants.[57] The Committee of Independent Experts has concluded that the Commission is only politically accountable when it concerns a person who is within the legal competences of the Commission. The allocation of tasks defines the competence and accordingly also the political accountability of the individual Commissioner, so the argument goes.[58] Reversely, the Commission is fully accountable for the civil service, at least at the level of the Director General, and should therefore be able to give directions to his or her Director General.

In this respect different categories must be distinguished. Individual Commissioners have relations with three types of bodies: personal cabinets, Directorates General (DG's) and agencies. Firstly, Commissioners have a personal office, a 'cabinet'.[59] They are staffed by civil servants who support their Commissioner in the execution of his tasks. One of their main tasks is to inform the Commissioner of matters in the portfolio of other Commissioners, as a result of the collective accountability of the Commission. Within the cabinet, one civil servant is appointed as a parliamentary *attaché*, liaising closely to parliamentary committees and parliamentary groups.[60] These personal cabinets are, however, heavily criticised. They are regarded as a contra-machinery with a dual administration that demoralizes the civil servants in the DG's.[61] A parallel can be made with several Member States, where cabinets or similar bodies such as 'political advisers' of a minister, independent of the traditional civil service, exist.

Secondly, and quantitatively more important, there are within the European civil service 27 Directorates General (DG's) in which circa 20.000 officials work. A Commissioner has the portfolio for one or more Directorates General (DG's).[62] At first sight this seems comparable to what is happening at the national level. National ministers have their own portfolios as well.[63] There are, however, some major differences. In contrast to national ministers in at least some Member States, a Commissioner does not head a DG[64] and therefore does not have a leading position within the hierarchical administrative structure. This leads to complex relations. There might be Commissioners with more than one DG, Commissioners without an assigned DG and even DG's reporting to more than one Commissioner. Some Commissioners do not, unlike national ministers, run their DG autonomously.[65]

---

57 Tomkins (1999) 757, Van Gerven (2000a) 103.

58 Committee of Independent Experts (1999b) par. 7.8.4-7.8.6. See also Van Gerven (2000a), 98-99.

59 Nugent (2001) 119-133.

60 Westlake (1997) 241.

61 Committee of Independent Experts (1999b) par. 7.5.8.

62 Nugent (2001) 134-161.

63 Nugent (2001) 7.

64 A DG is headed by a civil servant, a Director General. His appointment, like that of other higher officials, is subject to interstate bargaining. See Lequesne (2000) 48-49 and Nugent (2003) 119.

65 Christiansen (2004) 105.

In this confusing context it appears difficult to achieve effective accountability for the acts of the administration.[66] Commissioners are considered to be accountable for specific policies, but they do not have the legal position to make civil servants do what is needed to achieve the policy goals, since there is no direct chain of command between the Commission and the DG's involved.[67] This in turn weakens the position of the European Parliament. To hold the Commission and its Members effectively to account, a direct legal link between Commissioners and their administration is thought to be essential.[68]

3.3.4 Accountability for Agencies

Thirdly, an increasing number of civil servants operate in independent agencies. Agencies are a relatively new phenomenon in the EU.[69] Their powers differ substantially. Sometimes agencies are promoted because of their political independence, which places them in a better position to preserve policy continuity against the changeable preferences of variable parliamentary majorities.[70] On the other hand, agencies have been strongly criticised, because they lack a constitutional basis and are not subject to effective mechanisms of accountability. Especially the powers of the Commission to supervise agencies are still unclear.

At the European level, roughly speaking, two types of agencies can be identified: executive agencies and regulatory ones. Executive agencies are responsible for what the Commission has called 'purely managerial tasks'.[71] They assist the Commission in implementing the EU's financial support programmes and are subject to strict supervision by it.[72] Regulatory agencies are of a different nature: they are, according to the Commission, 'required to be actively involved in the executive function by enacting instruments which help to regulate a specific sector'.[73] From an accountability perspective the last type of agencies are the most important ones: they are put at arms' length of the Commission as well as other EU institutions.[74]

It is to be expected that more EU regulatory agencies will be created in the coming years. In the view of the Commission the creation of further autonomous regulatory agencies in clearly defined areas 'will improve the way rules are

66 Nugent (2003) 122.

67 Mehde (2003) 431.

68 Mehde (2003) 441-442.

69 Vos (2003) 113-147 with many references, Vos (2000) 1113 ff. See further Geradin, Munoz, Petit (2005).

70 Majone, Everson (2001) 129.

71 COM (2002) 718 final, 3. See for a more subtle typology Vos (2003) 119.

72 Council Regulation (EC) No 58/2003 (*OJ* L 11, 16.1.2003).

73 COM (2002) 718 final, 4.

74 Independent agencies have been created by both the Commission and the Council. See Curtin (2005) 88-119.

applied and enforced across the Union'.[75] Different from most of the presently existing agencies the Commission wants new regulatory agencies to have the power to take binding decisions in individual cases in application of regulatory measures. In 2002 the Commission published a first draft of a regulatory framework for the European Regulatory Agencies,[76] setting out the limits of their activities and powers, their responsibilities and requirements for openness and accountability. The manner in which agencies should be supervised by the Commission and other EU institutions was an especially important part of the Commission's proposals. This framework has not yet been established.

3.4 Mechanisms for Political Accountability

3.4.1 Parliamentary Powers

As stated above, accountability presumes authority on the part of the body or institution to whom account is given. It presumes scrutinising procedures, there must be some means of investigating, and scrutinising the actions of the organ held to account, of seeking information and explanation and enforcing remedies; agents must not only be called to account, they must also be held to account.[77] What means are available to Parliament to hold the Commission to account? What mechanisms are in place?[78]

Under article 200 EC-Treaty, the Commission must submit an *annual general report*, to be discussed by the European Parliament.[79] This debate is one of the highlights of the parliamentary year, but it appears to be of little practical consequence.[80] There also is an annual debate on the Commission's legislative programme.[81] Apart from this, the European Parliament has some other classical competences which can also be found in the Member States. The Parliament can *hear* the Commission[82] and it can put to it questions orally and in writing.[83] In each past-session, there is a 'Question Time',[84] in which a Commissioner replies to each question and MEP's can ask a limited number of supplementary questions.[85] Finally the European Parliament can set up *committees of inquiry*. These committees can investigate alleged contraventions of Community law or

[75] COM (2001) 428 final, 24.

[76] COM (2002) 718 final. It was in 2005 followed by a draft of an Interinstitutional Agreement for an regulatory framework for the European Regulatory Agencies: COM (2005) 59 final.

[77] Mulgan (2003) 9.

[78] Chalmers, Hadjiemmanuil, Monti, Tomkins (2006) 116 ff.

[79] Article 200 EC; article 112 Rules of Procedure of the European Parliament.

[80] Nugent (2003) 209.

[81] Rules of Procedure EP, Rule 49.

[82] Rules of Procedure EP, Rule 37. A debate may follow.

[83] Art. 197 EC.

[84] Rules of Procedure EP, Rule 109.

[85] Westlake (1997) 254.

accidents of maladministration.[86] A well-known example is the enquiry on the BSE-crisis, in which the Commission was held to account.[87]

Control by Parliament is made possible by the attendance of Commissioners at several occasions. These can include part-sessions of the Parliament, meetings of parliamentary committees and plenary meetings of the Parliament in Strasbourg. A Commissioner is almost always present in the plenary meetings during legislative votes.[88] According to Arnull, the Question Time as well as attendance of the Commissioners in Parliament seems to be influenced by the British parliamentary model.[89]

The growing role of the European Parliament has to a large extent been stimulated by *budgetary control*. The Parliament is competent to give discharge to the Commission in respect of the implementation of the budget. Article 276 EC-Treaty further provides:

> 'Before giving a discharge to the Commission, or for any other purpose in connection with the exercise of its powers over the implementation of the budget, the European Parliament may ask to hear the Commission give evidence with regard to the execution of expenditure or the operation of financial control systems. The Commission shall submit any necessary information to the European Parliament at the latter's request'.

In one instance, the use of this instrument has lead to a political crisis. In 1997 the Parliament refused to obtain discharge to the Commission over the financial year 1996. Budget control has also contributed to the strengthening of some national parliaments. Accountability in for example the United Kingdom and the Netherlands came to maturity after some political scandals in the 19th century with regard to public expenditure.

3.4.2 Transparency

There can be no accountability without transparency; rather accountability presumes transparency as a precondition. It is essential for every way of public scrutiny that public bodies are as open as possible about the decisions and actions they take. In this respect the European Union has often been criticised. According to the Committee of Independent Experts for example 'the whole tradition of secretiveness which characterises both the Commission and the other EU institutions, above all the Council', is a source of major concern.[90]

In recent years efforts have been made to increase transparency within the European Union. General rules on access to EU-documents have been adopted.

---

[86] Art. 193 EC.

[87] Harlow (2002) 99-100. See also Shackleton (1998) 115 ff.

[88] Westlake (1997) 241.

[89] Arnull (2000) 36-37.

[90] Committee of Independent Experts (1999b) par. 7.6.3.

In the context of enhancing the principle of participatory democracy, several provisions have been added to the European Constitution. Article 16A EC (as supposed to be amended by the Reform Treaty) stipulates in general terms that the Union institutions, bodies, offices and agencies shall conduct their work as openly as possible 'in order to promote good governance and ensure the participation of civil society'. Moreover, it provides for the Council meeting in public when considering and voting on a draft legislative act.

Transparency is also essential for accountability in a more limited sense. Parliament cannot scrutinize the Commission if it does not provide the necessary information on its policies, decisions and actions. Of course, there may be a need in exceptional cases to keep specific information confidential, but there are no clear rules in which cases and for which reasons the Commission is not obliged to inform the European Parliament.

3.5 Consequences: Censure

A last element of political accountability concerns the consequences of being accountable and being held to account. According to the working definition proposed in part I of this book, accountability also implies that one should be required 'to suffer the consequences, take the blame or undertake to put matters right if it should appear that errors have been made'. In a parliamentary democracy this means that in the final instance individual ministers or the government as a whole must resign if a parliamentary majority has lost confidence. The power of dismissal or censure operates as the ultimate deterrent in the accountability regime.

The Commission cannot be dismissed by the Council or by the Member States. Only the European Parliament can dismiss the Commission as a body. This mechanism, which also exists in a parliamentary system, was introduced to create counterbalance and to control a mighty and independent institution.[91] In order to dismiss the Commission, Parliament has to adopt a motion of censure on the policy of the Commission by two-thirds of the votes and a majority of its Members.[92] The motion can be proposed by one-tenth of the Members of Parliament. It will not be debated for at least 24 hours. Before the motion will be voted, 48 hours must have passed.[93] A motion of censure has never been passed to date.

The motion of censure against the Santer Commission in 1999 was defeated by 293 votes against and 232 in favour. The motion concerned the discharge of the 1996 budget and accusations of fraud, mismanagement and nepotism by

91 Note that the Commission was meant to be independent. See Constantinesco (2000) 119.

92 Article 201 EC. According to Weatherill and Beaumont 'the most draconian power that the European Parliament has'. See Weatherill, Beaumont (1999) 108. See also art. 9D EU and 201 EC (as supposed to be amended by the Reform Treaty).

93 Rules of Procedure EP, Rule 34.

the Commissioners or within the sphere of their responsibility.[94] In this case the European Parliament did not set up a committee of inquiry in accordance with Article 193 EC, but instead requested a non-parliamentary Committee of Independent Experts to investigate the accusations against the Commission. The Committee identified failures of individual Commissioners and condemned the failure of collective accountability by the Commission. The Commission resigned by a unanimous decision when it became apparent that the most culpable Commissioners would not resign alone and that the European Parliament would vote in favour of a motion of censure if the Commission did not resign.[95] An important lesson from the Santer resignation is that the Commission can politically be forced to resign without the necessity of applying article 201 EC. The Santer Commission anticipated on a motion of censure and resigned of its own accord.[96]

The European Parliament cannot dismiss an individual Commissioner.[97] However it can make clear to the President of the Commission that it does not have confidence in a specific Commissioner. While a motion of censure has to be addressed to the Commission as a body, there is nothing to prevent Parliament from adopting a resolution criticising an individual Commissioner, a resolution calling upon him to resign,[98] a 'motion of censure sauvage' against an individual Commissioner, a motion 'naming names' or a 'reprimand motion'.[99] However, formally speaking Parliament cannot force an individual Commissioner to resign if a Commissioner refuses to do so (as Cresson did in 1999). Parliament could then, as a last resort, only consider a motion of censure against the Commission as a whole. The impossibility of sending away an individual Commissioner has been criticized in literature.[100]

However after Cresson's refusal and the fall of the Santer Commission some changes took place. Prodi, at that time President of the Commission, extracted a promise from all Commissioners that they would resign if he should ask them to do so ('Lege Prodi').[101] Article 217 EC was amended accordingly with the Treaty of Nice. It now provides that a Member of the Commission shall resign

---

94 Corbett, Jacobs, Shackleton (2000) 243-245.

95 Weatherill, Beaumont (1999) 1061.

96 Nugent (2001) 88.

97 An individual Commissioner can, however, be dismissed when the European Court of Justice compels a Commissioner to retire on grounds of serious misconduct or because he no longer fulfils the conditions required for the performance of his duties. This procedure is set in motion by an application by the Council or Commission. See article 216 EC: 'If any Member of the Commission no longer fulfils the conditions required for the performance of his duties or if he has been guilty of serious misconduct, the Court of Justice may, in application by the Council or the Commission, compulsorily retire him.' See also Hartley (2003) 14.

98 Corbett, Jacobs, Shackleton (2000) 244.

99 Westlake (1994) 27.

100 Van Gerven (2000a) 103.

101 Clegg, Van Hulten (2007) 25.

if the President so requests, after obtaining the approval of the Commission. Although this does not imply any legal right of Parliament to send away individual Commissioners it can more easily put pressure on the President to replace an individual Commissioner. It indirectly strengthens individual accountability.[102]

The question is whether this is sufficient to achieve effective accountability. It has been argued that in 1999 the possibility to force the resignation of Cresson would have prevented the fall of the Commission.[103] The power of Parliament to send away individual Commissioners by itself could therefore be preferable. Other authors reject the proposal of individual censure of Commissioners. Magnette, for example, has argued that the solution of the 'Legi Prodi' is more balanced. It preserves the room for manoeuvre of the President of the Commission, while giving the Parliament more influence. The model can also be found at the national level. Experiences in Germany have shown that even when a Parliament is not able to dismiss an individual minister, the head of the government usually follows the claims of the Parliament when they are expressed by a large part of the assembly.[104]

4 Political Accountability in the European Union: What can be Learned from the Member States?

4.1 Introduction

As explained in the introductory chapter this book tries to identify common principles ('*ius commune*') and practices which have been developed in different national systems over many years or sometimes even centuries with regard to political accountability and to see to what extent these principles and practices are relevant for the further development of the European constitutional system. The basic question we want to address is whether we need a concept more or less similar to the national concept of political accountability in the European Union and if so, what it should look like.

In order to answer these questions we had to take two steps. The first step was to conduct the comparative research as described in the introductory chapter. So in part II of this book the concept of political accountability has been described and explained for eleven EU Member States. It has resulted in a comparative chapter in which we have summarized the most important results

---

102 Hartley (2003) 14.

103 Clegg, Van Hulten (2004) 26.

104 Magnette (2001) 306. As shown in chapter 13 of this book other Member States have the same model as in Germany with a dominant role for the prime minister.

and have tried to identify basic models and common principles within the Member States.[105]

We now have to turn to the second step which is the issue of migration or transformation: can the national concepts, rules, conventions and practices relating to political accountability as analyzed above, be of avail for the European Union? What are the similarities between political accountability at the national level and accountability mechanisms at the European level as described in the preceding paragraphs? Could we identify common principles of accountability that can be transformed in the political system of the European Union or must we conclude that there are no such principles and that the European Union must develop its own accountability concept irrespective of the national experience?

4.2 The Apparent Absence of a Clear *'Ius Commune'*

Looking at the foregoing chapters and exploring the possibilities of transforming national mechanisms of political accountability towards the European level, there are at least two major problems. The first problem is the apparent absence of a clear identifiable concept of political accountability in Member States under review. The second one regards the already noticed peculiarities of the EU system. These will be considered in turn.

The concept of political accountability has a longstanding tradition, at least in the Member States of EU-15. Its origins are closely tied to the rise of the parliamentary system in the nineteenth century or even further back. In the new Member States the transformation into a parliamentary system has taken place after the fall of communism. In most cases they copied more or less one of the existing models in Western Europe. Given this fact one can safely conclude that all the Member States who were part of the research have a parliamentary system[106] in which the executive is usually held accountable through the concept of ministerial accountability. This is nowadays still seen as an essential element of democratic government in all the Member States.

Accordingly, at this abstract level there seems to be some sort of an *'ius commune'* in Europe. However, taking a closer look it becomes much more difficult to identify precisely confined principles and practices common in all the systems involved. Roughly speaking one can say that there are two basic models of political accountability in the Member States which are, at least in theory, fundamentally different: the 'parliament-oriented' and the 'government-oriented' model.[107] The rules and principles based on constitutional theory vary widely in the Member States. Evidently this variety is closely connected with the historical, political and constitutional nature of each and every national system.

---

[105] See Broeksteeg, Van den Driessche, Verhey (2008) chapter 13, Political Accountability in the EU Member States: Different Concepts and Practical Implications.

[106] See regarding France, Ziller (2008) chapter 5, par. 3.

[107] See for more details, Broeksteeg, Van den Driessche, Verhey (2008) chapter 13, par. 3.2 and 3.3., and par. 4.3. and 4.4 hereafter. In daily practice the differences are much less. See hereafter par. 4.7.1.

Given the complex nature of the concept of political accountability and the different ways it has been put into practice in the Member States, one could assume that it is difficult to come to unambiguous solutions for the accountability deficit in the European Union. Nevertheless, by describing and analysing the systems in the Member States one can gain insight into the various models as they exist in Europe. If there would prove to be no single common denominator one could perhaps identify a few core models with various features; perhaps such an exercise could deliver options or guidelines which could inspire the European Union to develop and improve its own system. Another possibility is that one specific model can be concluded as more suitable to the EU system than others.[108]

4.3 The 'Parliament-oriented' Model of Political Accountability

In the comparative research at least two basic models of political accountability have come forward. Both models focus on the relationship between the government and the parliament, which is crucial in every parliamentary system. However, the perspective of both models is different. In the first model political accountability is closely related to the, at least in theory, superior position of parliament, while in the second model the emphasis lies more on the role of the government and its powers. The first model is in place in the majority of the Member States, which were involved in the research. The second model can be found in especially the United Kingdom, the Netherlands and Denmark. The position of Germany is somewhat unclear: perhaps one could conclude that Germany tries to combine the two models and lies therefore somewhere between.

In the first model political accountability is essentially about the confidence the parliamentary majority must have in the government. If at a certain moment this confidence appears to be no longer there, political accountability means primarily the acceptance of political consequences: the government (or an individual minister) must step down. In some parliamentary systems like in Italy and Spain, this 'parliament-oriented' concept of political accountability directly relates to the constitutional theory of popular sovereignty. As being regarded as the voice of the people the parliament must be dominant over the government in order to guarantee the latter's democratic legitimacy. So at the end of the day the parliament must have the tools to let the government do what the people want it to do and, if not, to force the government to resign.

If we try to transform this model towards the European Union we run up against major obstacles. As is well known in the system of the European Union democratic legitimacy is based on more than one source: next to the European Parliament there is the Council of Ministers as well as the European

[108] See for example Ziller (2001) 102-119. He states that the Swedish model of government seems to be more familiar with the European system than the standard European model of government.

Council which are considered to be representing the Member States and, at least indirectly, the people from the Member States. As a result the European Parliament cannot be regarded as the one and only 'bearer' of democratic legitimacy, at least not in the way as it is deemed to be the case in national parliamentary systems.[109] The dual source of democratic legitimacy within the European Union finds expression for example the way the Commission has been appointed. Different from national governments the composition of the Commission is not the direct and immediate result of the elections for the European Parliament, but the outcome of a complicated procedure in which the European Parliament has substantial influence but the Member States at the end of the day seem to have the final say.

The absence of a singular source of democratic legitimacy within the European Union has consequences in terms of political accountability. Applying the 'parliament-oriented' concept of political accountability as described above is in the European context not obvious. From a democratic perspective the European Parliament seems to be less legitimized to dismiss one or members of the executive than for example the British, the Polish or the Italian Parliament. This is not to say that the European Parliament should not have the power to send away the Commission as established in article 201 EC-Treaty. One could even argue that the collective accountability of the Commission towards the European Parliament in a way fits well in a 'parliament-oriented' concept of political accountability; in all the Member States with such a concept, a motion of censure can only be addressed against the government as a whole. However, the theoretical perspective is fundamentally different as in the European Union, the European Parliament, although being elected, cannot claim the final say. One could even argue that the European Parliament's power to send away the Commission is more an expression of the need for constitutional checks and balances at the European level than that it delivers democratic legitimacy to the Commission.[110]

4.4 The 'Government-oriented' Model of Political Accountability

At first sight the second model of political accountability seems to fit better into the European picture. In this model the concept of political accountability focuses more on the role of the government. It is true that also in this 'government-oriented' model the relationship between the government and the parliament is essential; this is inherent in every parliamentary system. However, the emphasis is different. In the 'government-oriented' model, political accountability is not or not primarily about the consequences the government

---

[109] We leave aside here whether or not Europe lacks the *demos* which according to some authors is indispensable for the functioning of the democratic system. See chapter 1, par. 1.3. In this sense Grimm (1995) 282. See also Van Gerven (2005) 41 ff.

[110] See for an uncoupling of accountability and democracy also Chalmers, Hadjiemmanuil, Monti, Tomkins (2006) 313.

should take from a vote of censure by a parliamentary majority, but far more about what happens in the preceding phases. The basic questions are more governmental in nature such as for which public services the government is exactly accountable for, which powers the government has to give effect to its political accountability and how exactly the government has to give an account to parliament. The crucial issue here is the scope of the government's accountability and the quality of the mechanisms by which the government give an account.

Transforming this 'government-oriented' model towards the European Union seems possible. If we look at the Commission as the institution, which is politically accountable, similar issues seem to rise as in national systems. We could draw various parallels between the Commission and national governments; we could look at legal powers or other instruments to make their accountability effective; we could compare the relationship between the government or the Commission and executive and regulatory agencies; we could also focus on processes or mechanisms by which national governments give an account and look whether such processes or mechanisms could be applied in and around the Commission. At first sight such an approach seems to be thinkable if not promising.

However, there is at least one preliminary question which has to be dealt with first and which seems to confront us with an insurmountable problem: can the Commission reasonably be regarded as a 'government'? As already emphasised before, the European Union is a multi-level governance polity with a complex interweaving of executive tasks at the Union and Member State levels. At the European level there are effectively more institutions performing tasks of an executive nature. The European Union has what is called a 'dual executive' where on the one hand the Council of Ministers and/or the European Council and on the other hand the Commission share executive responsibilities.[111]

One could argue that the fact that executive tasks are divided between different bodies is in itself not exceptional. In most of the Member States executive tasks are delegated to ministries and to different sorts of agencies which operate separately from the government. What, however, makes the European Union fundamentally different from a traditional parliamentary system is the Council of Ministers (c.q. the European Council). It is a hybrid body: on the one hand the Council is an institution of the European Union which has powers at the European level, on the other hand its members are representatives of the Member States who are accountable on the national level in the first place.[112]

However, if we should limit ourselves to the relationship between the Commission and the Parliament, there is no real parallel with a regular parliamentary system. One cannot separate this relationship from the context of the EU institutional framework as a whole. Authors like Magnette have shown convincingly that interinstitutional tensions are much more governed by national divisions and technical reasoning than by classical majoritarian atti-

[111] Par. 2.2. See for example Curtin (2004).

[112] See par. 2.2 and 3.2.1.

tudes.[113] As a result the relationship between the Commission and the European Parliament is substantially different from that between a government and a parliament as we know in the Member States. Because they are both supranational institutions and share common interests, they are more often allies against the Council than enemies.

The conclusion from all this seems straightforward. Because the constitutional position of the Commission and the Council *vis-à-vis* the European Parliament is fundamentally different and the relationship between the Commission and the Parliament cannot be separated from the context of the EU institutional framework as a whole, the parallel with a full-fledged parliamentary system is only limited. The Commission cannot be identified as 'the' EU government. As a result the possibility of transplanting the 'government-oriented' model of political accountability to the European Union seems to be limited as well.

4.5 What the Traditional Concept of Political Accountability Cannot Offer

Now we have explained why the two basic models of political accountability, as they have come forward in our comparative research, do not adequately fit in the political system of the European Union, we can now say more precisely what ministerial accountability cannot offer on the European level. What it cannot do are basically two things.

In the first place it is not able to fill the assumed democratic deficit in the European Union. The debate about democracy in the European Union is comprehensive, complicated and linked with many other issues than only the accountability of the European executive. One has to take into account the much broader institutional context of the European Union and for example look at the role of the European Parliament as such, the significance of the European elections, the particular position of the Council and/or the European Council and the influence of national parliaments. One has also to consider the potential of alternative models of democracy that perhaps could reduce the 'democratic deficit': next to the principle of representative democracy the Reform Treaty explicitly recognized the significance of the principle of participatory democracy.[114] Because the principle of representative democracy at least until now is relatively weak at the EU level, one could presume that alternative models are perhaps more promising.

It would therefore be too simple to say that if we would strengthen political accountability in the relationship between the Commission and the European Parliament, Europe would become more democratic. It is well known that there are fundamental differences of opinion about if there is a democratic deficit and

[113] Magnette (2001) 292-310.

[114] See art. 8B EU (as supposed to be amended by the Reform Treaty).

if yes, how it should be solved.[115] The answer to these questions depends greatly on how one thinks about where democracy in the European Union should come from: from the Member States, from supranational provisions or institutions or from a mix of mechanisms on both levels. And also by which mix of representative and participatory democracy should democracy be achieved. If for example one takes the view that democracy in the European Union should first of all come from the Member States and not from the European Union itself, strengthening political accountability of the Commission towards the European Parliament is not the solution for the EU 'democratic deficit'. On the contrary, from this perspective it should perhaps even weaken the democratic legitimacy of the European Union.[116]

The second thing the concept of political accountability cannot do in the EU context is closely related to the foregoing: it cannot solve the accountability deficit of the Council of Ministers (c.q. the European Council). On the European level it is very difficult to hold the Council to account, because its members are national ministers. So to a part of the EU executive the regular national accountability mechanisms apply in the first place.[117] However, these mechanisms at least until now have not proven to be very effective. In practice very few national parliaments succeed in effectively holding the individual members of the Council to account.[118] Besides, national parliaments cannot hold the Council as a whole to account.

The same is also true for the European Parliament. This is not to say that the Council could not give an account to the European Parliament. In this context one could point at Article 9B TEU, as supposed to be amended by the Reform Treaty, which says that the President of the Council shall present a report to the European Parliament after each of the meetings of the European Council. In line with this, one could also imagine that the President of the Council appears before the European Parliament, explains the Council's policy and answers questions on the decisions which have been taken. However, at the end of the

---

115 There is an abundant amount of literature on this issue. A summary can be found in Craig, De Búrca (2007), 133 ff (with many references) and Chalmers, Hadjiemmanuil, Monti, Tomkins (2006) 63 ff and 167 ff. Some authors question (Moravczik) or downplay (Majone) the democratic deficit in the European Union. See Moravczik (2002) 603-624 and Moravczik (2004) 336-365, Majone (1998) 5-28 and Majone (2000) 273-302. Other authors think that there is indeed a democratic deficit. See for example Follesdal, Hix (2005). See further on the democratic deficit Weiler (1999) 77 ff and 264 ff.

116 See for example Grimm (1995) 296 who draws the conclusion that 'full parliamentarisation of the European Union on the model of the national constitutional State will rather aggravate than solve the problem'. See further Weiler (1999) 84. Although he acknowledges the democratic deficit to a certain extent, he thinks that it is at least questionable whether strengthening the European Parliament will necessarily solve the legitimacy problem of the Community. 'It may even enhance them'.

117 Although it is not unthinkable that some principles of political accountability as mentioned hereafter, could be applied in the relationship between the Council and the European Parliament.

118 See for example Kiiver (2006). About the role of national parliaments see also Tans, Zoethout, Peters (2007).

day such accountability mechanisms will prove to be very weak. The European Parliament does and will not have any sanctions at its disposal if the parliamentary majority would find the Council's policy or behaviour unacceptable.

So, both on the national and the European level political accountability mechanisms *vis-á-vis* the Council seem to fail. This raises the fundamental question which role the Council should play in the political system of the European Union. In recent years, the executive tasks of the Council have been extended. Executive powers on several areas have been delegated in a haphazard way to the General Secretariat of the Council as well as to independent agencies which have been established by Council regulation.[119] This seems to increase the accountability gap even further. It anyway puts more pressure on the national parliaments to effectively hold the individual members of the Council to account.

4.6 What the Traditional Concept of Political Accountability can Offer

From the foregoing one could perhaps conclude that the national concept of political accountability is of little use in the EU context. The concept of ministerial accountability cannot be transplanted towards the European level unchanged, as if the European Union is a full-fledged parliamentary system. As has been explained in the preceding paragraphs the constitutional system of the European Union differs too fundamentally from a parliamentary model to accept the theory of political accountability in the same manner as in the Member States. However, as we reject the theory as such this does not mean that national experiences could not be a source of inspiration. We could also look at accountability issues from a more practice-based perspective and see if and to what extent parts of national systems or the underlying principles thereof can have practical effect in the EU system.

In our view a practice-oriented or pragmatic approach could be useful for two reasons. In the first place we have to put in mind that political accountability can at least to a certain extent be seen separate from whether there is a democratic deficit or not. The fact that the European Parliament is not a full-grown parliament does not mean that it is useless to see if the functioning of the present accountability mechanisms can be improved in daily practice. One could also aim at enhancing checks and balances within the political system of the European Union or at improving the learning capacity and effectiveness of the Commission and its departments. Bovens has convincingly demonstrated that accountability in the European Union can serve more goals than only strengthen European democracy.[120]

Moreover as was shown in the preceding paragraphs there are not only differences between the classical parliamentary systems and the European Union,

---

[119] Curtin (2005) 88-119.

[120] Bovens (2006) 24 ff.

but also important parallels. The Commission is organized much like a national government with the College of Commissioners as the core executive and the directorates-general as the equivalent of the national ministries.[121] Administrative tasks are more and more delegated to executive and regulatory agencies which to a large extent are comparable with their national counterparts. Finally the executive tasks of the Commission are subject to scrutiny by the European Parliament which, at least in theory, can force the Commission to step down.

Given these parallels we can consider what the European Union perhaps can learn from the development of traditional parliamentary models at a more practice-oriented level. Are their any basic experiences or mechanisms of accountability which apply both on the national and on the European level? Taking into account the experiences and the debates about how political accountability in the Member States works in theory and in practice, at least six fields can be identified with regard to which the European Union could perhaps learn lessons from the Member States. In a somewhat simplified way these can be formulated along the following practical guidelines:

- be clear about what 'political accountability' exactly means (par. 4.7.1);
- do not accept definitions aimed at evading accountability (par. 4.7.2);
- distinguish between collective and individual accountability (par. 4.7.3 and 4.7.4);
- establish a clear chain of command (par. 4.7.5);
- reduce fragmentation of the executive (par. 4.7.6);
- do not focus on resignation, but on the quality of the account (par. 4.7.7).

We will now briefly explain why these guidelines could be important and what they could actual mean in the EU context.

4.7 Practical Guidelines on Political Accountability

4.7.1 A Clear Definition of Political Accountability

Comparing the concepts of political accountability which are used in the Member States, it has appeared to be difficult to find a common denominator. As we already have explained above two basic models can be distinguished. Some Member States like France and Italy are focusing on the procedure for forcing the government, the prime minister or an individual minister to resign (the 'parliament-oriented' model). Others like the United Kingdom and the Netherlands put more emphasis on the minister's duty to account to the parliament for the work of his department and other civil services (the 'government-oriented' model). Both perspectives derive from various constitutional traditions and different theoretical concepts of democratic legitimacy.

However, looking at daily practice the picture seems to be easier to grip. If one tries to come to a synthesis common features can be distinguished, which

[121] Hix (2005) 40 ff.

are explicitly or implicitly present in the practice of almost every parliamentary system. A common definition of political accountability which applies in every Member State could be:

> the right of the parliament to be informed by the government which gives account of how it uses or have used its powers and, where appropriate, suffers the consequences, take the blame or undertakes to put matters right if it should appear that errors have been made.

This definition is not new; it largely fits in with accountability concepts as defined by others referred to in the introductory chapter.[122] Summarized the concept thus contains three basic elements:

- *being accountable:* the guarantee of the government being accountable to the parliament for the use of its executive powers;
- *calling into account*: the right of the parliament to call the government into account which results in the obligation of the government to inform the parliament and to explain and justify its conduct;
- *holding to account*: the right of the parliament to make a judgment on the conduct of the government which results in the obligation of the government to accept the consequences; this could ultimately mean resignation.

Perhaps this definition can help clarifying the debate on political accountability in the European Union. This debate is often unclear or sometimes even evasive. If we look for example to the European Commission's White Paper on European Governance 'accountability' is defined in a way that makes the concept almost meaningless.[123] According to the Commission it means that 'each of the EU Institutions must explain and take responsibility for what it does in Europe'. This definition raises questions. Who is exactly responsible for what? To whom and how are they are made responsible? What are the possible consequences of being responsible?

The White Paper on European Governance did not give even a beginning of an answer on these questions. But where the Commission in the meanwhile is totally silent about is the political accountability of the Commission itself; a political sensitive issue which attracted so much attention during the political crisis around the Santer Commission. Using a clear definition of political accountability inspired by what is common in the Member States, can help to clarify the debate on political accountability in Europe and to expose EU institutions like the Commission which apparently prefers to use vague or irrelevant definitions to serve their own interest.

---

[122] Harlow (2002) 6 ff, Oliver (2003) 48, Bovens (2006) 9. See further chapter 1, par. 3.2.

[123] *White Paper* 10.

4.7.2 Evading Accountability

What regularly happens on both the national and the European level is that by choosing a limited definition, one tries to evade accountability if something went wrong. A well-known example is the distinction which was made by some British politicians between *accountability* and *responsibility*: ministers would be *accountable* in the way that they could be challenged about any action of the civil service, but they would only be *responsible* if they are directly and personally involved. Another example also from Britain is the refusal of ministers to take responsibility for management failures in executive agencies. In this view a minister would only be responsible for policy matters, not for operational concerns. Fortunately both attempts to restrict the scope of ministerial accountability were rejected by the House of Commons.[124] Britain is in this respect far from unique. Comparable arguments to evade accountability have occurred in for example the Netherlands and Denmark.[125]

The same evasive conduct occurred in the run-up to the political crisis in the European Union in 1999. The Santer Commission stated that Commissioners were responsible only for matters of policy, and not for questions of implementation. The Committee of Independent Experts rightly argued that 'this distinction, if strictly interpreted, is tenable neither in law nor in fact'.[126] Apart from the fact that the distinction between policy and implementation can hardly be applied in practice,[127] it is also unacceptable in principle: the result would have been that no one could have been hold politically responsible for the fraud and mismanagement that took place in the Commission's Departments.

What one can learn here from experiences in the Member States is that at the end of the day a parliament will never accept artificial definitions of political accountability which are introduced by members of the executive and which in fact are aimed at evading accountability. There are good reasons for this. Using a restrictive definition as a result of which no one can be hold to account for failures made within the executive, is unacceptable. This is also true in the European Union. That the European Parliament is not a full-grown parliament and therefore political accountability differs from the traditional concept in a full-fledged parliamentary system, does not justify a blurred or restricted executive accountability. If we accept that the European Parliament can call the Commission into account, then the Parliament must be able to get a grip on the whole range of its executive activities.

---

124 Tomkins (2008) chapter 12, par. 2.2.3.

125 Broeksteeg (2008) chapter 8, par. 3.2.2.2. and Jensen (2008) chapter 4, par. 3.

126 Committee of Independent Experts (1999b) par. 7.9.1.

127 Except perhaps for Sweden. See Nergelius (2008) chapter 11, par. 3.

4.7.3 Collective Accountability

As has shown in chapter 13 of this book many Member States know both collective and individual political accountability. However the meaning of these concepts differs from state to state. It is closely connected with differences on the idea of political accountability and its role in the political system in general. Given these variations we have once again to distinguish between:

- the obligation to account for the government's conduct;
- the obligation to suffer the consequences.

On the first point there seems to be a consensus in the Member States on the effects of collective accountability in so far as collective accountability must result in ministers supporting and defending government's decisions in public even if they personally disagree. The purpose of this is that it enables the parliament and the public to know what the government's position is on a given issue.[128] It would be impossible to call the government to account if individual ministers would give different views or different interpretations on what the government policy or decision is. As a result collective accountability also implies that individual ministers do not discuss their disagreements in public.

The Santer Commission at the time defined its collective accountability more restrictively. According to the Commission it would imply that each Commissioner may not call into question a decision taken by the whole Commission and to refrain from disclosing what is said at meetings of the Commission. However, given the apparent consensus in the Member States as mentioned above this definition is too limited. It enables an individual Commissioner to evade responsibility by saying that a certain decision did not fall within his portfolio, but within that of some other Commissioner.[129]

The Committee of Independent Experts rightly argued a wider approach. Collective accountability also means that commissioners actively inform themselves on matters falling within colleagues domain's, discuss these matters during the Commission's meetings and *actively* support the Commission's policy once decisions have been made.[130] Unfortunately the critique of the Committee has not changed the Commission's view. The Prodi Commission published a Code of Conduct for Commissioners in which it replicated the criticized interpretation of collective responsibility articulated by the Santer Commission.[131] Taking into account our comparative research the arguments in

[128] Tomkins (2008) chapter 12, par. 2.1.

[129] Critical about this Chalmers, Hadjiemmanuil, Monti, Tomkins (2006) 332: 'Collective responsibility, for the Santer Commission, appeared to revolve around the notion of each Commissioner minding her own business, not rocking the boat, and not querying the work of (or any allegations of wrongdoing) in any other Commissioner'.

[130] Committee of Independent Experts (1999B) par. 7.10.2.

[131] This has not changed since then. See European Commission (2004). Principle 1.2. provides: 'Out of respect for the principle of collective responsibility, Commissioners shall not make any comment which

favour of this interpretation are weak in so far as it cannot be supported by what seems to be common in at least some Member States under review.

4.7.4 Resignation: Collective or Individual?

With regard to the second element, the obligation to suffer the consequences, there is much less consensus among national systems. In the majority of the Member States the parliament can only force the government as a whole to step down. Individual ministers only resign of their own accord or on request of the prime minister. This is for example the case in Germany, France, the Czech Republic and Italy. In some other Member States however, like in the Netherlands, the parliament can also take a vote of no-confidence on an individual minister. In such a system an individual minister must not only explain and defend his policy, but he can also be forced to resign by the parliament if a majority thinks that he is no longer fit to do the job.

The EU Treaty provisions on resignation of the Commission seem to be in line with which is common in the majority of the Member States under review.[132] As indicated above the European Parliament cannot dismiss an individual Commissioner; a motion of censure of the European Parliament can only be addressed to the Commission as a whole. However, after the refusal of Cresson to step down in 1999 and the fall of the Santer Commission hereafter, an important change took place. Article 217 EC-Treaty now provides that a Commissioner shall resign if the President of the Commission so requests, after obtaining the approval of the Commission.[133] Although this does not imply any right of the European Parliament to send away individual members of the Commission, it perhaps has become easier for the Parliament to put pressure on the President to replace an individual Commissioner. It can be argued that this treaty provision has strengthened individual accountability.

One could wonder whether this treaty provision is sufficient to achieve effective individual accountability. It has been argued that if the European Parliament would have had the power to force Cresson to step down in 1999, the fall of the Commission as a whole could have been prevented.[134] However, one could also take the position that article 217 EC offers a well balanced solution. It preserves the margin of manoeuvre of the President of the Commission, while giving the European Parliament some influence.[135] In practice this influence will probably be substantial. If the Parliament would adopt a resolution criticizing an individual commissioner or, more far-reaching, calling upon him to resign, it will be difficult for the Commission President to ignore it.

---

would call into question a decision taken by the Commission. They shall also refrain from disclosing what is said at meetings of the Commission'.

[132] Broeksteeg, Van den Driessche, Verhey (2008) chapter 13, par. 5 and 9.

[133] See also art. 9D (6) EU (as supposed to be amended by the Reform Treaty).

[134] Clegg, Van Hulten (2004) 27.

[135] Magnette (2001) 306.

From the parliamentary systems in the Member States one cannot deduce many arguments to adapt article 217 EC. On the contrary, in many Member States, like for example in Germany, it is not the parliament but the prime minister who may replace individual ministers. There are no indications that such a system leads to an accountability deficit.

4.7.5 A Clear Chain of Command

A precondition for being held accountable is that a Commissioner has legal powers to implement his policy. At first sight it seems as if the Commission has the same position as a national government. Much like a national government the Commission is a collegiate body whose members have their own portfolio. The directorates-general could be considered as the equivalent of the national ministries; they advise the Commissioners on policy matters and are responsible for the sound implementation of the policy decisions of the Commission.

These tasks have been endorsed and worked out in the Code of Conduct of the Commissioners.[136] However, if we look closer the legal position of the individual Commissioner is very unclear. Unlike a national cabinet minister an individual Commissioner, as already mentioned before, is not heading a particular Directorate-General. This gives a blurred picture. There might be Commissioners dealing with more than one Directorate-General, Commissioners without an assigned Directorate-General as well as Directorates-General reporting to more than one Commissioner.

As a result the portfolios of the Commissioners and the administrative structure are disconnected. There is no clear chain of command that links individual Commissioners with the civil service. This leaves individual Commissioners with the situation that they can be held accountable for things happening within their portfolio, but they do not have control over the civil servants who are actually dealing with these matters. From an accountability perspective individual Commissioners seem thus to have a weak position.[137]

The position of the Commission could be strengthened by setting a clear chain of command between an individual Commissioner and a clearly defined part of the civil service of the Commission. This will clarify what an individual Commissioner is precisely accountable for. In this respect it is helpful that according to the Reform Treaty (art. 9D (5) TEU) the number of members of the

---

[136] European Commission (2004). It says, amongst other things, the following: 'The chain of responsibility continues down to department level in the person of the Director-General, who is answerable to the Commissioner and the College for the proper implementation of the guidelines set by the College and the Commissioner and, in particular, for the management of the Directorate-General or Service in line with the distribution of powers as defined by the Staff Regulations, the Financial Regulation, the Rules of Procedure and the rules laid down as part of the administrative and financial reform of the Commission' (Par. 2.1).

[137] Mehde (2003) 423 ff.

Commission will be diminished to two thirds of the number of Member States. This will prevent the political accountability of the Commission becoming too fragmented and will thus enable the European Parliament to determine easier which Commissioner is accountable in a specific matter. However, one could take one step further and directly link an individual Commissioner with one clearly identifiable Directorate General or a specific division thereof. With such an organizational arrangement the position of the individual Commissioners would run parallel with the position of ministers in most of the Member States.

4.7.6 Reducing Fragmentation of the Executive

In general terms one could speak of a standard European model of government with political accountability as one of its common features. In this model a precondition for effective government is the hierarchical structure of the civil service. It enables the parliament to locate accountability at the top of each ministerial department. Traditionally only Sweden has a fundamentally different model: it is based on a constitutional separation between the cabinet and independent administrative agencies.[138]

In many European countries the standard model has been adapted during the last decades. One can see a growing tendency to cut the executive into smaller pieces. In for example France, Italy, the Netherlands and the United Kingdom there has been a haphazard process of establishing a great variety of agencies.[139] In the Netherlands there are almost four hundred agencies which are all different. In the United Kingdom one has, under the umbrella of the so-called quango-state, non-departmental public bodies, public corporations, National Health Service Bodies and Non-Ministerial Government Departments.

In some Member States like for example France or Italy the accountability of agencies is not a serious issue. On the contrary, it has been argued that at least in some cases there are good reasons for setting up agencies independent from politics. However, in other Member States agencies have become increasingly controversial. The most important reason for criticizing agencies nowadays is their lack of accountability. Ministerial accountability for the actions of independent agencies is limited: legislation has put them at arm's length from daily politics. Other accountability mechanisms are still controversial because they have not yet proved to be a full-grown alternative. Sometimes one even concludes a restoration of political accountability. In 2004 a commission in the Netherlands recommended to bring almost all the agencies back to the ministerial departments.[140]

In the Member States there is no consensus on which model of the executive should be enhanced. However, national experiences show that fragmentation of the executive is a serious concern. This goes for the European Union too. There

---

138 Nergelius (2008) chapter 11, par. 3. See also Ziller (2001) 102-119.

139 See for a comparative research Verhey, Zwart (2003). See also OECD (2002).

140 Werkgroep Verzelfstandigde Organisaties op Rijksniveau (2004).

is a considerable risk of getting into an obscure system of committees, agencies and policy networks which has become almost inaccessible to the outside world and who are in fact accountable to no one. Here the 'problem of many hands' arises: because many different administrative groups and entities contribute to the decision-making process, it is hard to identify who is, at the end of the day, accountable for the outcome.[141]

The problem of fragmentation seems to raise an important argument in favour of upgrading the Commission as the 'core executive' within the European Union. This means a Commission with clear executive and supervisory powers for the use of which the Commission as a body as well as individual Commissioners can be held accountable. The great advantage of the Commission as 'core executive' is clarity; one could at least presume that it will then be much clearer for the European Parliament, the Council of Ministers, the European Council, other EU institutions, the Member States and civil society whom one has to call to account for executive decisions of the European Union. The risk of a too powerful, unitary executive at the European level[142] is probably limited because of the comprehensive, multi-level system of checks and balances in which the Commission has to operate.

However, this issue has to be seen in a broader context. The debate about which role the Commission should play in the future is comprehensive, complicated and linked with many other issues than only the accountability of the European executive. One has to take into account the institutional context of the European Union and for example look at the role of other EU institutions, especially the European Parliament, the Council of Ministers and the European Council. Concentrating executive power in the Commission would moreover lead to a diminishing role of independent agencies. The academic debate on EU agencies shows that that there are several arguments pro en contra putting agencies at arms length of the Commission.[143] It has been suggested that clearly identifiable agencies are more visible to the outside world than obscure Commission divisions and therefore contribute to greater transparency and accountability. Leaving open whether this is true or not, it shows that just saying that the Commission should be the 'core executive' in the EU system is not a simple argument to make. However, while debating the future of the EU executive the risk of fragmentation should be seriously considered.

4.7.7 Focusing on the Quality of the Account

As we have seen above the concept of 'political accountability' in the Member States basically contains three essential elements: being accountable, calling into account and holding to account.[144] In practice it sometimes

141 Bovens (2006) 18. See also Curtin (2004) 15.

142 See Craig (2006) 344.

143 Vos (2000) 1113 ff.

144 See par. 4.7.1.

seems as if politics and public opinion are only interested in the last element. This can be the logical result of the concept of political accountability itself. In some Member States the concept is strongly focused on the parliamentary power to force the government or an individual minister to resign. However, this focus on resignation can also be seen elsewhere. More generally speaking one could say that the process of accountability in the political arena is more and more reduced to the question of who must get the blame for what has gone wrong. A political climate like this invites ministers to evade their responsibility and to shift the blame to others, particularly to the civil service.

The ultimate sanction of resignation is essential. Without the possibility of sanctions there can be no effective accountability. However, one intends to forget that accountability in daily practice is much more than imposing sanctions. It is much more about providing proper information, explaining the cause of events, debating the political issues and trying to determine whether and how the situation should be redressed. One could assume that that is where the public is probably most interested in: trying to find out why things has or has not happened, rectifying possible mistakes and establishing mechanisms to reduce the chance that similar errors would be made in the future.

Seen from this perspective it thus seems more fruitful to invest in the quality of the account than to focus on resignation. This applies perhaps even more to the European Union. As long as the European Union is not a parliamentary system and the European Parliament is not a real parliament, there are even fewer reasons to regard resignation of the Commission as the central issue, at least not to the extent as it appears to be in some Member States. However, what the European Parliament can do is to try to improve the quality of the mechanisms by which it calls the Commission and its individual members into account. This approach seems more promising, especially if one assumes that accountability of the Commission *vis-à-vis* the European Parliament is not or not primarily aimed at strengthening European democracy but at other goals such as enhancing checks and balances within the political system of the European Union and improving the learning capacity and effectiveness of the Commission and its departments.

5 Concluding Remarks

This book intends to contribute to the debate on accountability in the European Union. Its scope is limited; it mainly concerns the political accountability of the Commission towards the European Parliament. Other problems of executive accountability, especially the accountability of the Council of Ministers and/or the European Council,[145] are left aside.[146] However, as the fall of the Santer Commission in 1999 and the crisis around the nomination of the Barroso Commission in 2004 have shown, it would be a mistake to neglect or underestimate the importance of the relationship between the Commission and the Parliament. The accountability mechanisms as they exist in this relationship need full attention now and in the future.

Seen from an accountability perspective there is reason for concern. Writing on a publication on 'Accountability on the EU' Tomkins has concluded that 'it stands as testament to the Prodi Commission's success in effectively closing down the debate on political accountability in the European Union which the reports of the Committee of Independent Experts had seemed, for a short while, to have started'.[147] Nor in the Commission's White Paper on European Governance, nor in other documents or proposals which have been published since, has anything been said about enhancing the political accountability of the Commission. This is remarkable given the serious fraud and mismanagement which led to the fall of the Santer Commission in 1999. There is no reason to conclude that a serious debate on political accountability in the European Union is no longer necessary. On the contrary, since 1999, accountability has remained one of the main issues in the debate on European democracy and no real solutions have come up since then.

In trying to clarify what 'political accountability' could mean in the European Union and to improve mechanisms of political accountability, one should take into account the longstanding constitutional traditions in the Member States on this field. Article 6 EU clearly sustains this view: it says that the European Union is founded on the principles of freedom, democracy, human rights and the rule of law principles which 'the Member States have in common.' It would not make sense to look at accountability issues in the European Union while neglecting experiences in the Member States which have been gained in the course of many decades or even centuries. On the contrary, European citizens presumably expect that they will be governed by European institutions that are accountable and that the mechanisms by which European institutions can be hold to account are in any case not weaker than the traditional accountability mechanisms at the national level.[148]

Given the foregoing it is important to try to detect which constitutional principles we have in common in Europe and to see if and to what extent the European Union can build upon this *'ius commune'* not only to make the European executive more accountable, but also to strengthen the indispensable support of

---

145 See the book which has been published in the other sub-project (see chapter 1) Tans, Zoethout, Peters (2007).

146 Although it is not unthinkable that the results of this research and especially the principles of political accountability, could have a certain significance for the relationship between the Council of Ministers and/or the European Council and other EU institutions, especially the European Parliament.

147 Chalmers, Hadjiemmanuil, Monti, Tomkins (2006) 337.

148 See further chapter 1.

the Member States and its peoples for the decision making process within the European Union. It is self-evident that this cannot take place by simply copying one or more national traditions; as repeatedly said before the European Union is not a full-grown parliamentary system and it will not be in the foreseeable future. However, this research has shown that it is worthwhile to have a closer look at national mechanisms of political accountability in order to check more precisely if and how the European Union, in the spirit of article 6 EU, can built upon the longstanding traditions of national constitutionalism.

What are the main results of this research? The search for the '*ius commune*' on political accountability and the attempt that has been made to transform this '*ius commune*' to the European Union, has not lead to a recommendation of a clear model that the European Union should adopt. Taking into account the specific features of the constitutional system of the European Union this is perhaps an obvious result. However, the comparative research in this book did at least lead to two things.

The first one is that, although there is no common model as such, one can see common features of political accountability in the Member States, which are explicitly or implicitly present in the practice of almost every parliamentary system. A common definition of political accountability which applies in every Member State could be:

> the right of the parliament to be informed by the government which gives account of how it uses or have used its powers and, where appropriate, suffers the consequences, take the blame or undertakes to put matters right if it should appear that errors have been made.

Summarized the concept thus contains three basic elements:
- *being accountable:* the guarantee of the government being accountable to the parliament for the use of its executive powers;
- *calling into account*: the right of the parliament to call the government into account which results in the obligation of the government to inform the parliament and to explain and justify its conduct;
- *holding to account*: the right of the parliament to make a judgment on the conduct of the government which results in the obligation of the government to accept the consequences; this could ultimately mean resignation.

This definition can help clarify the debate on political accountability in the European Union. This is especially the case while this debate until now has often been unclear or sometimes even evasive.

This definition can be used as a starting point for a more practice-based approach. Taking into account the experiences and the debates about how political accountability in the Member States works in theory and in practice, some key issues can be identified with regard to which the European Union could perhaps learn lessons from the Member States. In the European Union comparable issues of political accountability seem to be at stake. In a somewhat simplified way these key issues can be formulated along the following practical guidelines:

- do not accept definitions aimed at evading accountability;
- distinguish between collective and individual accountability;
- establish a clear chain of command;
- reduce fragmentation of the executive;
- do not focus on resignation, but on the quality of the account.

These guidelines are aimed at implementing political accountability at a more practice-oriented level. They can be seen as a yardstick for both the national and the European level in order to make political accountability more effective.

Evidently this research is not the last word that will be said about accountability. It is an issue that is comprehensive, complicated and linked with many other issues than only the accountability of the European executive. Taking into account the broader institutional context of the European Union further debate and research will be needed to assess the value of our research for the future constitutional development of the European Union.

Bibliography

ARNULL (2000)

A.M. Arnull (eds.), *Wyatt & Dashwood's European Union Law* (London 2000).

BOVENS (2006)

M. Bovens, 'Analysing and Assessing Public Accountability': A Conceptual Framework, European Governance Papers (EUROGOV), no. C-06-01, 2006, available on <www.connex-network.org/eurogov> (viewed December 2007).

DE BÚRCA (2003)

G. de Búrca, 'The constitutional challenge of new governance in the European Union' (2003) *ELR* 28 814-839.

CHALMERS, HADJIEMMANUIL, MONTI, TOMKINS (2006)

D. Chalmers, C. Hadjiemmanuil, G. Monti, A. Tomkins, *European Union Law* (Cambridge 2006).

CHRISTIANSEN (2004)

Th. Christiansen, 'The European Commission: The European executive between continuity and change' in J. Richardson (ed.), *European Union: Power and policymaking* (London 2004) 99-121.

CLEGG, VAN HULTEN (2004)

N. Clegg, M. van Hulten, 'Reforming the European Parliament', <fpc.org.uk/fsblob/130.pdf> (viewed December 2007).

COMMISSION'S WHITE PAPER (2000)

Commission's White Paper, *Reforming the Commission*, COM (2000), 200, available on <http://europa.eu.int/comm/reform/refdoc/index_en.htm> (viewed December 2007).

COMMITTEE OF INDEPENDENT EXPERTS (1999A)

Committee of Independent Experts, *First Report on Allegations of Fraud, Mismanagement and Nepotism in the European Commission*, available on <http://www.europarl.eu.int/experts/default_en.htm> (viewed December 2007).

COMMITTEE OF INDEPENDENT EXPERTS (1999B)

Committee of Independent Experts, *Second report on Reform of the Commission, Analysis of current practice and proposals for tackling mismanagement, irregularities and fraud*, available on <http://www.europarl.eu.int/experts/default_en.htm> (viewed December 2007).

CONSTANTINESCO (2000)

V. Constantinesco, 'La responsabilité de la Commission Européenne: la crise de 1999', in P. Albertini et al., *La responsabilité des gouvernants* (Paris 2000).

CORBETT, JACOBS, SHACKLETON (2000)

R. Corbett, F. Jacobs, M. Shackleton, *The European Parliament* (London 2000).

CRAIG (1999)

P. Craig, 'The nature of the Community: Integration, Democracy, and Legitimacy', in P. Craig, G. de Búrca (eds.), *The Evolution of EU Law* (Oxford 1999) 1-54.

CRAIG (2000)

P. Craig, ''The Fall and Renewal of the Commission': Accountability, Contract and Administrative Organisation' (2000) *European Law Journal* 98-116.

CRAIG (2006)

P. Craig , 'The Locus and Accountability of the Executive in the European Union', in P. Craig, A. Tomkins (eds.), *The Executive and Public Law. Power and Accountability in Comparative Perspective* (Oxford 2006) 315-346.

CRAIG, DE BÚRCA (2007)

P. Craig, G. de Búrca, *EU Law. Text, Cases and Materials*, Fourth Edition (Oxford 2007).

CURTIN (2001)

D. Curtin, 'The Commission as Sorcerer's Apprentice? Reflections on EU Public Administration and the Role of Information Technology in Holding Bureaucracy Accountable' (2001) Jean Monnet Working Paper No. 6/01, Symposium: Mountain or Molehill? A Critical Appraisal of the Commission White Paper on Governance, available on <http://www.jeanmonnetprogram.org/papers/01/011801.html> (viewed December 2007).

CURTIN (2004)

D. Curtin, *Mind the Gap: The Evolving EU Executive and the Constitution, Third Walter van Gerven Lecture* (Groningen 2004).

CURTIN (2005)

D. Curtin, 'Delegation to EU Non-Majoritarian Agencies and Emerging Practices of Public Accountability', in D. Geradin, R. Muñoz, *Regulation through agencies in the EU. A new paradigm of European governance* (Cheltenham 2005) 88-119.

CURTIN, WESSEL (2005)

D. Curtin, R. Wessel (eds.), *Good Governance in the European Union. Reflections on concepts, institutions and substance* (Antwerp/Oxford/New York 2005).

EDITORIAL COMMENTS (1999)

Editorial Comments, (1999) *Common Market Law Review* 36 269-272.

EDITORIAL COMMENTS (2004)

Editorial Comments, 'Power to the people of the European Union – Right on?' (2004) *Common Market Law Review* 41 1475-1479.

EUROPEAN COMMISSION (2001)

European Commission, *European Governance. A White Paper*, Brussels 2001, available on <http://ec.europa.eu/governance/white_paper/en.pdf> (viewed December 2007).

EUROPEAN COMMISSION (2002)

European Commission, *Framework for European regulatory agencies*, Brussels, COM (2002) 718 final.

EUROPEAN COMMISSION (2004)

European Commission, *Code of Conduct for Commissioners*, SEC (2004) 1487/2, available on <http://ec.europa.eu/commission_barroso/code_of_conduct/code_conduct_en.pdf> (viewed December 2007).

EUROPEAN COMMISSION (2005)

European Commission, *Draft Interinstitutional Agreement on the operating framework for the European regulatory agencies*, Brussels, COM (2005) 59 final.

FOLLESDAL, HIX (2005)

A. Follesdal, S. Hix, 'Why There is a Democratic Deficit in the EU: A Response to Majone and Moravcsik', European Governance Papers (EUROGOV) No. C-05-02, available on <http://www.connex-network.org/eurogov/pdf/egp-connex-C-05-02.pdf> (viewed December 2007).

GERADIN, MUÑOZ, PETIT (2005)

D. Geradin, R. Muñoz, N. Petit (eds.), *Regulation through agencies in the EU: A new paradigm of European governance* (Cheltenham/Northampton MA 2005).

VAN GERVEN (2000A)

W. van Gerven, 'Managing the European Union: For Better or for Worse?', in B.S. Markesinis (ed.), *The Clifford Chance Millennium Lectures* (Oxford/Portland/Oregon 2000) 91-104.

VAN GERVEN (2000B)

W. van Gerven, Guest Editorial, 'Ethical and political responsibility of EU Commissioners' (2000) *Common Market Law Review* 1-15.

VAN GERVEN (2000C)

W. van Gerven, 'Het voor en tegen van een Europese Grondwet', in A.K. Koekkoek (red.), *Bijdragen aan een Europese Grondwet, Staatsrechtconferentie 2000* (Deventer 2000) 27-44.

VAN GERVEN (2005)

W. van Gerven, *The European Union: A polity of states and people* (Oxford/Portland/Oregon 2005).

GRIMM (1995)

D. Grimm, 'Does Europe need a Constitution' (1995) *European Law Journal* 1 284-288.

HARLOW (2002)

C. Harlow, *Accountability in the European Union* (Oxford 2002).

HARTLEY (2003)

T. Hartley, *The Foundations of European Community Law* (Oxford 2003).

HIX (2005)

S. Hix, *The Political System of the European Union* (Basingstoke Hampshire/New York 2005).

KIIVER (2006)

P. Kiiver, *The National Parliaments in the European Union: A Critical View on EU Constitution-Building* (The Hague 2006).

LEQUESNE (2000)

Ch. Lequesne, 'The European Commission: A Balancing Act between Autonomy and Dependence', in K. Neunreither, A. Wiener (eds.), *European Integration After Amsterdam* (Oxford 2000) 36-51.

MAGNETTE (2001)

P. Magnette, ''Appointing and Censuring the European Commission': The Adaptation of Parliamentary Institutions to the Community Context' (2001) *European Law Journal* 292-310.

MAJONE (1998)

G. Majone, 'Europe's 'Democratic Deficit': The Question of Standards' (1998) *European Law Journal* 5-28.

MAJONE (2000)

G. Majone, 'The Credibility Crisis of Community Regulation' (2000) *Journal of Common Market Studies* 273-302.

MAJONE, EVERSON (2001)

G. Majone, M. Everson, 'Institutional reform: independent agencies, oversight coordination and procedural control', in O. De Schutter, N. Lebessis, J. Paterson (eds.), *Governance in the European Union* (Luxembourg 2001) 129-168.

MEHDE (2003)

V. Mehde, 'Responsibility and Accountability in the European Commission' (2003) *Common Market Law Review* 40 423-442.

MÖLLERS (2006)

C. Möllers, 'European Governance: Meaning and Value of a Concept' (2006) *Common Market Law Review* 43 314-336.

MORAVCZIK (2002)

A. Moravcsik, 'In Defence of the 'Democratic Deficit': Reassessing the Legitimacy of the European Union' (2002) *Journal of Common Market Studies* 40 603-634.

MORAVCZIK (2004)

A. Moravczik, 'Is there a 'Democratic Deficit' in World Politics? A Framework for Analysis' (2004) *Government and Opposition* 336-365.

MULGAN (2003)

R. Mulgan, *'Holding Power to Account': Accountability in Modern Democracies* (Basingstoke 2003).

NUGENT (2001)

N. Nugent, *The European Commission* (New York 2001).

NUGENT (2003)

N. Nugent, *The Government and Politics of the European Union* (Basingstoke/New York 2003).

OECD (2002)
OECD, *Distributed Public Governance. Agencies, authorities and other government bodies* (Paris 2002).

OLIVER (2003)
D. Oliver, *Constitutional Reform in the United Kingdom* (Oxford/New York 2003).

ORGANISATION FOR ECONOMIC CO-OPERATION AND DEVELOPMENT (2002)
Organisation for Economic Co-operation and Development, *Distributed Public Governance: Agencies, Authorities and other Government Bodies* (Paris 2002).

RAPPORT-DEHAENE (1999)
Rapport-Dehaene, *Rapport à la Commission Européenne, Implications institutionnelles de l'élargissement* (Bruxelles 1999).

DE SCHUTTER, LEBESSIS, PATERSON (2001)
O. De Schutter, N. Lebessis, J. Paterson (eds), *Governance in the European Union* (Luxembourg 2001).

SHACKLETON (1998)
M. Shackleton, 'The European Parliament's New Committees of Inquiry: Tiger or Paper Tiger?' (1998) *JCMS* 115–130.

SHAW (2000)
J. Shaw, *Law of the European Union* (New York 2000).

TANS, ZOETHOUT, PETERS (2007)
O. Tans, C. Zoethout, J. Peters, *National Parliaments and European Democracy. A Bottom-up Approach to European Constitutionalism* (Groningen 2007).

TOMKINS (1999)
A. Tomkins, 'Responsibility and resignation in the European Commission' (1999) *Modern Law Review* 62 744-765.

VERHEY, ZWART (2003)
L.F.M. Verhey, T. Zwart (eds.), *Agencies in a comparative and European perspective* (Antwerp 2003).

VOS (2000)
E. Vos, 'Reforming the European Commission: What role to play for EU Agencies' (2000) *Common Market Law Review* 1113- 1134.

VOS (2003)
E. Vos, 'Agencies and the European Union', in L. Verhey, T. Zwart (eds.), *Agencies in a comparative and European Perspective* (Antwerp 2003) 113-147.

WALKER (2001)
N. Walker, 'The White Paper in Constitutional Context', in Symposium: Mountain or Molehill? A Critical Appraisal of the Commission White paper on Governance (2001) Jean Monnet Working Paper No. 6/01.

WEATHERILL, BEAUMONT (1999)
S. Weatherill, P. Beaumont, *EU Law* (London 1999).

WEILER (1999)
J.H.H. Weiler, *The Constitution of Europe. 'Do the new clothes have an emperor?' and other essays on European Integration* (Cambridge 1999).

WEILER (2001)
J.H.H. Weiler, 'The Commission as Euro-Skeptic: A Task Oriented Commission for a Project-Based Union. A Comment on the First Version of the White Paper', in Symposium: Mountain or Molehill? A Critical Appraisal of the Commission White Paper on Governance (2001) Jean Monnet Working Paper No. 6/01.

WERKGROEP VERZELFSTANDIGDE ORGANISATIES OP RIJKSNIVEAU (2004)
Werkgroep Verzelfstandigde Organisaties op Rijksniveau (Werkgroep-Kohnstamm), *Een herkenbare staat: investeren in de overheid* (The Hague 2004).

WESTLAKE (1994)
M. Westlake, *The Commission and the Parliament* (London/Dublin/Edinburgh 1994).

WESTLAKE (1997)
M. Westlake, 'The Commission and the Parliament', in G. Edwards, D. Spence (eds.), *The European Commission* (London 1997).

ZILLER (2001)
J. Ziller, 'European Models of Government: Towards a Patchwork with Missing Pieces' (2001) *Parliamentary Affairs* 54 102-119.